TRANSFORMATION

THE STORY OF
MODERN PUERTO RICO

BY

Earl Parker Hanson

"*. . . we are merely realistic.*"

—Governor Luis Muñoz Marín

SIMON AND SCHUSTER

NEW YORK 1955

F
1958
H3

FIRST PRINTING
LIBRARY OF CONGRESS CATALOG CARD NUMBER: 54-9797
DEWEY DECIMAL CLASSIFICATION NUMBER: 972.9505
MANUFACTURED IN THE UNITED STATES OF AMERICA
BY AMERICAN BOOK—STRATFORD PRESS, INC., NEW YORK

35581

For

LIDA SIBONI HANSON

Who has always recognized the difference
between Science and the human spirit
which created Science, motivates it,
and is therefore the greater of the two

"RIGHT SHALL AGAIN PREVAIL"

THIS IS THE STORY of a small island with few resources other than
the ingenuity and determination of its people. It tells how a backward, underdeveloped society has emerged from its past and today stands as a symbol of progress.

Puerto Rico is a significant bridge between the two cultures
of the Western Hemisphere. Before it emerged, it was pointed out
as a sorry example of the evils of either the Latin American
mañana spirit or of North American imperialism, or of both.
Today it is the best proof of the results of friendly intercourse of
these two cultures. In an era when extreme nationalism poisons
many underdeveloped lands, Puerto Rico kept its head and devised its own political status. Fully self-governing at home, it has
freely chosen to continue its association with the United States,
with common citizenship, ideals, and interests.

This is a story with numerous heroes and few villains. Upper-
most in its cast is Governor Luis Muñoz Marín, revered by his
fellow citizens as the founder of the Commonwealth and the leader
who inspired and guided us in our uphill path, promising not
much more than Churchill's "blood, sweat, and tears."

The author of this book is another important character in the
story of Puerto Rico's emergence. In 1935 I had the satisfaction
of working with him in the Planning Division of the Puerto Rico
Reconstruction Administration. The seeds of economic reform
were planted by a small nucleus of men through research, planning, and creativeness. Earl Hanson, as Executive Secretary of
the Planning Division, inspired us all to greater accomplishments.
When the forces of reaction tried to reverse the inevitable trend
and most of the Puerto Rican leaders and scientists left the PRRA

in order to back Muñoz Marín, Earl Hanson, who could have stayed with his continental friends, chose the side of his Puerto Rican brothers in spirit and resigned with us. Shortly after that, I had the pleasure of dedicating one of my articles to him and I mentioned then the hope that some day "right shall again prevail in Puerto Rico." It has happened, and we are all elated that one of Puerto Rico's staunchest friends has come back to us to see our development, study our progress, and tell the world about it in his own inspiring words.

RAFAEL PICÓ

Chairman, Puerto Rico Planning Board

Contents

Introduction

By CHESTER BOWLES

At a time when we Americans urgently need to burn deeply into our private consciences and public policies a sympathetic grasp of the hopes and strivings of the underdeveloped world, it is both fortunate and arresting that Puerto Rico can teach us so much.

It is fortunate because for us there is no area of readier access or more legitimate concern than this island homeland of over two million of our fellow citizens in the Caribbean. It is arresting because the remarkable recent transformation in Puerto Rico has not as yet been fully appreciated by the rest of the American public.

Professor Hanson's present work will do much to compensate for this deficiency. Explorer, researcher, geographer, technician, Mr. Hanson long ago achieved distinction and popularity as an authority in numerous fields.

Those familiar with his past books or public lectures may know that his career has ranged widely from Iceland, to Chile, to the Amazon, to Liberia. Until now they may not have known of his first-hand concern with Puerto Rico, first in 1935–6 when he was planning consultant and member of the executive board of the Puerto Rico Reconstruction Adminis-

tration, and again in 1952 when he organized an inter-university area studies course on the island, conducted jointly by the Universities of Delaware and Puerto Rico.

Thus the author can write with both whimsy and fervor, against a background of personal acquaintance with men and events. This intimacy has lent both persuasiveness and readability to his account.

In 1952 Puerto Rico and the continental United States formally entered upon a relationship that defies duplication, and often even description. As a political venture the Puerto Rican experiment in non-independent independence is totally unique, and Mr. Hanson shows with some care how indispensable for the Puerto Ricans themselves the maintenance of their peculiar status may be. He makes a good case that for them either statehood or complete independence would be impossible alternatives, equally ruinous.

But if constitutional patterns are not often transplantable, ingenious ideas often are. More than most Americans, those who live in Puerto Rico share the hopes and heartaches of that two thirds of mankind who remain ill clad, ill housed, and ill fed. Yet nowhere, except perhaps in the agricultural settlements of Israel or in some of the industrial and village projects of India, have there been pioneering efforts at economic development which match in promise the techniques recently evolved in Puerto Rico.

In India, I learned from the daily saga of success and setback, disappointment and reward, how significant such imaginative improvisation may be. In Gandhi's land I learned to appreciate the spirit of this other non-violent revolution in Puerto Rico, halfway around the world.

That the underdeveloped countries themselves have not been slow to recognize real achievement has been abundantly shown by the steady, two-way passage to Puerto Rico recently: an influx of inquiring visitors, and an exodus of trained experts.

For the good of all concerned, the United States would do well to live down her invidious, international reputation as a Gold Coast of plenty in the midst of a world slum. How better to do so than to introduce to the world the striking accomplishments of Governor Luis Muñoz Marín, who unhesitatingly calls his administration "a government of the poor for the poor." "Bread, Land, and Liberty," the motto of his Popular Democratic party, is the rallying call of awakening peoples everywhere in Asia, Africa, and South America.

For Puerto Rico has been a microcosm of evils recurring in much of the world. Indeed the same central problems seem inescapably to repeat themselves wherever people are emerging from colonialism:

the same determination to uproot absentee political control and sycophantic economic monopoly;

the same impatience for industrialization, an impatience that will not tolerate the leisurely, ad hoc, progress which occupied Western Europe and the United States for over 150 years;

the same necessity for developed water resources and multi-purpose projects for irrigation, flood control, and power;

the same imperative need for land redistribution and rural resettlement;

the same drives for improved sanitation, better health, increased literacy, and decent, low-cost housing;

the same immediate concern over population pressure;

the same disparity between the numbers and inclinations of university graduates and the ability of the society to absorb them and their talents appropriately;

the same dilemma of reconciling culture with progress.

For all that it accomplished as the local adjunct of the New Deal in the nineteen thirties, the Puerto Rico Reconstruction Administration early demonstrated the ineffectiveness of a rigid planning, which was benevolently prepared and supervised by a government outside the immediate context of local needs. Thus a decade ago Puerto Ricans learned a lesson which should now be a truism: that if a people are to be saved from whatever danger threatens them, whether it be the militant aggression of communism or the social scourge of poverty and disease, they will in the last analysis save themselves through their own indigenous power, pride, and responsibility. If outsiders are to be helpful, their help must take the form of friendly and unobtrusive support.

The preliminary failure of the co-operative movements in Puerto Rico showed how essential the psychological and cultural predispositions of a people really are to the success of an otherwise logical approach to a pressing problem. When, unlike comparable experiments in Israel and Mexico, the rigid disciplines of voluntary collective farming proved unacceptable, the Puerto Rican government wisely shifted to other expedients.

"We are neither radical nor conservative," says Muñoz Marín, "we are merely realistic." This pattern of adaptability is one which each underdeveloped country must learn for itself by trial and error. Each will have its own tangled web of false starts and dashed hopes. If it can surmount them with the flexible, non-doctrinaire improvisation of Puerto Rico, it will have learned another essential lesson.

Cultural innovations in education and family life represent departures from an older Puerto Rican tradition, and their accommodation to it is a complicated matter. The author's comments on these problems are of course his own, but no one will gainsay the importance of the issues he raises.

As observers from three underdeveloped continents go to Puerto Rico, there is much for them to see. They will want to look at the operation of the Water Resources Authority (Puerto Rico's "Little TVA"), the Transportation Authority, the Housing Authority, the Social Programs Administration, and the Planning Board's efforts to integrate the activities of other agencies. They will examine the history of the Develop-

ment Company and the Development Bank. They will become familiar with the role of the Land Authority and the "proportional profit" farms. They will note that the government has no fear of prolific, egg-headed research in the Economic Development Administration. They will appreciate, as Senator Taft himself once did, the usefulness in Puerto Rico of a little temporary socialism to promote subsequent private enterprise. They will study the government's devices for attracting outside investment and keeping it socially responsible.

When they do all of these things they will begin to grasp the striking advance of a people who in a few short years of public medicine have eliminated malaria, drastically reduced the incidence of tuberculosis, and dramatically increased life expectancy. They will respect the degree of achievement in innovations ranging from finance, agronomy, and power plants, to housing, village planning, and public works. They will learn how it is that Puerto Rico has been opening a new factory once a week, and how per capita income has been doubled in a few short years.

They will begin to appreciate the spirit of a people who have devoted one third of their slender budget to a widely flung educational program covering everything from vocational training to bookmobile units for rural areas. They will respect the magnificent sacrifice involved in Puerto Rico's substantial annual contribution from its public treasury to the worldwide Point IV effort. And they will be inspired by a program which can do all of these things while preserving and invigorating a democratic, indigenous culture.

That is why the words and works of Puerto Rico's governor could speak so eloquently if they were made available to Asia today. That is why the United States should take special pride in its own recent and enlightened co-operation with Puerto Rico's "Operation Bootstrap." That is why this test case in American attitudes toward the generic problems of

*underdeveloped areas could be so pertinent elsewhere, if
we wanted it to be.*

*Let us make full use of the opportunities given us by this
instance of special success. Here are the ingredients of attitude and policy which we owe to a world that needs them.*

CHESTER BOWLES

July 31, 1954

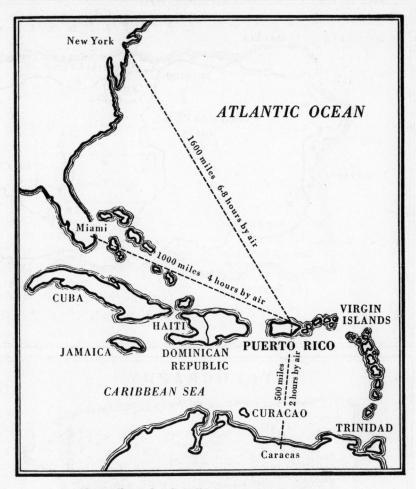

New York

ATLANTIC OCEAN

1600 miles 6-8 hours by air

Miami

1000 miles 4 hours by air

CUBA

HAITI

JAMAICA

DOMINICAN
REPUBLIC

PUERTO RICO

VIRGIN
ISLANDS

500 miles 2 hours by air

CARIBBEAN SEA

CURACAO

TRINIDAD

Caracas

Physically and culturally, Puerto Rico is the link
between Latin America and the United States.

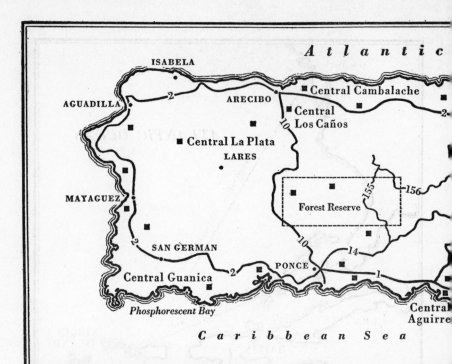

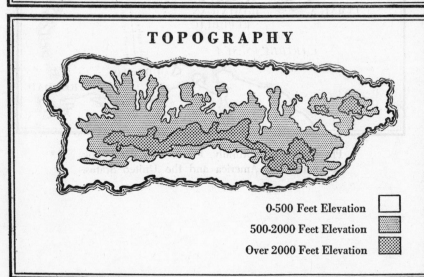

TOPOGRAPHY

0-500 Feet Elevation

500-2000 Feet Elevation

Over 2000 Feet Elevation

O cean

SAN JUAN

Luquillo Beach

LUQUILLO

CULEBRA

167

3

+El Yunque

FAJARDO

Central Fajardo

Forest
Reserve

CAGUAS

156

Vieques Sound

RRANQUITAS

CAYEY

4

1

3

VIEQUES

Central
Lafayette

GUAYAMA

3

PUERTO RICO
with Vieques and Culebra
• Cities ■ Sugar Mills —0— Highways
Scale 0 5 10 15 20 Miles

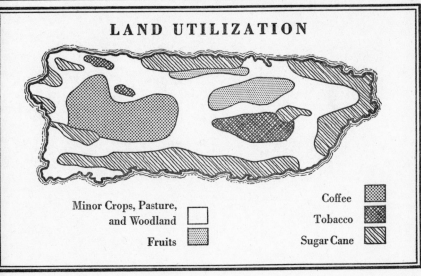

LAND UTILIZATION

Minor Crops, Pasture,
and Woodland

Fruits

Coffee

Tobacco

Sugar Cane

Foreword

IT WAS MY GREAT PRIVILEGE, in 1952, to take a class of seniors
and graduate students from the University of Delaware, including one high official from the Dominion of Pakistan, to
Puerto Rico for a summer-school course, the object of which
was to study Puerto Rico as an integrated, living social
organism.

We were especially fortunate in being able to go there that
particular year. For 1952 marked the greatest political turning point in the island's history. It was the Birth of a Nation
year, when Puerto Rico finally emerged from centuries of
colonialism and became a self-governing Commonwealth,
within the American Union and in compact with the federal
government.

Academically, the course was an interesting experiment in
the teaching of human geography as expressed through
regionalism and was based on the premise that once you dis-
sect any one society or region, and divide it into such com-
partmentalized specialties as physiography, history, sociology, economics, politics, technology, and folkways, you also
kill it and can no longer deal with a vital social organism.

Better than any other document I know, the memorandum
of tribute and appreciation, drafted at the time by my students, expresses the deep emotions which were stirred by the
emergence of a new political unit within the American scheme
of things.

UNIVERSITY OF DELAWARE
Newark, Delaware

FOR PUERTO RICO—TRIBUTE AND APPRECIATION

On the twenty-fifth day of July, 1952, and the first of the new American Commonwealth of Puerto Rico, we, the undersigned, wish to pay our tribute and express our deep appreciation to that Commonwealth, to its dignified and courteous men and women in all walks of life, to its government of able, energetic, and dedicated young men, to its leader and governor, to the university's students and faculty members with whom we have been associated during the past month.

Together we comprise a class of the University of Delaware which has been privileged to participate in a course given on the island by the Universities of Puerto Rico and Delaware, devoted to the understanding of Puerto Rico as a vital and complex society and a microcosm of modern world trends. With the exception of one member from Pakistan, we are all citizens of the United States; without exception, we are devotees of freedom, democracy, and decency in human relations.

As such we rejoice in the new powers and freedoms that will from this day on be exercised and safeguarded by some two million American citizens of Spanish heritage and language. The formalization of those specific powers and freedoms, celebrated today, resulted in large measure from the democratic sanity displayed by both participants—San Juan and Washington—in the evolutionary development of a new compact of citizenship. In the modern troubled world it is worthy of high respect and profound study as such, and not merely—great as the generosity was—as an act of generosity on Washington's part.

With deep sincerity and from overflowing hearts, we pay our simple fraternal tribute to the people and leaders of Puerto Rico, yesterday's as well as today's, for the patient fortitude and the dignified and decent manner in which they, as Puerto Ricans and American citizens, have met the challenges of past decades, the bewilderments, the ebb and flow of hope, the anxieties, the many fearful perils, and the troubles that at times flared into turmoil. We pay our fraternal tribute to Puerto Rico for the dignified loyalty it has shown in its relations with Washington, for the Constitution with its glowing Bill of Rights which its people have drafted for their future guidance and as a new charter of freedom, for the skill and spirit of deep humanity with which its leaders and people have shaped the forms of their accelerated modern evolution.

Through our presence and travels on the island, through the instruction that was granted us, and finally through the overwhelming hospitality that was extended to us by Puerto Ricans of all classes, from the highest officials to the poorest countrymen, we have been privileged to see and learn something of the many problems and obstacles, diverse and at times terrifying in magnitude, that the island has faced, and must continue to face, in its present uphill struggle toward a decent material sufficiency as a solid basis for democratic human brotherhood. We have seen, shared, and rejoiced in the mounting faith in the outcome of that struggle, displayed by the people of Puerto Rico, by students and observers from many parts of the world, and by men, business, and capital throughout the American Union. Because that faith is by far the most important single element for success, we pay tribute to Puerto Rico for its remarkable achievements to date and express our conviction that Operation Bootstrap, with all its tribulations and perplexities, with all its inevitable setbacks, will continue to mount to an inspiring success in solving Puerto Rico's many present problems.

If we took nothing home with us except the sense of fraternity and human identification which prompts this tribute, if we could in the future pass on nothing else about Puerto Rico to our own students and co-workers, our visit and work here would still have been outstandingly valuable to us. The reassuring example of one human society, however small and however it may be one of several such, working with fortitude, dignity, and energy toward its own salvation as a member of the great human world of interdependent societies, is the greatest gift—in the modern age of fearful tensions and paralyzing doubts—that Puerto Rico has given to us and to the world.

Written and signed in San Juan, Puerto Rico.

MOHAMMED AKBAR
Assistant Secretary, Ministry of Health and Works, Government of Pakistan
NANCY ALLEN
Teacher, Delaware Schools
JOHN R. BERRY, JR.
Student, University of Delaware
PATRICIA GEORGE
Lieutenant, N.C., U.S.N.
EARL PARKER HANSON
Professor, University of Delaware
MARGARET J. HARVEY
Teacher, Delaware High Schools
MARJORY WINTRUP
Teacher, Delaware Schools

HELEN IRONS
Teacher, Delaware Schools
JOAN McCAIN
Teacher, Delaware Schools
REBA E. PARK
Teacher, Delaware High Schools
KIRK L. PRESSING
Student, University of Delaware
RUTH PURDY
Student, University of Delaware
GLENOLA B. ROSE
Graduate Student, University of Delaware
RONALD THOMPSON,
Graduate Student, University of Delaware

Although the document expresses precisely my own feelings toward the Commonwealth of Puerto Rico and its remarkable people, it cannot—nor can anything else, for that matter—express my feelings of identification with, and gratitude toward, a large number of Puerto Rican men and women, and non-Puerto Ricans who have played parts in the growth of my story. Acknowledgments of the kind here given are always feeble; they are nevertheless necessary for reasons too deep to be dwelt upon.

Luis—Governor Luis Muñoz Marín—needs no special mention here. Thirty years ago, I first heard about Puerto Rico from him and from Muna Lee, then Sra. Muna Lee de Muñoz Marín, and now Miss Muna Lee, an honored official of the U.S. Department of State, known throughout the hemisphere for her work in cementing inter-American cultural relations. To Muna I want to pay special tribute as a person and an unfailing friend. She has contributed much to this book.

When I first met Luis and Muna in New York, their children, Luisito and Munita, were very small. Now they are very tall and are both staunch friends of mine to whom I owe much. He is Luis Muñoz Lee of San Juan; she is Sra. Muna Muñoz de Rosado, the wife of Julio Rosado del Valle, one of Puerto Rico's outstanding painters, whose murals are seen in the Caribe Hilton Hotel and will soon be seen in several other buildings being erected at the time of the present writing.

When I first went to Puerto Rico in 1935, I became associated with a number of young men, instructors at the University of Puerto Rico and consultants on Puerto Rican affairs. Today most of them occupy high positions in the Puerto Rican government. In fact, they virtually *are* the government; they and their associates comprised the group on which Muñoz called in 1941 to form a new government which was in those days revolutionary in nature. Outstanding among them is Rafael Picó, in 1935 professor of geography, today head of the Puerto Rico Planning Board, whose encouragement and constant help have been largely responsible for this book. Since he must often have shuddered as he saw the book developing during the past several years, and since he may still shudder at various things that are left in it today, I must here add that neither Picó nor anybody else in Puerto Rico has ever tried to dictate in any way what the book should say and contain. He and his associates have given me much valuable help, encouragement, and occasional advice; the book itself, with its faults and hoped-for virtues, is entirely mine.

Sol Luis Descartes, today the Commonwealth's Treasurer, Rafael Cordero, today the Comptroller, Jaime Benítez, now Chancellor of the University of Puerto Rico, and Estéban Bird, now one of Puerto Rico's leading bankers, are among those whom I remember most fondly from the old days, and to whom I owe much for help on this book.

Dr. José Padín was Commissioner of Education and Acting Governor when I passed through Puerto Rico in 1931. An account of my brief meeting with him then is given in Chapter VII. He is one of the finest men I have ever known, learned, courteous, courageous, uncompromising in matters of human integrity. Today he is the Commonwealth's honored Elder Statesman, and I am proud to number him among my friends. His help and encouragement in the preparation of this book have been invaluable.

Among those whose friendships I have cherished since the 1930's, and who have helped me in recent years, is also Waldemar Lee, a leading businessman who has played a strong part in building up the tourist industry. His wife, Marjory Ashford de Lee, daughter of Dr. Bailey Ashford, her sister, Gloria Guinness, and the latter's husband, Maurice Guinness of the Shell Oil Company, all formed parts of that fine company of men and women who made life so pleasant and challenging for me during the days of the PRRA.

James and Dorothy Bourne, who were liquidating the FERA when I first went to Puerto Rico, and with whom I then had many professional disagreements, are today among my warmest friends. My thanks go to them for helping me with the present book; also my apologies for those passages in the book on which I do not agree with them, and for which I here take full personal responsibility.

One of the Puerto Ricans whose friendship has been un-wavering throughout the past twenty years is Dr. Antonio Colorado. He played a valiant part in the great PRRA battle in 1936. Subsequently he went into exile in New York, where I was privileged to be associated with him in the preparation of the "New World Guides to the Latin American Republics" —indeed, had it not been for his tremendous contributions there might well not have been any guides. Today he is one of the most important pioneering members of the Common-wealth's Department of Education. He has also done much work on this book.

In 1936, I lived for a time with Tomás Blanco, one of the island's leading intellectuals. If today we no longer see eye to eye on the significance of what is happening in Puerto Rico, I nevertheless owe him a debt of gratitude for the stimulation that he has given me.

Dr. Antonio Fernós Isern, Resident Commissioner for Puerto Rico in the U.S. Congress, Dr. Juan Pons, Secretary of Health, Teodoro Moscoso, Secretary of Economic Develop-ment, Ramón Colon Torres, Secretary of Agriculture and Commerce, Enrique Bird-Piñero, of the Social Programs Administration in the Department of Agriculture and Com-merce, have all become cherished friends of mine and have contributed greatly to this book.

Thanks also go to Sr. Rafael Pol Mendez, not only for his valuable help and lavish hospitality, but also because he has built up the Los Caños co-operative into one of the leading such institutions in the world today. That means much to me, as a man who used to labor for the creation of a sound co-operative movement in Puerto Rico, only to be told that the Puerto Ricans were too individualistic ever to grasp and apply the principles of co-operation.

A special debt of affection and gratitude must here be acknowledged to Felísa—Doña Fela—and to her husband, Jenaro. In the old days we were united in bonds of friendship and support for Muñoz; today Felísa is world famous as Sra. Felísa Rincón de Gautier, mayoress of San Juan, who in 1954 was elected "Woman of the Americas." Knowing her and Jenaro has been a great privilege of my life.

My affection and gratitude for Jorge and Carmen Font Saldaña are also things apart and special when I contemplate my experiences with and in the Puerto Rican scene. Both have long been friends and inspirations to me. I can say the same of their children, among whom Martita has won a special place as a member of my own family.

Among those who will not be able to read these acknowledgments, but to whom they are nevertheless given with a full heart, are Jesús Piñero, the first Puerto Rican ever to be appointed the island's governor, and Antonio Lucchetti, the father of electrification on the island and the indefatigable head of the Water Resources Administration until his death in 1953. Jesús Piñero died in the same year. Both had been close friends and invaluable helpers of mine since we first met in 1935.

I have had many differences with Carlos Chardón; our paths have crossed, separated, and crossed again. I will always remember fondly the days when he was regional administrator of the PRRA and I was privileged to work with him. I sincerely hope that our paths may one of these days come together again, and stay together.

Drs. Raymond Crist, Clarence Senior, and Preston James

read the manuscript of this book and gave me valuable suggestions for changes and amplifications.

Morris Llewellyn Cooke, Otto Mallery, and Donald Stephens are here thanked as being among the many friends who not only enriched my life, but have also contributed much to the point of view developed in this book. All three have visited Puerto Rico, have seen the island through fresh eyes, and have illuminated my own viewpoint on it.

Ruby Black is outstanding among the Americans who twenty years ago formed a small band for the support of Muñoz Marín and of decency in Puerto Rico's colonial affairs. Thank you, Ruby, for your hospitality, your friendship, and your uncompromising stand in those dark days.

Finally, my profound thanks go to Charlotte Leeper. I first met her in 1935, at the home of then-Senator Luis Muñoz Marín. She was on the island for the purpose of starting a department of social work at the University of Puerto Rico, and she and I had many rousing arguments over the meanings of the various social upheavals which were in those days in their beginnings. Some years later, after we were both back in the States, we were married. Unemployed and poor, we had no real vacation, no honeymoon, until ten years after our marriage. Then we had it as guests of the insular government, on the occasion of Muñoz Marín's inauguration as the first governor ever to be elected by the people of Puerto Rico.

More than anything else, that great occasion brought out my feelings for Puerto Rico and its leaders and people, and caused me to write this book as a labor of love in the truest sense of the term.

E. P. H.

CHAPTER I

Transformation

A SMALL SOCIETY shook off the lethargy and anguish of its colonialism and began to reshape itself. It created no Utopia. It didn't solve a single human problem for all time—in the ultimate sense beloved and often demanded by scholars but never achieved by people. Its successes were those of real people in a real world—clashing and fearful. From any point of view those successes were remarkable.

In an election which amounted to a political explosion, human energies were released for creative purposes other than procreation. During the years that followed, through the complex processes of trial, error, invention, mistake, and occasional success, those energies came to be reasonably united and channeled into the concerted striving toward a better life. Standards of living began to rise, and with them hopes for future generations. Agricultural and industrial production began to soar. Education, geared specifically to the needs of the people, began to be regarded as an inalienable right. Physical health and life expectancy showed improvements so dramatic that they began to attract world attention. Colonialism was abolished as the society's prevailing political institution, greatly modified as an economic force, and virtually destroyed as an attitude of mind. Democracy began to take its place as a working reality.

1

That small society is not Denmark of the nineteenth century; it is today's Puerto Rico. The story of its anguish, explosion, and current effort is the burden of this book. It is an important story which should be better known than it is, if only because it reflects great credit and honor on the United States at a time in world history when the United States is under wide and vicious attack.

It is an important story, too, because a billion former and present colonial subjects in all parts of the Western world are today demanding the right to struggle for the things that Puerto Rico has begun to achieve. Those thousand million people in Asia, Africa, Latin America, and Oceania are not interested in radio polemics on political institutions. They are hungry and they demand the right and the opportunity to produce more food. They are unemployed and they demand the right and the opportunity to create jobs. They are ill and they demand public health facilities. They demand the right and the opportunity to create—through education and all the other processes which together make for a better life—a free and creative future for their children.

The story of modern Puerto Rico is the story of how such demands can be met, in decency, within the framework of capitalistic democracy, resulting in the immeasurable strengthening of that democracy. Hence, modern Puerto Rico —with all its faults, all its mistakes, all its glaring deficiencies —is a microcosm and a social laboratory of world importance.

More than two million people live on a tropical island a hundred miles long and thirty-five wide—about as large as Long Island—and on a few adjoining islands such as Vieques. Their density of population is more than 650 per square mile, which is one of the highest in the world for a predominantly agricultural society. Their birth rate is high; the population grows at an alarming pace. Before the onset of the modern era, in 1940, they were relatively helpless, as a colony of the

United States, to cope with their own urgent problems; at least they thought they were helpless, which amounts to the same thing. Their colonial economy operated more for the benefit of corporation shareholders on the United States mainland than for that of Puerto Rico's people themselves. The majority of those people suffered all their lives from malnutrition which amounted to a process of slow—and sometimes rapid—starvation. Most of them bore their hunger, their many illnesses, their abject poverty, their miserable housing, and their exploitation by a few large sugar companies with a hopeless fatalism.

Then, in 1940, they elected a leader who promised only to guide them on the long, tortuous, and sometimes perilous uphill road toward a decent life. With that election the Puerto Rican people expressed their determination to take hold of their own affairs, to create and fulfill their own promises, to shape their own destinies.

The casual visitor to Puerto Rico today may not recognize many of the outward signs of the enormous progress made since 1940, because he has no starting point for comparison. He may see only a few fine hotels, a number of equally fine homes, some paved roads, beautiful scenery, a few large housing projects, and the seething slums, rural and urban, which remain from the days of darkness and cannot, even today, be abolished entirely. The chances are that he will not see the dedicated and energetic officials who work day and night and never let go of the problems which have become their very existence. He may never stumble onto the people in the hills and on the coastal plain, discussing their own problems and the ways in which they might be solved through direct community action. But if he saw the island a few decades ago, and returns today, he will be all but overwhelmed by the changes observed and the far greater changes that are obviously in the making.

Whoever knew the island twenty years ago and sees it today, whoever saw, then, towns like Luquillo falling into decay, with jungles in the plaza, streets pitted, houses falling to pieces, and sees them now, built up, painted, repaired, with paved streets and well-planned new buildings; whoever walked the country roads then and saw the people dragging their feet in lethargy, sometimes raiding garbage trucks for food and as often carrying the coffins of their dead children, and sees them now—far more friendly and vital, at times complaining healthily about the bureaucracy of their government which seems to impede the progress that didn't exist twenty years ago; whoever compares the analytical reports of the recent past with those of today, examines their statistics, tabulations, graphs, and footnotes, on production, budget, education, public health, and the elections that express the people's will in political terms, will know immediately that he sees a new Puerto Rico, a Puerto Rico about which it has been said that it made more progress in the years since 1940 than previously in all the centuries since Columbus landed there.

Since 1940, Puerto Rico has, among other things:

Greatly extended its power network and launched a remarkable program of industrialization to give employment and to strengthen and diversify the economy.

Made strong headway in the diversification, modernization, and augmented production of its agricultural plant.

More than doubled its per capita annual income in terms of purchasing power and made strides in the improved distribution of that income among all the island's people.

Created one of the best public-health services in the hemisphere and reduced its death rate to a figure comparable to that of the continental United States.

Expanded its educational system and taken drastic steps toward its reshaping to fit modern needs.

Extended that great impetus to all classes of Puerto Ricans, to the point where thousands are today "civically employed" and are giving their thoughts and labor to the task of directly improving their lives instead of expecting their government to do everything for them.

Created social and economic conditions under which its former "explosive" birth rate has turned the corner and is rapidly declining, so bringing the society ever nearer the point where population will finally be in balance with the productive effort.

Abolished its former colonial status and created new forms of political relationships under which it is today an "independent" country within the framework of the United States, sharing the broader independence of the latter.

A program so effective and vitally important cannot, of course, be carried forward without opposition. The wonder in Puerto Rico is not that opposition exists but that it is weak. The Catholic Church, for instance, which once played a powerful role in Puerto Rican affairs, is not entirely happy over today's improvements. At least one of its high officials, Bishop McManus of Ponce, bewails the separation of church and state under the Commonwealth's constitution and repeatedly charges the entire program with being immoral. Nevertheless, the great effort rolls on and gathers momentum daily.

A gratifying side result of Puerto Rico's current orientation is a new and vital sense of identification with the United States. As never before, the majority of Puerto Ricans now sense and express a deep pride in their American citizenship and their status as members of the great American Union. Relatively few remain who still advocate independence apart from the United States. Most of these identify themselves politically as *Independentistas,* or members of the Independence party which registers minority votes but elects few if any officeholders. Its leaders hope to achieve sovereignty by peaceful means and in a spirit of reasonable friendship toward the United States. A very small handful, by now reduced to a few hundred, call themselves Nationalists, express venomous hatred for the United States, are fanatically dedicated to an abstraction called freedom, and make themselves felt and heard through bloodshed and terrorism. They were heard from on November 1, 1950, when two of them tried to assassinate President Truman, and again on March 1, 1954, when four of them sprayed the House of Representatives with bullets for the purpose of embarrassing the United States at the Tenth Inter-American Conference which opened that day at Caracas. Their cause and tactics win a certain amount of applause in communist circles and in some Latin American countries. In no way do they represent the thoughts and aspirations of more than an infinitesimal part of Puerto Rico's people.

Rexford Tugwell wrote as follows about the achievements of the Commonwealth's leaders and people, in the Annals of the American Academy of Political and Social Science, January, 1953:

"Seldom—in my experience or in my reading—have I encountered instances of such sudden, determined, and effective moods of enterprise as have risen and persisted in Puerto Rico during the last decade. Moreover, the movement seems to pervade all phases of economic, political, and social life, and by now to have reached so firm a resolution as to have more than an even chance of constituting the beginning of one of those progressive spirals that social theorists are learning to treat with so much respect. It is not too much to say that a transformation is in process which for a long time will be one of the wonders of human history."

Puerto Rico's first governor was Juan Ponce de León of Florida fame. The first governor to be elected by the people of Puerto Rico themselves is Luis Muñoz Marín. The political changes which preceded and followed his first election, in 1948, are parts of a world-wide trend. They correspond to the postwar granting of independence to the Philippines, India, and Indonesia, of dominion status to Ceylon, and to the evolution which makes dominion status for Nigeria and the Gold Coast almost a certainty for the near future.

In his first inaugural speech, on January 2, 1949, Muñoz said: "Colonialism is obsolete and is disappearing with relative speed from the face of the earth." Referring to conditions at home, he said: "The colonial system not only is going to disappear in Puerto Rico, but is already speedily disappearing, much more so than in other places. In what colony, in what part of the world or in what time, has there taken place an act like this? What colony has ever elected, with the free votes of its people, its own legislative and executive government? No greater tribute can be paid to the people of the United States, and particularly to their president and congress, than recognition of the unprecedented nature of their action. Traces remain of the colonial system in Puerto Rico, but it is evident that colonialism is being abolished rapidly in this community."

The inaugural celebration at which he spoke those words was undoubtedly the greatest celebration, the most overwhelming and spontaneous outpouring of the human spirit, in Puerto Rico's history. Those who attended it will never forget it. On July 25, 1952, I attended another celebration which marked the final liquidation of the island's colonial status, and the emergence of the new Commonwealth of Puerto Rico as a self-governing member of the American Union. In the intervening time, Congress had passed its Public Law 600, which permitted the people of Puerto Rico to draft their own constitution. Unique in federal legislation, that law amounted to the offer of a compact between Puerto Rico and the United States. It was not to go into effect unless accepted by the people of Puerto Rico; if the latter rejected it, Public Law 600 was to be a dead letter. Puerto Rico had held a plebiscite accepting it, as well as an election of members of the constituent convention. The latter had drafted the new constitution to replace the Jones Act—drafted in Washington—under which the island had been governed since 1917. The people of Puerto Rico had accepted the constitution, and Congress had ratified it early in July, 1952, after proposing one or two minor changes which the Puerto Rican Constitutional Convention accepted.

That series of events had created what is in effect a compact, freely entered into and accepted by both parties—by what had formerly been the ruling country and the colony. Under that compact the Commonwealth of Puerto Rico is today a self-governing member of the American Union, composed of American citizens and in all ways a member of the great American economic structure. Whatever dissatisfaction with it still exists in Puerto Rico, as among those who strive for an independence synonymous with national sovereignty, however the present Commonwealth status may or may not be Puerto Rico's ultimate political form, the democratic fairness with which the Congress had gone along in the evolutionary process creating the Commonwealth is deeply appreciated by almost all Puerto Ricans except the remaining handful of rabid Nationalists who saw their cause evaporating before their eyes and expressed their resulting fanaticism through the tragic shootings in the Capitol on March 1, 1954.

The new status became official on July 25, 1952, selected as Constitution Day because it was also the day on which General Miles had landed on Puerto Rican soil with his troops during the Spanish-American War. Throughout Latin America, long aware of Puerto Rico's unique status as the last former Spanish possession in the Western Hemisphere to come under the American flag, the event aroused much interpretive interest. One reason was that Muñoz used the occasion as a means of repaying the great debt which he felt the Puerto Ricans owed to the United States. To his co-workers, who were making feverish preparations for the celebration in the brief time available, he said:

"Invite several hundred guests of honor from the United

States and Latin America. Especially from Latin America. Invite them by telephone and cable. Charter planes to bring them here if necessary. Invite important political figures and journalists. Include some known Latin American enemies of the United States if they will come. We must show them something about the United States that many of them have never dreamed of. As Latin Americans, we owe it to Washington to do everything in our power to improve America's reputation throughout the continent."

The guests of honor came from Washington, New York, Baltimore, and Boston, from Havana, San José, Lima, Quito, Santiago, and Mexico, several hundred of them, at little Puerto Rico's expense. The government arranged a picnic for them at Luquillo Beach. Muñoz took the Latin Americans aside for a special talk, designed to alter a number of conceptions still current in Latin America about the United States being the colossus of the North, the Yanqui Imperialist, the Dollar Diplomat who showed his reputedly evil intentions toward all of Latin America in his treatment of Puerto Rico.

I didn't hear the talk and saw no copy of it. No copy was ever made. Muñoz talked informally to his fellow Latin Americans. I once wrote down the essence of what I thought and heard he had said, and asked him to check it. When I got it back, he had written on the margin: "I don't talk that way. This is a sales talk. You can't sell truth with sales talks. In fact, you don't 'sell' truth. You live it, express it, lay it out under the sun."

I asked him what he *had* said. He answered: "I simply told them our story. I told them about the anguish of our former colonialism and about our successful determination, since 1940, to abolish that colonialism and all its psychological and economic evils. I told them about the series of events, and about the Congressional fairness, which led to our present commonwealth status. I told them how that status fits our economic as well as cultural realities, with no implication of imperialism. I told them about the great social and economic progress which we have been able to achieve during the last decade and invited them to go wherever they wanted on the island and see the signs of that progress for themselves. They all knew us as Latin Americans who have remained Latin Americans in culture. I didn't have to sell them anything. I let them see Puerto Rico and draw their own conclusions about us and the United States."

There, obviously, was an important if informal international conference which did much to improve our good name in the hemisphere and may for years to come have important effects on inter-American relations. Two years before the Caracas conference, it established a point of view which was later to do much to offset the mad actions of four Nationalists in Washington on the day of that conference's opening.

Not only the Latin American nations, but all the "underdeveloped" parts of the noncommunist world are becoming realistically aware of the nature and deep significance of Puerto Rico's modern effort. That awareness is fostered systematically and consciously through the Commonwealth's active and voluntary participation in the world-wide Point IV program. The very conversation which Governor Muñoz Marín had with President Truman in 1949, arranging for that participation, was unique in Puerto Rican affairs.

For half a century after the Spanish-American War, the Puerto Rican people had virtually been beggars at Washington's door. No matter what the United States did, it seemed never to be enough. Virtually every Puerto Rican who went to Washington on an official mission, and many who went there for personal reasons, pleaded for the redress of wrongs, real or imagined, for more justice, more self-government, increased relief from mounting poverty. In San Juan they talked in those terms to their various governors, Americans appointed by Washington; in Washington they talked to all the Presidents, one after another; they saw the various Secretaries

of War and later the Secretary of the Interior; they button-
holed Senators and Representatives. Sometimes they were
heard sympathetically; sometimes their pleas were effective
in certain ways; sometimes—as in the case of President Cool-
idge who thought that the Puerto Ricans should be grateful
for what they had and not ask for more—they were rudely re-
buffed. That pattern was broken in 1949, when the first governor elected by the people of Puerto Rico saw the President
of the United States and offered favors instead of asking them.

In his inaugural address, Truman had made his sensational
"Point IV" statement, which went around the world like an
electric shock and came to be regarded, in many parts of
Africa and Asia, as the most important single statement made
by a world leader in the postwar era. "We must embark," he
had said, "on a bold new program for making the benefits of
our scientific advances and industrial progress available for
the improvement and growth of underdeveloped areas. More
than half the people of the world are living in conditions approaching misery. Their food is inadequate. They are victims
of disease. Their economic life is primitive and stagnant.
Their poverty is a handicap and a threat both to them and to
more prosperous areas."

Aptly, he had described the Puerto Rico of ten years earlier,
with equal aptness, the kind of program for which the people
and leaders of Puerto Rico had begged for decades.

There is no written record of the conversation between the
two when Muñoz visited President Truman shortly after the
latter's inauguration. In general, however, it went as follows:

The President said: "What can I do for you?"

"Nothing," answered the Governor of Puerto Rico. He said
to the President: "During the past ten years we have changed
from 'Operation Lament' to 'Operation Bootstrap.' We have
begun to do the things that you call for in your Point IV. We
have worked out techniques for doing them and are well on
the way to solving our basic problems. Within the framework

of the American scheme of things we have also strengthened and widened our democracy immeasurably. Now we want to do what we can to help you implement Point IV."

He went on to explain: "We believe that we have something to show and to teach the so-called underdeveloped regions and their people. If you will send us their representatives and your technicians, we will gladly show and teach them whatever we can—as result of our past ten years of experience. We believe that we will thereby also help to strengthen the good reputation of the United States throughout the world, because what we have done, and are doing, is to a large extent a result of American fairness, co-operation, and democracy."

Muñoz returned to San Juan and talked to his legislature. Even before the U.S. Congress had passed the legislation which made a small reality out of Point IV, little Puerto Rico, struggling to solve its own problems with inadequate means, poorer by far than the poorest state in the union, had appropriated $50,000 for the purpose of aiding the nation in its new world-wide program. No state, no other part of the American Union, has contributed financially to the Point IV program. Every year since 1950 our former colony has appropriated $35,000 for the same purpose, and similar appropriations are planned for the next six years.

Appropriate governmental machinery was set up in San Juan and Washington. Not only American technicians, but also official visitors from all the underdeveloped parts on the democratic side of the Iron Curtain, began to go to the island under the new official program. They go there today in a swelling stream. They visit the island for a few days, a few weeks, months, or a year. They inspect the various programs, talk to the leaders, exchange ideas, gain ideas. Some go on scholarships provided by Puerto Rico and obtain valuable training in a large variety of skills ranging from the planning of public works through agronomy, social programs, and housing, to such trades as printing and auto-mechanics. At the time of the present writing, approximately a thousand foreign visitors and students have either been sent to Puerto Rico by Washington or have been attracted directly by the island itself. According to official records, they have come from all of the Caribbean islands and from nineteen Latin American republics, from Burma, Egypt, Formosa, Guam, Hawaii, India, Indonesia, Iraq, Israel, Italy, Japan, Liberia, Gold Coast, New Zealand, Nigeria, Pakistan, the Philippines, Rhodesia, Spain, Tanganyika, Thailand, and the Union of South Africa.

Those men and women have made an international crossroad out of what a decade earlier had been "America's Cherished Slum." Many of them have borrowed the Puerto Rican idea and techniques, and even Puerto Ricans, for the purpose of extending the island's upward spiral to other parts of the world. Puerto Rican innovations and inventions, in such fields as education, public health, housing, and finance, have begun to appear in India and Pakistan, Indonesia and West Africa. The Dutch possession of Surinam has adopted modified Puerto Rican practices for the solution of its slum clearance and housing program. As part of its reconstruction work after the devastating hurricane of 1951, the island of Antigua has adopted the Puerto Rican-devised technical and social program for building thousands of new rural homes—of concrete, sanitary, hurricane-proof, fireproof, and attractive—at a cost of some $300 each.

Quite probably, Puerto Rico's current achievements and aspirations are understood and appreciated much better in the world's underdeveloped areas in Asia, Africa, and the Americas than they are in Wisconsin, Iowa, Massachusetts, or New York—especially in New York City, where the presence of hundreds of thousands of Puerto Ricans creates serious social problems. Terms like land tenure, improved agricultural production, industrialization, low-cost housing, public health, education, social justice, and democracy have a direct meaning to even the poorest of Asians and Africans that has long been clouded to the average American by virtue of our high standards of living, which lead us to take such things for granted.

There is a curious indifference in the United States to the nature and world implications of Puerto Rico's modern transformation—an indifference which stems in part from ignorance of what is going on. The notice given to the Luquillo Beach conversation with a number of outstanding Latin Americans is a case in point. Muñoz' words on that occasion were played up in a number of Latin American newspapers and did much to further new attitudes toward the United States in countries south of the Rio Grande. To judge from the complete lack of notice in the United States press, one would think that the North American journalists and public-relations men who were present at the picnic did not consider the informal conference as being worth reporting. As far as motion pictures were concerned, the conference was a wasted effort.

There were some motion-picture photographers at the picnic, busily directing and grinding away to make a film which is undoubtedly in good focus, correctly exposed, and with excellent color values. The subject which they considered important, however, was roast pig. They made pictures of twelve succulent pigs, roasting over a great bed of charcoal. They pointed their camera at a peasant, a *jíbaro*, dressed, incongruously for Puerto Rico, in a white shirt with a red sash, who chopped one of those pigs to bits with his machete. Carefully, and with several rehearsals, they photographed the *jíbaro* in the act of putting slabs of *lechón asado* on plates and handing them to various important persons from New York and Washington, who sniffed their appreciation and smacked their lips for the benefit of public relations and inter-American good will.

Great are the powers of the professional public-relations people, who know from "scientific" investigations exactly what the public wants. According to the motion pictures made at the Luquillo Beach picnic, the most important aspect of the emergence of a new commonwealth, with political connotations that are world-wide and deep, was the roasting and serving of twelve Puerto Rican pigs.

The Korean War brought out dramatically an aspect of Puerto Rico's transformation which is extremely important, not only to the United States, but to the entire noncommunist world.

Perhaps our greatest need at the present fearful moment of history is that for allies and friends. It has been said with much truth that all our guns and tanks, all our planes and ships, all our bombs, including atom and hydrogen, will do us little good if the starving, underprivileged billion of the democratic world's population decide to go over to the communist side. One of the most important aspects of the current breakdown of colonialism is the fact that it tends to win for our side the allegiance of millions of former colonial subjects who were previously either hostile or indifferent in times of crisis. Indeed, except for such professionals as France's Senegalese troops, colonial subjects have seldom been trusted to fight in wars; the Union of South Africa dared not accept Negro volunteers during World War II, lest they shoot their Boer officers instead of their German enemies.

That custom of mistrusting colonial subjects in time of war has long been applied in Puerto Rico and has long been resented there as an insult to Puerto Rican integrity and ability. Under Spain the island was an important strategic position for Spanish troops, but a backwash as far as the Puerto Ricans were concerned. They did not participate in Spain's wars in the New World. Under the United States it became an equally important strategic position for American troops, but only slowly were the Puerto Ricans recognized as Americans through the parts they were permitted to play in our wars.

During World War I the Puerto Ricans were segregated—in a manner culturally alien to them—into various units according to whether they were white or colored, and kept in Puerto Rico or Panama for garrison duty or as labor battalions. The Puerto Ricans were not permitted to play their full parts as Americans in the war, probably because they had so little to defend and were not trusted to defend that little with any real interest in their work.

During World War II Puerto Rican soldiers saw some action on the various fronts and apparently did an excellent job. It was not, however, until the outbreak of the Korean War that the island began to develop a military history of its own in the sense that Puerto Rican soldiers, in Puerto Rican units, as such, made outstanding contributions to military events.

From the second month of that war until early in 1953, the 65th Regiment of Puerto Rican Infantry was in the thick of the Korean fighting as a unit, identifiable as being entirely Puerto Rican. At the worst time of the war it covered the retreat of the U.S. Marine Corps, holding back the communists until the marines could take new positions. It was the only unit in the United Nations forces in which all casualties were consistently replaced by volunteers, with many at home waiting to be called into action. Its casualties were heavier than were those of any other unit on the United Nations' side. It was mentioned often in dispatches.

Those of us who were in Puerto Rico in 1951 and 1952 were impressed by the overwhelming pride that the island's people showed in their soldiers in Korea. Again and again, when batches of such soldiers returned from the front, the city of San Juan was bedecked with posters saying, "Men of the 65th, we are proud of you"; the government used all available government cars, and many private cars volunteered by their owners, for the purpose of returning the soldiers to their homes; the people turned out in droves to welcome them.

Here, obviously, was something new on the cultural scene. Whatever the reasons, the fact remains that, as soon as Puerto Rico had won the right to forge ahead and create a new society with a new life, as soon as the Puerto Ricans had achieved their present status as something more than second-grade, colonial American citizens, they also displayed an almost fanatical adherence and devotion to our side in the current world struggle.

The parade on July 25, 1952, brought out dramatically another contribution that Puerto Rico is making to American democracy and human decency.

Again, as on January 2, 1949, the flags were flying all along Avenida Ponce de León and from all the public buildings throughout the island. This time, however, there was a difference. They were hung from Y-shaped poles on which the Puerto Rican flag flew side by side with, instead of under, the Stars and Stripes. In the grandstand I was accompanied by a number of graduate students from the University of Delaware. On one side of me sat Mrs. Reba Park, on the other Mrs. Margaret Harvey, both teachers in Wilmington, splendid women, and both Negroes.

In the early, military part of the parade, with planes roaring overhead, were several contingents of Puerto Rican soldiers, men of the 65th, returned from the fighting in Korea. When Mrs. Park saw them she began to cry.

"Look at them," she said. "Look at those men. White officers and Negro officers; white soldiers, brown soldiers, and black soldiers, all mixed together, all doing a job together. What a wonderful people these Puerto Ricans are! Prof, I can't tell you what it means to me to be in a country where I can forget all about being a Negro."

She was paying tribute to an element of democracy which has been basic to Puerto Rican life since long before the drafting of the new constitution being celebrated by the parade. The lack of race prejudice which she noticed was old; the tremendous wave of applause which greeted the Puerto Rican soldiers was a sign of something new, but equally important.

The men of the 65th were the high point of that parade. The popular enthusiasm which greeted them came rolling out in great surges of cheering and applause, with overwhelming emotional force, from all parts of Avenida Ponce de León.

The inordinate pride indicated by that applause is perhaps more important to the United States than is any other single aspect of the island's modern transformation.

Hunger knows no argument, and for the many and complex social processes by which our present urgent problems can be solved—and loyalties to our side of today's great world rift increased—dramatically—as hunger is permitted and encouraged to decrease, Puerto Rico is a pilot area of transcendental importance.

The "progressive spiral" mentioned by Tugwell always demands the leadership and unifying influence of what Toynbee called "a powerful personality—a breaker of the cake of custom." This, in Puerto Rico, is Luis Muñoz Marín, a poet and erstwhile New York bohemian. Modern Puerto Rico's effort is largely the effort of Muñoz Marín. The story of modern Puerto Rico is that of Muñoz Marín, of his early struggles, his failures and defeats, and his final triumphant rise to undisputed leadership. The two are inseparable. Puerto Rico cannot be understood unless Muñoz is also understood.

He is a man with a faith in man's brotherhood and creative ability so strong that it seems mystical to some, naïve to many —so unshakable that he began to impart it to his people in 1940, and so gave them a new hope, and a new faith in themselves. Whatever the philosophical weaknesses of his faith in mankind, its strength in political leadership is attested by the hundreds of new factories which have been built on the island since 1948.

He is a man who has created within and for himself the image of the noble peasant and has put it to work with outstanding success. Sociologists make complex studies of the Puerto Rican *jíbaro* and find him every bit as faulty as are all other people, just as greedy or generous, just as wise, just as confused, just as lustful. Muñoz waves all that aside. He holds to his image of the *jíbaro* as a simple peasant, shrewd, wise in his earthiness, dignified, decent, and stubborn in his demand for more decency. The image works. The main source of Muñoz' political and personal strength is the simple, earthy, and dignified love which the *jíbaros* feel and constantly express for him, in return for his own abiding rootedness in the decent qualities of all people everywhere and the *jíbaros* in particular.

He is a remarkable political figure, skilled in politics, but in no sense a politician. A poet and popular leader, he is also, however, the head of a political party. Often he finds it necessary to be almost ruthless in his management of that party for the sake of greater democracy for his island's people. Again and again he must teach his politicians to give up petty, momentary political gains for the sake of greater public decency.

When Chester Bowles was U.S. Ambassador to India, he repeatedly invited and urged Muñoz to visit him there. No other American, he insisted, could do as much as could the Governor of Puerto Rico to improve relations between Nehru's republic and the United States. It is unfortunate that the pressure of affairs at home prevented the latter from accepting the invitation.

What Bowles had in mind was undoubtedly related to one of the most important aspects of Puerto Rico's current orientations. At a time when Radio Moscow, with antiquated facts, inverted facts, invented "facts," or no facts at all, blares forth world-wide and vicious attacks on the United States, using Puerto Rico again and again as the stricken proof of ruthless American imperialism, hundreds of foreign visitors from all parts of the noncommunist world constantly study the island itself as the most effective example possible of "America's answer to communism."

CHAPTER II

The Colony

Puerto Rico is a relatively small island, dramatically beautiful, passionately beloved by its inhabitants, which for more than four centuries was important to somebody else for reasons which did not directly concern the Puerto Ricans. Hence it was a colony, first of Spain, and later of the United States.

The story of Puerto Rico is essentially that of a people who began as Spaniards but soon, because they were not permitted to *function* as true Spaniards, lost much of their identity as such and became culturally amorphous; it is the story of how they slowly, in part for self-preservation, acquired characteristics as Puerto Ricans, but then had to reshape those characteristics again to conform with the demands made on them by an alien culture imposed from without; it is also the story of their final triumph in becoming true Americans without giving up their characteristics as Puerto Ricans —as soon as they were permitted, truly, to function as Americans.

Juan Ponce de León, whose bones now rest in San José Church, in San Juan, was a member of Columbus' second expedition when the latter landed in Puerto Rico for water. He returned in 1508 with a group of soldiers and settlers for the purpose of pacifying the already peaceful Indians and grabbing their lands for Spanish use. The tragedy of the Indians, however, was not quite as great as has commonly been supposed. Undoubtedly, some of them died of disease and overwork and gave way to Negroes, kidnaped in Africa. But indications are that the majority simply retreated to the island's central mountain range, leaving the coastal strip to the invading whites. For almost three centuries after the first settlement, the mountainous interior remained crown territory, unsought and unused by white settlers. In many places in the interior, today, physiognomies are almost pure Indian. Among the *jíbaros* there are obviously more Indian genes than is generally believed or can be accounted for by the prevailing doctrine of ruthless extermination.

Ponce went off in 1513 to discover Florida and to die in Cuba later. He was a part of the conquest that had begun to gather the furious momentum with which it rolled over Spain's new world in the west. Near-by Hispaniola and Cuba became the jumping-off places for that conquest. Cortés in Mexico, Pizarro and Almagro in Peru, added rich lands to the Spanish domain and vast quantities of gold to Spanish pockets and the nation's treasury, while their priests began the work of adding millions of souls to the Spanish heaven. The result was an electric shock, a wave of intense excitement throughout the European world and its growing possessions, the invention or postulation of Eldorados all over the American continent, and a whole series of expeditions—many of which came to beat themselves out tragically against hard and dismal realities.

Puerto Rico's settlers, too, were inflamed by that excitement. They had by now discovered that, whatever their land might be, their lives were poor and miserable. They wanted to leave and go on to great deeds. However, they discovered to their sorrow that they were premature conquistadors. They were doomed to stay where they were and only slowly did they develop that passionate, poetic love for their own soil which is so marked a characteristic of the modern Puerto Ricans. In 1534, when they were inflamed over the news of Pizarro's conquest and Peru's fabulous wealth, their governor, in order to prevent the abandonment of an important strategic position, threatened the death penalty for any attempt at departure. Not many were affected by that threat, but a few can be every bit as indignant as can many. In 1530, after two decades of turmoil and travail, there were 300 whites on the island and 1,500 Negroes—who didn't count.

Spain came to regard Puerto Rico almost exclusively as a fortress from which to guard the Caribbean and the Isthmus of Panama—the keys to Spain's American empire. The people of Puerto Rico became servants of the fortress. They contributed so little to the empire's wealth that funds for the island's maintenance and fortification were drained from the coffers of Mexico. Contributing little, they were neglected.

San Juan's great fortress of El Castillo del Morro was begun in 1540, completed in 1606, and was not proved obsolete until 1898, when a shell from Admiral Sampson's fleet penetrated one of its walls and exploded in an underground chamber.

The fort of San Cristóbal was begun in 1631, and during those early centuries the recorded history of the Puerto Rican people was far less one of internal growth and development than of tribulations suffered in the defense of somebody else's empire. During the sixteenth, seventeenth, and eighteenth centuries there were constant efforts on the part of the English, French, and Dutch to wrest the island from Spain. Towns and settlements were repeatedly sacked and burned by French corsairs during the 1500's, rebuilt and burned again. Sir Francis Drake attacked San Juan in 1595 in an unsuccessful attempt to capture a treasure ship that had put in on the way to Spain. The English took the city three years later, but had to abandon it after some months of occupation because of illness among their troops. The Dutch burned San Juan in 1625, and raids and attacks by French and English privateers occurred periodically until the last attack on San Juan harbor before the Spanish-American War, which was made by the English in 1797. And during those dismal centuries various hurricanes ravaged the island even more than did Spain's human enemies.

Writing about the early seventeenth century, the historian, now the Commonwealth's Assistant Secretary of State, Dr. Arturo Morales Carrión says: ". . . In the country, under the most primitive conditions of life, a people is gradually forging itself which seeks its elemental sustenance from the earth and lives by clandestine commerce. A social dichotomy arises between city and country, between the fortess and the hinterland. These are two worlds, obeying different motivations. The walled city is a creation of imperialism, bulwark of a political structure which embraces vast territories. It is a stronghold in seas of enemies and heretics. It develops, therefore, a psychology of suspicion, and its citizens do not venture on the surrounding waters lest the Dutchman catch them. Within its walls, the predominant elements of its society are at each other's throats: the bishops and the governors, the governors and the councils. The country, on the other hand, produces a much more homogeneous rustic society, which lives in a primitive manner and develops its own norms and customs, alien to the great imperialistic conflicts and disdainful of the rigid metropolitan commands. So Puerto Rico develops during the seventeenth century: a land largely virgin, exuberant and forested, with a small, pauperized population, which does not succeed in creating a plantation economy with a wide base of slavery, like that which is beginning to develop in the neighboring British and French colonies."

While the general restlessness of the age of revolutions was inevitably reflected in Puerto Rico's spirit and thinking, little

seems to be known today about the extent to which Puerto
Ricans sympathized with the causes of the new republics
emerging in North and South America. The island was one of
Spain's important bases for military operations during the
Latin American wars of independence, and so was much too
thoroughly policed for any expressions of sympathy with the
revolution. Moreover, the population—45,000 in 1765 and
156,000 in 1800—was growing so rapidly, swelled by a sudden
stream of immigrants, that it was all but impossible even to
define the term "Puerto Ricans."

After the Louisiana Purchase, many Spaniards and Frenchmen moved to the island from that territory to escape the rule
of Protestant, republican America. Corsicans flocked in after
Napoleon's fall. Frenchmen came from Haiti to escape the
wrath of their former slaves, tories from Venezuela and Co-
lombia, men who despised the revolution and sought in
Puerto Rico a haven of peace and authoritarian sanity. "They
came," writes Raymond Crist, "with their wealth, their slaves,
and their experience in tropical agriculture. The influx of capital was especially timely. After the other colonies achieved
their independence from Spain, Puerto Rico no longer received from the Viceroyalty of Mexico the money which, for
some two centuries, Spain had taken from the richer colony
and allocated to the impoverished garrison of Puerto Rico,
and which had served to cover the costs of the island's civil
administration."

When the revolutionary tumult subsided, Spain had only
two colonies left in America—Cuba and Puerto Rico. A number of Puerto Ricans living in New York and Havana were
ardent advocates of their island's independence, stirring up
all the trouble they could with intrigues and letters to the
press, but on the island itself such sentiments were sternly
suppressed. The nineteenth century saw a few sporadic dem-
onstrations against Spanish authority, but only one, the *Grito
de Lares*, is of importance to the present inquiry.

The modern Puerto Rican writer, Tomás Blanco, describes the event in the following terms:

"... On September 23, 1868, the Venezuelan Manuel Rojas and the North American Mathias Bruckman gathered some four hundred men in the town of Lares and proclaimed Puerto Rico's independence. The following day the revolt terminated —with the announcement that military forces had arrived from Aguadilla."

The incident, however, cannot be dismissed in so bald a fashion. Many real patriots either participated in the *Grito de Lares* or applauded it. If it demonstrated dramatically the futility of armed resistance, it also did much to kindle the flames of patriotism, through which, during the remainder of the nineteenth century, Puerto Rico was to achieve notable results in its dignified emancipation from Spanish tyranny. The lone-star flag of freedom which was designed by the Lares patriots is today revered as the official flag of the Commonwealth.

Because of its deep significance in the evolutionary development of Puerto Rico's struggles and culture, it is all the more regrettable that the republic proclaimed at the time came to be "revived" in a later day, in a bizarre play-acting fashion, by the Nationalist leader Pedro Albizu Campos, who claimed that it had never ceased functioning and that it represented the true government of the Puerto Rican people.

The nineteenth century saw a marked though erratic movement of liberalization on the island, of preoccupation with political and economic reform, of groping toward civil liberties—which in turn resulted in the emergence of a number of truly Puerto Rican political and cultural leaders. The island's population, which had hitherto been amorphous in the cultural sense, assumed shape and identity in the sense of becoming truly Puerto Rican. It also became specific and vocal about its grievances and began to force sporadic reforms from Spain. The old mercantilistic colonial rule was altered. Commerce with the United States and foreign colonies was authorized and established. Other reforms included freedom of the press, separation of civil and military powers, and the creation of cultural societies.

One of the eventual results was the creation of an important "revolutionary" newspaper, *La Democracia,* which came to be founded by Luis Muñoz Rivera, father of the island's present governor. Founded and used during the Spanish regime for the purpose of arousing the national consciousness of the Puerto Rican people and espousing their political emancipation, it was later to be used, under American rule, for the same purposes by Muñoz Marín.

An Autonomist party was formed, and while it was torn in dispute as to whether to collaborate with liberal elements in Spain or with the revolutionary elements in Cuba, it was nevertheless dedicated to the island's eventual self-government. Spain tried repressive measures, but the voice of the Puerto Ricans was now too clamorous to be stilled. Finally, in 1897, Muñoz Rivera obtained for Puerto Rico the first real constitution, the first real charter of home rule that the island had ever had.

That constitution, which was hailed with jubilation on the island, was in effect less than a year. It died with the ceding of Puerto Rico to the United States through the Treaty of Paris. During the years immediately following—when American governors with cultural and psychological orientations alien to those of the island clashed repeatedly with the Puerto Ricans who were frantically determined to preserve what few political and civil liberties they had won after four centuries as Spanish subjects—the idea arose in the United States that the Puerto Ricans were an unruly lot, ungrateful, "unfit" for self-government. Most of the rights and freedoms which had been granted by Spain in 1897 were abrogated during the first year of our rule. Many of the Puerto Ricans who had hailed us as liberators began to take a darker view of the situation.

Long before the Spanish-American War, Puerto Rico had relatively close commercial ties with the United States—and even with the thirteen colonies which preceded the United States. In the early days the trade consisted of illicit though exuberant smuggling to circumvent Spain's repressive economic rule. During the nineteenth century it became legal.

A sugar economy developed on the island, with relatively large estates on the flat and fertile coastal lands, with a number of poor and small mills, and with the United States as its most important customer. American farmers, however, began to plant beet sugar, and in 1870 they managed to protect their infant industry with a tariff. Puerto Rican planters went bankrupt and began to clamor for free trade with the United States. Much of their land reverted to cattle raising.

After the Spanish-American War, when Puerto Rico came under the American flag, it achieved the free trade with the mainland United States for which it had clamored so long. But then it found that its plant for producing sugar was so poor, antiquated, and inefficient that it couldn't take advantage of the situation. American capital, not Puerto Rican, came to reap the major benefits of the island's inclusion within the U.S. tariff structure.

That the United States should eventually take over Puerto Rico was almost a foregone conclusion the day it became certain that we would build the Panama Canal and would have to protect it from various strategic positions. Then we fought Spain, and Puerto Rico again had the unhappy experience of becoming somebody else's sentry box from which to guard somebody else's empire. It also, however, became an investment field for millions of dollars of American capital which poured into the island under the American flag and came eventually to dominate its entire life.

That capital poured primarily into the sugar industry and resulted in a remarkable transformation and modernization. Great new mills were erected; industrial efficiency was introduced in the sleepy, backward, poverty-stricken former Spanish colony; company towns sprang up; landed estates were created to safeguard the American investments. Many Puerto Rican planters sold their lands and so their means of livelihood. Others, who tried to hold out, were squeezed out of the picture. They found that credit for their operations was available only from the large sugar companies. When they borrowed, at high rates of interest, they eventually lost their lands anyway—through mortage foreclosures. Only a relatively few Puerto Rican planters managed to survive as *colonos*, selling their cane to the great mills.

Latifundia, the concentration of land in large estates, had long been the great curse of Spanish America—the principal feature of the medieval feudalism which Spain had once imported bodily into the new world. In Puerto Rico, however, latifundia had never amounted to much under Spain. Poor, hardly worth bothering with, the island had never attracted the capital and enterprise which later resulted in large landed estates. At the time of the Spanish-American War, the docility and friendliness of the Puerto Rican people—as contrasted with the revolutionary ferocity of the Cubans—had been astutely ascribed by American observers to the more or less equitable distribution of the island's land. Now, after the Spanish-American War, and as a result of the influx of American capital and corporate efficiency, latifundia became a marked feature of Puerto Rico's culture.

According to Estéban Bird's classic report on the sugar industry, published by the Puerto Rican government in 1941, the production of 70,000 tons in 1897 grew to over 1,000,000 tons by 1934. The acreage planted to sugar cane trebled during the first thirty-five years of the century, but the tonnage produced multiplied tenfold. By direct purchase, extending credit to small planters and then foreclosing on mortgages if it seemed desirable, by leasing lands for ten- or fifteen-year periods, by any and all means, four great American sugar corporations acquired fertile holdings on the island's level coastal plain that aggregated over 166,000 acres, of which 55,000 acres were held by one corporation alone. However, in 1934, the peak year of production, only some 76,000 out of those 166,000 acres were actually planted to sugar. The rest of that vast empire was either used for pasturing the oxen which drew the sugar carts or lay idle—held in reserve while thousands of Puerto Ricans who had no jobs, or jobs insufficient for their needs, were denied a place on which to grow a few stalks of corn and a few plantains toward the end of helping to feed their gaunt families.

There were other and smaller absentee corporations in the Puerto Rican sugar picture, American as well as European, but the Big Four were by far the most powerful, controlled the largest part of the sugar lands, and dominated the political scene. Their names and holdings were as follows:

Corporation	Acreage Controlled	Acreage Planted to Sugar Cane
Fajardo Sugar	47,600	22,000
Eastern Puerto Rico Sugar	54,700	20,900
Central Aguirre	34,800	20,000
South Puerto Rico	29,000	13,000
Total	166,100	75,900

American capital poured into other branches of the island's economy, into citrus fruits, tobacco, and transportation, but sugar—under its stimulation—came to dominate everything. Coffee, which had been the principal crop just before the

Spanish-American War, withered away in importance after World War I. No absentee capital flowed into coffee. The Puerto Rican coffee growers continued to own their land, but they lost their markets and so went bankrupt anyway.

By 1930, the island's social, economic, and political system was geared almost entirely to sugar. Transportation by highway or railroad was laid out to serve sugar; agricultural credit was obtainable only in sugar; with the exception of needlework—a sweatshop industry dominated in New York and based on the cheap labor of a stricken society—nearly all existing industries served sugar; business was geared to sugar and depended largely on sugar for its well-being; politics was almost completely dominated by sugar. Not only were the various U.S. appointed governors concerned with protecting U.S. interests, which meant sugar, but sugar permeated the island's political life. The political parties which received financial donations from sugar and its associated interests could survive; the rest could not. Thousands of laborers in the sugar industry voted as their bosses and foremen told them to, on pain of losing their jobs. Other thousands of workers and small farmers in the hills sold their votes at election time because they needed the money for buying beans and rice in the expensive U.S. markets. The insular legislature came to be composed quite largely of Puerto Rican sugar lawyers who were understandably loath to disturb the island's principal industry and their own sources of income.

Sugar, to be sure, paid the major part of the insular taxes, employed the major part of its workers, created the major part of its business, supported seventeen of Puerto Rico's twenty seaports in the sense that those seventeen handled sugar exclusively and had no warehouses or other facilities for anything else. But the time was to come when sugar's contribution to the economy was woefully insufficient for the island's needs, when sugar was frozen by the depression's agricultural quota system and so was not permitted to expand, and when any economic expansion outside of sugar seemed equally impossible.

A new way of life, modern industrialism directed and managed largely from beyond the island's borders, had been imposed on the backward, Catholic agrarian society with its old Spanish cultural orientations. The results, in material plant and productive efficiency, were impressive, though too large a share of its profits went into non-Puerto Rican pockets in the mainland United States. To be sure, a number of Puerto Rican fortunes were also made from the new order of things, and a small class of Puerto Ricans, directly or indirectly associated with sugar, began to show profits, savings, and standards of living which were in marked contrast with economic conditions under Spain. Millionaires appeared for the first time on the Puerto Rican scene. Those men, however, had good reasons not to invest their monies in new local enterprises not connected with sugar and its related activities. The direct benefits reaped by Puerto Rico as a society of men and women, outside of experience, taxes, and the low wages of a cheap-labor economy, were debatable.

The joker in all that was that it was basically illegal, insofar as the sugar corporations drew their strength from their large land holdings. The Foraker Act, the first organic act drafted by Washington for the island's rule, contained a curious provision, known as the Five-Hundred-Acre Law, under which no corporation was permitted to own or control more than half a thousand acres of Puerto Rican land. Ostensibly, that federal law had been designed to protect the island against the large corporations. Dr. Henrique Bird-Piñero, however, has uncovered strong evidence—not yet published—to indicate that its inclusion in the organic act was strongly backed by the American Farm Lobby, which wanted to protect the beet sugar interests against the growth of an appreciable cane sugar rival in Puerto Rico.

Unfortunately, the law contained no teeth, no provision

for enforcement. The weak and sporadic efforts to enforce it, made in Puerto Rico during the first three decades of American rule, as the evils of latifundia became ever more apparent, were dramatically unsuccessful. By and large the law was ignored or circumvented at every turn; only a few bold Puerto Ricans, notably Muñoz Marín as a writer in New York, clamored for its enforcement. Not until 1935 did Washington show an interest in reviving it and putting it to work. Not until after the revolutionary election of 1940 did Muñoz begin truly to enforce it, and so to lay the foundation for his program for the island's transformation.

With admirable energy we Americans began to clean up in Puerto Rico immediately after the war with Spain. Roads, schools, and public-health programs attested to that energy and the good will behind it. We made fiscal arrangements which were in marked contrast to the earlier Spanish looting of the island's wealth, and which today provide the means by which Puerto Rico is able to pull itself by its bootstraps out of its former morass.

The armed forces, which in Spanish days had been a drain on the island's economy, now began to contribute to it. Military and naval constructions, pay and pensions to Puerto Rican soldiers and sailors, benefits for their dependents, the operation of airports—all these and many more, mounting steadily in volume and importance from the Spanish-American War through World Wars I and II into the present era of fearful alert, have poured millions of dollars into Puerto Rico.

While Puerto Rico was given free entry into the tariff-protected American market, it was also stipulated that customs receipts from foreign vessels in insular ports need not be turned over to the federal treasury but might be retained on the island to help manage its affairs.

Having no voting representation in the federal government,

and on the principle of no taxation without representation, the Puerto Ricans have never paid taxes to Washington. Even today, their income taxes are paid exclusively to their own government, and excise taxes on goods manufactured locally —such as rum—remain in Puerto Rico instead of being paid into the federal treasury as they are from the various states.

From the beginning of American rule until the grim 1930's, the official statistics showed steady gains in trade, education, public health, road construction, and virtually all other matters to which official statistics are dedicated. The external trade grew from $19,789,000 in 1899 to $183,285,000 in 1930. We began to point with pride to the fact that, under the American flag, Puerto Rico had acquired more telephones per inhabitant, more miles of road, more seats in schools, more hospital beds, more of almost everything imaginable, than many another country in the Americas—whichever happened to be convenient for comparison. There were more jobs than formerly, and certainly the per capita income, calculated on the basis of total income divided by total population, was higher than it had ever been before. Since 1903 there had been a University of Puerto Rico, and a number of its graduates had been able to find jobs in the insular scheme of things, in government, the professions, public services, and the like.

The only difficulty about all that was that it didn't work out for the people of Puerto Rico. Writing in New York in 1929, Muñoz Marín called Puerto Rico "a land of flattering statistics and distressing realities."

The illness of Puerto Rico's colonial economy became apparent during the late twenties, even before the onset of the depression, when the Brookings Institution published its survey of the island, and when Bailey Diffie and his wife Justine, produced their *Porto Rico, a Broken Pledge*,* important as

* NOTE: The island's official name during the first three decades of American rule was Porto Rico, a matter which caused many Puerto Ricans to complain that we had robbed them even of the correct spelling of their name. It was changed to Puerto Rico during the early years of the Roosevelt regime.

the first passionate—though at times exaggerated—attack on the evils of Puerto Rico's colonial economy to be made by a non-Puerto Rican scholar. The Diffies pointed out that, while Puerto Rico usually enjoyed a favorable balance of trade in which the value of exports exceeded that of imports by about $10,000,000 annually, the balance of payments was seldom if ever taken into account.

The profits drained from Puerto Rico by absentee investors, the freight paid on goods exported from Puerto Rico or imported to the island from the mainland, rents on absentee-owned properties, and various other items, came, according to the Diffies and to Jack De Golia's study of the tariff and trade situation, to somewhere around $20,000,000. That meant that the economy as a whole grew poorer by some $10,000,000 per year—except for federal expenditures and the capital investment, which stopped about the time that the Diffies wrote their book.

Muñoz Marín pointed out in one of his articles that Puerto Rico's "favorable" balance of trade resembled that of a burglarized house, in which exports also exceed imports.

After 1930 Puerto Rico headed rapidly toward complete bankruptcy. Municipality after municipality could not pay its obligations in wages and salaries; the bonded indebtedness as well as private mortgages soared to unprecedented heights; personal suffering, amounting to near starvation, permeated the population.

Puerto Rico's statistics improved immeasurably, but there is a vast difference between people and statistics. Under the aegis of the United States, and in line with a common colonial phenomenon which demographers have never been able to explain satisfactorily, the birth rate also began to soar. The fact that sanitary measures were improved undoubtedly had something to do with the matter. The fact that poverty and hunger are often themselves contributors to a downward social spiral, in which a high and growing birth rate is another contributor, is also relevant. In 1900 the population was about 900,000; by 1940 it had risen to nearly 2,000,000. To be sure, the economy expanded during the century's early decades, but it was an artificial economy as far as Puerto Rico was concerned, devoted in too great a measure to other people's enrichment. Moreover, it didn't expand as rapidly as did the population—and it stopped expanding about 1929, when new capital stopped flowing into the island.

Throughout the first four decades under the United States, Puerto Rico remained truly a stricken land, disease infested, hungry, beset by poverty so far as the bulk of its population was concerned, virtually without hope.

Dr. Bailey Ashford, who served in Puerto Rico as major in the Medical Corps of the U.S. Army, described conditions in the coffee hills as follows:

"Rose [Director of the Rockefeller Sanitary Commission] saw the poor mud-stained laborer degraded by his disease and literally submerged in the monotonous routine of coffee culture, living from hand to mouth; his children starving and sick; and his wife, no better off than he, working a bit in the coffee grove and a listless bit in the bare shack. He saw the exquisite beauty of these tropical mountains with their sheer ravines and their limpid streams. He felt the cool damp of the coffee grove under the feathery shade of the guava tree. He talked with the plantation owners and found that only a tithe of his workmen were worth their salt, and that they were held on as laborers—with a wage pitifully low, it is true—because the owner hadn't the heart to turn his half-starved people off, sick as they were. He personally verified their ragged clothes, their lack of shoes, and their docile, animal-like constancy in the work of the *amo*, or master. He talked with the *jíbaros* and found a man who had descended almost if not quite to the level of the beasts, stumbling about by day over the slippery mud of the coffee plantation, sleeping cold and wet at night without bed or bed covering, eating what he could get, a fare limited principally to a mess of rice and beans, with codfish and tubers—and procreating, with no thought of the morrow, no thought of the hereafter, no thought of the future of his sons and daughters, not even a thought of a freer, better life; only a monotonous repetition of today, yesterday, and of the other yesterdays before it." *

Ashford wrote about conditions early in the century, shortly after the end of the Spanish regime. But in 1929, Governor Theodore Roosevelt, Jr., described the island's country people in much the same language. Even those who were employed by the sugar industry led a dismal life.

In 1935, sugar employed some 100,000 workers, or about 20 per cent of all who worked for wages. About 93,000 of these were farm laborers, most of whom worked four or five months a year, during the harvest season, and were idle the rest of the time. Most of the sugar workers lived in company houses, which were often better than were other rural living quarters; they traded in company stores at prices that were generally lower than those in other stores; they had credit at some of the company stores, which helped to tide them over the long dead season; their wages were usually somewhat higher than those they could receive elsewhere. Nevertheless, Estéban Bird charged sugar with gross injustices in its treatment of labor, while reaping impressive dividends for its absentee stockholders.

His reports read: "After making allowances for seasonality of employment, for supplemental labor of women and children and for the average number of idle days during the week, various agencies have estimated that the typical wage income of sugar laborers is around $170 per year." That was, of course, a tragic wage on which to raise and support a

* From *A Soldier in Science,* by Bailey K. Ashford. William Morrow and Company, New York, 1934. Copyright 1934 by William Morrow and Company. Quoted with permission of the publisher.

family, clothe it, educate it, feed it largely on imported foods at prices higher than those paid in the continental United States. Bird goes on to cite the earlier study made in 1929 by the Brookings Institution, according to which the average weekly wage of a Puerto Rican working-class family was "$6.47 per family, $3.49 per worker, and $.85 per person. Approximately twelve cents per day to cover all their daily requirements. These families spend 94 per cent of their weekly earnings for food, the largest single item being polished rice—*a coolie's diet*.

"Twelve cents per person per day," writes Bird indignantly, "is only four cents more than the food expense required for feeding a hog in the United States! No wonder these laborers have even lost combativeness to do what was witnessed in the United States during the recent depression—farmers in the West holding up trucks in transit laden with food, picket lines formed by a harassed and embattled farm group ready to combat by any means the desperate situation created by a social structure on the verge of collapse. Twelve cents per person per day explains why birth, sickness, accident, and death are suffered with a *helpless fatalism*.

"Twelve cents per person per day is the root of all evil; it ought to dispel the brutal contempt for this laborer held by many defenders of the present state of affairs who accuse him of laziness. Twelve cents per person per day plays a prominent part in a death rate of 575 (per 100,000) for enteritis and diarrhea, 237 for tuberculosis, and 221 for malaria in the sugar cane areas of Puerto Rico."

To Bird's statement should be added that tens of thousands of Puerto Ricans were totally unemployed during the depression and had no land on which to grow subsistence crops, and that thousands of women were working at home for the needlework industry, for pay that began in New York at sweatshop rates and was divided and fractioned by various contractors and subcontractors until at times, when it finally reached the workers, it amounted to three cents per dozen for hand embroidering and hemming handkerchiefs.

Twelve cents per person per day, and no cents at all for 150,000 unemployed, and three cents per dozen handker-chiefs, go far to explain the lethargy and spiritual corruption of Puerto Rican politics before 1940. The man who earned that twelve cents voted as he was told, lest he lose it. The man who didn't earn it voted as he was told because somebody paid him two dollars for so doing. From the United States, progressively lightening its political control through the decades, Puerto Rico had achieved a measure of home rule that was on paper notable as colonial affairs go. At twelve cents per person per day it tended to be a sham, operating largely for the perpetuation of evils and for the benefit of the entrenched interests which could afford to pay two dollars every four years for the vote instead of two dollars daily for the work.

CHAPTER III

The Anguish of Colonialism

DURING THE EARLY YEARS of American rule, mainland corporations had little difficulty in absorbing a large part of Puerto Rico's economy. Absorbing the Puerto Ricans culturally, as Americans, was more difficult and took longer—especially since thousands of them continued to starve on their feet. With their Spanish agrarian heritage, they differed from us in their language, their cultural orientations, their desires from life, their views on individual dignity and on personal, financial, and political morality. Only recently, and only dimly have we begun to realize that a man can be no less good an American because his language is Spanish, he considers Cervantes a greater writer than Hemingway, and has reservations about Lincoln's having been the only great liberator, since his own slave-owning grandfather had once been one of a group that petitioned Spain to abolish slavery in Puerto Rico, with or without compensation.

One of the most important aspects of Puerto Rico's modern transformation is the growth of the idea that several million people can retain their Spanish language and the basic aspects of their old Spanish culture and still be good Americans. Few Puerto Ricans doubt that Washington now—in contrast to its former attitudes—officially thinks so. Many doubt, how-

ever, whether the Puerto Ricans can long retain a relatively
pure Spanish language and culture while working in factories,
American style, listening to U.S. radio broadcasts, transfer-
ring their allegiance from coffee houses to bars and Coca-Cola
stands, and serving in the U.S. armed forces.

It is always risky, however, to refer to any people as "they."
The Puerto Ricans who were consciously concerned with culture changes during the early days of American rule and took
an interest in political and international affairs belonged to
the relatively small upper class. Some 80 per cent of the population consisted of the submerged poor. Most of these were
aware of their own suffering and serious personal problems,
but their patriotism was confined largely to a passionate love
for their island.

In a speech delivered in 1951, Muñoz described their feelings toward their country in the following words: "To the
Puerto Rican, *patria* is the colors of the landscape, the change
of seasons, the smell of the earth wet with fresh rain, the voice
of the streams, the crash of the ocean against the shore, the
fruits, the songs, the habits of work, and of leisure, the typical
dishes for special occasions and the meager ones for everyday, the flowers, the valleys, and the pathways. But even more
than these things, *patria* is the people: their way of life, folkways, customs, their ways of getting along with each other.
Without these latter things *patria* is only a name, an abstraction, a bit of scenery. But with them it is an integral whole:
the homeland *and* the people."

The process of Americanizing Puerto Ricans was, until
recently, held back by the fact that they were officially and
individually often regarded as being inferior to almost any
American fool who came along.

There have been a number of American ladies on the island,
wives of American lawyers, managers, technicians, or officials,
who have prided themselves on the fact that no Puerto Ricans

had ever set foot in their homes except servants. Descendants of the conquistadors, leaders of Puerto Rican thought and affairs, men with international reputations as scholars, were excluded from the guest lists of those ladies for the simple reason that the latter did not want people to think that they were going native.

Shortly after we stepped into the picture, the Puerto Rican government created a number of scholarships and sent several groups of young men to the States to study in various universities. The first of those groups seems to have raised serious problems in Washington. Some say that Washington's officials thought that they must be Indians, since they came from the West Indies; others, that the capital was simply determined to keep colonial subjects apart from first-class American citizens. Whatever the reason, the boys of the first group were sent to that great institution for the segregation of colonial subjects—Carlisle Indian School.

Non-Puerto Rican enterprises on the island, American sugar mills and plantations, business firms owned and managed by American or European capital, adopted employment and social policies which have long been common to colonialism everywhere. No matter how well qualified by education or skill, Puerto Ricans were not permitted to hold top-level jobs in such enterprises. For the lesser jobs they did hold, they were paid less than any imported American or European would have been. As colonial subjects, and with rare exceptions, they were not admitted to the clubs and social life of the resident Americans.

Meanwhile, however, a group of super-patriots began to rise among the Puerto Ricans, partly because they sincerely wanted to become Americans in spirit and culture as well as in fact, and partly because they often found it easier to do business and get jobs if they glowed with fervor over everything American. That Americanism, however, as preached by resident Americans, by many U.S. officials, and by the Puerto

Rican super-patriots themselves, had an odd twist to it. An American living in the States could, can, and does criticize many things American. In Puerto Rico, however, a man was not considered a good American if he criticized anything at all that came from the United States. Everything American had to be accepted as being best and unassailable, lest the Puerto Rican who criticized it be regarded as un-American —and so, in some cases, even lose his job. Any clerk in the Department of the Interior, any member of the military brass, any continental businessman, was in that manner perforce accepted as knowing more about Puerto Rico's problems than did the island's people and leaders themselves.

The new class of super-patriots, blindly embracing that odd kind of Americanism, was exemplified by a high official of the insular government who always flew the American flag in front of his house and lowered it daily, at sunset, with a great ceremonial to-do. Slowly, reverently, lovingly, he pulled on the halyard until the flag was in his arms. Slowly, reverently, lovingly, he caught each precious fold, lest some part of the flag touch the ground. Sowly, reverently, lovingly, he then looked around to see if anybody was looking—preferably an American. With or without an audience, but better with one, he hugged the flag to his breast, kissed it, and staggered into the house with his precious burden.

A salesman from Illinois was introduced to one of the super-patriots in San Juan. Asked what part of Illinois he had come from, he answered, "Springfield."

"Ah," came the impassioned answer. "You must indeed be proud. Springfield, Illinois, the home of Abraham Lincoln, the Emancipator, the greatest man who ever lived. Doesn't it fill you with reverence to have sprung from the soil made sacred by Lincoln?"

Whereupon the salesman turned to another man and said: "What's the matter with him? Is he nuts?"

The super-patriots gave rise to the story about the Americanometer, with which the irrepressible intellectuals amused themselves. That strange device, according to the story, was designed to measure the degree of people's Americanism. Having built a model, the inventor dug up the spirit of George Washington for the purpose of testing his machine. It registered an Americanism of 55 to 60 per cent, which was quite good, and in line with historical fact. Then he tried it on Abraham Lincoln and got a rating of 75 per cent, which also indicated a high degree of accuracy. Franklin D. Roosevelt ran it up to 90 per cent, which was almost perfect. But when the machine was tried on the flag-kissing official, the Springfield lover, and various other super-patriots, it always gave trouble. Invariably the Americanometer then began to smoke, spin, and dance from overwork; its needle began to stagger and strain upward and ever farther upward—up beyond 100 per cent, up beyond 150 per cent, up to 200 per cent—steadily upward until the whole machine flew to pieces in a terrible explosion from the vast pressure of Americanism behind it.

The super-patriot is still found in Puerto Rico, but largely among the older people. Today's leaders, businessmen, teachers, professional men, are people who don't need to embrace Americanism with quite so much passion. Born under American rule, and often educated in the United States, they had little difficulty in acquiring American ways and habits of thought. It was perhaps for that very reason that Puerto Rico's real revolution, which began in 1940 and has accomplished wonders in the abolition of the colonial psychology, did not get under way until the island society had acquired its first twentieth-century leader, reared in the United States, equally at home in both cultures, aided by a group of new helpers who were also brought up under the American regime and able to chart the island's remarkable progress as an integral part of the American scheme of things.

By the same token, once the Puerto Ricans had begun to

become Americans culturally it was impossible for them to remain colonial subjects.

Excluded from high position in American firms, Puerto Ricans were also excluded, during the first two decades of our rule, from high positions in their own government. Not until 1917 did Puerto Ricans begin to be appointed to such positions—although still for the purpose of carrying out policies that had been drafted in Washington; not until 1952 were the island's people entirely free to determine their own policies—within the framework of the American Constitution as interpreted by the U.S. Supreme Court—and to elect their own leaders for the purpose of carrying out those policies.

Puerto Rico's insular politics struggled always in the black shadow of the island's poverty, dominated by that poverty and the resulting frantic struggle for twelve cents. Men at the bottom of the social scale voted as they were told because they needed their paltry wages; men and women higher up found that the greatest single employer of white-collar workers was the government. There were virtually no industries to absorb the energies of those whom the university was turning out. When the economy stopped expanding in 1930, government became almost the only possible employer of the ever-swelling stream of maturing, educated Puerto Ricans who had to make their livings in one way or another.

Hence, although it was always carried along by glowing phrases devoted to high ideals, Puerto Rican politics became largely a partisan struggle for control of the budget—and so also of patronage. A man's living, his very life, the living and the very lives of his children, often depended on whether or not his party came into power or at least won some few crumbs of patronage. Neighbors were set against neighbors, ostensibly over matters of principle but in reality over the question of jobs. Tradesmen in the various towns, druggists, haberdashers, were patronized or shunned according to their political party affiliations.

With politics largely a struggle for bread and butter, politics also came to dominate the entire insular scene. Everybody was politically minded, down to the lowliest street sweeper, who might have been all for Puerto Rico's independence but gladly proclaimed to his party boss not only his loyalty to the party, but also, if circumstances seemed to demand it—in bad English or no English at all—his passionate love for the United States—in order to get and hold his job and to be able to recommend his friends for other jobs.

Under such circumstances it is surprising to find that Puerto Rico's political leaders and politicians have on the whole always been among the most honest to be found anywhere. Virtually all of them, during and since the Spanish regime, maintained high moral standards in financial matters involving their personal integrity; every one of them died poor. The island has never experienced great scandals involving large-scale graft as opposed to petty pilfering; the Cuban and Mexican pattern of graft-riddled large or small government offices had never developed in Puerto Rico.

On the other hand, it is true that elections, before Muñoz changed matters in 1940, were riotous displays of cynical *dis*honesty. Votes were bought openly and shamelessly, and all the more easily because the men who sold them needed the money for their gaunt families. All the tricks known to crooked political campaigners—false registration, the use of floaters, the registration of the dead—were employed by the various parties with enthusiasm. A friend of mine went to the polls rather late in the 1932 election, only to be informed that he had already voted—no fewer than twenty times and impartially the same number of times for each of the competing parties. Since all the watchers there were his personal friends, they allowed him to cast the twenty-first vote. Another friend voted in eleven different polling places in the

same election, under eleven names of registered members of
the opposition party, whose votes so went to the party of my
friend. In some towns, in several elections, the numbers of
votes cast exceeded the total populations of men, women,
and children.

There was the typical story of a group of political workers
who had spent a day driving about in a car, distributing campaign literature. They were driving home late in the evening,
with several hundred undistributed handbills still in their
car. As they passed a cemetery one of them threw all these
bills over the wall to the gravestones. A companion protested.
"Stop that," he cried. "Paper and printing cost money."

"Why not?" was the answer. "Those fellows vote, don't
they?"

Cultural anthropologists might well speculate on whether
or not the Haitian institution of the Zombie had its origin in
politics, where it has existed for a long time.

The men who were sent to the insular legislature might
have their own ideas on sugar's being the great benefactor or
the squeezing octopus; once they got into the legislature they
left sugar alone. In theory, the enforcement or repeal of the
Five-Hundred-Acre Law was one of the great issues of insular
politics; in practice it was untouchable until the years immediately preceding and following the great revolution of
1940. Certainly, the entrenched sugar interests were against
its enforcement, while the American governors could usually
be counted upon to side with those interests in the matter
and to veto any insular legislation which provided for the
law's enforcement. No matter how much power the insular
legislature had, that power was always overshadowed by the
veto power of a governor who was responsible to Washington
rather than to the people of Puerto Rico. Therefore, in matters
that really counted, the various legislatures tended to behave
themselves like bodies of loyal American citizens.

In 1929, in an article in *The Nation* calling on the newly appointed Governor Theodore Roosevelt, Jr., to implement and enforce the Five-Hundred-Acre Law, Muñoz Marín wrote: "Why has nothing been done about it [the Five-Hundred-Acre Law] so far? Because the governor of Puerto Rico can, by a ruthless use of patronage and election machinery, destroy any party if given sufficient time; because parties don't like to be destroyed; and because no governor has so far let it be known that such a policy, far from drawing reprisals from him, would enlist his co-operation." Before 1940, he could have said the same about almost anything that really mattered. The fact that a governor had the power to destroy any party or leader espousing a real idea meant that nobody except a rare Muñoz Marín would openly espouse it and work for it, as opposed to merely talking about it. In 1936 Muñoz was himself to feel the full force of the powers of political destruction vested in federal officials.

The one outstanding political issue to which all parties gave lip service was that of ultimate status. It dominated all political thinking and sent shudders up and down the spines of thousands of Puerto Ricans, depending on which kind of status was discussed. Not only had the United States promised Puerto Rico that its colonialism was temporary, not only is colonialism *always* temporary by its very nature and by the natures of men, but it was obvious that colonialism was not working well and had therefore eventually to be replaced by something else.

For obvious reasons, those connected with sugar or with their bread buttered on the sugar side, those who were in business on a relatively large scale, which again meant those whose bread was buttered on the sugar side, comprised the Republican party, which was and is closely allied with that in the States and advocated statehood as the island's eventual status. They had to. Statehood was the one form of political relationship which, under the thinking of those days, best safeguarded sugar. Under statehood Puerto Rico would always be within the American tariff wall. Under statehood, argued its advocates, Puerto Rico would have its best chances to develop to its maximum capacities.

At the other end were those who advocated eventual independence, some in a spirit of bitter hostility to the United States, some in a friendly spirit—as the best means of resolving difficulties to the mutual benefit of everybody. As an independent nation, they argued, they could make foreign trade treaties and so boost their business. As an independent nation, they would be outside the U.S. tariff barrier—which undoubtedly raised prices and greatly increased the burdens of the poor. The two political parties which during the 1930's advocated independence, though with radically different approaches and philosophies, were the Liberal party and the Nationalist party.

In between was the Socialist party, which advocated continued relations with the United States but refrained from defining the relationship and from raising the status question as a political issue. A local organization, hardly socialistic in the accepted sense of the word, Puerto Rico's Socialist party had no connection with the party of the same name in the United States. What ties it had on the mainland were rather with the American Federation of Labor.

However, while the question of ultimate status was the political issue par excellence, it was so only in debate. Parties advocating independence could obtain campaign contributions from business only as long as they could be trusted not to do anything about the matter. And early during the American regime a number of Puerto Ricans discovered that it was dangerous even to advocate independence—even though it had been clearly understood from the beginning that the Puerto Ricans were entitled to independence if they really wanted it. As they had discovered under Spain, they now discovered again that it is dangerous in a colony to express and act upon firm political beliefs. What pleases one governor and is encouraged by him may not please the next—and may draw reprisals.

During the early years of American rule, the various Washington-appointed governors governed with the help of the island's Republican party, which, while for statehood and therefore undoubtedly loyal, was also by far the minority party. Then Wilson was elected President and appointed, as governor of Puerto Rico, one Arthur Yager, a liberal-minded man who showed great respect toward local feelings on political status. He did not believe that the desire for independence amounted to disloyalty to the United States, and he was the first to co-operate with the majority party—Muñoz Rivera's Unionist party, which had strong leanings toward independence and had actually been in power since 1903. Yager also began the practice of putting Puerto Ricans into important executive jobs which had previously been filled almost exclusively by continental Americans. As a result, relations between Washington and the island showed a marked improvement.

Governor Yager also labored to have the original organic act, the Foraker Act, replaced by a more liberal basic law. The resulting Jones Act was a great step in advance which did not, however, please all the Puerto Ricans. Some of those who advocated independence objected to the fact that the act offered U. S. citizenship to the Puerto Ricans; they felt that the issue of eventual status would thereby be clouded. Others objected with good reason to the fact that the Jones Act, as had the former Foraker Act, provided that the curricula and policies of the island's school system be shaped by a Washington-appointed Commissioner of Education, responsible to Washington and devoting his efforts largely toward Americanization. They wanted school curricula to be determined by a Puerto Rican Commissioner of Education, responsible to the insular legislature and permitted to devote his efforts toward shaping an educational system designed to meet the needs and problems of Puerto Rican people.

Despite such objections, however, the Jones Act was passed. Both it and Yager's liberal and enlightened rule strengthened good will toward the United States immeasurably—until Harding succeeded Wilson as President, and Yager was succeeded in Puerto Rico by a new governor of the go-getter type.

This was J. Montgomery Reily, apparently appointed by Harding to wave the flag, shout hurrah, and stand for no nonsense. His inaugural ceremony, on July 30, 1921, was one of the most splendid and impressive the island had ever seen—being designed in part to show the Puerto Ricans who was boss, and in part to celebrate locally the return of republican sanity to national affairs. But at his first meeting with leaders of the Unionist party which helped Yager govern, Reily cut loose with a blast against all ideas of independence and announced that he would govern only with the help of men who were its avowed enemies, and would appoint Unionists to office only if Antonio R. Barceló, the party's president, renounced his earlier stand on political status. Then the governor went on a barnstorming tour to all parts of the island, in which, in town halls, schools, and village greens, he violently denounced the idea of independence.

That kind of thing did nothing to endear the United States to the Puerto Ricans. It is quite evident on the island even today that the individual desire for independence is not necessarily a reasoned matter, based on political logic and growing out of either personal hardship or dislike of the United States. More often it is an unreasoned and deeply emotional outcropping of pride in culture, ways of life, habits of thought— in individual mores and orientations backed by centuries of cultural evolution. These were not only threatened by the

American way of life, artificially imposed, but were now actively, if unconsciously, attacked by Reily.

Nevertheless, Reily's campaign was a powerful incentive toward Americanism of the super-patriot kind, while also strengthening the widespread feeling of permanent mistrust toward all U.S. officials on the island, no matter how well disposed toward the people of Puerto Rico. What had it availed men to go along with Yager, only to be later punished by Reily?

The question of education, which had created much controversy during the last decades of Spanish rule, continued to be a bone of contention during the first five decades under the American flag.

Near the end of the Spanish regime, in 1874, the governor (according to Enrique Lugo-Silva in his doctor's dissertation on the Tugwell regime) sent to Spain for a number of teachers. He specified that he wanted men and women who were "completely Spanish in sentiment, to inculcate in the pupils the most healthy Christian and moral maxims, especially to teach them to love the fatherland so that they may grow to be loyal subjects of Spain, good citizens, and fathers able to support their families." They were requested because of a reputed shortage of Puerto Rican teachers, but within a few months most of the latter had been dismissed from their posts for what would today be called subversive activities. The governor accused them of "radical and autonomistic views," doubtful morality, and membership in various secret societies. He claimed that they were hostile to Spain, that they transmitted that hostility to their pupils, and that they were "sowing a seed pernicious to the future welfare of the province and fatherland, the bitter fruits of which are already being reaped in the sister Antilla [Cuba]."

When we stepped into the Puerto Rican scene in 1898, one of our first steps was to enlarge the island's school system considerably and to reshape it toward the end of accelerated Americanization. Continental educators who knew nothing about Puerto Rico and its problems went to the island as commissioners of education and shaped curricula after continental patterns, regardless of whether they were suited to the island's needs. Puerto Rican children early began to learn about the United States; their social studies dealt with life in the United States rather than with the Puerto Rican life to which they must adjust themselves; most of the history taught them was the history of the United States; their books were written in English and designed for continental students rather than for Puerto Ricans.

Worse yet, it was decreed early that all the teaching in all the grades had to be done in the English language. That was supposed to be a good way in which to teach English to the Spanish-speaking Puerto Ricans, and to make them truly bilingual. It didn't work. Teachers who knew no English suddenly had to acquire it for fear of losing their jobs; thereafter they had to do their teaching in a language that was poorly mastered and foreign to them. Children who had never in their lives heard any language but Spanish were suddenly expected, on entering the first grade, to master the three R's and other subjects, taught to them in a language they knew nothing about, by teachers who spoke it poorly and had difficulty in expressing themselves in it. The result was not any sudden, miraculous mastery of the English language by the Puerto Ricans; it was confusion mounting toward intellectual chaos and compounded by resentment.

The flaws in that system were obvious to many Americans; with the best of intentions, however, they could do little about it. Not permanently at any rate, in a system of government in which any congressman had more power than did the most enlightened administrator.

In 1930 Dr. José Padín was appointed Commissioner of Education. He managed to install important reforms under the so-called Padín plan, in which all the teaching in the primary schools was done in Spanish, but English became a required subject of study. The plan was extremely popular and worked excellently, until the turbulent year of 1936, when the Nationalists embarked on a program of violence and assassination and in some American quarters got all the Puerto Ricans blamed for the acts of a few fanatics. That was the year when tensions began to mount, and relations between Puerto Rico and Washington became badly strained. Senator William H. King of Utah, as head of the Senate Committee on Territories, made a quick trip to Puerto Rico to see what was wrong. As a result of his visit, the English language, instead of remaining a desirable subject of study, again became a political football. The chain reaction set off by King resulted in a situation in which the Americanism and loyalty of many a Puerto Rican came to be judged, not by his knowledge of the English language, but by his attitude toward the fantastic reforms instigated by Washington; if he deplored those reforms because they were obviously bad pedagogy, he was widely accused of being un-American or anti-American.

Federal officials took King in tow on his arrival in Puerto Rico and organized a motorcade which drove to all parts of the island to show the Senator how the Puerto Ricans lived and what the United States was doing to alleviate their lot. But he seemed in no way interested in slums or in reconstruction projects, or in anything else except the question of whether little boys and girls spoke English. Every time his car stopped he dove out, accosted some child on the road, and asked: "Do you speak English?" Invariably, of course, he got no answer at all; even if the child had known a few words of English, he would still have been so embarrassed, and so frightened by the august Senator, that he wouldn't have been able to say anything. At crossroad after crossroad the cars stopped to permit the Senator to pick out some child and ask his unvarying question: "Do you speak English? Answer me! Do you speak English?" At crossroad after crossroad that rather direct form of academic research brought the same negative results, with the Senator growing ever redder in the face and ever more convinced that he had the solution to the Puerto Rican problem. Then, in the southern part of the island, he came a cropper, with disastrous results to the Puerto Rican educational system.

The road crossed a river, but the water was too high for the cars to negotiate the ford. The motorcade stopped while somebody went for a yoke of oxen to pull the various cars across. While it stood there, naturally, a group of boys gathered to gawk, and the Senator had his golden opportunity. He accosted the group, but almost immediately the boys began to dance around him, shouting like Comanche Indians.

"Do you spik Eeenglish? Do you spik Eeenglish?" yelled the young rascals, who ranged in ages up to sixteen. "Do you spik Eeenglish? Do you spik Eeenglish?" With fiendish bursts of derisive laughter and impolite gestures, they danced around the Senator in unholy glee. King dove back into his car to smolder in defeat, but the insult from the youngsters was to have far-reaching results.

He was not a man to let grass grow under his feet, and when he returned to Washington he began immediately to put pressure on Harold Ickes, the Secretary of the Interior. He demanded an immediate return to the stress on English in the Puerto Rican schools.

The top men in the Department of the Interior had never approved of Padín's policies regarding the English language. Now, prodded by King, they set out to change those policies. They accepted Padín's resignation as Commissioner of Education and began to look for somebody who could be trusted to do a better job of Americanization accelerated by ramming English down the throats of the bewildered children. They didn't have an easy time; no qualified Puerto Rican would

accept the job on those terms; finally, in 1937, they settled
on Dr. José Gallardo, an instructor in Spanish in a Charleston
college who met the one principal qualification of promising
to change the Padín system in favor of something more drastic.

Gallardo fumbled about with a basically absurd system in
which the teaching was done in English half of the time, and
in Spanish the rest. That led to so epic a state of confusion
that he had to change the system himself. Prodded by Senator
King, Ickes then sent him a nasty letter, in 1943, stating that
the bad Puerto Ricans still didn't know English, that Gallardo
had not succeeded in making them bilingual in six years' time,
and that the commissioner was not doing his job.

Now the shoe was on the other foot; Gallardo was a martyr,
and many of the Puerto Rican leaders, who had bitterly opposed him and his vacillating policies, rose to his defense.
Ickes backed down—being a thoroughly honest and decent
man—but the problem of English in the Puerto Rican schools
was still far from settled.

One of Gallardo's most astonishing ideas, early during his
regime, had been that of importing a number of American
college graduates to teach in the Puerto Rican schools, more
or less as Governor Sanz had in an earlier year imported
Spanish teachers. The Americans who went were eager for
adventure, but found the going rough. To be sure, they had
received excellent teacher training at such institutions as
Columbia University; they knew all about curricula and
methods; but they knew nothing whatever about either Spanish or Puerto Rico, and therefore found it difficult, to say the
least, to fit themselves into the Puerto Rican scene. Naturally,
too, they were resented.

Gallardo couldn't pay them according to prevailing American standards; trying that would have created havoc among
the Puerto Rican teachers whose wages were far lower than
were those in the United States. But in those depression years
many teachers were glad to get any kind of job.

That odd collection of Americanizers stepped into the island's educational scene, found it impossible even to communicate with their pupils in the only language that the latter knew, couldn't cope with disciplinary problems, and at times, naturally enough, got very little co-operation from their Puerto Rican colleagues and administrative superiors. All of the latter naturally resented the fact that jobs belonging normally to Puerto Ricans, already scarce enough, were being given to teachers imported from the ruling country, as well as the fact that here was a "God's Chosen People" element, sent down on Washington's insistence and favored by Washington —an element that considered itself superior to the Puerto Ricans and their system and was therefore hardly amenable to local administrative control. What happened to at least one of these teachers has been described in Wenzell Brown's astonishing book, *Dynamite on Our Doorstep*, in which Brown expounded the idea that all Puerto Ricans apparently hated and resented all Americans, and that Puerto Rico seemed about to blow up in a revolutionary blood bath.

Gallardo's chaotic second term expired early in 1945, and the Popular Democratic party, which had been organized in 1938 and in power since 1941, decided to find somebody else to lead a new educational policy. Ickes was ready to go along, but the appointee had to be confirmed by the Senate, which demanded a written guarantee of loyalty as expressed through the promise of a militant policy on stressing the English language. On those terms, again, no qualified Puerto Rican would accept the job. Through the obdurate, revolutionary stand of the colonial subjects, colonialism was breaking down rapidly in one of its most important manifestations. The letter that was at the time written to Secretary Ickes by Dr. Rafael Picó, Chairman of the Puerto Rican Planning Board, is evidence of the manner in which the colonial psychology was disappearing.

November 20, 1945

Hon. Harold L. Ickes
Secretary of the Interior
Washington, D. C.

MY DEAR MR. SECRETARY:

I should appreciate it if you would kindly withdraw my name as candidate for the position of Commissioner of Education of Puerto Rico.

As you are well aware, the position has been vacant for the past four months, and no new nomination has been submitted to the Senate since it returned my appointment to the White House last August. A United Press dispatch from Washington published November 11 in the local daily, *El Mundo,* quoted a spokesman from Interior as saying that although I am still considered for the position by the Department of the Interior, my name will not be submitted to the White House until I "clarify" my views on the question of the teaching of English in Puerto Rico. Recently other parties have also requested from me a statement on the subject that would satisfy Senator Dennis Chavez, the principal objector to my nomination in the Committee on Territories of the Senate.

I have refused to make the statement requested. I firmly believe that my position on the question of English was amply clarified in the public hearing held on June 11, 1945, before the Committee on Territories, and in the statement submitted subsequently to the same committee, a copy of which I enclose with this letter.

Briefly stated, I believe in stressing under any political status the teaching of English in Puerto Rico as an essential subject of our curriculum. With this aim there is no controversy either here in Puerto Rico or in the States. As to the methods for reaching this goal there is, and has been, a continuous controversy for at least the past twenty-five years. My contention is that the point in question is not a subject for political interference, but should rightfully be reserved for educators and experts on the methods of acquiring a second language. With all candor, I have to state that the consensus of educators familiar with the Puerto Rican problem is that the goal of better English is best achieved by stressing the teaching of English as a subject without interfering with the use of the mother tongue as the language of instruction in the other subjects of the curriculum. Although I sympathize with this point of view, as I stated in my extension of remarks, I postponed the outlining of a definite policy as to methods until I could have an opportunity to examine in the Department of Education the results obtained with the methods used by my predecessors in the Department.

Any further commitment on my part, I felt, and I still feel, is unwarranted and would handicap the freedom of action that I, or any other new Commissioner of Education, should have on entering the position. Puerto Rico needs a new educational policy, not only in the question of English, but throughout all the curriculum, so that our educational system will really serve the best interests of the community, which is engaged in a far-reaching program of social and economic reform. What I or any other self-respecting educator must insist on is freedom to develop the educational program required by our conditions, without political interference from any source, without strings attached to the position, and with ample advice from experienced technicians. In view of the recommendation of President Truman that Puerto Rico should be given a chance to choose its own political destiny, it is unbelievable that our right to shape an educational policy should be denied or curtailed at this time. . . .

In view of the fact that Senator Chavez' opposition has created an impasse harmful to the educational system of Puerto Rico, which has been without a responsible head for so many months, and considering that I will not have the freedom of outlining a real educational policy if I break the impasse by appeasing Senator Chavez, it is with regret, Mr. Secretary, that I must respectfully ask you to withdraw my name as candidate for the position of Commissioner of Education of Puerto Rico. . . .

Sincerely yours,
RAFAEL PICÓ

The new generation of Puerto Ricans which now controlled the government had broken the vicious colonial habit of accepting without question everything that came from the ruling country. The impasse mentioned by Picó remained for several years—during which the island remained without a responsible head of its educational system. Finally, in 1948, Congress gave the Puerto Ricans the right to elect their own governor, who could, in turn, appoint his own Commissioner of Education, responsible to the governor and people of Puerto Rico rather than to some accidental, obdurate Senator with fixed ideas but little knowledge of Puerto Rican life and affairs.

CHAPTER IV

Colonialism Bankrupt

WITH THE UNIVERSAL fertility of the poor, the Puerto Ricans kept shooting children like cannon balls at the rigid walls of their economy. The fact that the economy stopped expanding with the advent of the world depression, that it actually began to contract, increased the emotional need for the bombardment. Children kept coming; the population kept growing; the means for supporting the population diminished. In that vicious downward spiral, something was eventually bound to give. That something came to be the revolutionary 1940 election. Meanwhile, however, and despite Washington's best efforts, Puerto Rico reflected the general unrest which marked the entire Caribbean area during the 1930's. Tensions mounted; anti-American feelings increased noticeably. To many it seemed that independence was the only possible cure. They (and I) were convinced that if the United States did not soon do something drastic about Puerto Rico the colony would blow up in our hands like a firecracker that we had held too long. We were too prone to look to Washington for cures. But nothing really effective happened until Muñoz turned to his own people instead of to the ruling country, until he sought cures in the human spirit of the Puerto Ricans themselves.

In certain Puerto Rican circles, where the island's newly defined Americanism is now embraced with something of the fervor often shown by new converts toward their new religions, colonialism has by now become almost a dirty word. Mentioning it at all seems to be regarded as an ungracious act to discredit the United States, which has in recent years been of such great help in the Puerto Rican struggles for the improvement of life. By the same token, and in those same circles, it is increasingly fashionable to assert that standards of living began to rise almost the day the United States took over in 1899.

Whatever the statistics to back that contention, it is undoubtedly true that the total numbers of Puerto Ricans who walked in despair up and down the mountains and valleys of their beautiful island, with little food and less hope, increased noticeably during the first thirty years of our rule.

Hoover's governor, Theodore Roosevelt, Jr., discovered that fact some time before the depression's onset. Virtually all his predecessors had filled their official reports and public statements with statistics on mounting trade, unfavorable balances, increasing numbers of schools, telephones, and miles of roads constructed; they had waved the flag with varying degrees of enthusiasm and played with varying degrees of skill on the "here we are and watch us grow" theme. Roosevelt was the first to look at people instead of statistics, and to say: "This is awful!" Whatever the causes to which he ascribed the conditions he saw, it is to his credit that he saw them, and talked and wrote about them, and did what little he and his wife could to alleviate them through various kinds of relief and industrialization of the handicrafts type. He was the first high American official to propound the "Stricken Land" type of propaganda which proved valuable to Puerto Rico in one historical period, but is proving increasingly embarrassing and annoying today—for the excellent reason that it no longer fits existing conditions.

Writing under the title "Children of Famine" in 1929 and before the stock-market crash, he said: "Riding through the hills, I have stopped at farm after farm where lean, underfed women and sickly men repeated again and again the same story—little food and no opportunity to get more. From these hills the people have streamed into the coastal towns, increasing the already severe unemployment situation there. Housing facilities, of course, are woefully inadequate. Besides, the lack of funds and the increased work have rendered it impossible for our Health Department to cope satisfactorily with our increasing problem.

"We were and are a prey to diseases of many kinds. In the fiscal year ending June 30, 1929, 4,442 of our people died from tuberculosis. Our death rate from this disease was 4½ times the death rate in the continental United States. Our death rate from malaria was 2½ times the rate in the continental United States. Some 35,000 people in our island are now suffering from tuberculosis, some 20,000 from malaria, and some 60,000 from hookworm.

"This condition is all the more deplorable because the climate here is exceptionally healthy."

Governor Roosevelt wrote the above in the New York *Herald Tribune* and thereby annoyed a number of Puerto Rican businessmen, who claimed that his statements gave the island a bad name, were bad for trade, and scared away potential tourists—who were actually not going to Puerto Rico in any event because there were no adequate hotel facilities for them. He was quoted in the *Review of Reviews*, and again by Bailey and Justine Diffie. The latter added:

"Even the casual visitor finds it difficult to escape the continual piteous spectacle of poverty throughout the island. The inland districts, from the outskirts of the cane-ridden valleys to the tops of the mountains, seethe with human misery, and it is impossible to pass into or out of any city or town without traversing the fringe of unsightly, malodorous, filthy habitations which surround the more prosperous area. Every spot of arid or swampy land unfit for decent living has been seized by the gaunt, penniless population which stolidly accepts its fate and lodges where it can. . . ."

Governor Roosevelt and the Diffies described conditions that were not due to the world depression but had by 1929 become normal to the predepression economy. Too many Puerto Ricans lived largely outside their island's economic structure; the depression, when it came, only intensified their suffering and added to their numbers.

With the depression, in August, 1933, came the Emergency Relief Administration, first known as the Puerto Rico Emergency Relief Administration and later as the local branch of the Federal Relief Administration, first called the PRERA and later the FERA. Headed locally by James Bourne with the assistance of Dorothy Bourne, a skilled social worker, it became a tremendous and organized effort to spend a million dollars a month where the money would do the most good and under the rules for such spending that had been formulated in Washington. Its primary purpose was to keep the people alive, through providing millions on millions of meals—where the existing economy had given little to far too many people except a hopeless decline toward a shabby death.

That relief administration was, in Puerto Rico, colonialism's declaration of social bankruptcy; the need for it was increased greatly in 1934, when the Costigan-Jones Act put sugar production on a quota basis, reduced the island's total production of sugar, paid bonuses to the proprietors of sugar lands for *not* growing cane, but made no provision for the thousands of Puerto Rican agricultural workers who were thereby thrown out of their jobs.

Whatever the weaknesses of the relief organization from the philosophical point of view, it had one enormous strength which was to become apparent only later, after its liquidation.

Except for James and Dorothy Bourne at its head, and a few consultants who came from the States for general guidance, it was staffed entirely by Puerto Ricans. The cultural conflicts which later all but wrecked its successor, the Reconstruction Administration, caused by the presence of both Americans and Puerto Ricans in administrative and policy-making positions, the minds of the first geared to Washington and of the second to the island's needs, were entirely absent from the PRERA and FERA.

Partly in order to give employment to white-collar workers, partly for guidance in its efforts, the PRERA carried on widespread studies of living conditions. The administration's social workers uncovered countless evidences of unbelievable poverty. A few of the results are listed below:

In 1933, an investigation was made of the island of Vieques, belonging to Puerto Rico. Here 11,000 people, crowded onto 51 square miles of land devoted mainly to sugar (which belonged to somebody else and precluded any effective attempts at subsistence agriculture), were found to have a *total* income averaging $500 per week.

In June, 1935, a housing survey was conducted in two barrios (minor civil divisions) of the municipality of Utuado. All houses in these barrios were inspected. Out of a total of 598 houses, all but fourteen were recommended for complete demolition as being unfit for human use. Only thirteen houses had latrines; 585 were without sanitary facilities of any kind.

In 1934, the federal government had to deal with a juvenile crime wave. Teen-age boys began to enter post offices and to break mailboxes, always before witnesses. Since that was destruction of federal property, they were hauled into the federal court and sentenced to terms in the federal reform school at Chillicothe, Ohio. When one of them was sentenced, his family called in all the neighbors for a celebration which couldn't have been more joyful if he had won an appointment to West Point. The boy had made good! For a number of years he was going to a place where he would get an education, learn English, learn a trade, with adequate food, clothing, and housing. The crime wave stopped when the federal judge caught on to what was happening and stopped sending Puerto Rican teen-agers to Chillicothe.

Gangs of boys and girls, homeless waifs ranging in ages from four or five to perhaps fifteen, infested most of the cities and could not be dealt with by the authorities, lest the jails and limited institutions be filled to overflowing with children only too glad to be where they obtained enough to eat. A social worker, Rosa Marín, investigated some of them and found children of five who had not the vaguest idea of who they were, where they had come from, or who their parents were. They slept in hallways and alleyways—anywhere at all—and they earned their livings as best they could. They carried bags, dove for pennies in the harbor, and carried on a relentless campaign of petty thievery. They snatched things out of houses, siphoned gasoline out of the tanks of automobiles, stole hub caps, radiator caps, sometimes even tires from parked cars— anything that might bring in a few pennies at the junk yard. They also organized the car-watching business. If a man parked his car anywhere except in front of his own house, he was immediately surrounded by a group of boys clamoring to be allowed to watch it. It was then up to him to give five cents to one of the boys; when he did, all the rest went elsewhere and his car went unmolested. If a man, however, refused to pay the watching fee, irritated because it was "all a racket," he was likely, on returning to his car, to find all the air let out of the tires, or the tires slashed, or the gasoline drained out of his tank.

The police and judges knew several men, decent, law-abiding citizens deserving co-operation from the authorities, who went to jail regularly once a year, for a month before the cane-cutting season began. During the dead season between harvests they had become so weak and emaciated from hunger that they were unable to stand up to the grueling work of cutting cane in the tropical sun, and were in danger of losing the only jobs available to them. Therefore they made a practice of annually committing some petty theft a month or so before the harvest season—stealing a ham, or a loaf of bread, or a few cans of milk—always in plain sight of a policeman. The latter would arrest them, and the magistrate would sentence them to a month in jail—usually with his congratulations and his profound expressions of personal esteem—and society through its penal system would build up their strength by a month of adequate feeding coupled with treatments for malaria and other devitalizing ailments.

In his report on the sugar industry, Estéban Bird wrote: "On two occasions within the past year the writer has had the opportunity to realize the full significance of seasonal unemployment." He wrote about conditions in 1935, and he might well have added total unemployment to seasonal; for every man who in those days had work only four or five months of the year there was at least one who was totally unemployed. "While riding about five miles out of the town of Arecibo I stopped at a peasant's house for information. There were four children, an old man, and three young men sitting at the *batey* * in silence, anemic, barefooted, dressed in rags, wide-eyed, deadly quiet. With the usual courtesy of country folks in Puerto Rico, I was given the information requested. I asked how things were: 'Sir, we have not seen a coin around this house for two months. Our yucca and yams have been consumed. We have very little left of anything else and things are bad in Arecibo. We are waiting for work in the sugar plantations, but God, there is no end of waiting.' Helpless, counting the days before reaching the point of starvation, and easy prey to illness. Ten yards from their shabby thatch house, a

---

* A little land in front of a peasant's house. A front yard. A spot for social gathering, gossip, etc.

rich growing crop, thousands of dollars in the making for a fortunate small group who own the land, the railways, the stores. A challenge to social consciousness!

"The other case: the dead season again. Scarcely four miles out of San Juan, a small, shabby, and old wagon with doubtful wheels, pulled by a bony old horse, blocked the way and I was obliged to stop. Two women and several naked children were around it. They had buckets which were being filled with waste food out of old garbage cans by the driver. The ghastly-looking party departed with filled cans for a wretched house near the road. They looked so desperate that I asked the man at the wagon how it was possible that those people could afford to buy waste food for a hog. He smiled sadly, and in a broken voice answered: 'They are desperate, almost starving. I pass this spot every day coming from San-turce where I collect garbage for feeding hogs. One day they waved at me to stop and asked for some of it for feeding a hog. They promised to give me a quarter share when they slaughtered it provided I would give them a daily ration. I had your same doubts, and I asked to see the hog. They said that it was not around. I asked more questions; they broke down and confessed; they were starving, the children had gone without food for a day, they had been sent to town to beg for food, but they had failed. They wanted waste food to eat it themselves. I have reported them to the authorities, but they have not been here. I help them the little I can and give them waste food. They say they make soup out of it!' "

It is from such tales, written by the hundreds into the PRERA's case records, told by the hundreds by various observers, that one gains an inkling of Puerto Rico's plight during the early thirties.

A vast, sprawling organization, harassed by Washington's rules, under which relief was to remain essentially relief with no nonsense about changing the basic economy, frantically

training more and more social workers to tackle the insuperable task of evaluating the human needs that were only too
devastatingly obvious on every hand, the PRERA began its
enormous task with straight relief but soon branched also
into work relief, bending its efforts toward economic reconstruction and developing plans for future steps in that direction.

Its activities, beyond the work of handing out dole payments, meals, clothing, and other necessities, reached into
many branches of the island's life and may be summarized as
follows:

There was a program of public works, devoted to the construction of schools, hospitals and other public buildings,
bridges and the like. Important because Puerto Rico badly
needed more physical plant, this was also inefficient under the
Congressional rule that only a certain, relatively small, percentage of the funds could be spent for materials; the rest had
to be spent for wages. The program did, however, keep men
alive in the dignity of labor and concrete achievement.

In its agricultural program, the PRERA fostered home
truck gardens, provided seed beds and nurseries for the coffee
belt—which couldn't sell its crop in any event—eradicated bud
rot in the coconut regions, and gave facilities and instruction
for the establishment of canning centers in which women
could preserve their crops.

The co-operative movement that is today beginning to
gather real strength on the island had some of its earliest beginnings in the co-operatives for barter and exchange that
were sponsored by the PRERA in the rural areas, and in those
for the production and marketing of handmade art and crafts
products. Poor as those efforts were in relation to the over-all
need, poor as they necessarily had to be under a relief setup,
they were nevertheless invaluable in that they devoted relief
funds toward the fostering of a basic idea, largely new in

Puerto Rico, and the basic discipline of co-operation, which takes root only slowly and with difficulty in a stricken land.

Such ventures as fisheries and shoemaking were also inadequate by modern standards. Again, however, they developed various skills, planted new ideas in what had previously always been an agrarian society, and valuable social experimentation resulted.

The five thousand women who were kept alive in the Relief Administration's needlework industry had to be cautioned constantly by their foreladies to slow down, not to work too fast, lest the money spent for wages run below its politically prescribed proportion to that spent for materials. But those women sewed by hand, or pedaled away at their antiquated sewing machines, and made thousands of garments that were later given away in direct relief. The mattress ticking used in the needlework shops became famous. Somehow, the Federal Relief Administration had got hold of thousands of yards of such ticking, gaily striped, and had distributed it to various local agencies in the States and in Puerto Rico. I don't know what Bourne intended to do with it in Puerto Rico. I do know that agencies in a number of the states decided that the thing to do with mattress ticking was to stuff it with something to make mattresses for the poor who didn't have any—so perhaps even building up new desires which might help private industry in later years when people would again have money. But private industry didn't see it that way. It took the odd stand that government-made mattresses, even when distributed to people who had never owned mattresses in their lives and wouldn't be able to buy any if they *had* developed a desire for them, would be in competition with private enterprise and were therefore taboo. Hence an order went out from Washington to all local agencies including Puerto Rico that the mattress ticking must under no circumstances be used for making mattresses. In Puerto Rico it came to be used for making men's and boy's pants which were distributed widely as direct relief and were honored by having a *plena* * composed about "The Pants That Are Made by the PRERA."

Public-welfare activities included child welfare, mental hygiene and psychiatry, probation and parole, medical social service, research and planning, nutrition and home economics, recreation, social service training, social legislation and legal advice, interagency service, and direct relief. Again, regardless of their over-all effectiveness from the social point of view, those activities implanted or fostered a number of modern ideas that were relatively new to agrarian Puerto Rico and began to train a number of people who were later, after the 1940 revolution, able to go on with many important phases of the island's modernization and reconstruction. One of the most important was the program of free maternal health clinics in which women for whom it was mortally dangerous to have any more children could obtain advice and contraceptives for birth control. These clinics were swamped with clients. Sickly women from all parts of the island flocked to them, so showing that the demand for birth control was even then widespread on the island. Later, when the relief organization was replaced by the new Puerto Rico Reconstruction Administration, the maternal health clinics were taken over by the latter as being among the most important federal activities on the island. Just before the election of 1936, however, they were closed on peremptory orders from Washington, resulting from political pressure that had been brought to bear on Roosevelt.

Even in 1936, a large part of the population desperately wanted help toward the limitation of families. It was not they who objected to the dissemination of birth-control information and assistance. The men who put a stop to such dissemination were politicians in the Protestant ruling country.

* *Plena*—A Spanish-language folk song about some current event, corresponding roughly to Trinidad's calypso and stemming largely from the Negro element on the south coast.

In education the PRERA supplemented the efforts of the insular government by organizing unemployed teachers and other eligible persons for a broad program of child and adult education. Here, again, only a scratch could be made in relation to the actual need. Because funds were limited, only one child from any one family could attend a nursery school. That was good for the child in question, but hard on its brothers and sisters. It was heartbreaking to see the latter, pale, anemic, sad, and probably envious, watching the lucky child depart daily from home for the school in which he or she would obtain a free lunch as well as instruction and recreation.

When public medical care collapsed almost entirely, due to the financial difficulties of the insular government and the various municipal governments, the PRERA stepped in to operate a number of medical centers and dispensaries.

The efforts to improve housing conditions in rural as well as urban areas represented a small but real start toward the slum clearance program for which Puerto Rico has today become world famous.

From the long-range point of view, the PRERA program of planning and research, organized in part to harness the energies of the educated unemployed, may well have been one of the most important. It tended to focus attention on the island's real problems, on the programs and projects needed to solve those problems, and in many cases on the obstacles encountered in the attempts to do something effective. It is not to be implied, of course, that the first impetus for such activities had come from a federal agency. Many Puerto Ricans, in the government and out of it, had long been analytical about the many details of their own social and economic problem, and the various departments and bureaus of the insular government had for some years been systematically publishing such analyses. The important matter is that a federal agency now took up the work with the welfare of the island at heart, that federal funds were poured into it, and that dozens of Puerto Ricans, as a result, thereby became closely acquainted with many aspects of the Puerto Rican difficulty. That effort was one of several links in a chain that was to lead directly to the present stage, where Puerto Rico is outstanding in the scientific planning of its social progress.

The activities of the planning and development section ranged from investigations of the operations of the tariff, through employment and employability, to overseas trade. They included studies of abandoned children and mendicancy, agricultural surveys, research on mineral resources, and experimental projects on garlic, ginger, and vanilla as potential crops for Puerto Rico. They branched out into studies of nutrition, recreational activities, tuberculosis, of municipal expenditures and farm debts. Together they further clarified the pattern of a stricken society and the questions of why and how it was stricken.

Why could not Puerto Rico help itself out of its dreadful dilemma? Why did every local effort to remedy local ills seem foredoomed to failure? Why, with a certain amount of local capital available, did Puerto Rico not build factories to make at home some of the things that were being imported from the continent, so improving the balance of payments and giving local employment? Some answers to those questions had been given in the report of the Brookings Institution, published in 1930; others were found in the book of the Diffies; still others were scattered through the publications of the Insular Bureau of Agricultural and Industrial Research. The fact that the PRERA now tackled such questions meant not only that a number of Puerto Ricans began to be acquainted with that literature, but also that the education of Washington officials and employees regarding Puerto Rico was greatly furthered.

One of the island's difficulties was that, poor as it was, it was still the second largest market in the Americas for U.S.-manufactured goods, the largest being Canada. It was also a place where U.S. manufacturers could dump their seconds, their misfits, their out-of-style clothing, everything they could not get rid of at home. And in those days those manufacturers were not going to stand idly by when budding local industries threatened their profitable market.

The various American soap companies, for instance, sold so large an amount of their product that they maintained twenty-two representatives in Puerto Rico alone. And when a Puerto Rican began to make soap locally, the price of soap from the mainland suddenly dropped to such low levels that the local enterprise, having no lasting power, was forced out of business.

When Puerto Rican enterprise began to make candy for local consumption, the local price of candy imported from the States went down until the Puerto Rican factory closed.

Puerto Rico depended on considerable quantities of gasoline for its transportation system. All that was needed to cause the price of imported gasoline to go down was for a Puerto Rican to get the idea of importing crude oil and refining it on the island; the price of gasoline went up again after he had gone bankrupt.

The report on "Obstacles to Industries in Puerto Rico," prepared by the PRERA, reads in part: "A specific illustration of opposition from steamship companies is in the incident of 'Hicaco Cal.' Prior to the establishment of that lime-manufacturing plant at Fajardo, the freight on a ton of lime was $10.00. When mainland lime manufacturers pointed out to the steamship companies that a local plant was gaining considerable trade (at a more favorable price), the steamship lines reduced the freight rate from $10.00 a ton to $3.00 a ton in order that the mainland manufacturer could undersell the local plant."

When Puerto Ricans had the idea that it would be good business to establish a local industry to can locally grown fruits, they discovered that, in accordance with common practice, freight rates on the empty cans that would have to be imported were figured on the basis of cubic space instead of weight, while freight on filled cans was charged on a basis of weight. Under those circumstances it cost more to ship in empty cans than full ones, which meant that a local canning industry was virtually impossible unless and until there was also a local industry for making cans.

Under such conditions, with four steamship companies dividing the Puerto Rican trade on a gentlemen's agreement basis and able to manipulate their high rates, with several examples of dumping from the States fresh in everybody's mind, local capital had good reason to stay out of local manufacturing. Puerto Rico seemed doomed to remain stagnant—its people to remain less an agricultural people than cheap labor in a rural sweatshop of industrialized agriculture—unable and not permitted to marshal the many skills that are required for any program of diversified agriculture or industrialization.

Colonialism was evidently bankrupt. The exploitative colonial economic system, buttressed by colonial political status, had run its full course to the point where the majority of Puerto Rico's people suffered from slow or rapid starvation. A great political restlessness therefore spread over the land. Much of the feeling for independence which grew during the depression years had its origin in existing economic conditions. Many Puerto Ricans believed that the things that had to be done to remedy those conditions could not be done under the American flag. But those who advocated independence advocated widely varying kinds, to be achieved by different means—a few in a spirit of hatred toward the United States, many others in a spirit of friendship—as a matter of mutual convenience to the people of Puerto Rico and those of the United States. The two groups, the one small in number but fanatical in approach, the other large in numbers but sane and democratic in spirit and methods, came to oppose each other with much feeling. At the top of the social structure were the relatively wealthy, who, because of what it might do to them, rejected all thought of independence and intensified their struggles for statehood.

What few if any Puerto Ricans could foresee in 1935 was that the agony of the depression years would unleash new world forces and set in motion new evolutionary processes which would soon make it necessary to reshape many old patterns of thought. They could not foresee that the bankruptcy of colonialism would create political and psychological conditions under which it would soon be possible to do, after all —under the American flag and much better under that flag than under any other—the things which had to be done to save Puerto Rico.

CHAPTER V

Tragic Lunacy

THE RESTLESSNESS which swept the entire Caribbean area during the 1930's was less intense in Puerto Rico than in the neighboring islands. One reason was that the Puerto Ricans are peaceful by tradition and nature; another that the United States could spend more money for relief than could the other colonial and sovereign governments. But in Puerto Rico, too, strikes began to occur in the tobacco and sugar areas and political tensions mounted to a high point.

It was one thing to know that colonialism was moribund on the island; it was another to know what to do about the matter. Old political leaders tried frantically to adhere to ideas and methods which had served them for decades; new and younger leaders pushed forward with ideas and methods which may not have been new as far as the world was concerned, but were certainly new in Puerto Rico's history.

The most dramatic of the latter, the one who made the most noise though with the smallest amount of numerical support, was the Harvard graduate Pedro Albizu Campos. He took his basic political philosophy, not from Puerto Rico's realities and needs, but from a reservoir of widespread concepts of patriotism which have by now become classical and dogmatic through the oratory and oversimplifications of history.

77

The classical, dogmatic answer to colonialism is national-ism and national sovereignty, consciously or unconsciously defined as being synonymous with individual freedom. The classical means of achieving that sovereignty is through vio-lence of one kind or another, as in the various revolutions which created the twenty-one nations out of the colonial pos-sessions once held in the Americas by Britain, Spain, Portugal, and France. The classical American leaders to be emulated, if only in their primer and picture-book aspects, are such men as Washington, Bolívar, Miranda, San Martín, Sucre, and O'Higgins. The classical patriotic attitude toward the ruling country is one of bitter hatred expressed through constant de-nunciation of the grasping tyrant.

Those were the emotional ingredients of the various Amer-ican revolutions. In many parts of Latin America, emerging as nations with Spanish, Catholic cultures, and with oligar-chic Spanish concepts of liberty, the United States had come, during the nineteenth and twentieth centuries, to be defined as the classical culture enemy, as the materialistic, Protestant Colossus of the North.

Stir all those ingredients together in the person of a fiery orator, and you are likely to have an explosive mixture with a deep appeal to a certain number of poverty-stricken ado-lescents of various ages, bewildered and hurt through their second-class citizenship, ready to find emotional outlets through a blind but fiery patriotism. Albizu Campos saw and sees himself in the classical pattern. Throughout his career he has used a blind, emotional patriotism, coupled with fanatical hatred of the United States, almost as a smoke screen to hide the details and real nature of Puerto Rico's ills. In an age when colonialism is obsolete and interdependence emerges to replace nationalistic independence, when armies of liberation are no longer popular or possible, except in those colonial areas where Communists use them for their own ends, he has in his own way made war on the United States.

His followers call themselves Nationalists and began as a legitimate political party. As such, however, and as long ago as the terrible depression year of 1932, they could not survive the first and only election in which they participated. Since then the party has steadily lost members but has by the same token become more fanatical. Today it is in no sense a political party, but a small group of terrorists numbering at most a few hundred according to official Puerto Rican estimates.

I write this on March 9, 1954, a little more than a week after the world was shocked by the tragic outburst of four Nationalists in Washington. On March 1, the day of the opening of the Tenth Conference on Inter-American Affairs at Caracas, four of the latter, one woman and three men, suddenly stood up in the gallery of the House of Representatives, uttered a cry for Puerto Rico's freedom, and began to spray the House with bullets, wounding five Congressmen. They did not care whom they hit. According to the woman, Lolita Lebron, they were determined to be noticed in the world's press, in an effort to embarrass the United States at the Caracas Conference.

Almost unanimously, the people and leaders of Puerto Rico were hurt and bewildered by that tragic outburst and afraid of what it would do to them and their good reputations. They could not understand why it should take place at precisely the time when their society was better off than ever before in its history because of the fair co-operation it had enjoyed from the United States throughout the preceding decade.

The world has seen a number of active terroristic groups since the turn of the century. Russia terrorists shot czars; Irish terrorists shot Englishmen and Irishmen; today Mau Mau terrorists kill Kikuyus and white Kenya settlers. All these, however, had and have visible grievances. But it is now apparent that the better conditions become in Puerto Rico, the more fanatical the Nationalists are. They are perhaps unique as terrorists in that they keep fighting against evils which have been largely eliminated, in favor of old concepts which diminish daily in validity and are already outmoded in world affairs. Truly, they seem to fit the definition of a fanatic as a man who redoubles his efforts long after he has forgotten his aims.

The tragic events of March 1, 1954, were vivid reminders of another series of terroristic outbreaks which had taken place less than four years earlier.

On November 1, 1950, two Nationalists walked down Washington's Pennsylvania Avenue. Their names were Griselio Torresola and Oscar Collazo. They looked and acted like ordinary, poor, peaceful Puerto Ricans—until they came opposite Blair House where President Truman was then living while the White House was being rebuilt. Then they whipped out revolvers and began shooting at the guards in front of the temporary White House—as though in a mad attempt to shoot their way inside and assassinate the President. One guard was killed in the gun battle. Torresola was killed. Collazo was wounded and hauled away to a hospital and prison. On the second floor of Blair House, President Truman was warned away from the front window, where he had gone to see what the commotion was about.

For several days previous to the Blair House affair, the world's press had been aware of a series of serious disturbances in Puerto Rico.

On October 28 there was a break in the island's penitentiary, resulting in the murder of two guards and the escape of 112 inmates. The break also resulted in the concentration of many policemen from elsewhere at and near the penitentiary, leaving the rest of Puerto Rico relatively unprotected.

On Monday, October 30, five fanatical Nationalists attacked the *Fortaleza*, the governor's official residence, in much the same fashion in which two others were to attack Blair House two days later.

On the same day, some twenty-five or thirty Nationalists

made their way to the isolated little mountain town of Jayuya, attacked the police station, killed and wounded a number of policemen, burned down twenty-one public and private buildings, and caused most of the population of some 2,500 to take to the hills.

Simultaneously, small groups of Nationalists cut loose with gunfire in eight other towns and villages. In Santurce, a mad barber who for years had been shaving Don Pedro Albizu Campos barricaded himself in his house and began to shoot. It took a dozen policemen, an equal number of firemen—who forgot to bring their axes—and half a company of National Guardsmen to get him out and subdue him.

Casualties in that series of events came to: 7 policemen killed and 21 wounded; 1 National Guardsman killed and 11 wounded; 1 fireman killed and 1 wounded; 18 Nationalists killed and 11 wounded; 2 bystanders killed and 7 wounded.

Undoubtedly, the principal aim of that bloodshed had been to focus the world's attention on the Nationalists as self-styled Puerto Rican patriots, and to dramatize the fiction that a heroic people had suddenly arisen to throw off the yoke of the Yanqui oppressor. All who know and knew Puerto Rico, however, were thoroughly aware that the Nationalists comprised only an infinitesimal part of the Puerto Rican people, and that they in no way expressed any considerable part of the thinking and feeling of those people.

Governor Muñoz Marín said to me in 1953: "Never under any circumstances assume that the Nationalists represent any part of Puerto Rican thinking, or even symbolize any Puerto Rican aspirations which have validity in the present day. Psychologically, they are in no way Puerto Ricans. They don't even live in a real world. They live in an unreal world of their own creation. In itself, that makes little difference. If people want to live in an unreal world, I see no reason why they shouldn't. The tragic fact exists, however, that every once in a while real bullets come out of the unreal world and kill real people in the real world. That is, of course, bad and must be prevented."

The Nationalists' strongest moral support seems to come from communist circles, which do everything in their power to capitalize on trouble anywhere in the capitalist world, and from Latin America, which, while often still clinging to old dogmas of liberty and freedom, is at the same time woefully ignorant of what has actually happened in Puerto Rico in recent years. After the attempted assassination of President Truman, many Latin American papers carried editorials lauding the Nationalists as Latin patriots. At that time, only one strong Latin American voice was raised in defense of Muñoz Marín as opposed to Albizu Campos, the leader of the Nationalists. Dr. José Figueres, formerly—and now again—President of Costa Rica, said: "As an Americanist and a democrat, I feel it my duty to contribute to the rectification of an error which is being propagated throughout Latin America concerning the situation in Puerto Rico. The true exponent of Puerto Rico's heroism is Governor Muñoz Marín, who . . . has devoted his life to . . . the conscientious solution of his people's problems. In his work as a leader he is backed by an entire generation of able and patriotic Puerto Ricans. He has wide popular support. Puerto Rico enjoys a true and solid democracy. By the same token I regret that circumstances oblige me to assert . . . that the figure of Albizu Campos is a malignant hoax on public opinion in the Americas."

There can be no doubt that Pedro Albizu Campos was and is a very sick man whose illness was accentuated by his personal experiences in and with the United States, a man with much intelligence and charm who lived, like another Don Quixote before him, in a bygone age. He was and is an anachronism in the grand manner, representing a force that was strong in all of Latin America a few decades ago, the force of blind anti-Americanism coupled with fanatical devotion to old Spanish culture.

Albizu was born in Ponce in 1891. His father was a Basque caballero, his mother of Basque, Indian, and Negro descent. The fact that Pedro was illegitimate is said to have had a profound influence on his life and to have done much to create and sustain the venomous bitterness of his adult years. The fact that he is dark—though his physiognomy is more Indian than Negro—undoubtedly added to his hatred of the United States. In all his political speeches, he has ceaselessly and relentlessly attacked the United States on the race issue, and there can be no doubt that American racism has done much to feed the Nationalist cause.

Albizu attended Harvard University, from which he was graduated in 1917 with a bachelor's degree in law. As a student he had become passionately interested in the Irish movement and in the Irish Republican party's sniping tactics. At Harvard, too, he had met and married Laura Meneses, a Peruvian girl who had studied chemistry at Radcliffe and was to have a profound influence on his later career.

An APRISTA, member of Peru's violently anti-American revolutionary party, herself dark, bitter, and unstable, Laura Meneses of Arequipa is said constantly to have goaded her sick husband into plotting and directing acts of bloodshed in which he himself—it should be added—never participated directly.

During World War I Albizu registered for the draft in Cambridge but was allowed to transfer to Puerto Rico, where he was sure that no color line would be drawn. In that he was wrong. There *was* a Negro regiment, the 375th, a labor regiment, and Albizu was assigned to it as an enlisted man. Later he was admitted to an officers' training camp, came out with a commission, and was a first lieutenant in the 375th when he was discharged in January, 1919.

Acutely sensitive to the many snubs he had received as a Negro, he now began to devote his life to the cause of Puerto Rico's independence, expressing himself in the beginning through a weekly newspaper that he had founded for the purpose. He argued that the United States was a usurper with no legal standing in Puerto Rico, and that the section in the Treaty of Paris by which the island had been turned over to American rule was illegal, having never been ratified by its people. He also claimed that the republic proclaimed at the time of the *Grito de Lares* was still a legal fact, needing only to be revived as an actuality.

In 1927 and 1928 he visited eleven Latin American countries, seeking support, preaching Puerto Rico's right to be an independent republic, and doing his best to stimulate South American hatred and suspicion of *el coloso del norte*. Here he sought and accepted help from a wide variety of conflicting groups, from all groups which would unite with him on the sole basis of a common anti-American feeling. The known sad plight of Puerto Rico's people was a powerful argument on his behalf, and the ardent Catholic, Albizu Campos, the rabid anticommunist, sought and received support from many communist groups.

The APRA, Peru's Marxist but anti-Stalinist revolutionary party, was persuaded by him to include in its platform the independence of Puerto Rico. In Mexico and Cuba he received support from local APRISTA organizations, and later from other groups as well. Groups of traditional Catholics, who were, like him, afraid of and opposed to the United States because it was a Protestant country, came to his support. Native fascist organizations did the same, and special committees were formed in various republics to support him and his cause.

Those organizations became his foreign representatives and the foreign ministries and embassies of the Nationalist party and its chimerical Republic of Puerto Rico. They were also propaganda cells and centers for moral support. Often, in later years, the editorials and resolutions published in various Latin American nations in support of the Nationalists' terroristic acts stemmed directly from the groups which Albizu had wooed or organized during his Latin American travels.

Albizu's idea in those days was to gain international support throughout Latin America for pleading his cause of independence before the League of Nations. His plan was to win that independence through his impassioned oratory in Geneva, supported by resolutions from a large number of groups in many Latin American republics.

However, one thing was still lacking to make his case complete. That was popular support from Puerto Rico itself. The attempt to win that support was the next stage in his political life; its dismal failure led to years of confusion and distress.

On returning from his Latin American tour, Albizu joined the Nationalist party, which had been founded in 1922 as a protest against the oppressive measures of Governor J. Montgomery Reily. He was elected its president in 1930 and began to prepare it for the elections of two years later. A stirring orator, he made countless speeches attacking the United States and appealing to the selfless patriotism of his people. Violently he attacked the concentration of land in large estates and the absentee ownership of the sugar industry as the island's besetting evils and as signs of North American greed and ill will. He contented himself, however, with claiming that the United States had to get out. He formulated no economic program through which existing evils were to be remedied without widespread death from starvation.

He ridiculed the concept of overpopulation. Even then, with 1,600,000 inhabitants compared with today's 2,300,000, Puerto Rico was obviously and terribly overpopulated in relation to its restrictive and exploitative colonial economy. Not only did Albizu brand all talk of birth control as indicative of vicious imperialistic aims, but he went so far as to claim that he had definite proof that the Presbyterian Hospital in San Juan, and the School of Tropical Medicine, then operated in that city by Columbia University, were maintained by the

United States for the sole purpose of devising means through which the Puerto Ricans would eventually be exterminated through ubiquitous injection of the (nonexisting) cancer virus.

Albizu's arguments on the latter point had a certain amount of appeal to those sections of Puerto Rico's illiterate masses where he was then regarded as an infallible saint. Disseminated out of context throughout Latin America, they also had appeal there. As late as 1952, they were used by Radio Moscow as proof of American devilishness. Even during the early 1930's, however, the majority of the Puerto Ricans regarded them largely as indications of Albizu's insanity. The journalist and English scholar, Bill O'Reilly, was to sum up prevailing opinion accurately when he said that one quick glance at the population figures should convince anybody that we Americans are washouts as exterminators.

Nevertheless, people loved his fiery speeches. They cheered them and him wildly and they signed the petitions that were to make the Nationalist party truly a political party, permitted by law to go to the polls. This was the heyday of Albizu Campos, the day of his greatest apparent influence, the day in which the students of the university, fascinated by the role which Cuban and other Latin American students have traditionally played in movements for "liberation," voted him lay canonization as their Patron Saint. Albizu interpreted that obvious popularity as a certain sign of impending victory. He rode the crest of the wave—until it broke on the reef of the election.

When the returns were in, it was found that, out of 453,000 eligible voters, 384,000 had gone to the polls. Out of the latter, fewer than 12,000 had voted for Albizu personally, who had run for the office of senator-at-large. The Nationalist party, as such, had polled only 5,257 votes, or less than 2 per cent of the total. Under the law, 10 per cent was required for the party to remain a party and go to the polls at the next election without a preliminary petition inscription of the same size. Since the election of 1932, and especially since that of 1940 which brought Muñoz Marín to power as the island's leader, the Nationalists have lost steadily in numbers, as many of them were attracted by Muñoz' great promise and greater achievement, and so joined the latter's Popular Democratic party. It is extremely doubtful in any event whether more than a minute proportion of them had ever been in favor of bloodshed. The few who are left today are by far the most fanatical.

Whatever the election's meaning, it was obvious that Albizu's scheme was wrecked. He could not go to Geneva, before the League of Nations, and claim popular support for Puerto Rico's independence on the basis of a 2 per cent vote for his party and its platform.

Defeated in their efforts to create a real Republic of Puerto Rico, the Nationalists now built a sham one, claiming direct descent from that created in 1868 at the time of the *Grito de Lares*. Most Puerto Ricans regarded it as a tragic bit of play-acting, but many Nationalists, especially the younger ones, were deadly serious about it. Albizu Campos was President, with a number of busy ministers to conduct the affairs of state, with the foreign representation that the chief executive had built up in eleven Latin American republics, with an "Army of Liberation" uniformed in white pants and black shirts and armed, if at all, largely with wooden guns.

As far as political activities were concerned, the Nationalists seemed during the first few years after the disastrous 1932 elections to content themselves with making speeches, haranguing the Puerto Rican people on the streets, in the plazas, in halls, and over the radio, with an unceasing message of bitter hatred for the United States and everything American. President Roosevelt and Mrs. Roosevelt, Secretary Ickes, and other federal officials, the institution of colonialism, America's intentions toward Puerto Rico, the island's own officials and leaders—and especially Muñoz Marín—the absentee ownership of land and the morals of various prominent ladies —all these and many more came in for their full share of undisciplined blasting.

In 1935 an affair at the university set off the campaign of terrorism and assassinations which was to make Albizu Campos truly notorious. Although once canonized by the students, he had later cut loose on them with several vituperative speeches in which he accused the boys of effeminacy and lack of patriotism, and implied that the girls, because they had departed from the old, traditional Spanish patterns of behavior and dress and had taken on the freer American ways, were immoral. Most of the students then wanted to call a meeting for the purpose of formally declaring him *persona non grata,* although a small group of Nationalists among them opposed the idea and threatened violence if such a meeting were held. Feeling ran so high that it was agreed that all students would have to check their revolvers at the door before entering the hall. (It was quite a thing to study in Rio Piedras in those days.)

On October 24, 1935, the day scheduled for the student assembly of censure, a group of Nationalists, armed with revolvers and bombs, drove to the university to break up the meeting. They were intercepted by the insular police, and in the ensuing exchange of shots, a policeman was seriously wounded, a spectator and four Nationalists were killed, and one Nationalist was injured.

That was the beginning of Puerto Rico's recurring bath of blood.

The funeral of the Nationalist "martyrs" was held two days later, and there Albizu preached a violent sermon of hate against everything American and against the insular police as the tools of Yanqui imperialism. He called on his listeners to avenge the deaths of their four heroic comrades in arms, and he specifically mentioned, for assassination, Col. E. Francis Riggs, the Washington-appointed chief of the island's police force.

Col. Riggs was one of the most respected and beloved officials in Puerto Rico, a thoroughly decent man, democratic, informal with an outgoing personality, the antithesis of the stern *Guardias Civiles* who had run the island during Spanish days and of the aloof, segration-minded Americans who had followed them. It was said of him that he favored Puerto Rico's independence, which probably meant that he had no objections to it, being wise enough not to meddle in the question of political status. He was also on personally friendly terms with Albizu Campos. He found his entertainment, not in exclusive clubs reserved for continental Americans, but in the casino of the public Escambrón Beach Club, where he was likely to invite almost anybody, a rookie cop, a clerk, an official, a Puerto Rican, or a continental, to have a drink with him.

Riggs was also a devout practicing Catholic who went to Mass regularly. Among the police as well as in Puerto Rico as a whole, he was the most beloved police chief Puerto Rico had ever had.

On Sunday, February 23, 1936, Riggs was waylaid by two young Nationalists on his return from San Juan Cathedral, where he had attended Mass. They fired on him without warning, killing him instantly, and were immediately arrested and taken to the police station. Here occurred one of those inexplicable things which often have a profound effect on human affairs, and which was to help throw all Puerto Rico into confusion for the next four years. Arriving at the station, their prisoners disarmed, behind closed doors, the police suddenly reached for their guns and riddled the two Nationalists with bullets.

That lynching, that sudden, wild revenge, became a talking point on the island for years, condoned by some, condemned

by others. It was to create terrible tensions between San Juan
and Washington and was the starting point of the worst period in Puerto Rico's political history.

The details of that situation, the tensions created, their effects on Puerto Rican life during the last four years of repressive colonialism, belong in a separate account and are related
in Chapter IX. Suffice it to say here that Albizu, through the
assassination of Col. Riggs, created a situation in which all of
Puerto Rico seemed officially to be blamed by Washington for
the actions of a few fanatics, and all Puerto Rico was punished
accordingly. He himself and seven of his associates were tried
in the federal court, on charges of conspiring to overthrow the
government of the United States, and sentenced to relatively
brief terms in Atlanta Penitentiary. On his return to Puerto
Rico, in December, 1947, he again began his chosen work of
persuading fanatical adolescents of various ages to martyr
themselves by committing murder for what he and they considered Puerto Rico's holy cause. Meanwhile, however,
Muñoz had won the election of 1940; the Popular Democratic
party had gained political control; conditions in Puerto Rico
had improved immeasurably; the ranks of the Nationalists
had shrunk to correspond.

By now, however, Puerto Rico's colonialism had been drastically modified. Washington officials no longer thought it
necessary to take charge of every major move in and for the
colony. The Puerto Ricans had matters well in their own
hands; they tried Albizu for inciting to murder and sentenced
him for eighty years in a Puerto Rican prison. But again he
managed to win a certain international audience.

While in prison, he complained ceaselessly and bitterly,
writing letters to the Pan-American Union and to various
Latin American republics about the evil United States. Day
and night he kept wet towels on his head, his chest, and his
genitals—as protection against the atomic radiations with
which, according to his claim, the powerful United States was

inefficiently trying to kill him. He charged in his letters that Washington kept no fewer than three machinery-laden ships anchored on the coast of Puerto Rico, sending a steady stream of radiations against his poor frail body. There was, moreover, no use, according to his charges, in the Puerto Ricans' trying secretly to move him out of the way of that bombardment. For the three ships also carried radar equipment, focused directly on him, through which they could keep track of him and immediately pin-point his presence wherever he might be moved.

As late as 1953 at least one South American newspaper solemnly and indignantly protested against such diabolical actions on the part of the Yanqui imperialists.

Governor Muñoz pardoned him in September, 1953, in part because Albizu was obviously a sick man whose "martyrdom" won him a certain amount of sympathetic attention in non-Puerto Rican circles.

Muñoz had previously said about Albizu that "never in history has one leader exercised so strong an influence over so few people." Not until after the affair in the House of Representatives, on March 1, 1954, did it become evident to him and the United States government that they were dealing with a madman whom nothing could stop while he lived, short of incarceration. The ensuing roundup of Nationalists, in Puerto Rico, New York, Chicago, and other centers, may now, once and for all, put a stop to the group's terroristic activities.

In the tragic career of Albizu Campos and the men and women he inspired to terroristic actions, the most tragic thing is not that a handful of people could be so insanely fanatical; it is not that lives were sacrificed to concepts which had lost their validity; it is not even that the people of Puerto Rico, whom Albizu pretended to liberate, were on the whole his greatest enemies. The most tragic thing is what the actions of a minute few Puerto Ricans did to the lives and aspirations of some two million peaceful, law-abiding citizens. But much of the harm done sprang from the fact that the Puerto Rican colony had been imperfectly understood in the United States and by those entrusted with shaping and carrying out United States' policies toward the island. And in that respect there has been a tremendous advance since the assassination of Col. Riggs.

The difference between 1936, on the one hand, and 1950 and 1954, on the other, was that in the two latter years Puerto Rico was not officially punished for the acts of its minute but rabid minority. Here and there, after the shootings in Congress in 1954, one heard people in New York, Chicago, and California sneer at all Puerto Ricans as "they," from whom one could expect nothing better. Official Washington opinion, however, and the editorial opinions expressed in most American newspapers, recognized the real situation, spoke sympathetically and even admiringly of the great Puerto Rican effort to raise standards of living within the American scheme of things, and in no way blamed the island's people for Albizu's actions.

In 1950, the island's leaders realized that in 1936 Puerto Rico had suffered from inadequate public relations with the United States and from the ignorance resulting therefrom—a matter which the colony could hardly have helped in the former year. Energetically led by Muñoz, in what amounted to a veritable popular crusade, they and the island's people then did everything in their power to reaffirm their friendship for the United States and to make it plain that Albizu's Nationalists in no way represented Puerto Rican thought and feelings. The fact that Puerto Rico attained commonwealth status, and with it full internal self-government, only two years later, indicates how official American feeling had by that time changed toward the island.

Immediately after the terrible events of March 1, 1954, Governor Muñoz Marín and his wife took the first plane to

Washington, as a sincere gesture of grief and condolence toward the Congressmen who had been shot and a reaffirmation of loyalty to the United States. The visit aroused favorable comment in newspapers throughout the United States. The wives of the wounded Congressmen gave a luncheon for Mrs. Muñoz Marín. In Chicago, a number of Puerto Ricans, on hearing that Congressman Bentley needed a blood transfusion, gave their own blood as a show of loyalty. Puerto Ricans and friends of Puerto Rico went on record in the world's press to explain the true situation and to absolve Puerto Ricans, as such, from blame. Even in Latin America, where Albizu had previously had his greatest following and support, the editorial expressions of sympathy with him and his cause were so negligible as to be almost nonexistent. Since the shooting had been done for the purpose of embarrassing the United States at the Caracas conference, it is significant that Puerto Rico was specifically exempt, at that conference, from the meaning of the resolution condemning colonialism in the Americas. In official Latin American thinking, Puerto Rico is today no longer a colony.

The Nationalists grow fewer and fewer. Their leaders are in prison at the time of the present writing—Albizu Campos being in a prison hospital. The fanaticism of the remaining Nationalists may of course increase as their numbers continue to decrease. Nationalist cells may remain active—especially in New York and Chicago where Puerto Ricans are still regarded by some as an alien group with second-class citizenship akin to that of Negroes. By and large, however, the shooting on March 1, 1954, seems to have cleared up one important point: the motivations of these terrorists must not be sought in the realm of reason, but in that of abnormal psychology.

CHAPTER VI

Growth of a Leader

P UERTO RICO'S POLITICAL LEADERS during the island's first three decades under American rule were men who stemmed from the Spanish regime and were Spanish in their thinking, orientations, and philosophy. Patriots, men of energy and integrity, passionate in their love for Borinquen,* they were also men of the nineteenth century who many times failed to understand the twentieth as it impinged on their society after the Spanish-American War. They were often bewildered by the urgent task of bringing about a successful relationship with the United States through the *rapprochement* of divergent cultures. America of those days was lusty, cocky, all-knowing in its new role as a world power, worshipfully devoted to the spirit of *laissez faire* under which no man was wiser than the successful American businessman even though he happened also to be a crook. Americans on the whole were condescendingly sentimental toward those millions of people of all colors whom President Theodore Roosevelt called "Our Little Brown Brothers" and whom the modern GI's have dubbed "Gooks," but also both ignorant and disdainful of the latter's habits of thought and cultural orienta-

* The old Indian name for Puerto Rico, today used poetically as a term of affection.

tion. Leaders of the colony could not hope to cope with that psychology. They could not hope to change, overnight or in thirty years' time, their own traditions and orientations which stemmed from centuries of relationships with Spain. Their language, their thinking, their sense of social values and human dignity, often clashed with the American go-getter spirit. Their traditional, oligarchic sense of liberty and justice, their cultural demand for intellectual anl philosophical consistency, were often sharply at variance with America's exuberant, youthful faith in the correctness and superiority of everything American.

Even Luis Muñoz Rivera, one of the greatest of them all, found it difficult to cope with the American Congress after he had coped successfully with the Spanish Cortes. When he first went to Washington as the island's Resident Commissioner he knew almost no English; it is said of him with admiration that he became eloquent in the language through only one year of hard study. Nevertheless, his language differed radically from that of the American Congress. He could hardly be expected to grasp the semantics involved in the sudden, overwhelming outrush of American corporate enterprise, with all its political ramifications, with its dogma that "what's good for business is good for the nation," with its smug assumption that Puerto Ricans of all classes stood to gain most from the maximum gains of those branches of American business which had early established themselves on the island.

Known as Puerto Rico's George Washington, Muñoz Rivera was the man who had obtained from Spain the short-lived charter of home rule which had been set aside when the United States stepped in. He was the founder and editor-owner of *La Democracia*, a crusading newspaper, and was in his day the greatest and most honored political figure on the island. Unlike most political leaders, he lived in the hills, in the small mountain town of Barranquitas, instead of in the more cosmopolitan capital, San Juan. He was one of the group of men who, during the nineteenth century, labored to awaken the people of Puerto Rico to their own dignity, problems, and powers—and so to give them a measure of cultural unity. Politically he stood for Puerto Rico's autonomy. He was one of those who were jailed during the "Terrible Year of 1887," when a Spanish governor tried to set back the clock of cultural advance through a rule of terrorism and espionage, punctuated by prison sentences. He was the idol of the island's country people.

Muñoz Rivera was the father of Luis Muñoz Marín. The tradition of a hallowed name became an asset to the latter during the early years of his political life, though he never rode on his father's coattails and carved his own political destiny according to his own orientations and the norms and demands of a new age. The fact that Muñoz Rivera died in 1917 may also have helped the son, who thereafter did not have the drawback of having an illustrious father always at his side. Like virtually all Puerto Rican leaders, Rivera died poor. Except for a sporadic and always insufficient income from *La Democracia*, the son had to make his own way financially—often with considerable difficulty.

Born in San Juan in 1898, Luis was raised in New York and Washington, where his father was Resident Commissioner and where the son began early to be intimately acquainted with the workings and psychology of the American government. I know little about his early life; I have heard reports which boil down to the strong possibility that he was a brilliant boy, undisciplined and spoiled. At the age of fourteen he entered Georgetown University, where he studied law—probably with a certain degree of nonchalance. There is a story that he wandered into the Library of Congress during his student days, picked up a book on socialism and became an ardent socialist; certainly, his first political activities

in Puerto Rico were on behalf of the Socialist party rather
than his father's Unionist party.

Like many Latins he was greatly—and in his case bilin-
gually—interested in poetry. I am neither lover nor judge of
poetry, have read almost none of Luis', and would not be
able to tell, if I had, whether it is good or bad. One fragment,
however, is worth repeating here because it shows a deep,
early identification with Puerto Rico's submerged sugar
laborers. It is from the poem "Pamphlet," found in the *An-
thology of Contemporary Latin American Poetry*, edited by
Dudley Fitts.

> *I have drowned my dreams*
> *in order to glut the dreams that sleep for me in the veins*
> *of men who sweated and wept and raged*
> *to season my coffee. . . .*
> *The dream that sleeps in breasts stifled by tuberculosis*
> *   (A little air, a little sunshine!)*
> *the dreams that dream in stomachs strangled by hunger*
> *   (A bit of bread, a bit of white bread!)*
> *the dream of bare feet*
> *   (Fewer stones on the road, Lord, fewer broken bottles!)*
> *the dream of calloused hands*
> *   (Moss . . . clean cambric . . . things smooth, soft, soothing!)*
> *the dream of trampled hearts*
> *   (Love . . . life . . . life!)*

Edwin Markham was his close friend and neighbor when
Muñoz lived on Staten Island, and the latter wrote a famous,
and still standard, translation of "The Man with the Hoe,"
which appealed to his personal sense of human identification
and justice. Puerto Ricans today still call him *El Vate*, which
is an honorary title meaning "The Bard." Tugwell came to
fear the title, and a few Puerto Ricans still do, on the grounds
that American businessmen might hesitate to deal with a
society that is run by a poet. When I questioned him about
the matter in 1951, Muñoz laughed and said: "I am not against

poetry; I am only against bad poetry. I have always been a
poet and I still consider myself one—rather than a politician.
The only difference is that I no longer use verse as my medium.
My medium today is politics and my hope is that the future
will consider the results good poetry rather than bad."

In the sense in which a poet is one who at all times identifies'
with people rather than with established dogma—with the
problems, fears, and aspirations of live human beings instead
of with the ideological distillates of life—he has proved himself to be a great poet. Academicians at times call his speeches
and writings those of an illiterate man who seems to know
nothing about the various systems of thought by which the
world is supposed to be run. Humanists regard them as the
expressions of a vital and powerful leader who at all times fits
his own thinking to human realities as he finds them, regardless of academic dogma.

I haven't read his verse, but I know that his prose writings
are superb and that he is a great poet in the medium of prose.
During the 1920's he began writing articles on Puerto Rico, as
a free-lance journalist, for such periodicals as *The Nation,
The New Republic,* and H. L. Mencken's *The American Mercury.* By far the most brilliant and daring analyses ever written of Puerto Rico's ills and its relations with the United
States, they created a sensation on the island, though they
were also resented by the super-patriots as being radical and
even revolutionary in nature. As a free-lance writer in New
York, Muñoz became a new voice in Puerto Rican affairs; he
set new patterns of thought and captured a small but solid
and important following of the same intellectuals who are
today making history through the manner in which they conduct their government. There can be no doubt either that he
is today one of those rare political figures in high office who
are masters of the English language. His command of the
American vernacular has been felt by many a Congressional

committee and is illustrated by an amusing incident of the 1930's.

He had an appointment to see President Roosevelt, and in the latter's outer office was a new secretary who didn't know the Senator from Puerto Rico. Taking it for granted that Muñoz couldn't speak English, worried about the problem of translation, since no Spanish language interpreter happened to be handy at the time, the latter said: *"Est-ce que vous parlez français?"* He went on to ask, in French, whether the Senator would mind speaking French to the President, since the latter didn't know Spanish.

The answer came back without a trace of an accent: "What about English? Does he understand that?"

Years later, after he had become Puerto Rico's governor and had won a certain amount of international fame for his Operation Bootstrap, he was in a hotel in New York when an English correspondent of Reuters came for an interview. The latter brought with him an interpreter, who put the Englishman's first long question into polished and involved Spanish. Muñoz let him struggle through it, but then answered in easy, colloquial English. That seemed to have irked the correspondent, who was determined to get revenge. As he was leaving, after a lengthy interview in which Muñoz had talked eloquently about the problems, the qualities, and the achievements of Puerto Rico's people, he stopped at the door and fired back one barbed question:

"By the way, Governor, when do you think Puerto Rico will become *economically* free of the United States?"

Muñoz answered without hesitation: "I would judge, about the same time that England is."

I first became acquainted with Muñoz through his writings. I was an engineer, recently graduated from the University of Wisconsin, roaming the deserts and mountains of northern

Chile. A friend had given me a subscription to *The Nation*, then edited by Ernest Gruening. From five thousand miles away I was particularly interested in the latter's crusade against American imperialism in the Caribbean and the occupation of Haiti and Nicaragua by the U.S. Marines. I was also fascinated by a series of articles on various parts of the United States. Outstanding among them was an article called "Porto Rico: America's Colony," by one Luis Muñoz Marín.

I returned to the States in 1925, shortly after reading the article, and in New York I became reacquainted with a number of my old friends from Wisconsin—among them the Icelander Björn G. Björnson, Horace and Marya Gregory, and Vilhjalmur Stefansson, whom I had first met when he came to Wisconsin to lecture. Horace and Björn told me about a remarkable and stimulating Sunday-Evening-at-Home, conducted by a Puerto Rican writer with an American wife, invitation to which was extended exclusively on the basis of intellectual interests and the quality of having something to say. Stefansson, they said, often went there, and George Hubert (later Sir Hubert) Wilkins, the Lomen Brothers of Alaska, Vachel Lindsay, Sara Teasdale, William Rose Benet, and a number of Latin American poets, intellectuals, political exiles, and journalists. On the first available Sunday they took me to the gathering, introduced me to Luis Muñoz Marín and his wife at that time.

Luis had married Muna Lee, originally from Mississippi, in 1919. Now an honored official of the Department of State, known and beloved throughout Latin America for her indefatigable and effective work in inter-American, inter-cultural relations, she was then a poet, writer, translator from the Spanish, and a passionate devotee to all things Spanish. His marriage to an American, unusual in those days, showed an early trend toward a cosmopolitan kind of Americanism. With and through Muna, he had close contacts in New York with a number of outstanding American intellectuals, with promi-

nent Latin Americans, and with young and ardent Americans
—Anglo as well as Latin—who were later to become prominent.
Composed of poets, singers, novelists, engineers, journalists,
philosophers, that heterogeneous group met weekly at his
home for the sole purpose of stimulating each other.

Invariably present at the Sunday evening gatherings, as a
co-hostess with Muna, was a woman who soon became another of my valued friends. A mountain of a woman, dressed in
fantastic red plush, with dyed hair and mascaraed eyes, with
gaudy costume jewelry jangling on her arms, she had an in-
cisive wit which tended to frighten all who didn't know her
well—as it was later to throw the fear of God into the various
writers who worked with her. This was Constance Lindsay
Skinner, who had been raised in the Canadian wilderness as
the daughter of a Hudson's Bay Company factor, had become one of Hearst's first sob sisters and a close friend (and
worshipful admirer) of Jack London, and later had done
valuable historical research and writing on the American
scene. When I first met her she was writing boys' books and
stories. Later she originated the "Rivers of America" series
of books, became its first editor, and built it up to its well-
deserved prominence, importance, and popularity.

On my first visit to Muñoz' house, that terrifying woman
called me peremptorily to her side, asked my name, and said:
"Tell me about yourself, young man!"

I spilled over about Chile, the Atacama Desert, the Andes,
about mining camps and Inca graves, water holes, condors,
and lost Indian villages, Andean llama herders and Americans
living in mining camps for years without ever seeing or sens-
ing anything except their clubs, their bars, their camp politics,
and the inferior "natives" with whom one must under no circumstances have social contact lest one be regarded as going
native.

Like almost everybody at those gatherings, with the possible exception of myself, Constance had the rare quality of

being not only a good talker but also a good listener. After some minutes of apparently rapt attention, she began to chuckle.

"Young man," she said, "you are an explorer and I like you. I love explorers because they are bold, free men who recognize no boundaries—geographic, intellectual, or moral!"

Except for the moral part, her description of explorers fitted Luis and Muna's Sunday evenings to a T.

If Luis was interested in my observations on Latin America, and especially on North Americans running colonial mining camps in Latin America, I was nothing less than fascinated by his own activities for Pan-American unity and the Pan-American labor movement. One of those activities was as a revolutionary conspirator against Juan Vicente Gomez, the bloodthirsty tyrant of Venezuela.

In 1920, Luis had been in Puerto Rico, had made some speeches for the Socialist party, had become associated with Santiago Iglesias, the party's leader, and had so become actively interested in the labor movement. Correctly he and Iglesias had decided that Gomez was one of the great obstacles to the spread and success of that movement, not only in Venezuela, but also, because of what he represented, in many other parts of Latin America. Through Iglesias, Luis had access to money in Mexico, interested in labor and potentially available for a revolution against Gomez—provided that there be first some kind of organization, ready and able to carry the revolution through. In New York he devoted some of his energies to the difficult task of putting such an organization together.

Not that there was any shortage of revolutionists! Wherever one turned in those days outside of Venezuela, in New York, Paris, London, Amsterdam, one ran into exiles from Gomez' ruthless regime; whenever three of those exiles met, they formed a revolutionary junta. Luis took hold of one of those juntas, on Cherry Street in Brooklyn, and tried to make a revolution out of it. But he had his difficulties.

"What a junta!" he complained to me—who was fascinated. "I try to talk to them about the practical problems of revolution, but I don't get anywhere. We need a military leader. Where shall we get him? We need arms. Where can we buy them, and what kind? How shall we transport our arms to Venezuela? Where shall we get our men and train them? What shall our policies be? What promises shall we make to the people in order to persuade them to support us? How can we persuade the United States to recognize our new government after we have won the revolution? I come back to those questions again and again, but do you know what they do? Every meeting breaks up in a fight over what the flag of the revolution shall be. They never get beyond that confounded flag."

Then, suddenly, late in 1925 or early in 1926, a real, live, Venezuelan general appeared on the scene and began to come to the Sunday-evenings-at-home. This was Rafael de Nogales, an aristocratic *Andino* from Venezuela's mountains, obviously part Indian, who had been raised at the court of the German Kaiser and trained in a Spanish military academy. A dramatic raconteur, he held the gatherings spellbound with tales of his adventures—many of which seemed highly improbable, although, as often happens in similar cases, those that *could* be checked always turned out to be true.

Nogales claimed that his first military adventures had been in the Spanish-American War. Later he claimed to have been on the Japanese side in the Russo-Japanese War, and to have gone from there to Alaska to look for gold. When World War I broke out, his "innate Latin sense of liberty" overcame his German upbringing and caused him to offer his sword to the Allies. But the British wouldn't have him unless he first became a British subject, the French would have him only in the Foreign Legion—which was an insult—and one by one the

Allies turned him down for one reason or another. Finally his innate Latin sense of liberty drew him into the Turkish army, where he became Inspector General of Cavalry, a general of some kind in rank, and apparently very useful.

He had written a book, *Cuatro Años Bajo la Media Luna*, and he was now in New York to arrange for its translation by Muna Lee and its eventual publication under the title *Four Years Beneath the Crescent*. Small, dark, dramatically fierce, interspersing all his conversations with grunts, talking often about how he would rather roll up in a blanket under the stars than sleep in the finest bed made, obviously not a mental giant, he impressed Luis as being an odd kind of Boy Scout with a military record. He also had a startling habit of always carrying photographs of himself, dressed in uniform, with a Turkish fez on his head and a German iron cross on his chest, and of giving one of these to almost everybody he met. But he was undoubtedly a general and a Venezuelan who hated Gomez as a result of having had his Venezuelan properties confiscated by the latter. As such, he could be useful to the revolution, and Luis introduced him to his junta on Cherry Street.

After some indoctrination, possibly about the revolution's flag, the junta sent him to Mexico to arrange for the promised funds. That was the end of *that* revolution. The funds did not materialize, the offer of them was withdrawn, and not until some years later did Muñoz meet the man who had promised them and ask him what had happened.

"What happened?" the latter sputtered. "What kind of a man did you send me? How am I going to have faith in a man who claims to be a world-famous general and who, on first meeting, shakes hands with one hand and shoves a picture post card of himself at me with the other?"

The junta broke up, and Luis was out of the armed revolution business, never to touch it again. In 1931 I met him in San Juan. I was on my way to Venezuela and the Amazon for

the Carnegie Institution of Washington, and I wanted badly
to meet Gomez, as an interesting, if ruthless, character. Luis
thought he could fix it through the governor's office. Governor
Theodore Roosevelt, Jr., however, was on the continent for
an American Legion meeting, and Dr. José Padín, the Commissioner of Education, was acting governor. It took me some
years to understand why the latter was completely and even
dramatically unco-operative when Luis Muñoz Marín introduced me to him and asked him to give me an official letter
of introduction to Gomez.

General Nogales came later to have the misfortune of having his enemy, Gomez, die a natural death before Nogales
could get at him. That happened in 1936, when I lived in
Puerto Rico. After the tyrant's death, the Venezuelan government invited all its political exiles to come home. In Venezuela
they made Nogales customs collector at some port; I heard
that he grew enormously fat on the job and became famous
for his Gargantuan drinking bouts. He made a trip to Panama
and died there, of appendicitis, on the operating table. His
body was shipped to Venezuela, where nobody knew what
to do with it, and where it lay for a week in a warehouse in
La Guaira. However, an American newspaperman who had
known Nogales in New York raised hell about the matter.
Here was a man, he wrote, who had been a personal friend of
the German Kaiser's, who had risen to be a general in the
Turkish army, who had fought with distinction in many wars,
who had made history with his explorations in Nicaragua
and had hobnobbed with Sandino. Here was a man of whom
Venezuela had every right to be proud!

Great are the powers of publicity! The Venezuelan government took Nogales out of the warehouse and gave him a
splendid military funeral, preceded by a great parade in
Caracas. The Kaiser was dead by now, but Hitler (whom
Nogales had hated venomously) contributed to the funeral
in the form of an iron cross of carnations. If Nogales' life had

petered out for lack of wars to fight, he at least achieved a hero's burial.

In midsummer, 1926, Luis and Muna, and their two children, Luisito and Munita, moved to San Juan, where he became the editor of his father's old newspaper, *La Democracia*. Later I heard fantastic tales about that harrowing experience. The paper had fallen on evil days in competition with more modern, American-style papers. There were just enough subscribers who couldn't let their beloved *La Democracia* die to keep it barely alive; just enough loyal employees to get it out—for the same reason and also because jobs were at best scarce. The trouble was that the latter often had to work without pay and that they therefore considered themselves as having a personal stake in the paper.

Every once in so often Muñoz would write what he considered a brilliant editorial, only to have the typesetter refuse to set it because he didn't like it. Then, after having perforce rewritten the article to suit his typesetter (where could he get another under the circumstances?), he got it back a second time because it made use of the letter "f" too often. "We are out of f's," complained the harassed typesetter. "I can't let you have any in this article." So the editorial would have to be rewritten for a careful avoidance of words containing that letter.

That hit-or-miss journalism, however, began to establish Muñoz on the local scene as a man who had something original and vital to say. Muna, meanwhile, became associated with the University of Puerto Rico as publicity director and teacher of American poetry.

In 1928 I had a telephone call from Luis in New York. It seemed that Puerto Rico was in a bad way and needed industries, and that the major political parties had decided to send the son of Muñoz Rivera to New York as a one-man industrial

mission to look for American capital willing to invest itself in
the island's progress. That at least was the official explanation
of Luis' presence on the continent. A more probable explanation—since the quest for such capital in that year must have
seemed hopeless to everybody—is that the major parties sent
him north in order to get rid of him. As a journalist and a
potential political figure, as a man whose writings were winning him many followers, he was a menace to all the old-line
politicians. He did not think like a politician, in roundabout
terms of immediate expediency; he came directly to the point,
no matter how politically embarrassing it might have been;
he thought and wrote in terms of Puerto Rico's well-being,
and never in terms of party policies; he was not subject to
party discipline and was every bit as great an embarrassment
to the politicians of one party as to those of another.

Whatever the reason or reasons, the industrial mission was
a dismal failure in that it found no capital, but Muñoz stayed
in New York to work for a time as night editor of Latin
American dispatches to the Associated Press, at twenty-five
dollars per week, and to collaborate with Nogales on the
latter's journalistic writings. Every once in a while I saw him,
and we made the rounds together of various bars, talking
about everything under the sun, looking for stimulating company, and going as far as our joint funds would permit—which
was sometimes, what with parties going on in various parts
of New York, surprisingly far.

Luis was a man to whom money as such seemed to have
little significance. While a trencherman of the first order when
he could afford it, he never seemed to be unhappy when he
couldn't—a quality that came to stand him in good stead in
politics, where even his bitterest enemies were constantly
forced to admit that he was completely incorruptible. What
did seem to make him unhappy, however, was lack of company, lack of conversation, lack of people with whom he could
exchange ideas. He has a reputation even today as a man who

feeds on people, devours them, must have them about him, a vast variety of people, university professors, journalists, hillbillies, politicians, bureaucrats, farmers, soldiers, cops. And in those early, unhappy days in New York he began to show some of the qualities that mark him today—a great loneliness like that of a man who was never sure that he had a real friend, coupled with an even greater gentleness toward people. He is capable of explosive rages over specific situations, but not of personal rancor against specific individuals. Even in those New York days he had an almost childlike faith in men of all kinds, which, while it has been betrayed again and again, has by now grown into a great and almost religious respect for mankind and the brotherhood of man.

He loved to talk about his own ideas, the things he had written, the things he had done and planned to do, but never with arrogance. About his own achievements he has always been one of the most objective men I have known, a man in whom pride of achievement is mixed in equal parts with a great and balancing humility, one who illustrates perfectly the truth of Goethe's dictum that "Only clods are modest; the brave rejoice in the deed."

In 1951, when Muñoz was governor, a public-relations man in the Puerto Rican rum industry thought it a good idea to invite a group of New York bartenders to the island to acquaint them at first hand with the glories, the velvety smoothness, the divine taste, the tropical aroma, the versatility, of Puerto Rican rum. As governor, Muñoz invited the group to the *Fortaleza*. Unlike many of his predecessors, he is always ready to do what he can to help any commercial promotion scheme that will help the island—never one to stand on the dignity of his office, to shirk a job as salesman for his beloved Puerto Rico. Besides, one suspects that he has a special fondness for bartenders—or at least should have. When the delegation of bartenders had assembled in the governor's mansion, Muñoz mixed them one of his own unique and often startling

cocktail concoctions, and then held them spellbound—as he
does all who see him—with the brilliance and humanity of his
conversation. Some months later when he was in a hotel in
New York, he received word that delegates from the Bartenders' Union were downstairs, looking for him. He went to
the hotel's bar, took charge, and mixed them another concoc-
tion, probably even weirder than the first. With that, one of
them made a speech and presented him with a gold card,
engraved in blue, making him an honorary member of the
Bartenders' Union, New York, Local No. 16, and giving him
the right to a free drink in any bar served by a member of
that union.

"Earl," he said when he told me about the affair, "recognition always comes. It may come late, but it comes. But my
God, Earl, think of what we could have done with that card
twenty years ago!"

I can't write a coherent account of what he did in those
days. I saw him every once in so often, and then he disap
peared again. I knew that he was busy in Latin American affairs, that he attended occasional conferences in Cuba, that he
wrote regular articles for the Baltimore *Sun* on Latin America,
that he was interested in liberal causes where they impinged
on Latin America, and that his thoughts and conversations
always, invariably, came back to Puerto Rico and the plight
of the island's *jíbaros*. But I wasn't a part of that. We were
friends who moved in different worlds which touched only
occasionally. In some ways, however, we were also both
anchorless in the rather tragic manner of the Greenwich
Village intellectuals of those days. I know that I valued my
sporadic evenings and week ends with him because they
helped, momentarily, to dispel loneliness and intellectual frus-
tration.

Looking back today, one thing occurs to me. In New York
we regarded Luis as a cosmopolitan kind of New Yorker—
not as a man who had been raised bi-culturally and must often

have been emotionally torn between the two cultures. Every once in so often he would grow nostalgic about old Puerto Rican ways of life and apprehensive over what the American rule was doing to them. He told about the Holy Rollers and other hysterical American sects which were gaining footholds among the formerly easygoing mountain people. He lamented the American hustle and bustle, and the American commercialization, which were doing away with the old coffee houses and so also with the custom of conversation about important issues. I realize now that he was at all times deeply attached to what he rightly considered the finest aspects of the old Spanish culture, and that he wanted his people, somehow, to retain those aspects.

In later years, when I knew him in Puerto Rico, he would sometimes—when with only a few trusted friends—start to sing Rafael Hernández' *Lamento Borincano*, that profoundly moving dirge for the Puerto Rican *jíbaro* and the sadness of his lot. That song became his theme song during the early years of his great struggle. In those years, too, he was often criticized for spending too much time in various cafés, drinking with friends. I wonder. Were those cafés, with their alcohol, to him the equivalents of the old coffee houses? Did he go there in part to listen to the Puerto Rican music which had so powerful an emotional hold on him? There must have been much of all that, though he seldom showed it. To many of the upper-class Puerto Ricans, his café habits seemed like those of a profligate who threw his money away like a released adolescent.

There is the famous story of the time when he had twenty dollars in his pocket—a rare occurrence. He went to the Escambrón Beach Club, told his friends about his wealth, and called for a celebration. Twenty dollars demanded champagne! He invited people to join him, called for more champagne and more whisky, and talked about Puerto Rico's plight and the tragedy of the island's people. Naturally, the bill soared far beyond the original twenty dollars. When the party finally broke up, it was forty-five dollars. Muñoz asked all his friends if they had any money, but the most they could dig up was five or six dollars. They urged him to pay his twenty and let the rest go till some other day. He grew embarrassed.

"To tell the truth," he said, "I went to the men's room a little while ago, and there was a man who began to talk to me. I had never seen him before, but he told me so sad a story about his life and his troubles that I gave him the twenty."

In 1929 we spent a long evening together in Julius' speakeasy on Fourth Street and Waverly Place, drinking whisky sours. That was the time when the U.S. Marines were fighting Sandino in Nicaragua, and when liberal elements were up in arms over that manifestation of dollar diplomacy and American imperialism. We were sitting in Julius', minding our own business and discussing Puerto Rico, and South America, and Horace Gregory, and Stefansson, and the world in general, when a man joined us and told us that anybody could see that we were both Latin Americans. The news didn't astonish us, even though I am not—being dark enough, however, to pass for one. The man, with more than one of Julius' famous whisky sours under his belt, then sounded off about how he, too, knew something about Latin America, being a major in the Marine Corps and having recently returned from the fighting in Nicaragua. Then he launched into a tirade against Sandino, whom he regarded as a murderous bandit.

After a time Luis turned to me and said: "I don't think he knows who I am. Should I tell him?"

"Go ahead," I answered, without any inkling of what was coming.

"My friend," said Luis to the marine, "I am Sandino's brother, Socrates."

The effect was startling. It seems that Sandino really did

have a brother in Brooklyn at the time, and the major changed his tune immediately. Sandino, it now turned out, was a Nicaraguan patriot and it was too bad that the Marine Corps had orders to get him.

I didn't see Luis for many months after that evening. Not until twenty years later did I hear the rest of the story.

The American Civil Liberties Union was interested in dramatizing the position of Sandino and had gotten hold of Brother Socrates for the purpose of sending him around to address audiences and stir up sympathy. Despite his name, however, Socrates was not too bright and couldn't be trusted to make a very good impression. Arrangements had therefore been made for Luis to go with him—Socrates to show himself and Muñoz to do the talking. They were, in fact, due to go to Cuba the day after our talk with the Marine officer. I don't know whether Luis actually got there; Socrates, however, never did show up and the barnstorming tour was stillborn.

I saw Luis next late in 1930, at a dinner party in Washington. He didn't look well—either in the sense of physical health or that of financial affluence. I walked with him from the party to an old automobile that he had parked a few blocks away and asked him what he was doing.

Restlessly, driven by a devil, he was driving his car wherever the whim might take him, sometimes sleeping in the automobile and sometimes, when he had a little money, in a hotel. He wrote weekly articles for the Baltimore *Sun*, occasional articles for space rates for the New York *Herald Tribune*, and whatever else he might be able to sell. The funds were barely enough to keep him going, enabling him only to buy gasoline and eat bananas and hamburgers.

Ten years later, after he had won the 1940 election, he was interviewed by a *Fortune* writer and recalled his last days in the United States before getting into the Puerto Rican political scene. He described his rovings in his old car, and said:

"When I found I could do that, I knew I was a free man!"
Certainly, his life of those days proved later to have been
valuable preparation for the astonishing political campaign
of 1940, when he again had virtually no money and had to get
along as best he could.

In the United States, the tour of living from hand to mouth,
in and with a battered old automobile, perforce came to an
end with the approach of the winter of 1930–31. Winter is a
cold time in which to sleep in an old car. Luis therefore drove
to Lewis Gannett's country home in Connecticut, borrowed
the house and lived in it for a time, chopping his own wood
and cooking his own meals. When spring came he decided
to return to Puerto Rico and get into things again.

He drove his rattling car to New York, arriving there the
evening before his ship's departure. He looked up a promising
Latin American novelist, whom he had never seen but to
whom he had been introduced over the telephone by Dr.
José Padín. They spent the better part of the night in a small
restaurant, drinking innumerable cups of coffee and discussing Latin American letters, social conditions, and political
affairs. The other was Romulo Gallegos, who had just finished
writing his remarkable *Doña Barbara*, dealing with Venezuela's turbulent cattle plains and now widely considered the
greatest Latin American novel ever written. In 1947 Gallegos
was to become the first president of Venezuela ever elected by
the democratic popular vote; in 1948, because of his liberal
and humane policies, he was thrown out of office again by a
military junta, in a putsch which was neither opposed nor
resented by the oil companies; in January, 1949, he was invited from his exile in Cuba to attend Muñoz' first inauguration as Puerto Rico's governor. Ill health prevented him from
attending. The two friends haven't seen each other since that
night of their first meeting, in New York in 1931, when they
settled the world's affairs in a dingy restaurant.

When they parted, Luis found that his car had a flat tire. He went to a friend of his and Muna's, an embattled suffragette of the old school, and said: "Do you want an automobile?" Being assured that the latter did, he gave her the keys, told her where the car was, and urged her to help herself. Then he caught his steamer for Puerto Rico, fiddled about for a time, got into politics on the side of the Liberal party, ran for Senator in 1932, and was elected. The island has never been the same since!

I write this in 1954, almost thirty years after I first met Muñoz. It should be taken for granted that he is no longer the bohemian he was in those days. He has led his beloved Puerto Rico out of its former bitter travail and up the *Jalda Ariba*, the long, stony uphill road which he has repeatedly used as his campaign slogan. As a leader, he has taken responsibility for over two million Puerto Ricans and fellow Americans. He takes such responsibility more seriously than does or did any other political figure I have ever heard of.

He has created a government of dedicated, sober, responsible men and women, who, before he came on the scene, had no inkling of how to run a government. He sets that government an example of a dedicated, sober, responsible man.

Matured by both age and responsibility, he works harder than does anybody else in his hard-working government. In the *Fortaleza* he is every inch the governor, every inch the administrator. At his personal home, outside of San Juan, he relaxes. There he invites his friends, the people he must have around him for the purpose of sharpening his wits on those of others. There he can again become something of the old Luis —however mellowed.

As happens to many, the vicissitudes of life separated him from his first wife. Muna Lee is today no less respected and beloved by all who know her, in Puerto Rico, in Washington and New York, throughout Latin America, because she and

Luis were divorced a number of years ago. His wife is today Señora Inés Mendoza de Muñoz Marín, who is gracious and extremely active as Puerto Rico's first lady.

He has two daughters by Doña Inés. Thousands of Puerto Ricans say: "Don Luis has become a true family man, sober, sedate, responsible. He no longer smokes and he drinks very little. The New York cosmopolitan is dead. The former café bohemian no longer exists. Don Luis has come home to us. He is now truly one of us!"

By the same token he has in recent years become seriously concerned about current culture changes. Having led Puerto Rico on the road upward from the economic chaos and human suffering of colonialism, having begun the island's modernization and set it on the road to salvation through industrialization and other aspects of economic development, he is now increasingly preoccupied with what all that is doing to the old Spanish culture. He doesn't want Puerto Rico to become another New Mexico or California. He labors to persuade his people to preserve their cultural roots, to keep the Spanish language as their own—unadulterated by the Americanisms of which he is a past master, to cling to their Latin culture heroes instead of turning to Hopalong Cassidy, to retain their old, democratic, easygoing ways of life while also punching time clocks in factories. Sometimes he reminds one of Henry Ford, who, having done more than any other one man to change the American way of life, grew nostalgic for the old ways and went in heavily for American antiques and old-time American villages.

There, perhaps, in the emotional dichotomy of every man who was raised in two cultures, lies an explanation for Muñoz' essential tragedy. I have little personal doubt, too, that his deep emotional attachment to Puerto Rico's Spanish culture had something to do with his former strong advocacy of the island's independence.

CHAPTER VII

Lobbyist

THE STEADY WORSENING of conditions on the island, going hand in hand with the apparent impossibility, under colonialism, of doing anything about the matter, strengthened Muñoz' belief in independence as essential for Puerto Rico's salvation. That belief, however, differed radically from that of Albizu Campos in that it involved no hostility toward the United States. Indeed, while the Puerto Rican super-patriots regarded Muñoz as being anti-American, he was undoubtedly by far the most American, and the greatest real friend of the United States, among all the island's political figures. He made it clear at all times that he wanted independence "as a matter of mutual convenience to the people of Puerto Rico and the people of the United States," to be achieved by peaceful means and mutual agreement. When heckled about his views by a Congressional committee, he once startled the Congressmen by saying: "Without in the least wanting to belittle the memory of George Washington, I must say that I am unalterably opposed to the use of violence for the achievement of independence."

Moreover, he seems to have regarded the idea of independence, also, as a potential energizing flame to stir the people of Puerto Rico into action on their own behalf. When I saw him briefly in San Juan in 1931, en route to the Amazon Basin, I argued political status with him. He said: "Damn it, I want my people to *want* independence. It is degrading for a colonial people not to want independence. Once they do want it, they will be roused out of their present lethargy and will begin to struggle for the improvement of their own lives. Once they do that, they will set powerful forces in motion and may even be able to bring things to the point where independence is unnecessary and even bad. We will cross that bridge when we come to it. But as of now, for conditions as they exist today, independence is the only solution."

After the fateful year 1936, Muñoz began to change his views on political status, arriving gradually at his present stand that, under existing conditions, Puerto Rico's salvation depends on continued relations with the United States. Until some months after the end of that year, however, he could see no solution for Puerto Rico's problem except as going hand in hand with the achievement of national sovereignty.

He reasoned that the advantages of being within the American tariff wall accrued largely to the continental sugar companies; the disadvantages, consisting primarily of having to pay high prices for goods necessarily bought in the States and shipped to Puerto Rico in expensive American bottoms, were borne by all Puerto Ricans. He saw clearly that land reform, the enforcement of the Five-Hundred-Acre Law, was an absolute necessity; but, while he worked ceaselessly for such reform, he was also convinced that it would never be permitted by a colonial government devoted primarily to looking after U.S. interests on the island. He saw the desirability of establishing new industries in Puerto Rico, but considered it all but impossible under existing conditions. Industries devoted to the manufacture of goods for local consumption were menaced by the threat of dumping; other potential industries were fought (if covertly and indirectly) by the sugar companies which controlled the insular government and wanted no undue competition in the labor market. Under those circumstances no sane man would invest capital in Puerto Rico's industrialization.

Local foodstuffs agriculture, lacking adequate transportation, credit, and plant for distribution and processing, could not compete with the highly organized and industrialized foodstuffs agriculture of the continent; the result was that ever more foods would have to be imported, at rising prices that ever more Puerto Ricans could not afford to pay. Under the United States, moreover, Puerto Rico was perforce included within the terms of the Coastwise Shipping Act, which meant high freight rates to raise the costs of living and commerce still higher.

In other words, while the various steps for salvation were obvious, and while there was no legal reason why most of them should not be taken under American rule, the entire moral, political, and social situation seemed nevertheless rigged against anybody's taking them in the colonial scheme of things. In 1929 Muñoz asked Governor Theodore Roosevelt, Jr., first through an eloquent article in *The Nation*, and later directly, to assume leadership in a program of land reform, under which the Five-Hundred-Acre Law would be enforced through alienation of all the lands held in excess and illegally, and through their subsequent distribution to small farmers and laborers. He was laughed at for his pains, not only by representatives of the federal government, but also by most of the Puerto Rican politicians.

In the same year, in an article in *The American Mercury*, he unburdened himself as follows: "By now the development of large absentee-owned sugar estates, the rapid curtailment in the planting of coffee—the natural crop of the independent farmer—and the concentration of cigar manufacture into the hands of the American trust, have combined to make Puerto Rico a land of beggars and millionaires, of flattering statistics and distressing realities. More and more it becomes a factory worked by peons, fought over by lawyers, bossed by absentee industrialists, and clerked by politicians. It is now Uncle Sam's second largest sweatshop."

For such evils he saw no cure except through the political independence which he preached far and wide—as the *sine qua non* and the essential first step toward economic and social salvation.

Those were the arguments which he used on his followers while he was a Senator in the Puerto Rican legislature from 1932 to 1936. Believing in the evolutionary processes, he did what he could to shape the island's economy and psychology toward greater preparedness for sovereignty, while waiting for the right opportunity for achieving that sovereignty peacefully and in a friendly manner.

Some of his friends and followers, however, who backed him as a leader, could not go along with him on independence. As a sovereign nation, they argued, Puerto Rico would be outside of the U.S. tariff wall; if it had to pay duties on its sugar it would not be able to compete with Cuban sugar with its lower production costs; bad as the Puerto Rican sugar industry was in the social sense, it was still the mainstay of the island's economy and its collapse would mean Puerto Rico's economic ruin. As a sovereign nation, Puerto Rico could no longer hope to enjoy the federal subsidies and other financial favors which were all that held the island's economy together; their cessation, together with the postulated collapse of the sugar industry, would mean inevitable social and economic chaos. As a sovereign nation, Puerto Rico would have tremendous new governmental expenses, for an army and a navy and for a number of governmental functions that were now being carried by Washington.

There were, of course, answers to such arguments. If Puerto Rico got out from within the U.S. tariff wall, it could make trade treaties with other nations—and so still sell its sugar; by the same token, it could buy dried meat from Venezuela much more cheaply than codfish from Gloucester, rice more cheaply from Brazil than from Louisiana. Puerto Rico would be able to ship and receive goods in foreign bottoms and might even be able to create its own merchant marine, to overcome the high rates charged under the Coastwise Shipping Act. As for an army and navy: there could be no doubt that the United States, in view of the island's strategic location opposite the Panama Canal, would always retain a military foothold there; what need did Puerto Rico have for armed forces? Muñoz was fascinated by the decent and democratic Republic of Costa Rica, where the president received a salary of some $250 per month and could be seen at any time by almost anybody—if only while he was having his shoes shined at a public stand, or was drinking a soda in the nearest drugstore—where there were more teachers than soldiers, and where most of the men in the armed forces were primarily musicians whose first function was to play Sunday concerts in military umpah bands in the plazas of the various towns. An independent Puerto Rico could become as decent and democratic as that, with modest needs but also with means ample to fill those needs.

So the debate on independence flowed back and forth in those days. Actually, there was no clear-cut answer—while Puerto Rico kept sinking ever farther into despair. Muñoz, however, was never doctrinaire, adhering to any scheme of thought for its own sake. By 1940, he had come far enough to disavow independence as a campaign issue. Later, when conditions changed, he changed with them. Under circumstances and relationships as they exist today, vastly different from those of 1935, he regards independence as a potential evil and a threat to the essential liberties—of earning their bread and functioning in a free and democratic society—of the Puerto Rican people. When he now opposes an independence "separate from the United States," he claims that Puerto Rico shares America's far more abundant and secure independence.

When Muñoz returned to Puerto Rico in 1931 the island was at the lowest ebb in its history. The world depression was in full swing, but federal relief had not yet been organized. The investment of capital in sugar had stopped; the former inflow of money for lands and buildings had dwindled to nothing. Then, too, a disastrous hurricane had raised havoc in the coffee and tobacco regions and had redistributed houses, or bits of houses, all over the island.

Muñoz had returned to tend to private affairs connected with *La Democracia*, but it was inevitable that he should get into politics at the earliest opportunity. It was now, however, impossible for him to work with the Socialist party with which he had formerly co-operated. In one of those striking political realignments for which Puerto Rico had long been noted, the Socialist party had joined forces with the Republican for the purpose of going to the 1932 elections as a coalition. The love feast was not quite as fantastic as it would have been in the United States. Both parties stood for eventual statehood for Puerto Rico and differed only on the question of whether or not status should be an election issue. The Socialist party was, moreover, largely a labor party, closely allied with the A. F. of L. in the States and about as "socialistic."

Muñoz joined the Liberal party, headed by Antonio R. Barceló, an offshoot of Muñoz Rivera's old Unionist party, which had strong leanings toward independence. The fact that Muñoz insisted that an independence plank be inserted in the Liberal party's platform didn't mean much under existing political conditions—where ultimate status was often an academic matter as compared with the urgent necessity for winning elections and getting the patronage. What did mean something was the fact that his dynamic leadership and his articles about Puerto Rico in the States had won him the support of most of the island's intellectuals, that his father had been the idol of the *jíbaros* in the hills, and that he, both through his name and his leadership, might well be counted upon to capture a goodly share of the rural vote.

The election of 1932 gave the Liberal party a larger vote than was polled by any other, though the party was defeated by the fact of the coalition. Muñoz was elected Senator-at-large. His first local campaign, against slot machines and similar gambling devices, was of minor importance, though such machines are today not found anywhere on the island. Soon after his election, he transferred his major activities to Washington, where he became, unofficially, the greatest lobbyist Puerto Rico had ever had. He had no business being there, of course. His job was supposed to be that of preparing and debating legislation in San Juan; his old associate, Santiago Iglesias, head of the Socialist party, had been elected as the island's Resident Commissioner, or official representative in Washington; under the game's rules the coalition had charge of Puerto Rico's relations with the United States. Muñoz ignored all that, ran rings around Iglesias in Washington, accomplished wonders as a lobbyist, and drove the coalition politicians wild with anger.

Again, however, he played no facile political game. He wanted to persuade Washington to do something real for the people of Puerto Rico; he wanted to create a situation under which Washington, after doing whatever was possible to improve the island's economic lot, would willingly and in full friendship give his people a decent kind of political independence. That, of course, required a tremendous amount of lobbying and educating in the capital which the coalition could be trusted to oppose tooth and nail.

A considerable part of his success as a lobbyist, and of his strength as a leader on the island, came to stem from the fact that he had resumed the editorship of *La Democracia*, which gave him a newspaper platform, and that he had arranged for the services of a remarkable woman as the paper's Washington correspondent. This was an old friend of Muna Lee's named Ruby Black, recommended by Muna, an intelligent journalist who was intensely interested in Puerto Rico's cause, ran a news agency of her own, and was one of those several women journalists who were friends of Mrs. Roosevelt's and at times enjoyed what was almost a family relationship with both her and the President.

During the four years that followed his election, Ruby came to be Muñoz' indefatigable co-worker in Washington. As a journalist she had access to a great deal of information and gossip which she passed on in a steady stream of letters. In part through her, whether he was in Washington or in San Juan, Muñoz seemed to have much more information on what was going on in the capital than did the official Resident Commissioner. When he was in San Juan and wanted to send confidential messages to various people in Washington, he could rely on her to do the job. When he wanted information, she got it for him—whether through discreet snooping or through the expedient of interviewing people as a journalist. *La Democracia* came to have much better coverage of the Washington scene, under Ruby's by-line, than did any of the more powerful and successful papers.

Ruby and Muñoz were a strong team, and she became famous in Puerto Rico as a friend of the Puerto Rican people. Muñoz' political enemies, of course, did their best to discredit her—especially since that kind of working relationship was unprecedented in Puerto Rican political life. Some of them described her as a kind of Madame du Barry; others claimed that she was an illegitimate daughter of Muñoz Rivera, and so Luis' half sister; Albizu Campos went so far as to announce that she didn't exist at all, being merely a diabolical fraud and political invention of Muñoz', created by the latter for the purpose of covering his tracks. His Puerto Rican friends, however, came to know her well. Ruby's Alexandria home became a salon for any and all Muñocistas who came to Washington, and the latter talked jokingly about some day hauling down

the statue to Columbus in San Juan's Plaza Colón and putting
Ruby Black in his place as a twentieth-century discoverer of
Puerto Rico.

The case of Robert H. Gore was Muñoz' first dramatic political triumph, as well as his first resounding victory against the
hocus-pocus of colonialism.

Precisely as Puerto Rico had long been a dumping ground
for shoddy American goods, so it was also at times convenient
as a dumping ground for shoddy, third-rate politicians, for
whom the powers in Washington could find no other position.
That meant that, while the helpless island had received some
very good governors from time to time, like Theodore Roosevelt, Jr., it had also received a number of terrible ones, among
whom Harding's Montgomery Reily had been outstanding.
Now, in the election of 1932, Roosevelt had been elected, and
the Democratic party demanded its pound of flesh. According
to Hubert Herring, writing in *The Nation* in November, 1933:
"Two of the smaller Atlantic islands—Manhattan and Puerto
Rico—now have a common bond. President Roosevelt gave
both to Postmaster Farley. Farley picked Joseph McKee to
rule Manhattan and Robert Gore to rule Puerto Rico. Both
islands rebelled; Manhattan has achieved a rousing success,
and Puerto Rico will probably soon rid itself of Gore."

This Gore was a Florida politician with money who had
helped to start and finance the Roosevelt boom and demanded his just reward. There was no place for him on the
continent, so they made him governor of Puerto Rico. Padín
wrote me in 1953: "Gore defeated himself through his own
appalling incompetence. I believe that the appointment of
this man as governor of Puerto Rico is the most disgraceful act
committed by any President against Puerto Rico. . . . Roosevelt was a very irresponsible man at times. Of course, he
corrected his error, because he was a great man."

Getting him in was Farley's doing; getting him out again was Muñoz'.

Shortly after Gore's arrival in San Juan, Muñoz and Barceló called on him to pay their respects as representatives of the party that had polled the most votes, bringing with them a list of Liberal party members whom they wanted the governor to appoint to various positions. They soon discovered that (1) Gore was going to play ball with the coalition and didn't intend to give anything at all to the Liberals, and (2) he made it a condition of appointment that the incumbent give the governor his resignation, with date left blank, on the day he took office. They hastily withdrew their entire list and were in the happy position of having the Republicans and Socialists almost as indignant against the governor (over the insult of the resignations) as were they themselves.

Moreover, Gore seemed to think that the Liberals were anti-American. They stood for eventual independence, and they wished to have Spanish used as the language of instruction in the schools. All this gave Muñoz incendiary material for fiery articles and editorials in *La Democracia*, the most famous of which dealt with the matter of the undated resignations. Popular indignation against those resignations transcended all party lines, since they were a direct insult to Puerto Ricans as such, regardless of whether they were Liberals, Republicans, Socialists, or Nationalists. As a result, Gore made the mistake of denying that he had ever asked for them. Muñoz came out with a stinging editorial which is still being discussed in San Juan. Its headline was in English, and read: "Governor Gore, you are a damn liar." Muñoz dared the governor to sue him. The latter didn't. If for no other reason, Muñoz' headline was important for the Puerto Ricans. They now had a political leader who set an example of daring to stand up to the representative of the United States.

Gore went farther and appointed to the university's Board

of Trustees a man whom the students regarded as an illiterate politician. Hubert Herring claims that he did it because he suspected the entire university of being anti-American, and he wanted on the board a flag waver of whose Americanism he could be sure. This was one Alonso Torres, a labor man active and important in the coalition, who had on numerous occasions expressed his dislike for the university. Some years previously he had been chairman of a commission, appointed to make recommendations for improving the island's dreadful economic situation. Typical of the means that his commission advocated had been the one to get hold of a number of canary birds, teach them to sing the "Star-Spangled Banner," and sell them in the States. In the face of the public uproar against his appointment to the university board, he wanted to prove that he, too, was literate. Accordingly he wrote and published an article about dogs. One of the gems of that article was the statement that in Siberia, where transatlantic steamers cannot go because of the ice and snow, dogs pull sledges. However, the term "dogs" seemed to be too common for a literary man; accordingly, throughout the article, he called them "these felines."

As a protest against the appointment of such a man to the university board, the students staged a protracted strike which closed the university for several weeks and created serious emotional tensions. While the strike was on, with the blessings of the Liberal party but certainly not of the coalition, Muñoz went to Washington to see what he could do toward having Gore removed. He went directly to Roosevelt —gaining access to him through a simple maneuver that the latter must have used repeatedly when he wanted to talk to people whom it was impolitic for him to see officially. Ruby Black persuaded Mrs. Roosevelt to invite the brilliant Senator from Puerto Rico to tea; the President came in and sat down to listen while Muñoz talked to the first lady; eventually Mrs. Roosevelt left the room and the two men could chat in private.

After Muñoz had talked a while about the mess that Gore had made in Puerto Rico, the tensions he had created, the unnecessary but dangerous resentments against the United States that he was stirring up, Roosevelt interrupted him to object to the students' ("immature children") mixing into important political matters. "They ought to be spanked," he said emphatically, wishing they would stick to their studies and sports, and perhaps not unaware of the bloody role that the Cuban university students had, a little while before, played in the ABC uprisings that had brought the army sergeant Fulgencio Batista to power as President of Cuba.

"Mr. President," answered Muñoz, "I mentioned the student strike only in order to show that the opposition to Gore is nonpartisan; the students belong to all parties. Besides, the alumni passed a resolution backing up the students, and you must admit that most of *them* are probably over twenty-one."

The President admitted that they probably were.

"Not only that, but the parents passed a resolution backing up their striking sons and daughters—which almost never happens when our students go on a rampage."

With that Roosevelt let out one of his characteristic guffaws. "I'll admit that *they're* over twenty-one. They must be over twenty-one!"

The two men, alike in many ways, understood each other from their first meeting. Muñoz left the White House with the promise that Gore would resign. But week after week went by without news of the resignation. The storm against him raged unceasingly in Puerto Rico while Muñoz sat in Washington, making valuable contacts in the New Deal administration, waiting for the proper psychological moment to go home, but apparently getting no action on Gore.

Somehow, however, Muñoz got word that Roosevelt was disturbed by the unceasing campaign of vituperation against the governor in Puerto Rico; he didn't like being forced to withdraw a man under fire. Immediately, Muñoz sent a cease-fire cable to the San Juan Liberals who had been doing most of the agitating, and the storm subsided. Gore's resignation was announced not long thereafter, and Muñoz could take the first steamer home.

When he landed he found thousands of people waiting to welcome him at the dock. He was received as the triumphant conqueror, and the event of his return was the signal for one of the largest and most enthusiastic parades the city had ever seen—a parade that was all the more dramatic because Gore had returned a few weeks before from a trip to Washington and had been met by a crowd that had gathered to boo and hiss him.

The incident was infinitely more important than was the mere removal of an inept governor. A new way of doing things had been demonstrated, by a member of the minority party and even against the official wishes of the ruling coalition, which, however incensed it had been about the matter of the resignation letters, still liked the fact that it got all the jobs. A small, neat hole had been drilled through the armor of political hocus-pocus with which Washington's representatives had for decades protected themselves on the island. The one outstanding champion of Puerto Rico's people had proved, to those people as well as to his own political opposition, that he could exercise a considerable influence in Washington—where the President was also a champion of the people.

Moreover—and this was perhaps the most important aspect of the breakdown of colonialism—Washington itself was getting an education regarding Puerto Rico. Gore was the last governor appointed by the United States solely for the purpose of repaying political debts. The island had begun to spit and scratch, and to make Washington acutely aware of its realities; it could no longer be used as an out-of-sight-out-of-mind dumping ground for the exile of deserving Democrats.

Gore's successor was in some ways even more inept—especially since he had to deal with serious problems that were beyond his mentality. But he was not appointed for the cynical purpose of repaying a political debt.

General Blanton Winship was a handsome, correct, southern gentleman who had formerly been the Army's Judge Advocate General and had been on a legal mission in Liberia. He didn't look offensive and he didn't say much—in part because he didn't have much to say and in part because he was elderly and tired, and said openly that he wanted no headaches and planned to devote his governship to resting amid pleasant surroundings. They were to become less pleasant as time went on; the uproar against him was to grow greater than had been that against Gore; but Roosevelt was tired of sending governors to Puerto Rico only to have their recall demanded almost immediately.

It was during Winship's regime that the dead whale was washed up on the beach of San Juan, and even that poor carcass achieved political implications.

One morning, residents of Condado, an exclusive residential section, were awakened by an awful smell and looked out to see an eighty-foot monster lying on their beach. They called the city health department to remove it, but found that the department's jurisdiction stopped at the beach, while its carcass-removing capabilities were confined to dead cats, dogs, and at the most, horses. They called on the U.S. Coast Guard, but found that that organization, while claiming jurisdiction over the beaches, lacked the tools needed for whale removing. Then they called the PRERA and got a response.

Jim Bourne, the PRERA's head, had read the famous story of how Roy Chapman Andrews had once disassembled a whale on a Long Island beach and had later reassembled it in the American Museum of Natural History. He had a notion of doing something similar, but things didn't work out that way.

Bourne came down with his gallant men, with hawsers and

launches, picks, saws, and spades, and began to push and pull, hack and whack, saw and shove, grunt and groan, while a vast and delighted crowd gathered to watch. People flocked from all over to see the spectacle; hawkers set up carts to sell oranges and other delicacies; but the beast remained immobile, invincible, imperturbable. The wire services picked up the story and broadcast to England and the United States the account of Jim Bourne's gallant encounter with the whale; letters and cables poured in with advice; ancient New Bedford whalers offered to take themselves out of mothballs to go to San Juan to remove the behemoth of the deep. But Bourne was himself descended from a long line of whalers. He and his men sweated and hacked; but the whale remained where he was—intact. The stench grew so great that hawkers cut orange peelings into the form of face masks, which they sold to the onlookers for the purpose of protecting noses, but the whale remained placid and unmoved.

Finally somebody decided on dynamite, but that had to be used carefully because near-by residents might object to having a mess of evil-smelling blubber blown all over their houses. Bourne's dynamite expert stripped to underpants and descended into the carcass's interior to plant the charge just right; a long string of wires was laid out to the detonator, a safe distance away; the crowd was pushed back to be safe from flying blubber; everybody held his breath; dramatically Jim Bourne pushed down the detonator's handle; *but nothing happened*. There was muffled rumbling; the whale shivered a bit, and then settled down with a sad *whoosh* to just where it had been before—apparently undamaged.

That of course delighted the audience, which had meanwhile grown to vast proportions. "*Ah,*" said a thousand men and women almost with one happy voice, "*just like our governor!*"

But by now the honor of the federal government was at stake, and Bourne, its representative on the scene, was no

longer in the mood for nonsense. He had his men stuff the
whale with dynamite, stepped to his detonator, and let her
fly. This time he got results. The whale rose up and had itself
spattered all over the neighborhood on roofs, windows, lawns,
and onlookers. That, too, was in a sense prophetic of later
events, when the honor of the U.S. was again apparently at
stake and when those who felt themselves entrusted with it
resorted to political dynamite.

Some time after the Gore affair, Mrs. Roosevelt and Rexford Tugwell, then Washington's Undersecretary of Agriculture, visited Puerto Rico. Muñoz had meanwhile organized
a small discussion group which met on occasional Sundays in
the home of Dr. Carlos Chardón, chancellor of the university,
to discuss the island's sad plight and its possible remedies. He
invited the two distinguished visitors to meet with this group;
they were so impressed that Chardón and two others, Rafael
Fernández García, a professor at the university, and Menen-
dez Ramos, the island's Commissioner of Agriculture, were
eventually invited to Washington as a commission to draft a
comprehensive plan for Puerto Rico's economic reconstruction. Muñoz was asked to go along as an unofficial member.

Unprecedented in the island's history, this step stirred high
hopes and higher enthusiasm. Not only was the commission a
sign that Washington really cared about the plight of the
Puerto Ricans, but it was also the first time in history that
Puerto Rican technicians had been officially asked to advise
the ruling country on the island's problems and their possible
solutions. Previously, most of the wisdom for managing
Puerto Rican affairs had come from Washington, from the
office of the War Department and, directly or indirectly, from
the mouths of Congressmen.

The report of the Chardón Commission, hastily drafted and
in places almost naïve by modern standards, recommended a
number of steps and programs through which Puerto Rico's

economy was to be reshaped to function more effectively than it had previously for the benefit of the Puerto Rican people. It called for the enforcement of the Five-Hundred-Acre Law, for the redistribution of the land, for rural resettlement, for the governmental purchase and operation of at least one sugar mill to be operated as a yardstick for regulating future relations between grinders and growers, for certain kinds of relief (including hurricane insurance) in the coffee areas, for a program of co-operatives, for the extension of rural electrification, for the beginnings of Puerto Rican industrialization through the construction of a local cement plant, and for the construction of various university laboratories to aid in the training of Puerto Rican technicians.

The plan included a number of matters which had long been considered essential for Puerto Rico's salvation, but which, in the thinking of Muñoz and others, were regarded as impossible as long as Puerto Rico was a colony of the United States. Nevertheless, and in part because of Muñoz' energetic lobbying, it was accepted by Washington and became the master plan for the operation of a new federal agency, the Puerto Rico Reconstruction Administration.

The agency was provided with a "revolving" operating fund of $40,000,000, so set up that there would be no need to ask for more money every fiscal year. Puerto Rico was transferred from the War Department to the Department of the Interior because the latter could be trusted to do a better job of social and economic reform than could the Army. Dr. Ernest Gruening was appointed Director of Territories and Administrator of the PRRA. His record as a crusading liberal, an ardent anti-imperialist, and a friend of Latin America, was well known in Puerto Rico, where his appointment was hailed with jubilation. Dr. Carlos Chardón took leave of absence from his position as chancellor of the university and accepted that of Regional Administrator, to take charge of PRRA work in Puerto Rico under the general direction of Gruening. Those two, and Muñoz—who refused to take a job in the PRRA—were regarded at home as a triumvirate of saviors, as the true heroes of the Puerto Rican people.

Inevitably, the Chardón Plan and the creation of the PRRA had powerful political repercussions in Puerto Rico. The coalition of Socialists and Republicans then in power in San Juan played the sugar game and opposed the entire matter violently. It didn't help itself, however, when the Puerto Rican legislature, in 1935, passed a resolution which roundly attacked the Chardón Plan and presented its own hastily drafted "respectable" alternative to the President and Congress. Such antics of opposition lost the coalition much popular support, which at best had always been tenuous.

More, with the creation of the PRRA, which came to be a kind of government within the government, distasteful to the ruling coalition and probably also to the appointed governor, the Liberal party had stolen a march on its political opponents in the matter of patronage. Muñoz had labored hard to keep politics out of the PRRA operations, but even he could not stem the tide in job-starved Puerto Rico with its job-slanted politics. More and more, the PRRA came to be infested with Liberals; they were all over the place, their appointment to jobs condoned in part by the fact that the coalition had come out openly against the Chardón Plan and could so not be trusted to implement it.

The defeat of 1932, the setback to the Liberals when Gore had refused them any part of the patronage, had now been turned into a resounding victory. Muñoz came despite himself to be regarded as a political wizard who produced jobs and political plums where none had existed before. He and the Liberal party seemed invincible and unmistakably had the next election, of 1936, in their pockets. They reckoned, however, as did everybody else in Puerto Rico, without the terrible chain reaction that was to be set off by the shots that killed Col. Riggs in February of that year.

As this is being written, in 1954, the PRRA is finally being liquidated as a federal agency. It did much, but it failed to fulfill its great promise, largely because it was at best another phase of imperialism. Nevertheless, it was tremendously important. Enlightened imperialism is better than unenlightened, and very surely, though by anguished and tortuous routes, the PRRA paved the way for Muñoz' later triumphs and for modern Puerto Rico's emergence from despair.

CHAPTER VIII

Reconstruction

I BECAME IDENTIFIED with the New Deal in 1934. Previously I had spent one and a half years on a scientific mission in all parts of the Amazon basin and the Andes of northern South America—usually alone. On my field radio—needed for checking my chronometers—I had heard all the speeches of the 1932 presidential campaign, as well as a constant, unvarying stream of dramatic reports on riots and strikes, more riots, more strikes, farmers' concerted actions to forestall mortgage foreclosures, the growth of shacktowns everywhere, hunger marches, veterans' marches, the great Battle of Anacostia Flats, and the organized sale of unemployed apples on the streets of New York as a means of restoring public confidence in the nation's imminent prosperity. From my shifting vantage points in the Amazon jungles and the Andes of northern South America, the United States had seemed chaotic and on the verge of collapse. Alone for the better part of eighteen months, I had enjoyed the great boon of having opportunity and time to think. I became determined to get into things on my return, to participate in the affairs of my country.

Morris Llewellyn Cooke hired me for his Mississippi Valley Committee, and I learned something about the aims and techniques of sound governmental planning—as a means toward guiding the government in the sane and socially effective expenditure of its public funds.

Occasionally I ran into Muñoz, now a senator in the Puerto Rican legislature. He came to Washington on some business mysterious to me, held court afternoons in what is still known as the "senator's corner" in the Tap Room of the Hotel Washington, returned to Puerto Rico, but always came back to the capital. Finally he arrived with three others, bent on drafting a master plan for Puerto Rico's salvation. These were the members of the Chardón Commission. I came to know them well and became fascinated by the things they told and taught me about Puerto Rico's problems. It didn't take long before I began to pull wires for a chance to go to Puerto Rico in order to work with these men.

Here was a New Dealer's dream—a small society beset by powerful evils beyond its control—a relatively simple society, not too complex to be understood. I had seen much of colonialism in various parts of the world and had thought that I understood it. Here, in Puerto Rico, was a microcosm for all the world's colonial evils. I must by all means get into the great battle against colonial exploitation which the ruling country itself was now undertaking.

President Roosevelt created the Puerto Rico Reconstruction Administration for the remedy of colonial evils; the Chardón Commission returned to Puerto Rico to create an organization for the implementation of its report; the National Resources Committee sent me to the island as a consultant to aid the administration in its vital program for planning the work's consistent, intelligent continuity.

So began, for me, the most rewarding and most disturbing adventure of a life which has experienced far more than its proper share of such adventures.

With its revolving fund of $40,000,000 the PRRA set out to reshape a society. Today's Puerto Rican economists and statisticians often smile at the entire business, and at the PRRA as having been a drop in the bucket, naïvely dreamed up and naïvely administered. As often happens, they are wrong. However small in relation to the great need, however poor by modern standards, the PRRA accomplished a great deal. However small and bungling, it was tremendously important as the embodiment of a great idea, the substitution of action for mere talk, and a start toward realistic reform.

The PRRA had its serious faults, the worst of which stemmed from the fact that, even though its basic plan had been drafted by Puerto Ricans, it was still a packaged bit of salvation, benevolently handed down, and rigidly controlled, by the ruling country. Nevertheless, it was so great and sudden an advance over Washington's earlier actions opposite the island that its psychological effects were enormously beneficial.

There could be no doubt that the PRRA was—to the men and women who worked in it, to the people of Puerto Rico, to the sugar barons and the coalition politicians who opposed it viciously and violently—the expression of a great idea. Desperately as James Bourne had labored to make the PRERA and the FERA truly effective toward reshaping Puerto Rico's economy to fit Puerto Rican needs, he had at all times been hampered by directives from Washington. The relief organizations which had preceded the PRRA had been step-ups in federal subsidies, and stopgaps to hold the island society together through the period of its greatest travail. The new organization was aimed directly at reforming Puerto Rico's basic ills, in order to reduce the pressing need for federal subsidies. The reactions to it were therefore varied. Those who were for the idea to the point of dedication supported the PRRA with an almost religious fervor as one of the greatest rays of light in Puerto Rico's anguished history. Those who were against it because they gained from the status quo opposed it with equal fervor, buttressed with pious doctrinaire platitudes. Those many literates who cared nothing about ideas and lived only for the present and their own advantages in the present were prone to support or oppose it according to whether or not they got something out of it—while naturally also giving lip service to the idea pro or con.

The majority, however, perhaps 80 per cent, had no public voice—as through the papers and the radio—and half of them were illiterate. These constituted the politically dormant body of the underprivileged, the *jíbaros*, the small peasants, the starving laborers, the parents of the child-gangs which infested the cities. It was to that large submerged group, directly or indirectly, that Muñoz Marín addressed himself incessantly. "You must have a guiding idea in life," he told them, "and this is it. You must support the PRRA, work with it, even if it means giving up momentary personal advantages. The PRRA labors for your advantages, your freedom; it labors for your liberation—and that of your children—from abject poverty."

While refusing any official position in the organization, Muñoz incessantly, at all times and in all parts of the island, stirred his people to back the PRRA wholeheartedly. "You must support the PRRA," he said, "because you must support the things that it stands for and has set out to accomplish. It is committed to the enforcement of the Five-Hundred-Acre Law, which is basic to our very existence. The PRRA will break up the great sugar estates and make their lands again available to the people of Puerto Rico; it will purchase a sugar mill and use it as a yardstick to regulate relations between the sugar corporations and the planters; it will foster and strengthen co-operatives; it will fight the power trusts, aid our program for low-cost electricity, and help to bring the blessings of electric power to all the island's homes, rural and urban; the PRRA is committed to rural resettlement, industrialization, and minimum wages. Those are the things we have been struggling and asking for. The extent to which you now support the PRRA is also the extent to which you support a brighter future for yourselves and your children."

Whether among the *jíbaros*, or the sugar laborers, or the politicians, or the businessmen, or the professionals, or the sugar barons, there could be no doubt that in those days Muñoz *was* the PRRA, to be supported, or opposed as such, according to individual orientations. With the active support of Muñoz, the PRRA was in large part a Puerto Rican effort; without that support it would have been—as it was to become later—merely another federal money-spending agency to be accepted because it brought financial benefits and because the Puerto Ricans could not help themselves, in any event. Always, in all the Puerto Rican thinking of those days, there was that skepticism about anything that came from the ruling country; what one administration or official did, the next could undo—therefore prudence was advisable in backing any federal effort too wholeheartedly.

So widely and firmly was the PRRA regarded as Muñoz' baby, that there were persistent rumors (whether or not they were true is less important than the fact that a situation existed in which they could thrive) that sugar would pay almost any sum for his assassination—which was equally desired by the Nationalists, whose style he was cramping by saying good things about the United States. Many of his friends were armed and considered themselves his unofficial bodyguard. Even he had a revolver in his pocket when he sat long hours nightly in various cafés and cocktail lounges, discussing the PRRA's great idea and Puerto Rico's future with his friends and with anybody who happened to drift in.

While solidly backing the PRRA, however, Muñoz never once—in those days of 1935 and 1936—wavered in his stand for Puerto Rico's eventual independence separate from the United States. Determined to achieve that independence in a friendly fashion and as a matter of mutual convenience to both parties, he seemed to regard the PRRA as a generous gesture through which the United States had set out to undo some of colonialism's harmful effects, and through which Puerto Rico would—by that much—become better prepared for independence.

The Reconstruction Administration's start was turbulent, due to the fact that it was also a brand-new organization, staffed by new people, sent to Puerto Rico to replace the existing FERA. What was to become of all the thousands of people who had been kept alive through the latter's energetic relief activities? What was to become of the many Puerto Ricans who had labored hard and loyally for the FERA and as a result knew so much about Puerto Rico's needs? The tensions were felt at all levels, and even in Washington. Dorothy Bourne wrote me in 1954: "I think that the FERA's self-analysis toward the end of its existence might well have made possible a transition to the PRRA reconstruction emphasis without the break which made the PRRA a superimposed plan in many respects—in spite of having Puerto Ricans on its board. This, as you may remember, was the subject of Jim's final public statement, which resulted in his coup de grâce with Roosevelt, Hopkins, and Gruening."

The new federal policy amounted to an energetic war on the sugar monopoly. While the PRRA got under way, the Department of the Interior therefore also took steps toward the enforcement of the Five-Hundred-Acre Law, for which Muñoz had labored so long. The Republican party, which dominated the ruling coalition, actually opposed such enforcement with vehemence. It failed all the way down the line.

The first step in the federal effort was necessarily the substitution, for the existing conservative incumbent, of a new attorney general who could be trusted to take an interest in his task of making a working reality out of the Five-Hundred-Acre Law. That was Benigno Fernández García, a member of the Liberal party, brother of one of the drafters of the Chardón Plan, and a close personal friend of Muñoz'. Of course, the coalition howled. Hadn't the Republicans and Socialists won the election? Were they not entitled to the jobs? Where was justice? Besides, it now appeared that Fernández García was a dangerous radical who had once been active in fomenting a strike in the tobacco regions, in which tobacco fields and sheds had been burned.

Nevertheless, Fernández was appointed to the job and got to work immediately. His job of enforcing the Five-Hundred-Acre Law, and so of creating a basis for breaking up the big estates, was one of the most important to be done in those days. The legal battles which he started were the most important suits in Puerto Rico's history. The island's eventual victory broke the political and economic hold that the sugar interests had on Puerto Rico and paved the way for the program of reform and production which Muñoz was to start in 1941.

On January 28, 1936, Fernández García filed a complaint in the Puerto Rican Supreme Court against the Puerto Rican firm Rubert Hermanos, Inc., charging that this corporation held approximately 12,000 acres of land in violation of its charter and the Organic Act, and asking the court to impose a fine and order the corporation's dissolution. All the sugar interests rallied to the defense of Rubert Hermanos, all the liberal elements in Puerto Rico rallied behind their attorney general. The sugar lawyers claimed that the Five-Hundred-Acre Law, having no teeth for enforcement, was not meant to be enforced; having been ignored for decades, was a dead letter. Nevertheless, on July 30, 1938, more than two years after the filing of the first complaint, the Puerto Rican Supreme Court ruled in favor of the insular government.

The aroused sugar industry now carried the suit to the U.S. District Court of Appeals in Boston, which, on September 27, 1939, set aside the Puerto Rican decision. Puerto Rico then appealed to the U.S. Supreme Court. On March 25, 1940, the latter upheld Puerto Rico and irrevocably gave the insular government the right to enforce the Five-Hundred-Acre Law. That same year, Muñoz won the election with his newly formed Popular Democratic party. The great revolution was under way.

While that legal battle was being prepared and fought, the Reconstruction Administration began its important work. The administration had programs of aid to Puerto Rican farmers—in coffee, tobacco, cattle, coconuts, sugar, and all other branches of the stricken agriculture—never sufficient to meet existing needs, but still sufficient for gaining experience, making mistakes, and building up a body of knowledge. Through its program of low-cost housing, it gave marked impetus to the slum-clearance effort which is today, under the Puerto Rican government, one of the wonders of the world. Like the PRERA and the FERA before it, the PRRA gave aid to various branches of the virtually bankrupt insular government—especially in such matters as public health and education.

The PRRA bought tracts of land in the tobacco and coffee regions, divided them into plots of two or three acres, built a small concrete house on each plot—sanitary, hurricane-proof —in design the forerunners of the three-hundred-dollar rural house for which Puerto Rico is today famous—and sold them to rural homesteaders against long-term repayments. A rule had to be made according to which only one house—the one provided by the government—could be allowed on each plot; otherwise the PRRA would have started another series of rural slums, as sons and daughters grew up and brought mates to live in unsightly shacks on the family plots.

The homesteaders were organized into co-operatives, and on each large project the PRRA established a school, a hospital, a community center, and an agricultural experiment station. These community projects worked quite well, and are still in existence. After some years, however, it was found that it was difficult to manage them from Washington, under federal red tape. Contracts were therefore made, with the Mennonites in the one case and the Quakers in the others, under which those groups would administer the projects for the government. Later, during World War II and in line with the policy of liquidating the Reconstruction Administration as a federal agency, the projects and their buildings were sold to those organizations against long-term repayments.

In 1952 I took my Delaware class of graduate students to La Plata, but Mrs. Park and a few others said that they refused to go through the hospital or any of the private homes because that involved an unjustified invasion of people's privacy. On repeated urging—in part because I had been one of the originators of the project—a few of us visited one of the homes after all. The owner, a widow of the original settler who had moved to La Plata out of the dismal slums of San Juan, was offended because several members of the class had stayed behind out of delicacy. The inordinate pride with which she showed us her little concrete house, immaculately clean, nicely furnished, was matched by the poise and regal grace with which, as a hostess, she served us the inevitable cup of coffee. More than anything else, that visit brought home to me the enormous psychological and cultural importance of the Puerto Rican government's present energetic program of rural homesteading.

One of the provisions of the Chardón Plan was to buy a sugar mill and its land and to use it in part as a yardstick for determining and demonstrating fair relations between the mills and the independent growers of cane, the *colonos*, who had long complained that they were being cheated by the large corporations. It was also to be used for social experimentation and for education in the various means by which the farmers and people of Puerto Rico might eventually come to play a major role in the management of their most important industry.

The PRRA bought a sugar mill from a French corporation, the Lafayette *Central*, with some 10,000 acres of land. In the beginning, the mill was operated by the federal government; that did not work very well. Today it is operated by a co-operative of cane growers which has bought it from the PRRA. The ideas and disciplines of co-operation are now, at last, taking a strong hold in Puerto Rico—though not yet in the management of land.

The estate of Lafayette *Central* was divided into individual farms, which were sold, against long-term repayments, to a number of Puerto Ricans. These, in turn, were organized into a number of land co-operatives. A few years later, in 1940, the situation was studied by Estéban Bird, and the land co-operatives had to be dissolved. The principal reason for failure was that the Puerto Rican farmers were not yet ready or able to adjust to the rigid disciplines involved in farming their lands collectively—as is being done with outstanding success in various parts of Mexico today. So, again, a valuable lesson was learned by Muñoz. Had it not been for the failure of the Lafayette agrarian scheme, he might well, when he took charge in 1941 of enforcing the Five-Hundred-Acre Law, have tried to work the island's most valuable and productive lands through co-operatives. With that lesson, however, and in view of the fact that Puerto Rico could not afford failures in the most productive branch of its economy, Muñoz came to invent new means of handling the vexing problem of tenure, and to incorporate them into his present highly original land law.

The PRRA organized a Self-Help Corporation. Its function was to organize co-operatives, lend them money for capital, and administer them until the loans had been repaid—the idea being that by then the members might have learned the basic disciplines required for success. It was financed with federal funds, but turned over to the Puerto Rican government; one of the most difficult tasks was to set it up in such a way that the politicians couldn't touch it. Personnel questions in administration, membership, and management had to be handled according to qualifications other than political affiliations or influence. The idea of a government agency's being so organized that the politicians could not touch it with patronage and for the purpose of building up their political strength was itself so new in Puerto Rico that it was all but revolutionary. The politicians of all parties howled, but it did little good. The Self-Help Corporation still exists, still organizes and finances co-operatives.

It was obvious that the island's ultimate hope was tied up with industrialization, based in part on low-cost power. The PRRA built several hydroelectric plants and turned them over to the Puerto Rican government, to be incorporated in the nascent government power system which was before too many years to cover the island with an integrated network of power lines.

Because building materials are basically essential for any program of reconstruction, and because Puerto Rico was exporting inordinately large sums of money for cement from the continent, the PRRA designed and built a cement plant and sold it to the Puerto Rican government, to be paid for out of earnings. It was an immediate technical and financial success. Later it was enlarged. Still later, for good reasons to be discussed in a succeeding chapter, it was sold to a private Puerto Rican corporation. Today the island is not only self-sufficient in cement—despite the fact of its current vast building program—but is even exporting cement to the mainland and to countries like Venezuela.

The Planning Division, in which I served as Executive Secretary under Chairman Rafael Gonzales, continued a number of studies for other potential industries which had previously been begun by the PRERA and FERA. These dealt, among other things, with a bottle factory to serve the rum industry and a cardboard factory to use the bagasse, which is a by-product of sugar. These came to nothing under the PRRA. Some years later, however, when Muñoz had gained control of the government and had to do things quickly, the studies were taken off the shelves and dusted off to form the backbone of Puerto Rico's first real program of industrialization. The bottle factory, the cardboard and carton factory, the shoe factory, the clay products factory over which we had dreamed and worked in 1936 are giving employment, improving the economy, and smoking up the countryside today; financially and administratively they had their ups and downs, and the policies under which they are operated have changed materially; they were the beginnings, however, of the dramatic industrialization program for which Puerto Rico is today famous.

My own major interests were centered in the Planning Division, and today I derive satisfaction from the thought that that organization, to which I contributed my personal efforts, paved the way for the present Puerto Rican Planning Board, which is outstanding among such organizations in the Western world. But in 1935 the word "planning" aroused a messianic fervor in some, considerable skepticism in others, and downright antagonism in those who strove desperately to preserve the old order. In Washington, the National Resources Committee was publishing—among many other and more realistic things—a large number of varying reports which might well have been entitled "It's Nice to Plan—or, Twenty Nice Ways to Plan"; I was a bit of a crusader myself, determined to spread the gospel.

We built up a considerable staff, but most of the key men who did the actual work—some of them men who didn't think that planning was possible, but who did think that it was stimulating and exhilarating—came from the university. Some

took leaves of absence and worked with us full time; others
came when they could and worked by the hour. All of them,
as they delved into all the details of Puerto Rico's troubles, as
they developed possible remedies which could or could not be
applied under existing circumstances, became dramatically
aware—as they had never been before—of the tangled and
complex nature of Puerto Rico's problems. Being good men,
they were also challenged.

Together, while evaluating current and future PRRA operations, they made invaluable studies of the Puerto Rican
scene. Their scholarly, measured, carefully prepared reports
on the sugar industry, on land use and land tenure and their
social implications, on the effects of the tariff, on various
knotty economic problems, on problems of population and
demography, of taxation, came to constitute a solid contribution to the literature on a stricken society and its ills. Much
of it remained unpublished and was more or less forgotten
except by the men who had done the work. Some, like Bird's
sugar report, was revived after 1940 and published by the
Puerto Rican government as soon as it had achieved the
power for such publication. All of it was valuable and eventually effective.

With no inkling of the serious troubles we were headed for,
Estéban Bird and I organized a needlework co-operative,
devoted to manufacturing women's underwear for the continental market. The organization amounted to a promise
which we held out to the five thousand nervous women who
had been thrown out of work through the closing of the
FERA's needlework shops. However, setting out to break into
the industrial scene with a shop which was to be owned by
the workers, we couldn't employ five thousand women; we
couldn't employ five hundred; we began with a few dozen
and hoped for the best.

We had trouble in finding a forelady for the shop; one after
the other was tried and was found to accept workers and

members only if they had been endorsed by politicians of various parties. They were immediately discharged and could not understand why. After all, they had acted only in accordance with an old Puerto Rican custom. We obtained a few designs and for a time ran the shop ourselves in our spare time. We studied women's underwear at all odd moments; in San Juan and Washington I spent much time in front of show windows displaying such goods; people must have thought me odd. The C.I.O. organizer, Teresa Angleró, attacked us viciously because, while we were paying much more than was the established industry, with bonuses scheduled out of profits, we weren't paying $1.00 per day. We invited her into the shop, told her to organize our women, gave her an office, gave her access to the books, told her to study our problems of finance and management, and to stop making wage demands calculated to wreck the co-operative. After I left Puerto Rico, Bird carried on alone. Within a few months he had a going concern, with an established brand of underwear, the "Linda" brand, and with an office in New York for distribution, designing, purchasing, and cutting materials. Then the sweatshop industry, which had been laughing up its sleeve at the bungling efforts of these amateurs, closed in and obtained a court order for the co-operative's dissolution on a technicality of one kind or another.

While all that and much more was going on, sugar and its friends were, of course, not idle. Not only the Big Four in Puerto Rico, but the entire industry, through its organization, the Association of Sugar Producers, became thoroughly aroused over the entire federal effort and fought it tooth and nail. The number of letters which poured into San Juan and Washington when special occasions arose, the similarity which all those letters displayed in contents, logic, and tone, gave rise to the strong belief that sugar maintained a large and well-oiled letter-writing machine which would swing into action, with thousands willing to lend it their names and efforts, the minute the word went out from the association.

A number of newspapermen went to Puerto Rico to write up the entire effort as being downright un-American socialism. Whether or not they were directly or indirectly influenced by the sugar interests is, of course, a matter for conjecture. What is known is that sugar hired two academic economists of high reputation to prepare a learned, objective, scientific, and impartial report to prove that Puerto Rico would have to continue as it was going—fed by the American taxpayers while bossed and exploited by sugar. Occasionally a nice, friendly representative of the sugar industry would come to San Juan to sound us out and discuss matters in a nice, friendly manner. The best jobs I have ever been offered were offered to me by those men; later, after the PRRA had blown up from its internal tensions and I had tendered my resignation to Secretary Ickes, when I left federal employ and was in the market for a job, sugar had lost interest in my valuable services.

The sugar corporations also began to adopt an unofficial though powerful line of talk—in part undoubtedly a threat—to the effect that they were on the verge of pulling out of Puerto Rico entirely. Such talk, plus the campaign against the sugar monopoly, plus the depression, sent the value of sugar stocks tumbling. A number of Puerto Ricans, apparently not intimidated, then bought thousands of shares of the stock as investments which they have never since regretted. In such manner, even before the court fights had been won and the program of real reform begun, absentee ownership in sugar came to be reduced materially.

On looking back on those days, I consider it one of the marvels of human relations that the sugar interests are today among the staunchest supporters of Muñoz—who has accomplished many times more than had even been envisaged by the PRRA, but has also brought to Puerto Rico a new prosperity which sugar shares.

Attacks from sugar did the PRRA no great harm. They were expected, and Washington officials recognized their source and meaning. Internally, however, the PRRA had serious weaknesses which were eventually to contribute greatly to its destruction as the embodiment of a great Puerto Rican ideal and effort. Those weaknesses stemmed from the rigid control which was exercised by Washington over all its activities and policies, and which convinced its Puerto Rican officials and leaders that they were in the end merely hired men.

There was a prominent personnel element in the PRRA which could not possibly exist in a similar Puerto Rican organization today, and which came eventually to cause all kinds of trouble. That was composed of non-Puerto Rican lawyers, shipped down by Washington as watchdogs for Washington's aims and interests. They dominated the entire organization—eager lawyers, young and hard-working, socially conscious, every one of them a graduate of Felix Frankfurter's Harvard Law School. (Indeed, at one stormy hearing held after the PRRA's tensions had come to a head, I saw and heard them get together to discredit all Puerto Rican lawyers by filling the record with testimony purporting to prove that nobody could be a good lawyer, and especially not a lawyer with a social conscience, unless he had been trained at the Harvard Law School.) They were men who knew some law and considered themselves advanced liberals and crusaders in their own right. However, they were completely dogmatic in their liberalism and sought to substitute general principles for real knowledge of the people and society concerned. By and large, they were a clannish lot who knew nothing about Puerto Rico, knew no Spanish, and associated largely with other Americans in San Juan rather than with the Puerto Ricans.

They were Washington's—and so also Ernest Gruening's—direct representatives on the scene. In a great new organization dedicated to the pious principle of giving all the positions of responsibility to Puerto Ricans, these young lawyers held all the ultimate power.

The fact that the power was held by Washington officials who could and did at any time override the Puerto Rican officials was a great structural weakness which was vaguely felt at first but contributed much to the great debacle of 1936. The organization's moral collapse in that year, through circumstances which grew directly out of Col. Riggs's assassination, did much to force Muñoz, in 1941 and after he had won control of his government, to take matters firmly in his own hands and create a new government composed of men who had learned from bitter experience that the job of saving Puerto Rico could be done *only* by Puerto Ricans who had the power as well as the responsibility. Indirectly, the experience with the lawyers contributed to the growth of the present conviction, widespread in the Puerto Rican government, that "the trouble with us in those days was that we were too prone to blame others for our troubles and to look to others for our salvation. Nothing was really accomplished until we took hold ourselves." By the same token, the lawyers may well have contributed to the resurgence, in 1936, of the demand for independence—as presumably the *only* status under which the Puerto Ricans could do things for themselves without interference from a lot of nice, idealistic, busybodying and meddlesome continental Americans.

CHAPTER IX

Disintegration

I T IS IMPOSSIBLE for anybody to judge accurately how many
Puerto Ricans were in those days in favor of the island's
political independence, either as a reasoned political doctrine
or as a vague but powerful emotional expression of discontent
with the lot of colonial subject and second-class citizen. There
are, in any event, so many kinds of independence, and so
many varying conditions under which one kind or another
may or may not seem desirable, and so many degrees of
timidity and outspokenness among people, and so many vacil-
lations among people as circumstances may change, making
independence seem more or less desirable, or making it more
or less safe to speak one's mind, that the most carefully regulated public-opinions poll would yield results that are far
from the actual mark.

Whatever their feeling, however, there can be no doubt
that most of Puerto Rico's people were one with Muñoz in his
disavowal of violence for the achievement of independence.
The island's entire history bears out the common observation
that the Puerto Ricans are essentially a gentle people, molded
by suffering, courteous, with a great dignity and an innate
intelligence deeply rooted in realities.

To such a people, devoutly peaceful, the top leaders of the Nationalists were largely strangers, fanatics whose murderous activities were culturally alien. Almost unanimously, the people of Puerto Rico condemned the assassination of Col. Riggs in February, 1936—not because it was ostensibly perpetrated in the name of independence, but because it was murder. A society which had never experienced or advocated the agonies of armed revolution, which had never participated in a war in the sense of sending its sons en masse to the front, which knew nothing of gang killings except through the movies and the press, which listed "murders of passion" as the worst in its category of crimes, could not understand—let alone condone—the planned, cold-blooded killing of the most democratic and beloved chief of police it had ever had.

That society was, however, due for a terrible shock when Washington began to act as though, on the one hand, all Puerto Rico was to blame for Riggs's assassination and, on the other, Albizu personified all desire for independence, and all independentists were therefore actual or potential assassins.

After Riggs's assassination a spate of articles appeared in the Latin American press—especially in Cuba, which is in the sugar business and perhaps for that reason all the more interested in Puerto Rico's potential independence—to the general effect that the noble but suffering people of Puerto Rico had at last grown tired of their Yanqui oppressors and had adopted the desperate methods of armed resistance. In Congress, too, the Puerto Ricans came to be described in various speeches as "they," though not as a noble and patriotic lot. The general tenor was that the United States had treated the Puerto Ricans with every consideration, had given them more freedom than was enjoyed by any other colonial people on earth, had given them the PRERA and the PRRA—and those ungrateful wretches had in turn killed Col. Riggs. Not only in Congressional speeches, but also in a number of U.S. editorials, the Puerto Ricans came again to be described as a

volatile, undisciplined, ungrateful lot, unfit for self-government and undeserving of American kindness and generosity.

The first cloud in the sky, which was in 1936 and 1937 to
turn black with thunderheads, appeared in the form of a
violent quarrel between Dr. Gruening and Muñoz Marín.
Muñoz was in Washington at the time of Riggs's assassination,
and Gruening asked him for a statement condemning it. He
said that the assassination could have terrible consequences
for Puerto Rico, and that it was necessary to make clear that
the Puerto Rican people, as such, were in no way behind it.
Muñoz, as the outstanding spokesman of the island's people
and the one political figure closest to Washington, was definitely the man to make such a statement.

What followed was historically important and completely
understandable at the time. It cannot be understood today
unless the tensions and the colonial atmosphere of 1936 are
also understood. There could and can be no doubt that Muñoz
wholeheartedly condemned the action of the Nationalists as
murder and tragic lunacy. He was the same man then that he
was in 1950, when he jailed the Nationalists after the Tragic
Week, and in 1954, when he flew to Washington to express to
the President, the Congress, and the American people, his
deep sorrow and that of the majority of Puerto Ricans over the
fanatical acts of four Nationalists in the House of Representatives. But the entire political and emotional climate of 1950
and 1954 differed radically from that of 1936. In that year
Muñoz felt himself, whether rightly or wrongly, in a difficult
position, if only because he, as a colonial subject who advocated independence, was virtually ordered by a ranking
representative of the ruling government to make a statement
with powerful political connotations—both in Washington
and on the island.

I don't for a moment believe, as some claimed, that Muñoz
refused because he was afraid that a disavowal of the killing

might be interpreted, in San Juan and Washington, as a disavowal of Puerto Rico's eventual independence. The reasons he gave seem clear and valid enough. "I agree," he said in effect, "that this is a terrible thing which may have serious consequences for all of us. But so is the lynching of the two disarmed assassins behind the closed door of the police station. If you people in the federal government condone that lynching and back up the police, you will do another terrible thing in that you will throw out of the window the processes of law, you will thereby make the police an armed branch of the federal government, and you will give a direct slap to Puerto Rico's judicial processes and attitudes. I cannot publicly condemn the one and not the other. On the other hand, if you back up the police, and I attack the lynching as well as the assassination, I will in effect be in a position of attacking the federal government, which can also, at a time like this, have serious consequences for Puerto Rico. The action of the police should therefore be condemned by a spokesman of Washington. I will," he said to Gruening, "gladly make a strong statement about Riggs's assassination, if you will make a parallel statement about the lynching of the assassins."

Gruening refused flatly, and the police came, in fact, to be supported by Washington officials. From that moment, however, Gruening turned on his old associate. In Washington, Muñoz found himself less welcome than he had been before; many people in Puerto Rico—not the *jíbaros*, not the peasants, not the starving laborers who had no real voice in any event, but the politicians and the politically minded in San Juan and other cities—began to wonder if it was not safer to go along with the powerful Gruening than to continue giving allegiance to Muñoz.

The shots which killed Col. Riggs, planned by a small group of terrorists precisely because relations with Washington had improved immeasurably, precisely because hundreds of thousands of Puerto Ricans were grateful to Washington for the PRRA and so undermined the Nationalists' cause, precisely because the Nationalists were a minute and shrinking group in the island's life, were to open a rift, deep and wide, between San Juan and Washington, and to have far-reaching disintegrating effects.

Regardless of variations and shadings in local feelings, it was almost inevitable that in Washington the independence issue should be confused and identified with that of Albizu's violence. That precipitated more confusion in Puerto Rico.

It had been tacitly understood since the first days of American rule, and lately reaffirmed by both Roosevelt and Ickes, that the Puerto Ricans were entitled to independence if they wanted it. By the same token it was understood on the island that the matter of asking for independence was one that was properly up to the Puerto Ricans—who could tell much better than could anybody in Washington when and if the time seemed right.

Now, on April 23, 1936, news came like a thunderclap from Washington that Senator Millard Tydings of Maryland had introduced a bill in Congress providing for the island's independence. What made things worse was that it was regarded as an administration bill, which meant that Dr. Gruening, as Director of Territories, must have been aware of it even if he had not—as came to be widely suspected—written it himself. To be sure, the bill was nicely worded as a liberal document in that it provided for a plebiscite through which the people of Puerto Rico should be permitted to vote on whether or not they wanted independence. It added a joker, however, by defining the kind of independence on which they would be allowed to vote, in such a manner as to *spell ruin and certain starvation for the island when achieved*. The bill gave the island almost no time in which to readjust its economy from the colonial to the independent. It threatened, within a few short years, to turn Puerto Rico out from behind the Amer-

ican tariff structure, without providing sufficient time or
means for creating an economy that could function outside of
that structure. Muñoz summarized the resulting indignation
when he said that the bill was a return to the old Mexican
ley de fuga, or law of flight, under which the Mexican police
used to arrest people, then tell them magnanimously to run
away, and then shoot them in the back for trying to escape.

The question of who had drafted the bill, and of how it had
come to be drafted, agitated Puerto Rico for years and was
not cleared up until the publication of Ickes' diaries in 1953.
There Secretary Ickes had written as follows on March 21,
1936: "Another matter that we considered which was of
special interest was whether a bill should be introduced in
Congress providing for a plebiscite in Puerto Rico on the question of independence. . . . I expressed myself as being strongly
in favor of such a bill. I pointed out that if Puerto Rico wanted
its independence, it ought to be granted it, but if it should
vote against independence, then such agitation as had been
going on in Puerto Rico recently would be put an end to for
probably twenty years.

"There is a bad situation in Puerto Rico. The chief of police
was assassinated recently and two or three local officials were
also killed. There is reason to believe that there is a general
plot to assassinate other island officials, including the Governor. . . . I strongly urged its [the bill's] immediate introduction, although it might not pass at this session of the Congress,
because of the quieting effect that I anticipated it might have
on Puerto Rican public opinion. I told the President that we
had drafted such a bill in my Department and he authorized
me to send it to Senator Tydings, with the suggestion that he
introduce it, although not as an administration bill."

What Ickes had not had time to figure out was that there are
many kinds of independence. There is a vast difference between the kind which permits the former colony, in friendly
relationship and with time and means, to create new internal

conditions under which it can function apart from the mother country, and a bill which defines independence in terms of complete ruin. The words "although not as an administration bill" come as a surprise at the present time. In Puerto Rico it had been understood from the first that it *was* an administration bill. The question of who had written it, while not entirely cleared up, is certainly illuminated. If such an important piece of legislation was drafted in Ickes' Department, and if the Director of Territories—while not actually pounding the typewriter—did not have full personal responsibility for it, then Ickes was not the administrator he was known to be.

Again, Ickes' reasoning showed the fallacy of regarding all Puerto Ricans as "they," of blaming the entire island for the acts of a few fanatics. His assumption that "such agitation as has been going on in Puerto Rico recently would be put to an end for probably twenty years" was to lead him to a series of major surprises.

At best, the bill was regarded as an insult to Puerto Rican *dignidad*, intelligence, and integrity. At worst, it clouded and confused the issue of status by willfully defining independence in the worst possible terms. The enlightened and liberal Washington administration, which more than any other had repeatedly assured the Puerto Ricans of their right to independence if they wanted it, seemed now to be showing its hand by ill-naturedly telling the island that it could damn well starve, too, if it did happen to want it.

The result was electrifying. In Puerto Rico one began to hear even ardent Republicans, advocates of statehood, 150 per cent Americans, say: "If that is the best we can expect from Washington, we have no choice but to be for independence at any cost!" The newspaper *La Correspondencia* accurately expressed public sentiment when it editorialized in the following terms: ". . . if the American government is in an angry mood and imposed it as an act of vengeance, let independence come, even if that costs us our lives." *El País* said: "The displacing of the American flag ought not to be a disorderly act, but should be done respectfully and following a friendly understanding."

Why, the question was widely asked, had no Puerto Rican been consulted on the terms of a bill which so vitally affected the island's destiny?

Dr. José Padín, as acting governor in Winship's absence, made a hurried trip to Washington to protest to Roosevelt, not against the idea of a plebiscite on independence, but against a "punitive" bill, suddenly and without warning imposed from without on a stricken people already confused and demoralized through the irresponsible acts of a few fanatics. He pleaded that the bill actually tended to strengthen the Nationalists' position, not to weaken it. He got nowhere. Roosevelt acted as though he was sick and tired of the entire Puerto Rican issue and wanted to brush it away with the one impatient gesture that he had asked Tydings to make for him.

In the PRRA we called a hurried meeting with Chardón and the key men of the Planning Division. I took the stand that Gruening's letter, creating the Planning Division, had specifically listed among our duties that of advising in matters of federal policy opposite Puerto Rico, that we could not take it for granted that Gruening, the Director of Territories and the PRRA's administrator, a famous liberal of long standing, had been behind—or even aware of—the disreputable Tydings bill, and that it was now our clear duty to prepare for him a detailed, objective report on what the Tydings kind of independence would do to Puerto Rico. There were some objections, but I insisted—may heaven forgive me—that if we didn't do what we could to enlighten Washington on the bill's dangers, we would in the end have only ourselves to blame for whatever might happen; on the other hand, if we did prepare the report I requested we would at least have done our parts and our duties as men at a time of crisis.

We worked four days and nights, analyzing the island's ills in terms of the Tydings bill, arguing policy, constantly holding our feelings in check in order to make it truly an objective report. We wore out one after the other of the secretarial staff and brewed gallons of coffee to keep going. I no longer have a copy of the report. I don't know if one is still in existence; but I remember its general contents. We dealt with the economic side, pointing out what would happen if the sugar industry—as it inevitably would under the bill's terms—were to collapse with nothing else ready or in sight to take its place. We dealt with the question of overpopulation in the face of the imminent complete collapse of the main feature of Puerto Rico's economy. We reviewed the history of the independence movement in the light of a long line of promises and statements about independence which had been made by Presidents and other federal officials since the first day of American occupation. From every conceivable vantage point, we dealt with Puerto Rican realities; from every conceivable vantage point it was clear that the terms of independence provided for in the Tydings bill would double and treble the island's prevailing starvation and could result in nothing short of chaos.

We sent the report to Gruening in Washington, but the results were not at all what we had expected. Instead of being patted on the back as one of a group of nice fellows who had worked loyally to furnish their chief with important facts, I received a cable resoundingly slapping me on the wrist for having dared to meddle in the matter and ordering me in no uncertain terms to collect and burn all copies of the report which might still be in San Juan.

To the men who had prepared the report, the cable was a direct slap in the face. "We seem to be nothing but puppets," they said. "Why were we placed in apparently important research, advisory, and policy-shaping positions, if our first really serious and important job is to be rejected rudely and ordered destroyed?"

In Washington, the Resident Commissioner, Santiago Iglesias, an ardent exponent of statehood, attacked the bill bitterly on the floor of the House of Representatives. The Tydings bill failed to pass. Several subsequent bills providing for statehood, and one aimed at making Puerto Rico an incorporated territory of the United States, failed equally to pass. No basic legislative advances were made in Washington regarding political status until after the revolutionary election in 1940, in which Muñoz went to the polls on the unheard-of platform that political status was in no way an issue, that the issue was internal economic betterment to be accomplished by the action of the Puerto Ricans themselves. Nothing definite was accomplished politically until the majority in Puerto Rico had realized that the need for bread is life's ultimate reality, transcending in importance the meaning of various political abstractions.

About this time Dr. Gruening became concerned with political activities within the PRRA, which were forbidden to federal employees under the Hatch Act. He instigated a series of inquiries into such alleged activities, some of which he headed himself—somewhat on the order of modern loyalty investigations. As a result, some of the outstanding Puerto Ricans in the organizations—all of them, it may be added, supporters of Muñoz Marín—were separated from the federal pay roll; one of them, Rafael Fernández García, one of the three drafters of the original Chardón plan, was discharged *with prejudice.*

A stench of fear arose within the PRRA and smothered all enthusiasm and creative effort. Many employees, whose bread and butter depended on Gruening, were afraid to be seen with Muñoz. If for one reason or another they felt impelled to discuss something with him, they parked their cars blocks from his house and sneaked in the back way.

Eventually, late in 1936, the entire situation flared into violent explosion. Dr. Carlos Chardón, one of Puerto Rico's heroes, resigned his position as regional administrator—unable to function any longer in his impossible position between Puerto Rico and the federal government. A group of us met in Font Saldaña's house and sent a cable to Gruening, signed, as far as I remember, by over fifty respected men, urging Gruening not to accept the resignation but to come to Puerto Rico to discover for himself the real grievances which had prompted it. Instead, he sent a lawyer or two and a small-time politician, apparently instructed "to break up the Puerto Rican solidarity and the conspiracy" which I, as a "renegade American," was accused of having organized.

A number of Puerto Rican officials, who had been indignant until that moment, now changed their tunes and began to sing the praises of Gruening, who controlled the jobs. Others, several dozen of them, resigned in a body in sympathy with Chardón, even though most of them had no other jobs to turn to. Some of these moved to New York in search of employment; some found whatever they could in Puerto Rico; some managed to return to their old jobs in the university. All who stayed, however, went underground in the sense of thereafter keeping quiet about Washington—until Muñoz won the 1940 election and pulled them out of hiding again.

Whatever the anguish of those days, it was obvious that colonialism, as a psychological institution, was breaking down rapidly. Young men who had studied in the United States and had taken on American ways were no longer willing, as had been their fathers, to accept as best and unassailable everything that came from Washington. The enlightened PRRA, the best that either ruling country had ever given to Puerto Rico, proved actually to be the seedbed for Puerto Rico's final, determined revolt against colonialism. The fact that the United States, which in those days was under so black a cloud in Puerto Rico, was eventually to gain immeasurably in prestige—on the island and in the world as a whole—is to me "one of the wonders of human history."

While all that was going on, Albizu Campos and a number of his followers were arrested and brought to trial—on charges of conspiring against the United States. On those charges they had to be tried in the federal court, under a federal judge, and again there was much indignation. Many Puerto Ricans felt that the Nationalists should have been tried on murder charges in a Puerto Rican court, and that their trial in the federal court not only showed an insulting lack of confidence in Puerto Rican justice, but also injected serious language difficulties. Moreover, the trial skirted dangerously on political matters. There were many who wholeheartedly condemned murder, but could not understand how and why the striving for independence, no matter what the means, could be fairly construed and punished as conspiracy—in a situation in which Puerto Rico had repeatedly been told by Washington that it was entitled to independence if it wanted it.

The Nationalists had two trials. The first resulted in a hung jury, composed largely of Puerto Ricans. The second, before a jury composed of two Puerto Ricans and ten Americans—several of whom knew virtually no Spanish—resulted in the conviction of Albizu and seven others. The leader and one other, Luis Velázquez, were sentenced to six years in Atlanta Penitentiary, to be followed by four years of probation. The rest were sentenced to four—and in one case five—years in Atlanta, also followed by four years of probation. The trials created a certain amount of public sympathy for the Nationalists, as martyrs and patriotic Puerto Ricans, which they would not have enjoyed as murderers. Whatever sympathy they enjoyed, however, was blown away the following year, when two Nationalists tried unsuccessfully to assassinate Governor Winship, and so established the "party" as being definitely dedicated to a program of violence.

Governor Blanton Winship, a southern gentleman in the finest sense of the word—correct, hospitable, polite, decent and pleasant in his personal relations—was certainly not the man to rule Puerto Rico in those turbulent days. Like thousands of his class, he was utterly bewildered by the New Deal and all it stood for. A retired general, he tried to do his duty as he saw it, but he was completely baffled by the PRRA, incapable of understanding its aims, its basic philosophy, and what it meant—or should have meant—to Puerto Rico. Discussions of the knotty problems of land tenure, of co-operatives, of the need for industrialization, dealt with matters which were to him beyond ken and vocabulary. For Puerto Rico he had one panacea, and only one: a tourist industry. San Juan's evil-smelling and unsightly slums must be cleared because tourists would not like them and their dwellers told in no uncertain terms to go back to the hills from which they had originally streamed into the city in a desperate search for something to eat. San Juan's water must be purified so tourists would not get sick. Great pageants must be staged by the Puerto Ricans for the purpose of attracting tourists. Everybody on the island must willy-nilly plant flowers—even at the expense of corn and cabbages—for the purpose of beautifying the island to please tourists. He even coined a slogan, presumably designed to play a powerful role in the island's economic rehabilitation. It said: "You may not find a pot of gold at the end of the rainbow, but you can always find a garden of flowers."

Placing such a man in the impossible position of governor, while at the same time extending the turbulent New Deal to Puerto Rico through the PRRA, had been another of President Roosevelt's thoughtless and even irresponsible acts. Poor, bewildered General Winship was to reap more than his full share of popular indignation; his direct and transparent thought processes—obviously those of a nice, refined southern gentleman who would have been bewildered to hear himself accused of harboring the master-race psychology—came even to be classified and labeled in popular thought. "El Winshipado" became a term to describe the worst attitudes to be found in the ruling country.

Unfortunately, one of his first concerns as governor, long before the Riggs affair, had been the police. These had previously been a genial body of men, servants of the Puerto Rican public, who caught burglars and occasional murderers, arrested swindlers, directed traffic, and in general had little trouble in keeping order in a society of likable, genial, peace-loving men and women. The military man, however, demanded discipline for its own sake. He enlarged the force, bought it tear gas, machine guns, and what not, procured a fleet of shining red automobiles for mobility, and sent it to summer camps for intensive training. There can be no doubt that he did it largely for the sole purpose of strengthening the police and making it more effective as a civic organization —simply because his military training had taught him that that was the thing to do. However, in view of the tragic events which followed the Riggs assassination, he came to be widely charged with having militarized and brutalized the police and having transformed it from an arm of the insular government into a tool of the federal government's most reactionary officials.

Because tensions were mounting, people all over the island wanted to meet and discuss the Puerto Rican situation. On several occasions, groups in various towns, not Nationalists, but ordinary peaceful Puerto Ricans, asked permission to hold meetings; the permission was granted by the local mayors whose duty it was to consider matters of that kind; eventually it was rescinded by the governor, who sent his police to enforce the decree.

Regardless of his reasons, he played with emotional dynamite and did much to increase ill will and suspicion toward the United States. A people which has painfully, throughout four centuries, labored and struggled for civil rights, for a measure of self-government, for the right of free speech and free assembly, is bound to be unduly sensitive in those matters and to become indignant over any apparent infringements from a representative of the ruling country.

April 16 is Puerto Rico's *De Diego Day*. De Diego was one of the island's heroes and an early advocate of independence. The fact that the Nationalists claimed him as their patron saint—more or less as the American Communists often do honor to Thomas Jefferson—did not detract from his standing as a beloved Puerto Rican patriot and historic figure. It had long been the custom on his birthday to hold a solemn Mass in his honor in the San Juan cathedral and to pay homage with a visit to his grave. Now, in 1936, the governor gave orders that the Mass must not be held. The cathedral remained locked and was surrounded by policemen; people were allowed to visit De Diego's grave only one at a time, with a heavily armed guard standing by, composed of the police force and soldiers—not the National Guard, which was made up of Puerto Ricans, but soldiers of the regular army. Meanwhile, police cars, bristling with machine guns, patrolled all of San Juan's streets while Puerto Ricans of all classes cowered in their homes. Again, everywhere, one began to hear people say: "We are loyal Americans. But, by God, if that damned fool stays long in the *Fortaleza*, some trigger-happy cop is going to lose his head and will force us to start shooting in defense of our lives, rights, and liberties."

Fear, resentment, and indignation came to a head as a result of the shameful Palm Sunday affair of 1937. The Nationalists requested, *and received*, official permission to hold a parade in Ponce on that day. They began flocking to the city from all parts of the island—and so did the police, heavily armed with revolvers, tear gas, and machine guns.

About a hundred Nationalists, in their white pants and

black shirts, in which it was difficult if not impossible to hide arms, and with their wives and sweethearts in the Women's Auxiliary, assembled for the parade, surrounded by the police and watched by a large group of curious spectators. At the last minute, after they had assembled for the start, they were told that permission for the parade had been revoked.

They started marching despite the police order, and immediately a fusillade of shots rang out, which kept on, according to the varying testimony of conflicting witnesses for a period of up to half an hour. In the melee, fifteen Nationalists were killed, one bystander, and two policemen, the latter probably by their own cross fire. A total of fifty-five people were wounded.

Governor Winship immediately ordered a government investigation, but there was little popular faith in it—not only because the government itself, which would do the investigating, was considered by many as being one of the parties responsible for the shootings, but also because the governor had already made a public statement in which he definitely justified the conduct of all the police and other government officials who had been involved. As expected, the governor's investigation disclosed that the Nationalists had fired the first shot and all others thereafter which had hit policemen, and cleared the police of all blame in the matter—lauding them, in fact, for their excellent behavior.

But then the American Civil Liberties Union of New York was persuaded to send Arthur Garfield Hays to Puerto Rico to organize a commission of inquiry into the Ponce affair and into the question of civil liberties in general. The commission held extensive hearings and announced its findings in a public meeting in San Juan—permission for which had been granted only after Hays's defiant insistence. These findings were that, despite the governor's public statement that the Nationalists had fired the first shot, there was no evidence whatever that any of them had been armed; the police had undoubtedly fired first and killed each other with their own cross fire, and the whole thing amounted to a *brutal, bloody, and unpardonable massacre*—even though it was recognized that the Nationalist party contained the elements of fanatical fascist gangsterism.

It was further concluded by the Hays committee that civil liberties had been seriously and arbitrarily curtailed in Puerto Rico during the preceding year.

The Inés Mendoza affair was a by-product of the Hays investigation. Miss Mendoza had for years been a capable teacher in the island's high schools; she now appeared voluntarily before the commission to testify that in her opinion the old habit of doing all the teaching in the English language was bad in that it served mainly to confuse the children. Virtually all Puerto Rican teachers felt that way, but she was the only one who had the courage so to testify in public. When her contract was thereafter not renewed, and she was thrown out of the public-school system, there was again widespread indignation over the fact that Puerto Rican professionals were apparently not permitted to criticize policies that had been arbitrarily handed down from Washington.

Some years after the 1940 elections, when Puerto Rico had a new lease on life and started energetically to set its own house in order, all the island's teachers openly condemned the old attitudes toward English, and the educational system was changed to correspond. By that time Inés Mendoza was the wife of Muñoz Marín. Today she is highly respected as the first lady of Puerto Rico, but largely forgotten as one of the island's earlier fearless fighters for civil rights.

The Tydings bill had given rise to the United Front, a group of earnest intellectuals who held meetings in all parts of the island to explain to the people that independence was not necessarily as terrible a thing as the Maryland Senator had pictured it, and that the issue must under no circumstances be discarded.

Muñoz went to Washington late in 1936, where he drafted what he considered a workable independence bill, which he persuaded a congressman to introduce. He wanted first to have the people of Puerto Rico vote on the idea of independence; then, if the vote were favorable, to have the terms of such independence worked out jointly by Puerto Rican and federal leaders, and then to have another plebiscite on the specific independence so developed. In effect, he proposed the development of a political compact between Puerto Rico and the United States. His object was to educate Congress in the meanings of various kinds of independence—to teach Congress that political sovereignty need not mean economic ruin, either for sugar or for the Puerto Rican people. The bill was stillborn; it never got out of committee. But it did result in the beginning of a new education for Muñoz; it started the thought processes under which he eventually came completely to disavow the separate-independence formula for political freedom as spelling anything but ruin for the island. It began to dawn on him that Puerto Rico's possibility for economic well-being depended solidly on the continuance of free markets within the American tariff structure; that no Congress, no matter how well disposed, could possibly grant anything better than most-favored-nations status to an independent Puerto Rico, that Puerto Rican sugar could not possibly compete with Cuban if it had to pay duty in the American market; that the collapse of the sugar industry, with nothing on hand to take its place, would mean complete ruin for the island; that the Tydings bill had perhaps not been too far from the mark after all when it had defined separate independence in terms of economic chaos and starvation.

But it was to take time, and much effective effort, before

those dawning suspicions grew to the full convictions which
the governor of Puerto Rico displays today. The postwar
granting of independence to the Philippine Islands seems to
have been the clinching argument. Muñoz realized that
Puerto Rico, having no geographic frontier, no industries
except sugar, no natural resources to speak of except land,
climate, and too many people, would be utterly ruined by
the kind of independence which had been granted to the
Philippines. He began to think of something new—of political
freedom within the American economic structure.

In Puerto Rico, in 1936 and 1937, Muñoz precipitated a
bitter political struggle within his own Liberal party, between himself and the party's president—Antonio Barceló.
Muñoz wanted the party to boycott the 1936 election on the
grounds that the Tydings bill had clouded the independence
issue which was one of the principal planks in the party's
platform. Barceló, the politician who had felt sure of victory
because the Liberal party had, after all, brought the PRRA to
Puerto Rico, objected. The party went to the election—and
was again defeated by the Coalition of Republicans and
Socialists. Barceló blamed Muñoz.

The latter organized a splinter group within the party,
called the Authentic Liberal party, tried to use it for captur-
ing control, and demanded that Barceló resign and hand over
to him the insignia of his leadership. Barceló wrote him a long
and sorrowful public letter, addressed to "My Young Fellow
Patriot," advising him that if he wanted to be a real political
leader he ought to go out and scratch for followers as others
had done before him, accusing him of having been a disrup-
tive influence, and expelling him from the party.

There were rumors—how correct they were I have no way
of judging—of a private deal between Barceló and Washington, in which the Puerto Rican had been promised much
federal patronage for his party, despite its defeat, if he ousted

Muñoz—the implication being that no Liberal could get a federal job if the stormy senator stayed in the party.

Whatever the truth of those rumors, it *is* true that Muñoz' political fortunes had hit rock bottom. The rocket which had soared so brilliantly was now a dead stick in the opinion of all the political dopesters—who had no inkling of the enormous prestige that he still enjoyed among the *jíbaros*. The latter didn't count politically, in any event. Their votes were bought, and Muñoz had no money—no matter what his prestige. The consensus of opinion, both in San Juan and in Washington circles interested in Puerto Rico, was that: "Muñoz is through. No respectable party will take him now and there is nothing left for him except to join the Nationalists and try to take control of them while Albizu is in jail. And that—definitely—is political suicide!"

The historian Arturo Morales Carrión, writing in the present tense about the events of 1936–37, expressed himself as follows: "The island now suffers days of intense political reaction. Albizu's extremism not only prejudices the evolution of the independence thesis, but also confuses and disperses the groups devoted to economic and social reforms. Without the energetic popular support which Muñoz had aroused in the beginning, federal aid degenerates into a bureaucratic activity with sparse results. Psychological fatigue, disillusionment, and disorientation spread in the urban centers. Muñoz, who for a moment had been the great promise, disappears from the urban scene. His star is in deep eclipse, and he is now seen only as the leader of a routed faction, a political bohemian who had pilfered the treasure of a name and an illustrious tradition."

CHAPTER X

1940

REGARDLESS OF CIRCUMSTANCES, it was probably inevitable that Muñoz should eventually be ousted by any party which had taken him in—no matter how brilliant his record. Political parties need money to survive; in Puerto Rico such money came largely in the form of donations from the sugar industry and its associated business activities; sugar didn't mind giving money to a party which advocated the enforcement of the Five-Hundred-Acre Law, to be followed eventually by independence—as long as it confined its efforts to advocating and didn't do anything real about the matter. But Muñoz was no lip-service politician. He stated his political theses and then set out to implement them. He regarded politics, not as a career or a means for personal enrichment or advantage, but as a convenient means for carrying out the ideas which he, as a poet and a patriot, had formulated.

I remember talking to his chauffeur in 1936, when Muñoz was still a senator. "Señor," said the latter, "I have driven for nearly all of the big political figures on the island, but I never again want to drive for anybody except Muñoz Marín. He is the only politician here who always says exactly the same things to people who ride in his car with him that he does in his public speeches."

A man like that, who made no private political deals of any kind, couldn't stay long in an organized political party which felt that it depended for its survival on the generosity of the sugar industry and the good will of the federal government.

It was known, of course, that Muñoz enjoyed great popularity among the hill people who could numerically swing an election. But it was also a political truism that they would not vote unless they were paid. Some would vote as directed, in return for two dollars; some would accept money only from the party of their choice and allegiance; most would refrain from voting unless they received their money.

In 1925, when the cost of living, and so also of votes, had been somewhat lower, Muñoz himself had written as follows in *The Nation*, then edited by Ernest Gruening: "A politician on the village square was trying to arrange for a hundred badly needed votes. The illiterate *jíbaros* around him all belonged to his party but refused to vote unless given fifty cents apiece. It appears that the politician could only dispose of a quarter for each voter. 'Of course,' he was saying, 'you understand that I am not trying to corrupt your consciences because there is not enough money in the world to buy the sacred conscience of the humblest man. It is understood that you are Unionists. You are also good citizens and cannot refuse to cast your ballots. I simply want to give each of you a quarter that you may drink the health of our glorious party and enjoy yourselves a bit before you go home, and all I ask is that you vote right now, before I leave.' The *jíbaros* refused to budge. They wouldn't vote for any other party, that was certain; they were loyal Unionists (followers of the erstwhile independence movement), but if they didn't get their price they were going home without voting. 'But how am I to know that you are really Unionists if you don't vote?' the politician queried reasonably enough. The answer came, solemn and shrewd: 'We don't care whether you know it or not. God knows it.' They didn't vote."

In the same article he had written further that the *jíbaros* are "passionate, shrewd in their simple dealings, susceptible to religious quackery, and manage to carry a surprisingly heavy load of generosity along with that of their poverty. They have developed a naïve armor of suspiciousness that enrages the politicians and rural confidence men who try to prey upon them."

It was to those people that Muñoz, rejected by Washington and his own political party, written off by nearly all the politically wise as being politically dead beyond chance of resurrection, was now to address himself—without a cent for purchasing votes, with hardly a dollar with which to support himself and his family. Early in 1937 he was forced to give up his home in the Condado section of San Juan and move into the crowded old walled city, into the building of *La Democracia*, to eke out an existence for himself, wife, and two children on the few dollars per month that the paper managed to pay him, on contributions from his few remaining friends, plus Muna Lee's small salary at the university.

Crisis had narrowed down his open friends to a small nucleus of those who were held to him by the qualities of integrity and personal dedication which are the essence of leadership—and who in one way or another felt that they could afford to continue working with him. Among them were a few "fanatics" who placed integrity and dedication above financial security, a handful of men who were financially more or less secure and untouchable, and some who had previously worked with Albizu Campos, had no jobs to speak of or to lose, and were now captured by Muñoz' ideas.

These men and women now organized themselves into the new Popular Democratic party. Their official slogan was "Bread, Land, and Liberty," and their emblem, designed by Dr. Antonio Colorado, was the profile of a countryman wearing the traditional Puerto Rican straw hat, the *Pava*. In the beginning they were derided by the sophisticated; the Popular Democratic party was considered a bit of political play-acting, almost as foolish and unrealistic as Albizu's Army of Liberation had been; most of the island's newspapers except Muñoz' own *La Democracia* referred to it, if at all, with quotation marks around the word "party."

Before too many years, however, the *Pava*, the hillbilly hat, was to attain something of the same intense emotional significance that another piece of headgear had attained in France more than a century before. Except for the fact that the other was associated with bloody violence, *La Pava* is today's equivalent of the French Revolution's Liberty Cap in that it also stands for revolution, for the dignity of man and the greatness of the human spirit.

The platform of the Popular Democratic party was unique in that it said nothing about ultimate political status. Indeed, it was stressed throughout the campaign that status—independence, statehood, or dominion status—was in no way a campaign issue; the *Partido Popular* bid for the vote entirely on the issues of social-economic reform. Muñoz and his followers campaigned for the enforcement of the Five-Hundred-Acre Law, for legislative steps in making sugar a public utility and so assuring that independent cane growers would receive fair prices for their crops, for effective steps toward the improvement of the banking system toward the end of liberalizing credits to farmers and businessmen, for land to be given free to landless agricultural workers, for the promotion of local industries, for social legislation to protect the island's workers, for slum clearance, for reforms in the school system and the extension of education.

Other parties, to be sure, also advocated social reform and improved social justice—forced to do so by Muñoz' bold public declarations. It was widely recognized, however, that the Muñoz party was the only one that really meant what it said and was in a position, if voted into power, to carry out its campaign promises. It was the only party participating in the 1940 campaign which had no commitments or financial ties of any kind and was beholden to nobody except the people who voted for it. Its only great difficulty seemed to be that it had no chance whatever—for precisely those reasons—of *being* voted into power.

The 1940 election was to be the one great and crucial test of Puerto Rican democracy. Muñoz had never been rejected by the electorate; the question now at issue was whether the electorate would again support him even after Washington and local political committees had rejected him. The electorate's continued support despite those setbacks in his political fortunes was the one important turning point in the island's modern revolution.

The Popular Democratic party's small group of loyal workers labored feverishly in San Juan, reproducing its symbol as often and as widely as their small means permitted, and running off thousands of petition forms on the presses of *La Democracia.*

Up in the hills, meanwhile, in the small towns, in the village meeting places, in small meetings in private homes, Muñoz began his tremendous work of campaigning, talking to the peasants, appealing to their natural common sense, winning friends and followers. Finally, on July 22, 1938, he could announce that sufficient signatures had been obtained in Barranquitas and Luquillo to register the party in those two municipalities. Barranquitas had been his father's birthplace and is still revered as his shrine; it was a dramatic place in which to begin.

Eventually the party obtained twice as many signatures on its registration petitions as it needed to function as a party on an island-wide basis. But still it was not considered as having a chance in the election. In 1932 Albizu Campos had also received many registration signatures—but had failed miserably when it came to getting the vote. Besides, it was known or suspected that the other three parties actually urged their constituents to sign Muñoz' petitions. Since he couldn't win, it could do no harm to see to it that he went to the elections; every old-line rural ward heeler felt so sure of his personal following that he thought that any votes that Muñoz *might* win must necessarily be taken from the ranks of the opposing old-line rural ward heelers; the *Liberales* felt that he could take votes away only from the Socialists and Republicans, and vice versa. Most of them, while laughing at him, therefore also welcomed him in the field and did what they could to assure his actually going to the election.

The campaign became a tremendous educational effort, to teach the people of the hills, the *jíbaros*, the peasants, the real meaning of democracy and the real strength of their vote provided they used it freely and did not sell it.

Starting with countless meetings and discussions with the *jíbaros*, in their little homes and in village greens, with small groups and in an informal, non-oratorical manner, and building up to larger and larger audiences as he came back, again and again, to every corner of the island's mountains, by car, on horseback, on foot, Muñoz received attention from the beginning, not only because of his reputation, not only because he was the son of Muñoz Rivera, not only because of his clear and simple logic, but also because his naturalness set him off from other political leaders and their *dignidad*. At one point early in his campaign he stopped his car by a stream, got out, undressed, and took a bath—simply because he was warm and wanted to cool off. The *jíbaros* who saw him said: "This man is just like ourselves. He doesn't try to impress us with his dignity, and he doesn't mind if we see him taking off his clothes."

Not being able to pay him, he had lost the driver who had served him so faithfully in his more prosperous days. But he had to have a driver, and when he asked his friends to find him one, he gave the latter's specifications as a man who needed no salary, didn't have to eat, and could drive a car without gasoline. Somehow, he seemed to have found such a paragon.

He had made a speech and was due for another in another part of the island. He said to his driver: "How much money do you have?"

"I have seventeen cents."

"Good. I have nine cents. Get all the gasoline the money will buy and drive as far as it will take us. Maybe somebody will help us at the other end."

The driver said: "When do we eat? And on what?"

Muñoz, who is famous as a trencherman, answered: "Somebody will feed us."

In various parts of the island friends and admirers with modest homes gave food and lodging to Muñoz and his driver. He took up collections among the poverty-stricken country people—five cents here, a few pennies there, a quarter from some particularly rich *jíbaro*—but the money so received was never used for his own expenses. It was a contribution to the party treasury, however small. He wanted to establish the principle that the *Partido Popular* was the people's own party, to be supported by them, and not the usual organization of questionable largesse which came out of the cities at every election to distribute political bribes.

At a political meeting he felt thirsty, reached for a bottle of Coca-Cola, and began to drink. A man said: "This man is different. Another politician would be wearing a coat, necktie, and hat, and would try to impress us by having the Coca-Cola brought to him on a tray, with a glass, and by drinking from the glass. This man leaves off the coat, hat, and necktie; his clothes are wrinkled and full of sweat because he has come far and worked hard; he drinks his Coca-Cola from the bottle. He acts like one of us and I am for him."

But Muñoz would have none of it. "Just a minute," he said. "I appreciate your support, but I happen to drink out of a bot-

tle only because it is convenient and there doesn't seem to be
a glass around here. But if you people supported me for that
reason, if you voted for candidates because they drink out of
bottles instead of glasses, every political son of a bitch on the
island would run around sucking on a bottle all the time. But
that is not the way you vote. You vote for principles that I will
explain to you, and that is why we will win this election."

Beginning with all the small towns and settlements in the
island's interior and descending to the coastal cities only near
the end of his long campaign when he felt fairly sure of the
mountain areas, he explained Puerto Rico's plight in simple,
intelligent terms. His campaign issues were social and economic reform, and not ultimate political status, which could
wait. He talked about his party's determination to redistribute
the lands of the sugar estates, by legal means under the Five-
Hundred-Acre Law and in such a way that it would not spell
the ruination of the sugar industry. He talked about the need
for social reform to protect the workers' interests, for minimum-wage laws and other pieces of social legislation, for
slum clearance and low-cost housing. He wrote and distributed a pamphlet, now famous, *El Catecismo del Pueblo* (*The
People's Catechism*), explaining not only the issues at stake,
but also the power of the vote when used correctly for the improvement of one's personal life. Again and again, at meetings, he would pick out some older man and ask him: "How
many times have you voted?"

"Ten times, Don Luis."

"Did you ever see any change in your life as a result?"

"Never, except that things grew worse."

"Then for heaven's sake, give us a chance. Lend me your
vote, just once. You can take it back later and give it to your
old party if you don't like what we do with it."

"Give us a chance; just one chance to show what we can
do!" became almost a campaign slogan, repeated in hundreds
on hundreds of meetings, to tens of thousands of men and

women, in private and in public, verbally and in print, in homes, town squares, and village greens. "All we ask is this one chance!"

He talked at great length about the practice of selling votes. Indeed, to him that question was the crux of a veritable spiritual campaign, a struggle for the substitution of "clean consciences" and their clean political expression for mere political trickery and tactics. He is still dedicated to that struggle—in other phases of the island's life and long after he had put an end to the purchase of votes by the "simple" means of ending once and for all the habit of selling them.

"Nobody can really blame you for selling your vote," he told his listeners. "Two dollars is extraordinarily hard to come by and will buy a lot of beans and rice for yourselves and your starving families; who can blame you for wanting to provide for your children? *But,* you must look at this thing clearly. Do you want two dollars or do you want justice? You can't have two dollars *and* justice, and this time you have to make a choice. Forego the two dollars and vote for us, just this once, and see what happens!"

"If you sell your votes," he explained, "somebody has to put up the money with which to buy them. After that, whoever wins the election is tied to the fellows who gave him the money to buy your votes. That is why you have seen many political parties win while you have never won. The only way in which your votes can count to diminish your hardships is by not being sold, so that the party that triumphs shall not owe anyone except you."

"You can't have two dollars and justice!" was repeated again and again and again to all who would listen and some who would not, to those who nodded their heads in solemn agreement as well as those who sneered. Throughout his campaign Muñoz pounded away at complete honesty; again and again he also preached against taking two dollars from sugar and then voting for him anyway. It is not known today how many, when the voting took place in November, 1940, followed his advice in that matter. What is known is that votes are no longer bought in Puerto Rico today—simply because the poor have discovered their dignity and political power and now refuse to sell their votes with the same tenacity with which they once refused to vote without pay.

The 1940 election marked the turn; its results were to prove so overwhelmingly beneficial that, by the next election of 1944, vote-selling had become almost universally recognized as a social evil, to be suppressed, if it appeared at all, through community disapproval. Writing in *Reader's Digest* about the latter election, J. P. McEvoy said:

"One sharecropper was given a new pair of shoes by an opposition party worker, presumably in the hope that these would win him the vote. Says Muñoz Marín, 'As the sharecropper came into town on election day with his new shoes he presented a shining contrast to the bare feet and broken-down footwear of his fellow countrymen. But no one said anything to him, no one even reproached him. They just kept walking all over town after him with their eyes fastened on his well-shod, corrupted feet! Dozens of people, then hundreds of them. That's all!'"

In the same article, McEvoy quotes Muñoz as telling "about the druggist who also owned a farm and who tried to persuade an agricultural worker on election day to accept five dollars in exchange for going home and not voting. The worker was a Popular, the farmer-druggist a Liberal. The worker stepped out into the street and shouted: 'Listen everybody! I have just been promised five dollars by this druggist if I would promise not to vote. I have no money but I can work—and I now offer this druggist to work fifteen days for nothing on his farm if *he* will go home and not vote.'"

Carefully, in meeting after meeting, village after village, during the campaign for the 1940 election, Muñoz explained the meanings of politics to his people. He told them that they had heard politicians talk before, year after year, in campaign after campaign, and that it never meant anything real. "Don't ever trust a politician," he said. "Not even me. How do you know that I won't swindle you out of taking somebody else's dollars and then saddle you with just another gang sold out against you? You don't, and there is nothing that I can say to convince you. Nevertheless, if you give us the one chance that I ask for, if you now throw out the rascals in San Juan and vote us in, and if we then prove to be every bit as great a set of rascals, you will have learned how to use your vote for the purpose of tossing rascals out of office, and you can toss us out in turn in the next election. Can you sell such power for two dollars?"

He said: "Always, politicians have made you vague promises—as I do here when I talk about justice. What do they mean? This time we want you to *know* what they mean. We are not campaigning for a set of loose and rattling planks in a platform. We are campaigning for specific things, even for specific bills. We have drafted our bills, for land reform and other things, even before you elect us. Read them, discuss them, amend them by writing to us—now, before you vote us into power. They are your personal bills, designed to change your personal lives. You are entitled to know exactly what you are voting for."

That, of course, amounted to gambling—on a really large and adventurous scale—in colonial politics. How could Muñoz know that, if he managed to win the election and came to control the insular legislature, his enemies in Washington would not send him another reactionary Governor Winship who would play the sugar game and veto the bills as fast as the legislature passed them?

Muñoz was getting results in that he was being talked about —in the hills, where it counted. But one man couldn't work fast enough; the island's radio facilities were not available to him; he had to invent new ways of spreading his voice. Somehow he acquired a recording machine. Whenever he made a speech thereafter, it was recorded and thirty or more records were hurriedly pressed from the master and played in thirty or more villages throughout the island.

He founded a rural newspaper, *El Batey,* published for free distribution whenever he had the time to write an issue. In this he hammered away incessantly at the issues involved, at land reform, social legislation, industrialization, health and education—preaching incessantly, too, against the old vice of selling the vote. There was so great a demand for the paper that it soon grew from a one-page affair to one of four pages; the demand and the consequent circulation grew dramatically until there was one issue with a million copies. That was more than the circulation of all the other Puerto Rican papers combined. The island's ultraconservative businessmen, who knew well that Muñoz had no chance whatever of winning the election, and who would have shivered in their boots had they for a moment thought that there might be such a chance after all, knew a good advertising medium when they saw it. In no time at all, *El Batey* was amply supported, through advertising, by the political enemies of the Popular Democratic party.

All this time, too, Muñoz was perforce also busily building up a political machine. The old leaders, the Creole *caciques,* the rural ward heelers, numbered about four hundred—belonging to all the parties. Before he was through, Muñoz had a machine composed of nearly four thousand local leaders, men whom he had picked in all the small and large places, men who had caught his ideas and whom he could lead by those ideas, unpurchasable men who could not purchase anybody else either, *jíbaros* themselves who could work among their fellows as *jíbaros.*

The party's constituent assembly was held on July 21, 1940, at the Sixto Escobar athletic park in San Juan. Lugo-Silva writes: "The gathering has been described as one of the greatest spectacles ever seen in Puerto Rico. More than 3,600 delegates from the entire island were present, among them rural delegates who took part in the deliberations and in the resolutions adopted by the assembly."

On the fifteenth of September the party held a mass meeting in Santurce, a suburb of San Juan, at which were approved all the bills to be passed in case the party won at the polls. Before a crowd of more than 15,000 persons, each Popular candidate for the insular legislature took an oath to vote for the bills which aimed at social and economic justice for the long-exploited masses of Puerto Rico—regardless of what the federal government might say.

When election time came, Muñoz was helped immeasurably by the new election law that had perforce been passed by the coalition in 1936—under popular insistence growing out of putrid scandals. That law is today regarded as a sign of Puerto Rico's growing democracy. First drafted and passed by the opposition, it had proved to be one of the several means by which Muñoz' party had come to power. Today it could conceivably serve the opposition equally well for a possible return to power. The Popular Democratic party has the power to tamper with it, and so to safeguard its position. It has not done so. There have been only minor changes in the law since 1940, and they were made with the full consent of all the parties.

Under that law, first tested in 1940, there is now one polling place for approximately every 150 voters. These may go to the school, or whatever building serves for the purpose, at any time they want before one o'clock; after that time, nobody is admitted, and the voting begins. The names of the registered voters are read off in alphabetical order, and they go, one by one, to the curtained booth to cast their secret ballots. Each man or woman steps out of the assembled group in full sight of all the rest, in a situation in which everybody watches everybody else. People may leave after they have voted, but nobody may enter the polling place until all the voting is over. By that system, all floaters, repeaters, and ghosts are rigidly excluded.

On election night, November 5, 1940, Muñoz sat at home with his old friend and loyal supporter, Jorge Font Saldaña. The latter had been one of those who had resigned their PRRA jobs in 1936, in indignation and in support of Muñoz. Since then, he had had four terrible years, at times barely eking out an existence for himself and his family, but never for an instant diminishing his support of the leader. Now the two were waiting for the returns to come in. They came first from Bayamón, which was traditionally Republican. But this time the Republican vote had been reduced considerably, while the *Populares* had made a real showing.

"They are doing it!" cried Muñoz. "They are doing it! They have refused to sell their votes!"

Returns came in from one of the mountain districts. The Popular Democratic party had won there.

Profoundly moved, Muñoz began to cry. "They are doing it, Jorge! Those wonderful people. They are starving and they haven't let me down. They haven't sold their votes!"

A few more returns came in. "We needn't wait for the whole picture. We're in! We've won! The *jíbaros* aren't selling their votes, and there is not a chance in the world of our not winning the election."

That, of course, called for celebration, but Muñoz had only a very little wine in the house and no money with which to buy more.

"Listen, Jorge. Do you have any whisky at home?"

"I have about half a bottle."

"Go get it. Telephone your house and ask your wife to bring it. Tell her to hurry. We have to celebrate."

Jorge telephoned his home and got the cook.

"Please ask Doña Carmen to come down here and bring that half bottle of whisky that's in the pantry!"

"The whisky! The whisky! Praise be to God!" The cook knew immediately what the order meant. "We've won! We've won!" She ran to the window. "Listen everybody out in the street. We've won. The *Populares* have won the election."

Long before all the returns were in, there was jubilation in all parts of the island. "The *jíbaros* didn't sell their vote! We have won the election. Don Luis has won!"

When the final count was completed, it was found that the *Populares* had received ten of the nineteen Senate seats, a majority of one. They received eighteen seats in the House, as against another eighteen that went to the coalition. But there was another group, the *Unificación*, which had won three seats in the House. With some judicious trading to line up this group on his side, and with constant use of the caucus to make sure that all his party members voted as a bloc, Muñoz, who became President of the Senate and the island's political leader, could expect to swing the legislature.

It was no overwhelming victory; the *Populares* had won 38 per cent of the total vote and had barely managed to gain control of the legislature. But it paved the way for future overwhelming victories; in 1944 they were to receive 64 per cent of the total vote, and their strong hold on the island's electorate has never diminished. The victory of 1940 also paved the way for future reforms and programs so drastic that today's Puerto Rico bears only slight resemblance to that of twenty years ago.

The deep and abiding love between Muñoz on the one hand and the *jíbaros* on the other, which began to manifest itself during the 1940 campaign, has never diminished. During the 1948 campaign, when Muñoz ran for the office of the first governor ever to be elected, there was an old *jíbaro* in the

Isabela region who promised the Virgin that if Don Luis was elected he would make a pilgrimage to kneel at the latter's feet. Don Luis *was* elected, overwhelmingly. Then, for a time and because the politicians in San Juan were driving him mad, he retreated to Ellsworth's Treasure Island resort, where he gave instructions to his guards that they were to admit nobody except members of his family and *any* jíbaro *who might want to see him.*

The old man at Isabela sold his last two chickens in order to raise forty-five cents for bus fare. He arrived at Treasure Island, barefoot, his faded blue denims patched but immaculately clean, his *Pava* on his head. When he told the governor-elect about his promise to the Virgin, Muñoz said:

"You have made a promise, and a man must keep his promises. It is up to you to kneel. But I have made no promise one way or the other, and there is no reason why I shouldn't kneel too. Let's both kneel!"

And then, after the poet had knelt with the peasant and when the latter was ready to leave, Muñoz' family told him about the chickens and the forty-five cents.

"He sold his last two chickens," they said. "He doesn't have return fare. The least you can do is to give him ninety cents for his transportation."

But Muñoz' answer was: "When a man offers you his soul, do you give him change?" He refused to give him money, but there was no reason why he shouldn't give him transportation. He sent the old man home in his own car.

It was during his 1940 campaign, too, that Muñoz began seriously to question his former ideas about Puerto Rico's independence. Whatever one said about ultimate political status, it was clear that the poor would be at the receiving end of whatever status might emerge from Puerto Rico's turmoil; Muñoz now discovered that the various ideas about status that had been so ardently discussed for so many years by the intellectuals meant little to the rural poor except as something that the politicians talked about. What was it these people wanted? They wanted the same things that all other people want the world over. They were hungry and they wanted food. They were sick and they wanted medical care. They wanted education and opportunity for their children. They wanted the human dignity that was too often denied them. Most of them would be content to take such things from any government that would provide them, no matter where it might be centered.

Muñoz discovered that there was little use in talking about political sovereignty to the rural poor who had never before seen signs that they might themselves someday come to exercise that sovereignty, and who could not grant that their Creole *caciques* would function any better as ward heelers under independence than they did under colonialism. He discovered that the various economic and other arguments for independence had little meaning for poor farmers who expected always to remain farmers and were hungry only for more and better land so they could be better farmers and provide better for their children.

It was, of course, known that he had previously stood for independence separate from the United States. He was questioned on the matter at one of his meetings and began to discuss it while explaining again that political status was in no sense a campaign issue. A powerful Negro stood up in the front row, confronted Muñoz, and said in a ringing voice:

"Don Luis, you give us independence, and . . . "—he drew his finger dramatically across his throat—"we die!"

More, he discovered that there was among the *jíbaros* very little of the hatred for the United States which had been preached by Albizu. Those people might hate their boss at the sugar mill—if he was a son of a bitch—but they hated him for that reason and not because he was an American or drew his power from the American regime. In fact, they were often, and simply, proud of their American citizenship, of the fact that they could go to the States without passport whenever they wanted and had the means, that they were, through that citizenship, one with the world's most powerful democracy. Moreover, while the sugar boss might be a scoundrel (though more often a Puerto Rican than a continental), they sensed that the United States as such, and the great body of Americans, were *not* scoundrels. If they had a real complaint against the sugar boss, they might even go to court and win the case—and what poor man could do a thing like that, for instance, in the sovereign Dominican Republic? They knew that the United States had given them roads, schools, hospitals, and health programs—not enough, to be sure, but certainly more than Spain had given them during four centuries. The United States had given them the PRERA, the FERA, and the PRRA in their hour of greatest need—which were again not enough but were far more than they could expect, under independence, from their own politicians.

Muñoz also began to realize that, in the event that he did achieve the island's independence, well over half of Puerto Rico's men and women might easily want to retain their U.S. citizenship—of which nobody would be able to rob them. What would he do with that tremendous body of "foreigners"?

So, slowly, began the mental process which eventually led to the new idea of a permanent tie with the United States as defined by existing realities rather than by any political doctrine. Statehood was out of the question because it would be ruinous; independence began to loom as being equally out of the question.

Ten years later, still led by Muñoz, the Puerto Rican people were to vote in a plebiscite for a compact with the United States under which they would become self-governing under a constitution written by themselves, and for a form of political relationship (devised in the colony) that was unprecedented in world affairs, unheard of and undreamed of by political scientists.

CHAPTER XI

Tugwell

THE AUDACITY with which Puerto Rico's colonial voters, in 1940, handed the ruling capital a package program for their own economic salvation—carefully worked out, widely discussed, sworn to by all of the winning party's candidates, voted upon by the people in what could be interpreted only as a mandate to Muñoz—is probably unparalleled in modern colonial history. Previously, all major decisions affecting the island had been made in Washington. Moreover, the tenor of the entire situation was unmistakably such as to inform Washington that the Puerto Ricans were now ready and determined to take matters into their own hands, to create for themselves the reforms for which they had in vain begged the United States during the preceding decades, and to do this without regard to their political status—even as colonial subjects. There must have been men in Washington in those days to whom the entire matter proved again that Muñoz was essentially an irresponsible political adventurer.

The latter's first step opposite the federal government was, however, to write Roosevelt a letter of congratulations for his third election to the Presidency, in which Muñoz also mentioned his own victory and outlined the aims and policies of the Popular Democratic party.

Roosevelt answered in part: "The purposes of the Popular Democratic party as you have outlined them are highly praiseworthy and should result in vastly improved social and economic conditions for the island. I particularly appreciate your pledge of co-operation and assure you that this administration stands ready to do all in its power to assist in finding a solution for the problems of Puerto Rico."

Secretary Ickes, however, was the man to do the actual assisting pledged by Roosevelt; the extent of his happiness is not known. Certain is it that the stubborn, autocratic curmudgeon was a thoroughly decent and honest man who had Puerto Rico's well-being at heart, was in no way fooled by the pious doctrinaire platitudes of the sugar lobby, endorsed most or all parts of Muñoz' platform in principle—but didn't want Puerto Rico to blow up in his hands over a revolutionary program. Whatever Muñoz might be, say, or do, Secretary Ickes still had the ultimate responsibility, in Washington, for Puerto Rico's well-being, under a governmental system in which Washington appointed the governor with veto power, and Congress could revoke laws pertaining to Puerto Rico. He could in no way wash his hands of that responsibility.

On the other hand, there are indications that he had always held Muñoz in rather high esteem, at least as an honest man of integrity, that he had no particular love for Dr. Gruening, and that he was well aware of the widespread mistrust and almost universal dislike with which Gruening and his anti-Muñoz views had come to be regarded in Puerto Rico. At the height of the troubles, early in 1937, Ickes had accepted Gruening's resignation as administrator of the PRRA. The secretary was aware that, when the news of that resignation reached San Juan, the entire staff of the PRRA, hundreds of men and women, had poured out of their offices into the open air in a great, spontaneous demonstration of relief. Shortly thereafter, Ickes had himself taken hold of Puerto Rican affairs for some months, while Gruening, as Director of Territories, had gone to the Pacific, apparently to dedicate light-houses and arrange for the annexation of various uninhabited islands for strategic purposes. Eventually Gruening had resigned as Director of Territories and had been sent north as Governor of Alaska.

In 1936, when I once insisted to Ickes that Muñoz was the one hope of the United States in Puerto Rico, the one man who could hold the island together and prevent an American debacle, I had the distinct impression that the Secretary of the Interior was inclined to agree with me but was powerless to do much about the matter. Gruening had many staunch supporters in the Department, and seemed, moreover, to have President Roosevelt's ear. After 1937, of course, it was impossible for Ickes to give support to a Puerto Rican leader who had been ousted by his own party and apparently (until the 1940 election proved otherwise) had no political following whatever.

Now, with all kinds of people buzzing all kinds of things into Ickes' ear—many of them to the effect that Muñoz was unstable, unreliable, a political dilettante, no matter how brilliant—the secretary had to catch up on history and make up his own mind about matters. Some very serious questions had been raised by the 1940 election. Muñoz had stormed out of his exile with a land bill that seemed to be nothing less than dynamite. Would he, in power, prove vindictive? Would he treat the sugar companies as squatters, illegally occupying lands to which they had no rights under the Five-Hundred-Acre Law? Would he prove so irresponsible as to try to throw them out without recompense? If he did intend to pay them, where would he get the money? Why hadn't he asked the federal government to step in, as through the PRRA or one of the agricultural agencies, to handle the delicate question? What did Muñoz intend to do with the sugar lands once his government had laid its hands on them? How did he intend to manage them without ruining Puerto Rico's principal industry, and so also the island's economy? Did he intend to divide up Puerto Rico's richest lands into small parcels and so start a downward spiral of "Haitianization"?

Those were real and valid questions for the man who held the federal responsibility and had not had the opportunity to follow Muñoz' thought processes in detail, or to keep abreast with the latter's astonishing campaign in the hills. Ickes now had to wrestle with this important problem: Should the governor of Puerto Rico—by this time Admiral Leahy had succeeded Winship, and Guy J. Swope had succeeded Leahy—sign Muñoz' various drastic bills or veto them—not because Ickes was against Muñoz' basic program but because he opposed its specific forms? If the governor did veto the bills, and especially the land law drafted to implement the federal Five-Hundred-Acre Law, what would happen to U.S. prestige on the island? Would such a veto, in the face of Muñoz' unmistakable mandate to carry out reforms in land tenure, be interpreted to mean that the United States did not, after all, favor the enforcement of its own law? Would it play into the hands of the Nationalists and so increase materially Puerto Rico's apprehensive unrest, of which Ickes had already had more than plenty? If the governor did veto the law, what kind of a program could Washington, in view of the PRRA's failure, offer the people of Puerto Rico in its place? There was obviously not much time, in any event, for the formulation of any such alternate program, and the chances were that it would not—since it would have come from Washington—have been accepted wholeheartedly by the Puerto Ricans.

The secretary therefore borrowed Rexford Tugwell from New York, where the latter had been engaged in city planning, and sent him to Puerto Rico to investigate the entire business and advise the United States on what to do—especially about the land law. A political scientist, a brilliant and distinguished academician in his field until Roosevelt's election, Tugwell had previously, until 1937, been one of the outstanding New Deal leaders and intellectuals. As Assistant Secretary, and later Undersecretary, in the Department of Agriculture, he had had much to do with problems of land tenure. He was known to be friendly to Puerto Rico's aspirations, had indeed been the one federal official who had in 1934 made it possible for the Chardón Commission to go to Washington for the purpose of drafting its plan for reconstruction. As a man of firm, and even arrogant, convictions, however, as one of the most irreconcilable New Deal philosophers, he was cordially hated by a great many men in the government.

Tugwell's reaction to Muñoz' land law was curiously revealing. He seemed astonished that the law's main features showed signs of real intelligence. He seems to have regarded the law as a sudden flash of inspiration on Muñoz' part, and not as something with which the latter had lived through twenty years of struggle and thought. He disliked certain other features, but could do little about them, in dealing with a bill which had in toto been submitted to the electorate even before the election, and which every incumbent of the Popular party had sworn publicly to uphold if voted into office. To his credit be it said that he recommended that the governor sign the bill. Swope did sign it and several others; the great Puerto Rican revolution was legally under way.

Tugwell had gone to Puerto Rico as an investigator. Eventually he was made chancellor of the university; a little later he became the island's last continental American to be governor. On the island he is today regarded almost universally as by far the greatest non-Puerto Rican governor that San Juan has ever had. His regime was one of great turmoil, great tensions, but still greater achievements. If the latter were primarily those of Muñoz and his followers, it is nevertheless true that he backed to the hilt a program which was in those days revolutionary, and that no governor before him had ever given so much of himself, so freely, for the furtherance of a great idea.

This was the situation: The entire philosophy as well as the main details of Puerto Rico's reshaping had been worked out by Muñoz and his followers long before Tugwell had ever come on the scene. As far back as 1920 they had begun to be formulated in the head of the stormy free-lance journalist in New York. They had been buffeted, shaped, and reshaped throughout the succeeding two decades, as a result of Muñoz' political fortunes and misfortunes, through the lessons taught by the PRERA, the FERA, and the PRRA, through years of high hope followed by tragic disappointment. Throughout the 1930's, the philosophy and details had taken shape in the heads of Puerto Rican intellectuals, trained investigators, who had made detailed studies of their island's ills, had learned from bitter experience how those ills could *not* be cured, and had now drafted a program geared to all the conceivable realities, under which cures might after all be accomplished. Tugwell was not in Puerto Rico to explore, chart, and follow new paths for the island's salvation, but to lend his sturdy help to, and shape effectively through his administrative experience and skills, the following of paths which had long been surveyed and charted by Puerto Ricans. From his own writings during and immediately after his governorship, he seems to have been almost unaware of that great reality; in his own mind he seems to have been the leader, a fact which worked against Puerto Rico in that it laid the island's new program open to vicious attacks from his many personal enemies in Congress, who were actually after Tugwell rather than Puerto Rico.

Outside of the strong backing which he gave Muñoz, Tugwell's really great personal contribution to Puerto Rico's reshaping was that of the political scientist who could take a revolutionary philosophy and program and translate them into definite government structures and actions. He knew how to create and run a government machine to accomplish great things. Muñoz and his followers did not—until Tugwell taught them.

Who were these men whom Muñoz now pulled out of their various exiles and entrusted with the job of forming a new government? They were eager, incorruptible young men, dedicated to a great idea, but they were also poets like their leader. They may never have written verse, but they were poets nevertheless, in their various fields of economics, law, sociology, geography, etc., creative men who identified with people and refused to be guided by dogma. They could make their way through scholarly essays peppered with footnotes and graphs, but what did such men know about the mundane matter of creating and running a stable and effective government? Tugwell taught them. He could not teach them anything about decency and honesty in government: those things were already present in the quality of the men who had assumed control with Muñoz. But the complex and yet efficient working structure of Puerto Rico's present government, as one of the most socially effective found anywhere on earth, is Rexford Tugwell's great achievement on the island. And even his bitterest enemies, in Congress and out, cannot deny the desirability of such a government—or deny him credit for creating its complex machinery.

There is an idea current that he took to Puerto Rico with him a number of New Deal officials, that the latter flocked from Washington to Puerto Rico after the need for winning the war had replaced the need for reshaping the country. A few such men did go to Puerto Rico with Tugwell, but always as specialists and for relatively minor positions. They did not shape policy or draft major plans. Muñoz and his Puerto Rican associates did not permit it. They had had more than enough of well-meaning men from Washington who, as in the

PRRA, tried to impose their dogmas on the island's human realities.

One of Tugwell's greatest mistakes was to write a book while he was fighting his battle. The book was published shortly after his departure from Puerto Rico, under the title *The Stricken Land;* with some justice, a number of Puerto Ricans said that it should have been called *The Stricken Rexford.* The book indicates his discovery of what many a continental had discovered before him—that the Puerto Rican road is rough for the non-Puerto Rican Man of Destiny. Throughout some seven hundred pages it records less the struggle of Puerto Rico than the minutiae of the struggles, the agonies, the rationalizations of Rexford Tugwell, and the clashes between Tugwell, the highly trained political scientist, and Muñoz, the poet, both of whom were driving at exactly the same goal. Throughout the book he shows a lamentable lack of knowledge of what had gone on in Puerto Rico before his own advent on the scene and indicates repeatedly that he thought it was Tugwell rather than Muñoz who had invented the terms for Puerto Rico's salvation. To the latter he often gives credit for what Tugwell considers brilliant flashes of insight and near genius, but he is also almost consistently irritated by the latter's refusal to bow to the governor in matters of basic policy. The book should not have been written until, after some four or five years, its author had had a chance to develop an objective point of view on his own Puerto Rican experiences. Nevertheless, he is today no less respected, and even revered, in Puerto Rico because his unfortunate book reveals him to have been "A god who is omniscient, but not omnipotent!"

The war created tremendous problems for the island, which was of special interest to the enemy because of its strategic importance. Submarines sank dozens of ships loaded with the necessities of life. The importation of foods was drastically curtailed, and prices rose sharply. The ghastly spectacle of air-raid alarms—and in one case a hurricane warning—dispersing long bread lines was all too common. On the mainland the war created conditions of unprecedented employment and prosperity for the civilian population; in Puerto Rico, lacking industries and partly isolated by the submarine campaign, it did exactly the opposite. The needlework industry collapsed because of transportation difficulties, as did the citrus-fruit industry, while most of the other branches of the economy were seriously impaired. Unemployment soared even higher than it had during the depression; mounting relief was an imperative necessity.

On the other hand, the island's rum industry soared to unprecedented heights of prosperity which it has never even approached since V-J day. On the mainland the production of whiskey and other liquors was drastically curtailed because the alcohol was needed for the war effort; Puerto Rican rum—the manufacture of which had gotten under way about 1936—came largely to take their places. In New York and elsewhere it was in those days often impossible to buy a bottle of whiskey unless one bought one or two bottles of rum along with it; the Puerto Rican distillers reaped a golden harvest, the taxes on which financed Puerto Rico's forward-looking program.

Under its organic law, defining relationships between the island and the mainland, excise taxes on goods manufactured in Puerto Rico were permitted to remain in the insular treasury instead of being covered into the federal treasury as they are in the forty-eight states. These excise taxes now soared; Puerto Rico's budget, which before 1940 had been around $22,000,000, shot up to as high as $150,000,000; with such funds the government could build factories, purchase lands held in excess of five hundred acres by the sugar corporations, provide machinery for the working and distribution of those lands, stimulate its public-health service, implement its new social legislation, foster co-operatives, and engage in all the multiple activities of a stricken society reshaping itself, while also contributing to wartime relief. The accident of the war, and the resulting prosperity of the rum industry, got Puerto Rico's "Operation Bootstrap" off to a flying start during those first four turbulent years of the Tugwell regime.

Morally, too, the war contributed to Muñoz' great effort. Whatever was said—and it was plenty—about that kind of program's being socialistic and un-American, military men knew that a hungry, unemployed, discontented civilian population is a serious military problem in a location of strategic importance. Muñoz' leadership and his effective program of reform and economic improvement held the island's people together despite their wartime hardships and greatly strengthened their loyalty to the ruling country, which now permitted and abetted the new Puerto Rican effort.

In his inaugural address Tugwell had expressed his basic philosophy as governor, which differed in no respect from that of Muñoz as political leader, in the following words: "In bettering public health, in educating children, in bringing power, light, sanitation into people's homes, in building more homes for the underprivileged, in providing all kinds of needed work, in the conservation of soil and other resources, in the use and tenure of the land, in the search for higher wages and greater social security—in all these we shall find work enough crowding in upon us in the years to come."

The Planning, Zoning, and Urbanization Board, today known simply as the Planning Board, was created as an agency for charting the island's progress and for integrating all the government's functions in order to give general, integrated direction to their respective efforts. Under the leadership of Dr. Rafael Picó, a geographer, that organization is today becoming world famous for the imaginative effectiveness of its operations, which, among many other things, prevent wasteful duplication in programs planned and executed by the various government agencies.

Previous to the creation of the Planning Board, the passage of Muñoz' land law had created an insular Land Authority as an agency to carry out the new government's land policies arising from the enforcement of the Five-Hundred-Acre Law. As money became available, the government now began to purchase lands from the sugar companies and to work them in such a way that the companies could stay in the manufacturing business of operating mills. The administration of those holdings, their partial redistribution to small farmers, planters, and squatters, the active program of social services and community improvement which is carried on as part of the Land Authority's work, described more fully in Chapter XIV, are the fruits of a social inventiveness which today promises to have its repercussions in India and Pakistan, Indonesia, Africa, and the Latin American republics—in all the lands which have for several years sent observers to Puerto Rico.

Muñoz knew well that industrialization was, on the one hand, essential to Puerto Rico's continued growth and development and, on the other, apparently impossible under existing conditions—requiring the investment of large sums of private capital which were simply not forthcoming. As pointed out in Chapter IV, Puerto Rico's economic climate was not conducive to such investment. Nevertheless, factories *had* to be built if the society were to survive. Hence, the government created the Development Company, modeled after Chile's *Corporación de Fomento,* and the Development Bank for the purpose of making industrial credit available. The government's aims in creating those institutions were similar to those of the Chilean organization. In recognition of the fact that industrialization was essential, the government took the stand that private capital should at all times be favored for the purpose, but that, when and where private capital did not come forward for building and operating factories, government would do the job. The government, too, would pave the way for private enterprise, would make investigations through which private enterprise might be encouraged in the industrial field, would, under certain circumstances, give various kinds of direct and indirect financial aid to potential private investors in the Puerto Rican scene.

From the PRRA, the insular government had already acquired the cement plant that was to provide the building materials so badly needed for all kinds of constructions, and a private company in Ponce had built another cement plant. Now, under the leadership of Teodoro Moscoso, the Development Company, constantly hampered by the fact that machinery and materials were hard to obtain during the war, enlarged the cement plant and set out to create more industries.

The rum industry needed bottles; the government built and managed a glass factory which started operations in January, 1945, two and a half years after the creation of the Development Company.

A factory for the manufacture of pulp board and paper from waste paper and bagasse (the fibrous end product of sugar-cane grinding) was built next door to the glass factory —justified for construction during the war because its operations would cut down considerably the amount of shipping needed for supplying Puerto Rico with essential materials.

A clay-products factory was built, in the beginning turning out glazed tiles but later turning its efforts to the production of washbowls and toilet bowls for the government's enormous program of slum clearance and low-cost housing.

Because it was evident that the tourist industry could someday be built up to the point where it would contribute materially to the island's economy, the Development Company participated in the founding of the Puerto Rico Travel Association, to promote the interests of *turismo*.

A shoe factory was built by the government in the southern part of the island.

Meanwhile, the government collaborated with the university in arranging for research toward further industrialization —especially in the utilization of the sugar industry's by-products, while the Development Company also promoted the training of Puerto Rican technicians in such mainland institutions as M.I.T. The improvement of labor relations, and education of both labor and management in the social aspects of those relations, became a special concern of the Development Company, which soon discovered that government-operated enterprises, in a democracy in which a number of legislators may well be labor leaders on the side, are particularly vulnerable to strikes and feather-bedding demands.

Although not created during Tugwell's administration, the Water Resources Authority completed its final organization during that period. Organized for the purpose of providing cheaper electricity to the island, hydro-generated wherever possible to reduce the importation of fuels, flung over all of the island in one great network of distribution lines, T.V.A. style, that agency, through its low-cost power, has by now become effective in attracting a number of privately financed industries to Puerto Rico. It is also, however, intimately concerned with the conservation of water and soil resources, having been created for the purposes of "conserving, developing, and utilizing, and aiding in the conservation, developing, and utilization of water and energy resources of Puerto Rico, for the purpose of making available to the inhabitants of the island in the widest economic manner, the benefits thereof, and by this means to promote the general welfare and increase commerce and prosperity. . . ."

A Transportation Authority and a Housing Authority to work toward the substitution of decent dwellings for the evil-smelling, unsanitary slums were among the other government agencies set up by Tugwell and Muñoz for the purpose of carrying out the mandate of the people for an improved life.

Such drastic steps, and many more, naturally aroused constant charges of statism and socialism. Muñoz' often-repeated answer to those charges was: "We are neither radical nor conservative. We are merely realistic." Puerto Rico discovered what such nations as Chile had discovered earlier and what many an emerging society such as India and Pakistan is discovering today—that a modern underdeveloped society cannot, under existing realities, find salvation by following doctrinaire patterns.

Throughout four centuries the Puerto Ricans had been a stricken people, starving, disorganized, not permitted by the rulers to take effective steps toward the improvement of their lives, lethargic and fatalistic as a result. Now, in 1941, they resolutely set out on new paths of achievement; during the eight ensuing short years, they laid the solid foundation for the great effort which is today attracting visitors and students by the hundreds from all parts of the world; their greatest gain during those years was, however, psychological. New energies were released for new creative enterprises; the former lethargy gave way to new hopes for some two million men, women, and children; the exhilaration of a hard uphill struggle with great rewards in sight took hold of the island's people; Muñoz and the Popular Democratic party gained daily in popularity bordering on adulation.

Among the lower classes, that is, which comprised well over 80 per cent of the population. The upper classes, the wealthy landowners, the ultraconservative businessmen, were in a turmoil of fear and tried their best—ably abetted by the coalition of the Republican and Socialist parties—to hamper the Puerto Rican government at every turn. At one point they sent a delegation to Washington, composed of the island's most powerful businessmen, to demand that Puerto Rico be given a strong military government because, as they claimed, the island was being led straight into un-American socialism.

In the 1940 election, the coalition had won the office of Res-

ident Commissioner, Puerto Rico's official representative in
Congress. That worthy was Bolívar Pagan, and he did everything in his power to hinder Muñoz and discredit him in the
eyes of Congress. At one Congressional hearing in Washington, he tried to embarrass the latter by asking him, before
a number of Congressmen, if his program did not amount
to socialism and so was against the American way of life.
Muñoz answered that he didn't know whether or not it was
socialism; he did know that it was badly needed and was
proving effective for dealing with Puerto Rico's ills. As for
the socialism, however, he wanted to refer the assembled congressmen to the Honorable Bolívar Pagan himself, to the man
who had asked the question, because the Resident Commissioner was *the head of Puerto Rico's Socialist party*.

The embattled 150 per cent Americans also used the F.B.I.
for the purpose of confusing and hindering the government
program. Agents of that organization were, of course, all over
Puerto Rico, investigating everything constantly. When they
asked questions about a candidate for some job, they usually
went first to the super-patriots of whose loyalty and respect-
ability they were certain. The latter then told them that the
candidate was, or had been, an advocate of Puerto Rico's
eventual independence and must therefore be regarded as being un-American and a poor security risk. Since a large percentage of Muñoz' following at the upper level was or had
once been in favor of independence, since the F.B.I. investigators could not be expected to understand that such sentiments did not necessarily mean that they were anti-American,
and since it did not seem to be clearly recognized that a large
number of independent countries and peoples were wholeheartedly on the side of the United States during the war,
that practice created a number of irritations, and some serious
obstacles. At the lowest political level, such use of the
F.B.I. seemed like a device for having Republicans appointed

to jobs in a government devoted to carrying out tasks and programs which were anathema to the Republicans.

Shortly before the 1944 election, which was to test Muñoz' real popular strength after four years of political domination through the slim margin that he had won in the legislature of 1940, the island's Republican opposition made its prize mistake, which proved also to be its dying gasp as a political force. Stocks of food had run perilously low; people were starving, and continued government relief was imperative. However, the funds earmarked directly for relief were running out; new funds were delayed through the opposition's political tricks. Confronted by that dilemma, and since one cannot stand idly by while people starve, the government began to use other funds which, according to the Republicans, could not legally be used for the purpose. In a grandiose gesture of righteous indignation, a Republican judge then ordered Tugwell's entire Executive Council, his cabinet, to be arrested and put into jail for contempt.

One suspects that the Puerto Rican people took the gesture with a hearty laugh; certainly, the cabinet members did not seem perturbed over their sudden acquisition of jail records. They telephoned their wives and asked them to come to the jail with playing cards, pajamas, possibly a spot or two of liquor, and above all with photographers. Certainly with photographers!

In commenting on the incident, Tugwell wrote: "Never in all my political experience have I seen a campaign document so effective as the picture of those commissioners looking out determinedly from behind the bars of La Princessa. To the *jíbaro* and *obrero* [worker] it was plain that the members of his government, all *Populares* but one, had suffered the humiliations of prison in order to protect his right to an income during unemployment. The whole effort of the *Populares* to redistribute social benefits in Puerto Rico was thus symbolized. It seemed not unlikely, after this incident, that the *Popular* victory might be so great as to be embarrassing. It was difficult to see how the *Coalición* could win anywhere at all."

As predicted, the election proved a clean sweep for Muñoz' party. In Tugwell's words, the Coalitionists "ended not only with an infinitesimal representation in the legislature but also without any adequate explanation of their political insanity. They were completely bankrupt."

There is room for doubt, however, whether, as Tugwell seemed to think, the foolish action of a judge and the picture of a cabinet in jail had much to do with the landslide. In 1940, Muñoz had said to the electorate: "Lend me your votes— only once, unless you like what we do with them." During the succeeding four years he had done many dramatic things with those votes and for the voters. Every election since then has been a landslide for him and his party. The Puerto Ricans have loaned him their votes again and again, in ever-increasing numbers. Evidently they did and do like what he has done with them. In view of that tremendous and deep-rooted human reality, shallow, mechanistic interpretations of election results seem out of place.

Nevertheless, it is interesting to note that the judge who in 1944 had given the *coup de grâce* to his party's hopes by jailing the entire cabinet was Marcelino Romany, who was later, in 1952, to win international fame by breaking the tensions of the Republican convention in Chicago with his earnest parliamentary efforts.

Tugwell's book is full of accounts of how his enemies in Congress, ably abetted by Puerto Rico's reactionaries, tried their best at all times to get at him by hindering and embarrassing the Puerto Rican program. That was important then; it is no longer important now, when Congress has co-operated so wholeheartedly in the program's political evolution. Indeed, the opposition of those days, by a Congressional minority, seems on the whole to have worked out for the benefit of Puerto Rico in that it served to bring the island's plight to the attention of Congressmen. Two Congressional committees visited Puerto Rico in a spirit of bitter hostility to Tugwell; once there, their members were awed by the spectacle of all but universal poverty, of sick, suffering people and reeking slums. Muñoz gave them eloquent expositions on the problems to be solved, the many difficulties encountered, and the goals to be achieved.

One letter, which is today a historic document in Puerto Rico, attests to the Congressional education regarding the island. Senator Robert A. Taft had gone to the island as a member of a committee presumably hostile to Tugwell. As a man of real integrity, he eventually gave the Puerto Rican program what was—considering its source—its greatest boost.

The glass factory, designed, financed, and owned by the Puerto Rican government, was being built during Taft's visit, but was having trouble under wartime regulations in obtaining machinery from the continent. The island's super-patriotic Republicans pointed it out to him as one more instance of state socialism, of government's going into the manufacturing business. So well had he come to realize Puerto Rico's desperate needs, however, that he surprised everybody by coming out strongly in favor of the project. On his return to Washington, on March 12, 1943, he wrote a letter to Donald M. Nelson, Chairman of the War Production Board.

DEAR MR. NELSON:

I understand that the Puerto Rico Glass Corporation, in part financed by the government-owned Puerto Rico Development Company, has applied for priorities on glassmaking machinery.

I have just been in Puerto Rico with the Subcommittee of the Senate Territories Committee, investigating social and economic conditions there. In view of the number of people crowded into a small island, I believe that the only possibility of a decent standard of living lies in the industrialization of the island. The construction of a glass factory will not only give employment to many who would otherwise be out of employment, but it will make it possible to continue other industries now shut down for lack of glass containers and cans. The rum industry and the canning industry must have some assistance, and glass containers can no longer be shipped from the United States because of the shortage of shipping.

The situation in Puerto Rico is not like that in the United States because there is no war work to which the employees of these industries can turn. Furthermore, in view of the shortage of food, canning is essential to provide more food for the people themselves. I have never been very strong for government-supported industry, but the situation in Puerto Rico is such that I believe the government has a proper function in promoting the development of new industry.

I hope that every consideration will be given to the application of the Puerto Rico Glass Corporation.

Sincerely yours,
ROBERT A. TAFT

Tugwell resigned in 1946, in part, it must be said to his credit, because his continued presence as governor—in the face of the bitter Congressional opposition to him—proved embarrassing and harmful to Puerto Rico. It had been his hope to have a bill passed by Congress during his incumbency, under which the people of Puerto Rico could thereafter elect their own governor instead of having to put up with any more in the long line of appointed governors from outside the island. The bill, however, had no chance of passing at that time. He did persuade Truman to appoint a Puerto Rican as his successor. Jesús Piñero, a sugar planter who had long been an ardent supporter of Muñoz, became the island's first native governor.

Piñero had been Resident Commissioner in Washington, elected as such in 1944 to replace Bolívar Pagan. On his appointment to the governorship he was replaced in Congress by the able, astute, and energetic Antonio Fernós Isern, who had during the preceding four years done wonders as Puerto Rico's Commissioner of Health. Fernós managed to get a bill through Congress providing for the popular election of future governors.

In the election of 1948, Muñoz ran for the governorship. He promised no wonders in his campaign; he promised his people only increasing opportunity to struggle the long, stony, difficult uphill road on which they had started in 1941. Four other candidates ran against him; the island's entire press was solidly against him; his own *La Democracia* was long since dead, and he had no newspaper until the last few weeks of the campaign, when one was started by his friends. The opposition controlled the entire press and made full use of the radio facilities for a ceaseless, vituperative campaign, some of it slanderous and aimed directly at Muñoz in person. When the returns were in it was found that, as one of five competing candidates, he had won over 60 per cent of the total vote.

Unmistakably he had another mandate from the people.

His inaugural parade and ceremony, on January 2, 1949, was the greatest, most enthusiastic celebration in Puerto Rico's history.

CHAPTER XII

Resources and the Physical Base

THE SMALLEST and most easterly of the Greater Antilles, about as large as Long Island, New York, Puerto Rico rises abruptly out of the sea. There are no surrounding banks and shallows to provide areas for commercial fishing. The Milwaukee Deep, immediately north of the island, is one of the deepest parts of the Atlantic Ocean.

Puerto Rico consists of an interior complex of mountain ranges, which rise to a maximum height of nearly 4,500 feet above sea level, surrounded by a fertile coastal plain. The *jíbaros* live in the mountains, growing coffee, tobacco, and subsistence crops. They are poor but prolific, harassed by life, but stubbornly independent in their thinking. The flat lands of the coastal plain can be worked by heavy machinery and support industrialized agriculture devoted largely to the production of sugar cane. Its thousands of workers are not farmers; they are wage earners in what was once a vast rural sweatshop.

About 1,500 miles southeast of New York, a thousand miles from Miami, and five hundred from Caracas, Venezuela, the island lies in the north tropical zone, at eighteen degrees north latitude. It is some 1,200 miles north of the equator and four hundred south of the Tropic of Cancer. Some academic geographers, whose number is now happily decreasing, maintain that the supposedly debilitating influence of the tropical climate will forever prevent Puerto Rico from amounting to much. The island's history since 1941 is an eloquent refutation of that kind of argument.

Enthusiasts like to describe Puerto Rico as a tropical island with a climate which they call "eternal spring." As elsewhere in the tropics, temperatures are more or less uniform throughout the year and usually vary more between night and day than between summer and winter. In San Juan, where most tourists and visitors make their headquarters, the difference in average temperature between summer and winter is only 5.7 degrees; the highest ever recorded is ninety-four degrees, the lowest, sixty-two. For the island as a whole, the greatest extremes ever recorded by official thermometers are a remarkable low of thirty-nine degrees in the mountains and an equally remarkable—to Puerto Ricans, though not to residents of Kansas City or Minneapolis—high of 103 degrees on the south coast. During the summer of 1936 I had to make occasional trips to Washington but was always glad to return to the Puerto Rican tropics for the purpose of cooling off. And if one can cool off in summer by moving to San Juan from almost any point in the continental United States east of the Rocky Mountains, one can cool off still more by moving from San Juan to the mountains, where, at three thousand feet elevation and over, temperatures are some ten degrees lower than on the coast. For such reasons, and because the mountain scenery is breathtaking and the mountain people are good people in the word's finest sense, the mountainous interior may one of these days become an important resort region.

The springlike climate is conditioned by the trade winds which blow steadily from the northeast and bring the rains. The topography conditions the distribution of those rains. Having crossed the northern coastal plain, the trade winds hit the central mountains and are forced to rise. In rising, they cool off, and in cooling, they must drop a large share of the moisture which they had previously picked up from the ocean and which now waters the sugar estates on the northern plain. The south coastal strip lies in the rain shadow. There the winds descend from the mountains. In descending, they warm up and usually absorb moisture from the ground instead of dropping it. For that reason, the south coast is relatively arid.

San Juan has a total annual rainfall of about sixty-five inches, an average of 214 days of the year with rain, but only five days per year without sunshine. The rains come in quick tropical showers, cool off the air and the ground, and then give way almost instantaneously to clear skies and pleasant sun. Visible from San Juan in the southeast is the mountain El Yunque in the Trujillo range, on which the National Forest Service administers one of the world's most famous examples of tropical rain forest. El Yunque is seldom free from its cap of clouds, and seldom does a summer day go by without torrential rains. The total annual rainfall there, only some twenty-two miles from San Juan, is nearly two hundred inches. The island's southwest, on the other hand, is semi-desert, with an annual rainfall of thirty inches or less.

Along the north coast, the botanically minded traveler sees vast acreages of sugar, grown without irrigation, as well as mangroves growing in swamps. In El Yunque National Forest he sees giant tropical tree ferns, mosses, orchids, and the great variety of trees and other forms of vegetation which have given El Yunque the name of being the most diversified of all the world's tropical rain forests. In the southwest he sees cacti growing in arid soil, but also vast acreages of sugar cane —grown, however, with the help of irrigation.

In all parts of the island, the visitor also sees thousands on thousands of small houses, little shacks, here and there built of concrete but more often patched together from old pieces of wood, tin, and rags. Those houses are small, not only because of the people's poverty, but also because of the lavishness of their climate. For the Puerto Rican poor live outdoors; they have most of their social life near the little country store, the *colmado* down the road, or on the *bateys* in front of their homes. A man's house is a convenient place in which to keep his *viejita*, his little old woman, and his children—a place of headquarters for his family, and only occasionally a shelter against inclement weather.

But, if it is patched together from scraps of debris, as are so many homes of the island's poor, this house is of little use when the weather really becomes inclement—which means when the hurricanes blow. Then he and his family crawl into the little shelter that he has built outside, a small, low affair, sometimes built of lumber and corrugated iron, but often of sticks, palm thatch, and sod, resembling an army pup tent in shape and not much larger in size.

Hurricanes, with their terrible destruction, are constantly on the minds of all Puerto Ricans and are named—probably in rebuke—after the saints on whose days they occur. So, if one mentions San Felipe, a Puerto Rican will not think of a man who was born in 1233, was so humble that he hid when the Cardinals wanted to make him Pope, and showed the gift of tongues at the Council of Lyons. Instead, his mind will automatically turn to the terror of 1928, when a wind named San Felipe blew down the coffee trees and their shade trees, wrecked thousands of houses, and killed a number of people. The ever-present danger of hurricanes is behind much of the government's present preoccupation with concrete houses, which are not only far more sanitary than are the old patch-work affairs, but also stand up under the wind and don't have themselves scattered all over the island. As standards of living improve, and therefore also the quality of the island's housing, as the Planning Board continues to make progress in its effort to have all of Puerto Rico's new construction made hurricane-proof, the personal and economic danger from high winds will decrease materially.

During the fifty-five years from 1899 to 1954 the island has experienced only three destructive hurricanes, but at least twice as many warnings which brought on feverish activity of preparation. The unforgettable sound of an approaching hurricane, in Puerto Rican cities, is the sound of hammering, as all other activities are dropped and men by the hundreds nail boards in front of their windows to keep them from being blown in. During the Tugwell regime, when German submarines virtually cut Puerto Rico off from the mainland, there was an all-pervading fear of a possible hurricane which would have created unprecedented destruction by wrecking houses at a time when lumber, nails, and other materials for post-wind reconstruction were not available.

Two anecdotes show the Puerto Ricans' ubiquitous awareness of potential hurricanes. In 1934 a continental lady artist went to the island to paint. She spent her first day in San Juan, painting a picturesque corner of Fort San Cristóbal, with some colorful signal flags flying. That afternoon, when she returned to her lodgings, she showed the painting to her hostess, who spotted two red signal flags with black squares in the middle, one hung above the other.

"Did you really see those flags?" asked the hostess.

"Oh, yes. They were there. Pretty, aren't they?"

"My God! That's the warning signal for hurricanes!" She telephoned the Weather Bureau, and, sure enough, the flags were flying and a great wind—which didn't materialize after all—was expected.

When Muñoz was a Liberal party senator, living in the Condado section, his son, Luisito, was a teen-ager who occasionally got into mischief with other teen-agers. One day as the boy's mother sat in her living room, Luisito dashed in with two or three of his friends, all of them obviously frightened, and ran upstairs to hide under beds. They were followed by an irate policeman, waving a piece of paper. It seemed

that the boys had amused themselves by tacking signs on all
the trees and light posts of a near-by square saying, "Hurricane due at six o'clock tonight!" It seemed also that this was
a major crime, since the neighborhood residents were frantically telephoning the Weather Bureau for confirmation or
denial of the terrible news.

The policeman was evidently a nice enough fellow and said
that he would refrain from arresting the youngsters if they
would do something to deny their false report and to assuage
the agitated feelings of local citizens. So the boys got to work
again and painted another batch of signs which they tacked
up on the square. Those signs read: "Hurricane postponed
because of lack of wind!"

If a number of scholars are pessimistic about Puerto Rico's
chances for raising standards of living, because the tropical
climate is supposed to rob Puerto Ricans of their energy, they
grow even more pessimistic when they study the island's
natural resources. They seem to believe that any society's
chances for the good life depend directly on the abundance
and diversity of those resources, found within that society's
borders. There is something to what they say, but when they
come to Puerto Rico they seem to forget that the Commonwealth is an integral part of a vastly greater society, lavishly
supplied with resources. Forgetting or ignoring that fact, they
examine the island's resources alone and find that it suffers
from a truly dramatic paucity of such materials as metals,
fuels, timber, and even arable soils.

The U.S. Soil Conservation Service, as quoted by Harvey
Perloff in his book *Puerto Rico's Economic Future*, had
pointed out that "only some 845,000 acres out of the island
total of about 2,103,000 acres of soil areas are well adapted to
a permanent agriculture and that most of this land requires
complex or intensive soil conservation practices if production

is to be sustained." Perloff goes on to say that, as of 1949, about 1,000,000 acres were actually in crops, and therefore Puerto Rico, in mid-1949, had 2.2 persons for every acre of tillable soil. "This compares with about three arable acres *per person* in the United States—a highly industrialized country with much less dependence on agriculture."

It has in recent years been fashionable among demographers to claim that—especially in a predominantly agrarian society—2½ acres of arable land per person (and not 2½ persons per acre) is the *minimum* required for the creation and maintenance of decent standards of living.

The dense forests which the early Spaniards found in Puerto Rico's interior have been cut down long ago; there are no commercial stands of timber.

There are no fuels suited for industrial development. There is neither coal nor oil that anybody knows about. To be sure, the mangrove swamps and the prunings of the shade trees in the coffee regions have long sustained a primitive hand industry devoted to making charcoal for home use, but that is socially wasteful and worthless as a base for industrial expansion. On the other hand, falling water that can be harnessed to produce electric power *is* available; the Puerto Rican government, since about 1936, has done everything within its limited means to develop that important resource as a base for industrialization and rural electrification.

Perloff lists the mineral resources. There are scattered deposits of silica sands suitable for the manufacture of glass products, and there are adequate deposits of limestone suitable for manufacturing cement and fertilizers. There is also pottery clay. It will be remembered that the limestone began to be utilized in the PRRA days for manufacturing the cement that has played so tremendous a part in the island's modern building boom, and that the new government, during the Tugwell regime, pounced on the glass sands and the clays for the desperate, immediate creation of new industries which staved off impending disaster.

There are some small known deposits of manganese, of iron ore, and of copper, lead, zinc, and gold. The manganese has been mined in a small way in the past, and the iron ore was mined and exported for a year or two, in what was—as things go in the world—a small and insignificant operation; for the rest of the mineral resources there seemed, and seems, to be no economic future at all.

Whatever other mineral resources are known today, or are being sought in a program of reconstruction that cannot afford to overlook a single bet, are probably insignificant from the industrial and economic point of view.

The relatively small space and the paucity of natural resources form parts of the so-called population problem which seems to haunt almost everybody who has anything at all to do with Puerto Rico. Many otherwise good men permit themselves to be frightened by the facts that Puerto Rico today has a total population of 2,300,000 people, that its overall density of over 650 per square mile is the world's highest for a predominantly agricultural country, and that its birth rate is so high that demographers call it explosive. To be sure, as discussed in a later chapter, the birth rate has in recent years turned the corner and is now dropping rapidly, while migration to the continental United States is doing much to relieve the pressure on the island; it is nevertheless also true that at present Puerto Rico's growth of population makes it necessary for the island's planners and executives to create some 18,000 new jobs every year to keep pace with the multiplication of Puerto Ricans. The figure grows smaller annually, but Perloff is still correct in saying that Puerto Rico is "in an Alice in Wonderland situation in which one has to run very fast in order merely to stand still."

In his introduction to Perloff's book, Jaime Benítez, chancellor of the university, wrote:

"The population of Puerto Rico is over six hundred persons per square mile, fifteen times greater than that of the United States. Population pressure in the United States would begin to compare with that of Puerto Rico if all the people of the world—over two billion men, women, and children—landed there overnight and if, by the same nocturnal magic, all available mineral resources were eliminated, heavy industry disappeared, and agriculture became the main source of employment. I do not say that mainland ingenuity would be incapable of solving such a riddle. The solution might be so adequate and audacious as to keep under control unemployment, illiteracy, and disease and at the same time foster production, efficiency, and democracy.

"In their own microcosm the Puerto Rican people and their leaders are trying to carry out a comparable task. And it is a task which is both worth while and exhausting."

Benítez' argument is dramatic and applies in part to conditions also found in Asia and other parts of the modern world. Before too many years, however, considering the interrelated nature of things, it will sound as though somebody had correctly said that the United States would be in a hell of a shape if the entire country had the same density of population that is found on Manhattan Island.

Today it is precisely the overwhelming demands made by 2,300,000 people which create the need for Puerto Rico's astonishing upward spiral—and the energies of those people which energize the spiral. A comfortable 200,000 people, or half a million, could not create the island's modern progress because they would have no need for it in the first place and would lack the essential labor force in the second.

In view of the paucity of natural resources, agriculture, no matter how limited the island's arable soils, must remain the principal foundation for Puerto Rico's economy. And, despite all modern effort at the diversification of crops, sugar cane, grown on the flat coastal lands where machinery can be used to multiply the efforts of men, will for a long time remain the island's main crop, the mainstay of the entire economic structure. It has many advantages over other crops, aside from the facts that it has been thoroughly established through the investment of millions of dollars and that any rapid change would therefore create chaos. Sugar cane yields a high return per acre, which is all the more important in a crowded society where every square foot of available land should somehow be made to yield maximum profits. It requires much labor per acre, which is equally important in a society which works energetically to find or create gainful employment for every one of its employables. It recovers rapidly from hurricane damage. It has a reasonably steady market which can be expected to grow as mainland populations grow and their food habits change toward ever more candy bars and soda pops. It can compete with other areas in that market, at least under existing political conditions.

No crop is any better than are the conditions under which it is marketed. Puerto Rican sugar finds a ready market in the United States because the Commonwealth remains within the American tariff structure and does not have to pay duties on its shipments to the States. If Puerto Rico were an independent nation, if it so had to pay duty on its sugar, even on a most-favored-nation basis, the island could not compete with Cuba in the American market, and the chances are that much of the Puerto Rican sugar industry would go bankrupt. Favored as Puerto Rico seems to be as a sugar producer, Cuba is even more favored. Cuban production costs are lower than are those in Puerto Rico; the difference is made up by the fact that Cuban sugar pays duty on shipment to the United States.

Cuba's soils are richer than are those of Puerto Rico, requiring less fertilization; they are more friable, more easily worked by machinery. Because Cuba does not have a central mountain chain, its rainfall is more evenly distributed than is that of Puerto Rico; Cuba does not need to irrigate at considerable expense for the purpose of producing cane in any of its various locations. With no interior mountain system, Cuba's flat sugar lands are much larger in contiguous extent than are Puerto Rico's and can so be worked all the more efficiently by modern industrial methods. Cuba has a railroad instead of a mountain chain running down the middle of the island, with branches reaching out to the coast; such a transportation system is more efficient than is Puerto Rico's, which runs around the outside of the island, with winding, perilous roads crossing the mountains here and there. Cuba, too, draws on seasonal labor from Haiti, Jamaica, and the Bahamas at harvest time, importing thousands of workers when the cane is ready to be cut and returning them to their homes when the job is done, to last out the seven months' dead season on somebody else's relief. Crowded Puerto Rico can make no such happy agreement but must pay its sugar workers enough to keep them alive, at home, the entire year.

It is possible that those conditions have something to do with the fact that the advocates of Puerto Rico's independence have so many well-wishers in Cuba, just as the independence of the Philippine Islands was at one time endorsed by the U.S. farm lobby, which wanted to protect its beet-sugar holdings against undue competition from tropical cane. Since the economics of independence would seriously handicap, if not bankrupt, Puerto Rico's sugar industry in competition with Cuba's for the American market, Cuba might expect to inherit Puerto Rico's share of the total American sugar quota in the event that the other island should achieve national sovereignty.

So exclusively has Puerto Rico's development been based on sugar cane since the turn of the century that all other crops have become precarious and more or less sick in the economic sense.

Up in the mountains, at the western end, is the island's great coffee region. Coffee, formerly the traditionally Puerto Rican crop, produced almost entirely by Puerto Ricans with no in- flux of absentee capital, enjoyed relatively high prosperity until World War I. Then, beset by hurricanes and by world economic changes over which the Puerto Ricans had no con- trol, it withered away in economic importance. The San Felipe hurricane of 1928 seemed to sound its death knell. After 1940, however, under the government's carefully planned promotional activities, which included the organiza- tion of co-operatives and the development of improved meth- ods of production and marketing, it began to come back, in the beginning for supplying the insular market of over two million Puerto Ricans who regard coffee as their traditional and indispensable drink. In 1951, when for some unexplained reason the price of coffee virtually doubled overnight in all the American chain stores, Puerto Rico was in the happy position of having an exportable surplus of coffee as well as of bananas, the trees of which, together with those of moun- tain oranges, are widely used for shading the coffee trees.

That summer, Puerto Rico's Commissioner of Agriculture, Ramón Colon Torres, invited me on a three-day tour of the island for the purpose of showing me something of agricul- tural problems and progress. We stopped for lunch at the government's seed-producing station near Isabela and heard the disturbing news over the radio that a hurricane had been spotted some three hundred miles south, that it was headed straight for Puerto Rico, and that it would probably hit us the following noon. In the evening we were on the south coast, prepared to spend the night at the home of the manager of one of the government's sugar plantations, but at ten P.M. Colon could stand the strain no longer.

"Earl," he said, "I have to call off the rest of the trip. I must get back to San Juan."

We drove in his Packard as fast as traffic would permit, plunging up into the mountains and across them toward

Caguas, slewing around great mountain curves, pelted by fierce gusts of rain and advance winds. The Commissioner of Agriculture was almost crying.

"My God," he said, "what a country! For the first time in thirty-five years we have an exportable surplus of coffee. We have a bumper crop and the markets are just right. Twenty million dollars worth of coffee, and another twenty million dollars worth of bananas. Forty million dollars for the Puerto Rican economy after all these years of hard and patient labor and suffering and bankruptcy and near-starvation in the coffee regions. Forty million dollars—and one goddamn wind comes along and blows it all to hell!"

We arrived in San Juan some time after midnight and the hammers were pounding everywhere, and the next morning my wife and I went to the barroom of the Condado Beach Hotel—which, with all its windows boarded up, was as good a place as any in which to await a hurricane. But Puerto Rico was lucky that summer. The hurricane missed the island, veered toward the west and caused terrible destruction in Jamaica and Yucatán, leaving Puerto Rico its bumper crop of coffee and bananas.

Farther east in the mountain areas, near the city of Barranquitas, is the tobacco district, where, as in sugar, absentee capital established itself early in the American regime. Here, too, is a great region for subsistence farming, where country people, working in the sugar fields, can grow a little to eat to keep them alive during the long dead season. From that district, daily during the cane-cutting season, men stream by the thousands into the fertile Caguas Valley to the east to harvest the cane and return nights to their little mountain homes.

Rafael Picó in his excellent *Puerto Rico's Geographic Region*, lists citrus fruits, grown between the sugar lands of the north coast and the mountains, as among the important Puerto

Rican crops. These, however, have now all but disappeared
from the scene, partly because of competition from Florida,
and partly because during the war no ships were available for
shipping grapefruit to the continent, causing the abandonment of large plantations. But pineapples are rapidly replacing citrus fruits in economic importance. Properly treated,
they yield a gross of about three times as many dollars per
acre as does sugar cane. Canning pineapples and freezing
their juice are among the new industries that modern Puerto
Rico has created; they are still small as industries go and when
compared with Hawaii, but they represent a significant
beginning.

As pointed out earlier, less than half of the island's total
area is in productive use; the rest is eroded or covered with
scrub forests and is too steep to be planted. But a land as
heavily populated as is Puerto Rico cannot afford, consciously,
to leave a single half acre idle and unproductive.

The frontier of crowded Puerto Rico consists of its unproductive lands, for which some form of economic utility
must be found. That need has given rise to numerous surveys
of its soil, geology, and present land use, and to many bold
schemes and experimental projects. Eroded lands, for instance, may be brought back through the planting of proper
grasses, which, in turn, may support dairy cows, granting
proper safeguards against overgrazing to prevent a recurrence of erosion—but only after somebody has invested considerable capital in the construction of dairies and other plants
for handling milk and milk products.

Hilltops covered by scrub forests, which today yield a
revenue only to the moonshiners who there distill their illicit
rum, may perhaps someday yield more legitimate economic
fruits by being planted to bay trees, the leaves of which are
distilled into bay rum.

Every possibility for expanding the island's agriculture is
considered by Puerto Rico's modern planners and technicians,

who must be constantly on the lookout for anything and everything that may serve the needs of a society with rising standards of living. Many things are tried; some succeed, but more fail in the end. Developmental work done by the PRERA had once made vanilla a paying crop. It did well until some years after World War II, when it could no longer compete with vanilla from Mexico, with its lower wages. Citron was a profitable crop during World War II and for some years thereafter. However, when Sicily, after the war, again began to export citron, Puerto Rico's markets dried up because of higher production costs. Catesby Jones is at present nursing along, in Puerto Rico, some clones of pepper which he had previously imported from the East Indies. Pepper is the most recent of the Asian spices to be introduced in the New World. It promises to become an enormously profitable crop in Puerto Rico, paying gross returns which range from $200 per acre at the lowest recorded price of pepper in the American market, to somewhere near $6,000 at current prices.

The possibilities and occasional actualities of failure, however, can be no deterrent. An effort must be made to make every square foot of Puerto Rican land productive in one way or another, be it with high economic yields or low. And that requires careful planning, carefully integrated, and patient development and research.

Sugar is successful in Puerto Rico in part because it is an industrialized crop. The basic problem of economic improvement is not that of agriculture *versus* industry, but agriculture *plus* industry. And in dealing with that problem, despite the paucity of its natural resources and precisely as in the case of sugar, Puerto Rico enjoys one resource of tremendous importance. That is the political status under which the Commonwealth forms part of the over-all American economy.

Within the American economic structure, Puerto Rico can draw on the common fund of money, capital, and credit. American capital invested on the island today, to take advantage of low-cost power, or momentary government concessions to new capital, or momentarily low—but rising—wages, or growing local markets, or swelling industrial raw materials as Puerto Rico improves its production, or federal exemption of income tax on monies earned in Puerto Rico, is no more exported from the United States than is New York or New Jersey capital which for one reason or another is invested in the Tennessee Valley, or Texas, or Georgia. And American capital is a great stimulant. As it finds local conditions to its liking, as it creates new wages, new profits, new savings, it also creates a swelling fund of local capital which begins in turn to be invested in the Puerto Rican effort and to reduce the percentage predominance of outside capital.

Similarly, manufactured goods produced in Puerto Rico are no more exported when they are shipped to the States for sale than is Milwaukee beer when it is shipped to New York or San Francisco and distributed throughout the United States with the help of national advertising.

Within our economic structure, for instance—to quote an extreme example which has nothing to do with such physical resources as iron ore—Puerto Rico can today dream of someday creating a great free harbor at San Juan, humming with assembly plants which receive sheet iron, motors, mudguards, bolts, gears, and other parts of machinery in the knocked-down state from the mainland, and assemble them into autobiles, tractors, and locomotives for distribution to a rapidly growing Latin American market.

Hundreds of new industries have been established in Puerto Rico since the government, in 1948, decided to make an energetic bid for U.S. capital for that purpose, offering such temporary inducements as tax exemption and co-operation from the Puerto Rican government. Scores more are being established every year. They would not, could not, be established if Puerto Rico were not an integral part of the American economic structure.

Those hard and stubborn facts did much to change Muñoz'
thinking about independence, and do much every year to
make political independence apart from the United States
economically less desirable. To be sure, there is now a new
Independence party on the island which seems to hope, someday, to persuade Washington to give Puerto Rico some kind
of national sovereignty, and which garners a considerable
share of the minority votes at election time. Nobody can even
guess, however, how many of its members actually want
Puerto Rico's independence, or would want it if they were
suddenly confronted with its imminent possibility and the
concomitant fact that many existing industries would have
to close shop on the achievement of independence. Nobody
knows how many belong to the Independence party merely
because they want to register a protest vote which they don't
want to give to the Republicans. Some seem to switch to the
Independence party from the Popular-Democratic because
they think that their rents should be lower than they are in
government housing, or their pay higher than it is on government projects, or their hours shorter, or because Muñoz didn't
give them the jobs to which they feel themselves entitled.

Whatever the feeling, whatever the changing voting
strength of the Independence party, it is undeniably true
that the more Puerto Rico progresses in its present remarkable upward spiral within the American scheme of things, the
more difficult it will be to achieve national sovereignty, and
the more disastrous such sovereignty may well prove *if*
achieved.

CHAPTER XIII

Neither Radical nor Conservative

D URING THE TUGWELL REGIME Puerto Rico's leaders had often groped fearfully in the dark, their programs shaped by the past but not yet tailored to the future. They knew that they had to form a kind of government new to Puerto Rico, one that would shake off the colonial psychology and strike out boldly for itself even though Puerto Rico was still technically a colony. With Tugwell's help, they did a brilliant job. They knew that they had to begin to industrialize, regardless of whether or not private capital was forthcoming for the task. They did the best they could under the circumstances, with government capital, but had no idea whether or not it would work through the years to come. They knew that they had to break the political hold of the sugar industry and at the same time divide up the great estates—or at least the profits accruing therefrom. Neither doctrinaire knowledge nor successful precedent gave them an adequate formula for accomplishing this. They invented their own formula, translated it into law, began energetically to implement it, and prayed to heaven it would work. They had precedents for the manners in which they tackled such problems as social legislation, transportation, industrial and agricultural credit, the generation and distribution of electric

227

power, but they still did not know whether those manners of handling things would work in Puerto Rico.

If nothing else, they had to worry about the fact that Puerto Rico was still a colony, still ruled by a governor with veto power, appointed by Washington, and was still handicapped by the fact that what one governor did, the next could undo. The storm against Tugwell that had raged in Congress, plus the fact that newspapers on the mainland ran occasional articles claiming that the Puerto Rican program was pure socialism, were ominous signs. Washington still had the power, and how did the men of the Popular Democratic party know that Washington would not send them, as Tugwell's successor, a governor ready to undo everything the *Populares* had accomplished, so collapsing the structure of their work like a house of cards? Fortunately, they were successful in persuading Washington to appoint Jesús Piñero to succeed Tugwell, the first Puerto Rican to be the island's governor, an old friend of Muñoz', and one who was wholeheartedly in favor of the latter's program; a Puerto Rican of the opposite side, a political opponent of Muñoz', would have been worse than almost any governor from the mainland who could be imagined.

The interim of Piñero's regime, from 1946 to 1948—until the time when the island was at long last able to elect its own governor and chose Muñoz Marín—was devoted in part to the task of revising old policies and shaping new ones for the long pull of the future. It was now necessary to take stock, to develop an over-all social, political, and economic philosophy, a creed to live by which would be no less American for being essentially Puerto Rican, growing out of the island's needs. Even that was difficult in a colony unused to such things. All of the island's former official creeds had been tailored variously in Madrid or Washington.

The first, "socialist" stage of industrialization through government investment and management could not long endure within the scheme of things American. Not only was it counter to American mores, but it tended to cut the island off from many financial resources which might otherwise be available. It was plainly evident, moreover, that the Puerto Rican government would not be able, through socialism, to keep pace with the rising tide of demands made upon it. Budgets were higher than ever before, but the demands on those budgets grew more rapidly than did the monies available. More money than had ever been imagined during the days of sugar colonialism was needed for education, public health, public services of various other kinds, public works, communications, and the like. The growth of population alone made it apparent that a government which created new industries out of its own limited funds would never have sufficient capital available to come anywhere near the mounting need for ever more new industries.

As a part of the United States, Puerto Rico therefore wanted its share of private capital that was piling up in the United States, ready and eager to invest itself in productive American enterprises. Much of the former indignant preoccupation against the absentee ownership of means of production began to give way to the realization that absentee *monopoly* rather than absentee ownership had been the great curse ten years previously. The new economy could be healthy even though financed largely, in the beginning, by absentee capital—as the early development of the United States had been financed largely by British capital and guided in its technical phases by British skills. The development of such an economy would undoubtedly raise wages and standards of living, which was the first goal of the Puerto Rican government.

A new policy was therefore adopted in 1948, under which the government could offer certain inducements to attract new capital for investment in the Puerto Rican effort, including tax exemption for some years and various kinds of technical and social co-operation and help. This worked so well, and was so much more effective than had been the former stage of industrialization under government ownership and management, that the government eventually, in 1950, sold its own factories for some $10,000,000 to the island's leading industrialist. This was Luis Ferré, whose family had long managed a large iron works in Ponce, making and repairing machinery for the sugar industry. The sale of the factories to one man, and the most powerful Puerto Rican industrialist at that, naturally drew a certain amount of criticism. However, the government had found no other buyers, either in Puerto Rico or in the mainland United States. Ferré did have the advantage of being a Puerto Rican rather than an absentee capitalist, and the money received through the sale could well be used elsewhere, through government investment, to prime the pump and further the over-all productive effort.

As happens everywhere today, when underdeveloped countries begin to develop themselves economically, the new government policies grow directly out of the needs and circumstances of the people, as interpreted by their leaders—not out of established doctrine of any kind. As Muñoz repeated again and again, they were "neither radical nor conservative"; they were merely realistic. The task of providing a badly needed, integrated philosophical framework for the guidance and unification of the island's many new departures in its life, for the information and guidance of continental Congressmen, editors, and potential investors in the Puerto Rican effort, became one of the greatest of many tasks assumed by Muñoz Marín after he had become the island's first elected governor.

In his first inaugural speech, on January 2, 1949, he dealt at some length with the problem of Puerto Rico's ultimate political status. But, as always, he came back to the place of status in the general scheme of things. "A political status, of course, does not exist in an economic vacuum. Thinking on a political status cannot be developed in a vacuum of economic or cultural thought. Ways of living and working; the forward-looking habits in a community; the religious vision; the land and its crops, and the factories, and the tools, and the techniques, and the raising of children, and the cultivation of the understanding, and science, and art, and recreation, and health habits, and sustenance, and clothes, and sheltering roof, and justice, and light, and generosity, and serenity, all these together, and their political status, and more, are the life of a people. The manner of expressing all these together in harmony is the ideal of life of a people. And the spontaneity and dynamism with which they are expressed constitute the people's integral liberty.

"Of course, certain aspects of integral liberty are closely related to the possibility or impossibility of other aspects. If a community does not develop an economy which is founded, or has hopes of being founded, on a victorious productive effort, it will see other forms of its life and liberty impeded, or decayed, or destroyed. From this comes our great dedication, which we should further strengthen on this day, to the task of constantly increasing production in Puerto Rico—more rapidly than the growth of population; more rapidly still to absorb unemployment; more rapidly still to go on raising the standard of living and security; and more rapidly still so that the present imperative need for aid shall not become permanent."

His political enemies, and especially Bishop McManus of Ponce, who talked against him during the 1952 gubernatorial campaign, have accused him repeatedly of being an arrant materialist, laboring for things of the stomach as against the soul—a charge which caused Padín to write me that "it is easy to say that man does not live by bread alone when one's belly is full of bread." In reply, Muñoz said in his first inaugural speech: "It can be said that people should not place high things of the spirit in balance with material things. I not only admit this, but energetically affirm it; they should not. But it is not a mere material convenience to be free from want, to have paths of hope that liberate from hopelessness; and, above all, the narrow national concept is not a high value of the human spirit in the times of anguish and creation in which we live. A people ought to be ready to make great material sacrifices in order to create an understanding of deep and clean human fraternity, which is a high ideal of the spirit; and to dissolve the hardness which permits it to contemplate insensibly the misery of others, which is a high ideal of the spirit; and to give root to attitudes that lead man to be more creative than acquisitive, which is a high ideal of the spirit; and to destroy bitterness of race, language, and culture, because to destroy them is a high ideal of the spirit."

In his first legislative message as governor, on February 23, 1949, Muñoz referred to the new spirit that his people had developed since 1940. He quoted an old adage: "If youth but knew and age but could," and pointed out that it no longer applied to Puerto Rico's society. ". . . At this moment in the life of Puerto Rico a miracle is taking place in its personality as a people which makes the adage turn out to be false. In taking over new powers after 450 years, the country feels old because of the abundance of those years, and it feels young and strong because of the powers it assumes."

He referred to the momentous political and economic implications of the island's new directions toward a more abundant life, and of the new demands that the island's people now made, not only on the conscience of all branches of the government, but on the "conscience which is well informed." "This country," he informed his legislators, his politicians, "does not need a government which is merely less bad than another; what it needs, and what from the eloquence of its action it has shown itself to deserve, is a government that is a good government. It does not expect perfection, for that is not a human possibility, but it does expect devotion.

". . . The people expect of you and me at this propitious moment the ultimate degree of the most enlightened good faith. The first condition of this good faith is the absence of personal motives in public life, arising as they may from greed or pride, ambition or vanity. . . . There is nothing more censurable in the eyes of the people than to take a public action or to assume a public attitude because of motives connected with careers or ambition or personal position. That is the great sin against the spirit of the people. This is true because it leads irrevocably to demagogy, which in its turn arouses irrational passions of group against group, be they economic, or racial, or religious, or groups which contribute one type of knowledge necessary to the work of government against groups which contribute another type. . . . Certain it is that the votes of the people do not authorize this, nor will they authorize it at any time the people be consulted. You know that personal interests play absolutely no part in my public life. And I can tell you that my life would be of no use to our people if day after day I were forced to be on the watch for demagogy."

In advising his politicians, who by habit and circumstances had their eye on the immediate vote, to plan for the future as well as the present, he said: "Apparent justice for a few which makes ineffectual the work of government for the many would not be justice. . . . In considering who are the many and who are the few, our vision must not be limited to groups existing in any given situation in this present year or in this present generation. It should be a vision of the people as a whole, who have continuity throughout the years and generations. . . . The future generations do not vote [today], but a democracy whose sole preoccupation was those who vote would be spiritually a very unsound democracy and could scarcely be transferred from one generation to another. On the other hand, we cannot allow the future to exercise despotic powers over the present, thus justifying all the harshness which our lives encounter in order to make excessively smooth the lives of those who have not yet been born."

The people demand that we act according to the dictates of a "conscience which is well informed." In the governor's preoccupation with that conscience which is well informed, in his constant, restless demand for information, lies one explanation for an outstanding characteristic of modern Puerto Rican life.

The systematic investigation of the island's social and economic problems and research leading to the clearer understanding of those problems are, of course, not new in Puerto Rico. They began during the nineteenth century with the establishment of the island's several cultural societies. However, during the Tugwell regime, and especially since the beginning of Muñoz' governorship, they have soared to such unprecedented importance that Puerto Rico is today a veritable researcher's paradise. The Planning Board carries on a large number of research projects designed for guidance toward specific actions; the university's Social Science Research Center and other units delve with varying degrees of judgment and success into a number of aspects and problems of the island's life; such special projects as the island-wide land-use survey conducted a few years ago under Dr. Clarence Jones of Northwestern University are calculated to produce the information on the basis of which Puerto Rico can develop a comprehensive and integrated land-use program and agricultural policy; the Economic Development Administration employs a staff of research experts to probe special economic problems; studies are being made, or have been completed, on such diverse matters as the educational system, patterns of living of Puerto Rican families, the structure of the Puerto Rican family, money and banking in Puerto Rico, the problems of the Puerto Ricans in New York, etc.

In that feverish activity, continental Americans have begun to play a new role in Puerto Rican affairs. Where they had once assumed most or all of the high policy-making positions in government and private enterprise, they are now hired by

the Puerto Ricans—whenever their specialized technical qualifications for a given task seem better than are those of available Puerto Ricans—for the purposes of research and fact-
finding. A new element in the island's life, they are popularly
referred to as either "The Vienna Boys' Choir" or "The Flying
Saucers," according to whether they indulge in hymns of
praise or in stratospheric pyrotechnic displays of unknown
origin and meaning. They vary greatly in their effectiveness,
but their total contribution to the Puerto Rican effort has
been and is enormous. Puerto Ricans acknowledge today that
they will forever be indebted to such men as Harvey Perloff of
the University of Chicago, Clarence Senior of Columbia University, Clarence Jones of Northwestern University, Simon
Rottenberg, Biagio di Venuti, Frederick Bartlett, Raymond
Crist—to mention only a few. All of these are men who have
been able to adjust to the Puerto Rican way of life and who
use people and the problems of people as their basic working
materials. Others, those who look down on the Puerto Ricans
and use scholarly abstractions as their basic working materials, don't work out as well. One of the latter Flying Saucers
is now locally famous for his statement that "the only trouble
with the Puerto Ricans is that they don't have a mathemati-
cally oriented culture," which led one Puerto Rican to ex-
claim: "Poor Muñoz, to have to depend on such people for
the implementation of his great philosophy."

Having talked about "an attitude, a norm, a way" in his
message of 1949, Muñoz discussed the task in hand. "The task
is production, justice, health, education, knowing how to live
together." He called for "more of the good life within reach
of more people every day, and education as to what is meant
by the good life. Good living does not always mean the good
life. Frequently it is far from being so. And the evil life of misery and insecurity is never the good life, although many good
people live that life. Bent as we are on production we must

ask ourselves: Production for what? Economic production for its own sake, without a life objective to guide it, only leads modern man to gluttony for worldly goods and to spiritual confusion. We produce so that people will have more of the good life, and here it is well to make clear whether we understand by this the mere multiplication in the consumption of trivial objects which titillate our appetite for acquisition, or whether we are to apply this term to the creative ideal of abolishing extreme poverty and broadening security and liberty in the lives of all men. I believe that in an economy based on high production there can be a good minimum standard of living for all as well as a high level for those who can legitimately attain it."

The essential and many differences between man as a *creative* being and man as a mere *acquisitive* being seem to have been major and important items in Muñoz' philosophical speculations in recent years—talked about constantly to small groups and large, to gatherings of voters and meetings of legislators, to friends in the privacy of his home and Puerto Ricans in all walks of life.

In that first legislative message as governor he laid down the essentials of an integrated program of development—essentials that were and are reflected in the attitudes of his government as an integrated body of legislators, administrators, experts, and specialists, working together for the common good rather than as a number of competing departments.

"The battle for the good life should not have all its emphasis placed on industrialization. Part of it must be placed on agriculture. In Puerto Rico there is still much land which is not in use, or is used ineffectually. Morally it is a serious offense to put obstacles in the path of using the soil in a community that has little of it, or to refuse to understand its better uses."

Of industrialization he said: "We shall continue giving ample opportunities to new industries and shall prefer that it be private initiative which establishes and controls them, as long as they live up to the civic responsibilities which should accompany every action which affects the lives of many."

There are many Americans today who believe that the current Puerto Rican industrial effort is based on cheap labor and may collapse when the cost of labor rises as standards of living are improved. To those, Muñoz said: "This government does not believe that wealth must paradoxically be founded on hunger. Wealth which arises from hunger is only for the few who obtain it. Starvation wages are not going to be an incentive for industrialization in Puerto Rico. It is well to say also that to wish to fix higher wages in an industry than that industry can pay is unconsciously to favor the proposition that there cease to be any wages whatever in that industry. Unemployment is a lower wage than the lowest of wages."

He addressed himself to those who seem to believe that Puerto Rican industrialization can be achieved only at the expense of labor in the mainland United States, with its higher wages and higher standards of living. After making it clear that most of the capital for new enterprises should, if possible, come from Puerto Rico itself, he said about continental capital invested on the island: ". . . It is not the policy of the government over which I preside to seek to close factories in the north in order to open them in Puerto Rico. Puerto Rico is part of the economy of the United States, and to close factories there does harm here just as to keep them from opening here does harm there. We are acting on the basis of the modern conviction that the more production there is anywhere in the world, the better it is for the whole world.

"The dynamic production of the United States," he said, "develops billions of dollars of new capital every year. What Puerto Rico is trying to bring about is that a relatively small amount of this new capital be invested in this particular part of the American economy which has so great a need for development in order to improve living conditions, achieve greater security, and so as not to depend for an unlimited period on federal aid. It must not be understood by this that we have no right to federal aid. All the states and territories have a right to it. But most of them do not depend on this aid for survival. We have a right to this aid and by means of it we shall achieve the right of not depending on it."

Enlarging on the matter of new American capital in a later message, on March 20, 1952, he said: "The economy of the United States generates more than twenty-five billion dollars of new capital each year. Out of this new and enormous capital wealth Puerto Rico is legitimately seeking an investment of thirty or forty million dollars of new capital a year—I repeat, of *new* capital, not transferred capital. The American citizens living in Puerto Rico comprise 1½ per cent of the population of the United States. And our industrial plan calls for less than one fifth of 1 per cent of the new capital generated, not without the modest collaboration of Puerto Rico, by the American economic system every year. It would seem clear that, as good citizens, we need have no fear that the industrial system of the United States is in danger of destruction at the hands of Puerto Rico."

He talked about health activities and education as being vitally necessary, in part for improving standards of living and in part for the purpose of giving impetus to economic expansion. For such ends, he implied, the government would need money—and ever more money. Where was that money to come from? It would come "from six sources, most of which are not at the present time being adequately used: (1) taxes which are collected; (2) taxes which are not collected; (3) federal aid; (4) the issuing of insular and municipal bonds; (5) economies effected by running the government more efficiently; (6) civic action in the community to solve its own problems. There has been only very slight action on the part of the community, except through the government, in creating on its own initiative a school, or a co-operative, or in helping to purify the waters of a river, or to provide a library, or to provide food and shelter in cases of extreme necessity."

With that statement he laid the foundations for a number of governmental activities. About uncollected taxes he said: "Probably the greatest source of the funds which we need lies in the taxes which according to law are owed and which are criminally evaded." He referred to the energetic efforts being made by his government to collect such taxes, and his preoccupation with the matter was to lead to a later complete "scientific reassessment" of all Puerto Rican properties—not by the usual rule of thumb methods, but by a rigid set of evaluated norms and standards, pioneered and developed by the island's Secretary of the Treasury, Sol Luis Descartes.

However, among the taxes which are not collected are those which are legally not paid because the government has specifically granted temporary tax exemption to certain new industries. While affirming that the tax holiday for those industries would stand, as originally agreed, until 1962, because "tax exemption is a contract that cannot be violated by subsequent legislation," he also said in his message of 1952 that "the system of tax exemptions for specific industries is not the best method, although it is the only one in the present circumstances that can produce results. It would be more desirable to develop a general taxation system that would stimulate economic expansion in agriculture and services as well as in industry, and that would apply to both new and already established enterprises. Under the economic conditions that still prevail in Puerto Rico it is not easy to develop such a system, due to the fact that low taxation is one of the main factors stimulating investment and expansion. This expansion, however, is impossible without preserving certain standards of health, education, security, and social services, which cannot be maintained on the proceeds of low taxes. This is the contradiction that we face, and our people deserve credit for the way that they are handling so serious a dilemma."

His third source of revenue, federal aid, was also dealt with at length in the message of 1952, partially in answer to the critics who still maintain that the modern Puerto Rican effort is sustained largely by a shower of federal gold. He said: "On the eve of the new constitutional relationship between Puerto Rico and the United States, it seems especially appropriate to look at bit into the future. Although the federal government spends a good deal of money in discharging its functions in the island, the sums it specifically contributes to aid Puerto Rico are relatively small. Two thirds of the federal funds spent in Puerto Rico are for the army, for the navy, and for payments to veterans. These expenditures are made, not with the purpose of aiding Puerto Rico, but because of the military needs and commitments of the whole Union. In Puerto Rico, as in each of the states, there are a number of federal agencies of a civil character whose funds are not in any way granted to or handled by the Government of Puerto Rico. Such agencies are the Post Office, the Office of Immigration, the Lighthouse Service, etc. Other agencies use federal appropriations jointly with Puerto Rican appropriations for road building, vocational education, certain health services, etc. These federal funds, properly termed grants-in-aid, do not exceed seventeen million dollars this year. Taxes on rum shipped to the United States may be properly described as Puerto Rican taxes levied on Puerto Rican industry. Customs duties, paid by Puerto Rican importers, go into the Treasury of Puerto Rico but they are not designed in all respects to serve the best interests of Puerto Rico. Sugar compensation payments are uniform throughout the American sugar industry and they are everywhere subject to restrictive conditions."

And then, having pointed out that "federal grants-in-aid are not the decisive factor in the economic struggle of our people," he began to discuss the possibility of soon contributing more than formerly to the Treasury of the United States. "A large factor [in the economic struggle] is that Puerto Rico is a part of the American Union and does not contribute to the Federal Treasury and to the running expenses of the Union. Obviously the right to be a part of a union of peoples and states without paying a proportionate share of the common expenses involved cannot be maintained as a principle. The respectable principle is that those who can pay should pay their share into the common treasury. There is also the principle that great associations help, during the period when help is required, those members of the association that cannot at the time pay their proportionate share. This is a great principle, a profoundly Christian and civilized principle, which in our case is based on common citizenship. There is another great principle that no taxes should be collected from people who do not have adequate representation in the bodies levying the taxes.

"If we take these three principles together, the possible future development of our people emerges rather clearly. Puerto Rico ought to pay its share into the Federal Treasury as soon as it is in an economic position to do so, in the same way that it is now contributing morally to the good democratic reputation of the Union. It would, however, be un-Christian, uneconomic, un-American, and extremely foolish to exact such a contribution to the Federal Treasury if that were to mean aggravating instead of ameliorating poverty, surrendering health to disease, closing instead of opening schools, lowering instead of improving standards of living, increasing instead of decreasing unemployment, and abandoning hope to desperation. But a day will come when this will not be so. And when that day arrives we ought not to wait until we are asked to share in the expense; we should rather be the ones to propose the sharing and to pay for it ourselves in the exercise of our own democratic authority and our own sense of responsibility as members, in a new way, of a great Union."

The question of economies in government was one to which he was to return in his next legislative message, delivered on February 23, 1950. There he promised to present an over-all plan for such economies, but warned against the idea that governmental economies are desirable for their own sake. "A government of the poor and for the poor is not a government which invests little or spends little on legitimate services. That might perhaps be a government of the rich and for the rich, who, because they were rich, would be unwilling to contribute of what they had and would not need to have others contribute to what they had. A government of the poor for the poor is a government which should use all its economic powers, without haggling, but within a strict and careful system of priorities, to raise the country's production as rapidly as possible to the point at which extreme poverty and insecurity will disappear from the life of man."

One suspects, however, that the last of the six listed sources of revenue, actual as well as hidden, was and is the one that fascinated him most as a pioneer in government and a leader of men. For if the island's various communities could be encouraged and aided to tackle for themselves some of the many problems for the solution of which they had previously—and often in vain—looked to the government, then he would have achieved another great upsurge in the one resource which outranks all others in importance—the human spirit.

Chapter XIV tells of some of the ways in which the Puerto Rican Department of Agriculture and Commerce encourages and helps new rural homesteaders to band together for self-help and community action toward the solution of their pressing problems. Studied by hundreds of observers from many countries, various social techniques of that action have in recent years been applied in several other parts of the world.

Muñoz, however, wants the philosophy of self-help and community action to be disseminated throughout the island—systematically—in an educational effort for which the government is responsible, and without the sacrifice of old cultural values. In that connection, and in relation to education, he said in 1951: "How are we going to channel our education so that, as qualities and manners typical of industrialism and necessary to its functioning are developed in our culture, we do not allow to be blotted out, lost, or confused those other qualities so deeply rooted in our culture which have played a part in the great good we have been able to accomplish, and which are probably profoundly necessary, whether we know it or not, to our happiness, to our good life? This is the mission of our education; it is the mission particularly of the Community Education Project we have established which has already begun to carry on its work with my personal supervision and co-operation."

In Chapter XIX are recounted some of the first strides that have been made during four brief years by the Community Education Project in the awakening of civic consciousness toward civic problems.

Muñoz likes to say: "To govern is to invent," and he has devoted a considerable part of his effort to the social invention required when a society strikes out on new paths. Former President Aguirre Cerda of Chile, and long before him, Sarmiento of Argentina, used to say, "To govern is to educate." In 1940, the Puerto Rican people were taught how to use their vote honestly and constructively. Later the politicians were taught how and why to respect the vote and well-being of the people. Today the people are being taught how and why to do for themselves many of the things for which they actually don't need politicians, legislators, budgets, or government enterprise.

CHAPTER XIV

Agriculture

THE NEW DEAL of Henry VIII was deeply rooted in the agrarian problem; too many English lands were in large estates, absentee owned and controlled by Rome. The Haitian revolution, which resulted in the establishment of a republic in 1804, grew out of the agrarian problem of too many large estates owned by Frenchmen but worked by an enslaved black rural population. Denmark's remarkable transformation of the nineteenth century began with problems growing out of the agrarian situation of large estates, as did Ireland's revolutionary upheavals. Mexico's great nineteenth-century leader, Juarez, dealt primarily with the problem of breaking up the large estates and dividing the land among the people; the Mexican revolution of 1910—which is still far from finished—began again with the breaking up of those estates. Observers have made a good case out of the claim that China's fall to the Communists was facilitated by the landlords and their great landed estates. The matter of large landed estates and resulting serfdom for millions undoubtedly had much to do with the Russian revolution of 1917. Chile's modern restlessness grew in large measure out of the system of landed estates in the Central Valley, handed down from the days of the early conquest.

Somewhere, in most real revolutions in modern history, the problem of latifundia has played a vital part; often it becomes the greatest single talking point of the revolutionary leaders; always, after the revolution's inception, the question of what to do about that problem becomes the one most urgent and most pressing. The Haitians slit the throats of the landowners, divided the land, and created a new class of landowners—small, impoverished, with economic means sufficient only for a bare, miserable survival, and none for growth. The Danes, on the other hand, broke up the large estates and gave social and economic strength to the small farmers through a co-operative movement which transformed Denmark into a model of democracy and social justice. The Mexicans created small landowners but found that the latter were soon again gobbled up by the more powerful former landlords; only now are they making strong headway with the government-sponsored co-operative movement which gives group strength to the poor.

Twenty years ago in Puerto Rico the agrarian problem of large, absentee-owned sugar estates was regarded as *the* most urgent basic problem that the island had to deal with; the enforcement of the Five-Hundred-Acre Law was regarded by Muñoz and his followers as the *sine qua non* for effective social reform.

Forty years after the passage of that federal law, making it illegal for any corporation to own or control more than five hundred acres of land, fifty-one corporations were operating illegally 249,000 acres of the island's best lands—either owned or leased by the corporations—an average of 5,000 acres per company. One corporation, the Eastern Puerto Rico Sugar Co., held over 50,000 acres.

Congress had added the Five-Hundred-Acre Law to the first Organic Act to the tune of oratory, expressing the fear that U.S. corporations might come to own all the valuable land on our newly acquired island, reducing the condition of the population to one of "absolute servitude." Having no teeth, the law had been ignored throughout four decades; Puerto Rico's population had been reduced to absolute servitude; the first job of the Popular Democratic party after achieving power was to remedy that condition by breaking up the large estates. More difficult, however, was the task of deciding what to do with the land once the estates had been broken up.

The modern dilemma in land tenure, encountered especially in sugar, is this: Social justice may seem to demand that the available land be divided as equitably as possible, among as many people as possible—which means in small lots. Industrial efficiency, however, and the use of heavy machinery and of expensive mills demand that it be worked in large parcels. A landed peasantry with small holdings, smaller capital resources, and no credit at the bank might for a time be able to eke out a bare subsistence, but this Haitianization would degenerate into utter misery as the population grew, the land became poorer, and the peasants, at the mercy of more powerful economic forces, eventually again lost even what little land they had.

A co-operative movement, similar to those in Denmark and Mexico, would seem to be the answer. But the creation of a strong, smoothly running co-operative movement requires years of hard and patient work, with many dangerous setbacks. In 1941 the co-operative idea had not yet been sufficiently entrenched and implemented in Puerto Rico to be trusted with the task of taking over an important share of the main branch of the island's economy. The failure of only one year's crop would have spelled disaster. Hence Muñoz' ingenious land law provided for acquisition of land by the insular government itself, to be used in various ways. Some of the land was to be incorporated in proportional profit farms owned and worked by the government to produce sugar cane and perhaps other cash crops; some was to be sold to small farmers in lots of up to twenty-five acres; more, while owned by the government, was to be given in usufruct, in small home parcels, to landless agricultural laborers who might thereby develop a rootedness and an identification with the soil. Lands that were relatively useless for other purposes were to be turned over to the insular forestry or conservation services. In addition, the Land Authority was given the power to acquire swampy and barren lands and to engage in reclamation projects for the purpose of adding to the island's arable areas. At present (1953), the Land Authority holds 98,000 acres of land, of which 48,000 are under cultivation—largely in sugar cane. That acreage, resulting from the acquisition of the largest of the former private estates, is about half the total land which had formerly been held by corporations in violation of the Five-Hundred-Acre Law. There is no pressing need for the government to condemn and buy all the sugar lands held illegally. The fact that the government has demonstrated its power to acquire such land when necessary, and to work it efficiently, is enough to assure both workers and planters a fair deal in the industry and to keep the sugar industry out of Puerto Rican politics. Under those conditions, the government might well use its available funds for purposes other, and more pressing, than that of acquiring more land—for stimulating manufacturing, spreading education and health services, etc. Today the government owns and operates about 10 per cent of the island's total cropland area and about 25 per cent of that area in sugar cane. Of the rest, some is still held by corporations in technical violation of the Five-Hundred-Acre Law, while some is owned and worked by the remaining private planters, who are called *colonos*.

The government farms are unique in that they are operated on a profit-sharing basis. Their managers share in the profits and also receive wages. The thousands of workers receive basic wages as prescribed by law, plus shares of the profits, distributed in proportion to the hours worked during any one season; at times these profit bonuses amount to more than 15 per cent of the wages earned; in 1952, the proportional profits paid out in addition to wages exceeded $600,000.

The sugar corporations are today primarily industrial enterprises, in the business of running the mills, while government farms and private planters supply most of the cane. For a time the corporations were regulated through being declared public utilities, subject to control in such matters as their treatment of the cane growers. By now, however, they have adjusted to the new scheme of things and seem to function well without the minute regulation that is accorded public utilities. They receive their cane, are certain of it, and retain maximum safeguards for their investments. In fact, while their investments have been drastically reduced, their percentage profits remain high.

While the technical operations of the proportional profit farms seem on the whole to be excellent, with ever-increasing yields per acre, and with economies made possible through such means as the operation of a central pool and repair shop for machinery used by all, their social functioning still leaves much to be desired. The hard facts remain that many of the laborers on the farms have not yet developed any rootedness in the soil, that they still tend to regard the whole venture as a government-operated means of taking up the unemployment slack, that that viewpoint creates a great demand for feather-bedding and impedes the introduction of labor-saving machinery, that the Land Authority has to deal with some sixteen labor unions which are as militant in their immediate demands as they are often shortsighted in relation to the long pull, and that the two sugar mills which the Land Authority has bought and is operating have had far more than their share of labor troubles—despite their benevolent policies.

That situation will, of course, be eased as Puerto Rico succeeds in creating ever more jobs—in agriculture, manufacturing, construction, and government services; for the present it contributes to the need for the labor education which is being

pushed energetically. As far as the Land Authority is concerned, it calls for rapid progress in the other phases of its
activities, to create as large as possible a body of agrarian
workers, rooted to the soil and replacing the former landless
sporadic day laborers.

Since the program's inception, under Title VI of the land
law, over five hundred farms have been sold on easy terms,
for a total of $475,000, to small farmers who receive help from
various insular agencies and from the Federal Farmers Home
Administration for the purpose of getting on their feet as independent agricultural producers. At the same time, under
Title V, no fewer than 26,500 small parcels of land, now used
by a total population of more than 100,000, have been given
in usufruct as home plots to formerly landless agricultural
wage earners; the former company towns are being replaced
as rapidly as possible by communities of rooted homeowners.
These are the famous *agregados*—squatters. They own their
houses, but title to the land is retained by the government in
order to prevent the program's defeat through a wave of real-
estate speculation.

Before the land is parceled out, its future uses are carefully
studied and planned by the Planning Board. It should be
suited in size for the creation of villages with some two hundred families and about a thousand inhabitants, conveniently
located in relation to the workers' places of employment. Not
only does such village grouping permit economy in the provision of such services as electric power, good water, sew-
erage, etc., but it also facilitates the fostering, through
co-operatives and community programs, of an integrated community spirit.

Among the people who in any one case are eligible for settlement in one of the newly planned villages, those who actually receive use of the land are determined by drawing lots.
The problem of housing on these plots was for years serious.
No matter what the Planning Board might wish to see, the

workers, though earning several times more than they had earned previously, simply did not have the money for building decent homes. In the early days, unsightly, unsanitary, rural slums began to spring up as rapidly as Title V lands were distributed. Then, a few years ago, Luis Rivera Santos, executive director of the Social Programs Administration, caught an idea from Jacob Crane of the Federal Housing Administration and developed a plan for building sturdy and sanitary concrete houses for the astonishing price of three hundred dollars each. The engineers laughed at him; he wouldn't be able to build the foundations for three hundred dollars; the houses themselves would cost well over a thousand. Rivera Santos went to Muñoz and said: "In 1940 you asked us to vote for you, just that once, to allow you to show us what you could do. I did vote for you, and now I am asking you to vote for me for the same reason. Give me just this one chance." As a result, Rivera obtained $10,000; he built twenty-seven houses with the money and had a surplus left.

Today a man who builds his home under that program makes a down payment of thirty dollars and has ten years in which to pay the rest at the rate of $2.25 per month. The government then lends him a cement mixer and prefabricated, demountable forms. It donates plans for the house, transportation of materials and equipment, and supervision, while selling him the cement and reinforcing steel at cost. Then, with the help of his family and neighbors, he builds his own house. In the back he must build a latrine in order to help the government solve the serious problem of hookworm. The Insular Department of Health has erected thousands of such latrines at a cost of some sixty dollars each; Rivera Santos is now erecting them, through his self-help program, at a cost of fifteen dollars.

Often, too, the owner gets enthusiastic help from neighbors in flimsy rural shacks who may not even be eligible for the new homes. Puerto Rico's constant fear of hurricanes contrib-

utes much to such neighborliness. Comes a hurricane, and
the man in the shack will have the right, in return for his help
in construction, to move his family for safety into the new
concrete house should his own home be blown away.

After the new settlers have moved into their homes, the
Social Programs Administration works with them constantly
toward the end of fostering the basic principle of mutual aid
and self-help.

Co-operative stores spring up, replacing the company
stores at which the sugar workers had formerly done most
of their trading; credit unions provide lasting power over
the dead season; where formerly the sugar companies had discharged workers for daring to plant even a few miserable
stalks of corn in their front yards, individual or community
subsistence gardens are encouraged, planned, planted, and
worked with the best technical help available from the Department of Agriculture. Home handicrafts are fostered, for
extra income, in collaboration with continental industries. If
the community lacks a road it is encouraged, through community action and with government help, to build one; some
of these new communities have built community centers,
school lunchrooms for their children, milk stations, rural libraries. For such activities, the responsible agency provides
plans which have been worked out by the Planning Board.

The Land Authority's Social Programs Administration and
the Division of Community Education of the Department of
Education, described in Chapter XIX, are among the most
vital and important new agencies created by the government;
the hundreds of Point IV visitors who go to the island annually, from countries which have Puerto Rico's basic problem
of small income with which to meet large needs for social improvement, are almost invariably impressed by their work and
carry their lessons back to such places as India, Indonesia, and
various parts of Africa and Latin America. For a number of
years, too, all the housing experts whom Washington was

sending to various parts of the world under the Point IV program first went to Puerto Rico to study the important social innovations under which that inventive island was solving its rural and urban housing problems.

While the Land Authority got under way because co-operatives in the early years could not be trusted to keep the sugar industry going efficiently, the co-operative movement itself, fostered by energetic government action, has now also matured to the point where it has become of great significance to the island's life and economy. Two sugar mills are now owned and operated co-operatively by independent Puerto Rican planters, the *Central* Lafayette and the *Central* Los Caños. The latter is one of the best and most efficient on the island; the cane growers' co-operative, which operates it under the management of Rafael Pol Mendez, is the largest such organization (in sugar) in the world.

Originated and financed by the PRRA, this organization has already repaid most of the money first loaned to it by the federal agency and now has so much money on hand that it is in doubt whether to repay the entire obligation before it is due or expand, buy another mill or two, and so spread the co-operative movement farther. At the time of the present writing it has over six hundred members who annually deliver to the mill quantities of cane that vary from fewer than a hundred tons to over 5,000. New members come in as the co-operative builds roads to various parts of the island, providing access to lands which had formerly been too remote from mills to permit the planting of sugar cane.

The mill was bought in 1940; since then the co-operative has invested $1,200,000 in improvements which have raised its daily capacity from 1,200 tons of cane to 2,500 tons. In 1951, Sr. Pol was expecting a new power plant which would not only improve the mill's operations considerably but would also permit the co-operative to sell electric power to the government's Water Resources Administration during the slack season.

In addition to receiving relatively high wages, constantly adjusted and readjusted to current prices for sugar, the workers in this mill share in the co-operative's annual bonuses out of profits, live in model homes provided by the co-operative, and receive free insurance, free hospitalization and free medical care. The co-operative also maintains a school bus to the high school of near-by Arecibo, and, in addition, operates a vocational school in that city, in which the children of its members and employees, as well as the general public, can learn to become carpenters, electricians, mechanics, welders, etc. For its members, the *colonos* who produce its cane, the co-operative maintains an energetic educational service, not only in the principles of co-operation, but also in modern agricultural practices which will increase the yield of their lands. At the same time the organization's technicians carry out a program of research, aimed at developing new uses for such by-products as molasses and bagasse.

Traditionally, the Puerto Rican sugar crop is shipped in a semirefined condition, to be refined on the mainland. When a Puerto Rican sugar producer some twenty years ago built a modern refinery, the howl from mainland refiners was considerable. Washington then made a ruling that only a small part of the island's sugar quota, 126,033 tons out of a total that was set at 910,000 tons in 1934 (and increased to 1,080,-000 tons in 1951) could be shipped in a refined state; the rest must be shipped in crude states for the purpose of protecting established mainland refineries. That remnant of economic colonialism irks the Puerto Ricans. They point out that if all the sugar produced on the island could be refined there, the Puerto Rican economy would gain by some $12,000,000 annually, and some 8,000 men would find new employment in the refining alone.

It was inevitable that sugar should receive the major attention of the island's planners who direct what Muñoz calls "the
battle for production." Not only was and is it Puerto Rico's
economic mainstay, but it is also by far the most popular crop.
It is in effect a weed, which needs almost no care from the
time of planting to the time of harvesting; it is produced for
a smoothly running industrialized system, with a mill standing ready to receive the crop and credit available as soon as
the crop is planted; its prices fluctuate less than do those of
other crops; the federal government, moreover, pays attractive subsidies to all American sugar planters. One result is that
there is usually overproduction, beyond the quota, resulting
in a surplus which has hitherto been sold to such nations as
Germany; another result is that there is constant pressure for
an increase in the quota to keep pace with the growing population of the United States.

As Puerto Rico is opened, as roads are built to formerly inaccessible areas, providing transportation from farm to mill,
more and more cane is planted on lands where its production
is uneconomical—but still far more economical than had been
the former isolated subsistence agriculture. That gives a momentary boost to the over-all economy, but it also leads to
serious problems of soil erosion and overproduction.

The island's planners are thoroughly aware of the dangers
in that trend, if only because they are also aware of the danger
inherent in a single-crop economy. They know that, under
sound and accepted government policies and careful management, using only the best grades of cane, the lands best suited
for sugar, and the most modern agricultural practices and
mechanized methods available, the island *could* produce as
many as 1,500,000 tons annually on far less than the 360,000
acres which now produce several hundred thousand fewer
tons, making available some 60,000 acres for other crops.
Achieving that desirable end, however, may mean the eventual adoption of agricultural zoning laws to regulate the uses

to which various types of land, in various localities, may be put.

But what uses? That is always the main question. The government, which is doing everything in its power also to help the planters of tobacco and coffee, is thoroughly aware of the need for diversification. It cannot, however, tell a farmer not to plant sugar, tobacco, or coffee unless there is another crop, at least equally attractive, to which he can devote his land and labor. On the surface, the question of what to substitute for the cash-export crops from which Puerto Rico derives its living seems simple. The island now imports about $90,000,000 worth of foodstuffs per year, which amounts to a considerable drain on its financial resources. Why not plant foods, and so cut down the drain?

It is not simple to tell a thing like that to a farmer, or to create conditions under which the farmer may be inclined to listen. Sugar is a successful crop largely because it is streamlined and industrialized. Were it not for the expensive mills, the highways, the credit facilities, the certain markets, and all the other aspects of a complex and highly organized system, no sane Puerto Rican would dream of planting cane. The problem then becomes one of industrializing *all* agriculture, of building roads, canneries, and other processing plants, of creating modern marketing facilities with adequate storage capacity, of creating the machinery for agricultural credit through which it is possible for farmers to modernize their operations, of putting the island's entire agricultural life on the same organized, streamlined basis that sugar enjoys today and that is taken for granted in most branches of continental agriculture.

It is obvious, as pointed out in Chapter XII, that some means must be found under which every acre of land can be made to pay the highest possible return—consistent with good conservation practices. Under conditions as they exist today, with the industrialization program only barely getting under way, corn pays a return of only some thirty dollars per acre, while sugar pays two hundred dollars. It is therefore almost impossible to convince Puerto Rican farmers that it is not more sensible to plant cane and import two hundred dollars' worth of corn than to plant corn and reap thirty dollars' worth. The problem is to make corn or some other crop pay two hundred dollars or more per acre. That problem is at present not at all agricultural in nature. It is basically a problem of distribution, industrialization, and the credits without which no farmer can practice new methods.

The case of the UP 3 sweet potato is an example of the manner in which agriculture is being rationalized, step by step, if not in accordance with some nonexisting over-all plan. The university had developed a sweet potato with outstanding qualities, better in many ways than any other in existence. Nobody would plant it, however, in part because marketing facilities were poor and unreliable, and in part because—for that very reason—neither government credit nor private credit was available for foodstuffs agriculture. Since UP 3 is especially excellent for canning, the government looked about for somebody to erect a cannery. Then, of course, it ran into the ubiquitous vicious circle. Nobody would invest in a cannery because the potato was not being produced; the government would not permit a potential canner to purchase and operate his own land, plantation style; no individual farmer would grow the potato because there was no cannery to provide a relatively certain market. Finally, however, the government did find a mainland canner who agreed to erect a plant in Puerto Rico on condition that he could protect his investment with a guaranteed yield from three hundred acres planted to UP 3. With that, bankers were persuaded to extend credit to farmers planting the crop within transportation radius of the projected cannery. In 1951, I visited the government's seed-producing station at Isabela and found it busy with thirty acres of its land, growing seed potatoes and persuading farmers to put in the crop against the construction of the projected cannery. Others were studying the situation to decide on the best location for the plant, not only for optimum profits for the investors, but also in relation to soils, roads, and for the optimum over-all benefits of Puerto Rico as a society.

The plant was opened in 1953, at Isabela, operated by the Marydale Products Company.

The efficient operations of the proportional profit farms have resulted in another, and similar, kind of diversification. Constant research results in constant improvements of cane varieties, and so in ever-increasing yields per acre. That means, since the government farms are held strictly to their quotas, that more and more land is available every year for purposes other than growing sugar. Moreover, some of the farms have by now been completely mechanized, with tractor trains replacing the former oxcarts for hauling cane to railroad or mill. Land formerly used for pasturing oxen—the sugar companies used to pasture their oxen on land worth a thousand dollars per acre—is now available for other purposes. One result is the extension of pineapple culture—which requires more field labor than does sugar, but grosses six hundred dollars per acre under proper conditions. Another is the development of canneries for pineapples in line with the island's current industrialization program. A third is a decided potential boost for the newly established dairy industry through the availability of excellent cattle feed in the dried leaves and parings of pineapples.

The manner in which agriculture is intimately tied in with industry is dramatically illustrated by the new Caribe plant, erected with private Puerto Rican capital for concentrating, canning, and deep freezing the juice of oranges and pineapples. That plant, employing the strict quality control which is essential for modern industrial operations but difficult for a poor and backward people to learn, now offers new incentives for planting pineapples while also providing a new source of revenue for the coffee planters who have long used a sour mountain orange for shade for their coffee trees. The product of the Caribe plant is excellent, and so popular on the island that it is not yet being shipped to the continent. In 1952 its owners were installing equipment for drying and grinding the orange peelings and pineapple cuttings for sale to dairy farmers as cattle feed.

A quick glance at the Puerto Rican trade statistics reveals that some $11,000,000 worth of milk products are imported annually, and that a dairy industry would therefore be highly desirable. Such an industry has indeed sprung up during the past decade and is now second in economic importance only to sugar, but it can still be improved and increased immeasurably.

What are some of the difficulties? Capital is needed for the erection of plants for bottling and processing milk; industry's inexorable demands for quality control—as for instance to assure that fresh bottled milk is truly fresh when it reaches the consumer—imposes disciplines which are difficult for a non-industrial society to acquire; the amount of land available for grazing cows, not better suited for more lucrative purposes and with access to roads over which milk can be shipped, limits the number of cows which can be grazed—a situation which in turn calls for an energetic road-building program for which funds are lacking, for the improvement of dairy stock, for the introduction of improved grasses, and for the creation of more industries, the by-products of which can be used as cattle feed.

Puerto Rico imports some $16,000,000 worth of meat and meat products annually, plus $9,000,000 worth of lard. Why did not, and why do not, Puerto Rican farmers supply those products themselves? For the same reason that the milk industry has a difficult time in getting started. Lacking modern slaughterhouses, refrigerating plants, smoothly running transportation facilities, industries for canning and the processing of by-products, Puerto Rico cannot hope to compete with the highly organized mainland meat industry, any more than a man who builds automobiles at home can compete with General Motors. Such things will come however, and until they do come there is no reason why Puerto Rican farmers should not improve their income and the health of their families by raising more pigs and goats than they did formerly, on a home basis rather than an industrialized one.

In 1951 the Secretary of Agriculture took me to the impressive experimental farm operated by the University of Puerto Rico in the Lajas Valley. There, besides doing many other things—among them experimentation which indicated that sugar production in the Lajas Valley could be doubled through the use of irrigation—the agriculturalists were raising dozens of varieties of hogs and goats for the purpose of producing strains best suited for Puerto Rican conditions. As always, however, that activity raised secondary problems. Not only do goats have a devastating habit of killing shrubs and young trees—so creating conditions of soil erosion which have in historic times, for instance, contributed materially to the fact that Palestine is today largely desert—but both goats and hogs must eat, and their eventual energetic distribution to Puerto Rican farmers demands the energetic provision of fodders. At the Lajas station it was found that the oily nuts of the royal palm are excellent hog feed. However, since there are not enough royal palms on the island to support an appreciable hog culture, some other source of feed must be developed —perhaps again from the by-products of various new processing plants.

The U.S. military forces maintain sizable camps and other establishments in Puerto Rico, but only recently have these begun, in a small way, to buy some of their foods from Puerto Rican farmers. Such foods were not formerly available in sufficient quantities, sufficiently safeguarded through grading and quality control, to meet the needs of large purchasers. Marketing facilities, and the related facilities for credit and transportation, had not been sufficiently organized to encourage the local production of foodstuffs, locally consumed, and so to reduce the island's annual export of millions of dollars for fresh or processed vegetables imported from the mainland.

The large tourist hotels in San Juan, which in themselves are an attractive potential foodstuffs market for Puerto Rican farmers, still import the bulk of their foods from the mainland. They must be sure of a steady supply of good quality. Under present conditions, for instance, it is far easier, safer, and less expensive to have breakfast oranges flown in from Florida, reliably graded and packaged, than to send a man out daily to various small and dingy markets to paw over the available oranges, grading them as he goes, picking twenty good ones here and thirty there with no guarantee that he will find the required quantity after spending the entire morning doing nothing else. And that goes also for such things as asparagus, strawberries, and avocado pears.

The great bottleneck in Puerto Rico's foodstuffs agriculture is the lack of organized and rationalized marketing. A man may be an excellent truck farmer but he will not go far if he has to spend days on end peddling his crop through the city in a pushcart and going from house to house ringing doorbells. His alternative is usually to take the crop to one of the local markets. Lacking facilities for grading, storing, or processing, he brings it in at about the same time his neighbors bring in theirs. The resulting glut, aggravated by the fact that existing facilities do not permit the rapid distribution of vegetables throughout the island, depresses prices and creates much periodic waste. Under such conditions it is in no way the farmer's fault that he is not a good credit risk and that he would rather devote his land and labor to raising sugar cane—

leaving some 60 per cent of the island's consumed foodstuffs to be bought on the continent and imported at high prices.

Co-operatives, being fostered energetically by the government, can do much toward solving the distribution problem in the urgent drive toward diversification; some of them have already begun to ship graded fresh vegetables to New York— a matter that is often easier, more feasible, and more profitable than distributing them in Puerto Rico. A system of chain stores, organized for central purchasing, would also help considerably and would, by providing steady markets, go far toward releasing credit for foodstuffs agriculture; at least one such chain store corporation has been asked to consider establishing itself on the island, but the problem is the old Puerto Rican one: the chain stores will not go there until they are sure of a steady, dependable supply of produce; the produce will not materialize until the stores are there; meanwhile sugar is a far better bet for a farmer than are vegetables.

There again, the government is now stepping into the picture under its present policy of using government funds wherever needed for the purpose of priming the pump for private capital. Near San Juan there is being built, for $23,000,000 of government funds, a great central marketing establishment, combined with a slaughterhouse and adequate storage, processing, and distribution facilities. This will function as a clearing house, buying produce and meats from Puerto Rican farmers, storing them as well as imported foods when necessary, and distributing such foods throughout the capital's metropolitan area—to hotels, wholesalers, retailers, restaurants—under conditions that guarantee the consumer the same grading, the same quality control, the same health safeguards that he has come to expect on the mainland.

There is no doubt that this project will greatly stimulate foodstuffs agriculture on some of the rich bottom lands near the capital. After that agriculture has been stimulated and the central market is a going concern, the government may well sell it to a private operator and use the money again for breaking the vicious circle in some other branch of Puerto Rico's economy.

The lack of agricultural credit is one of the great obstacles to agricultural modernization. Regardless of his education and the relative success of an energetic agriculture extension campaign, no farmer can practice sound methods and at the same time conserve his soil unless he can borrow money for fertilizers, tractors, and the like. Unless he does practice sound methods, however, he cannot borrow the money.

Some years ago government experts called together a group of bankers and asked them to develop a program under which they might diversify their credit facilities to include crops other than sugar. They were told that their strength was based on the island's economic strength and that it was greatly to their advantage to go along with the government in financing an island-wide effort toward diversification, going hand in hand with an energetic program of soil conservation. They answered that conservation was none of their business and that, if they extended credit to the existing chaotic agricultural system, they would soon go bankrupt.

The government people then began to talk about the island's many reservoirs, which provide water for Puerto Rico's spectacular program of electrification.

"Are you interested in those?" they asked.

Of course the bankers were interested in the reservoirs, which produce the power to run hundreds of factories.

"Some of our reservoirs," they were told, "are already filling with silt because, for lack of a sound conservation program, the soil is being washed down from the hills. What will happen to you when they are all filled up and our industrialization program collapses for lack of cheap power?"

That was a new thought to the bankers and a thoroughly

disturbing one. They have now organized a committee which is working hard on the problem of expanding the agricultural credit structure.

Meanwhile, however, the question of private credit versus government credit for farmers is being debated. A private bank is likely to give credit to a farmer who is a good risk, on a short-term basis and on the strength of his current planting. The bank is interested if he is a good farmer and has planted what looks like a good crop which has a chance of being sold at a profit at harvest time. Whether or not he mines the soil, wears it out, commits the social offense of permitting it to be eroded to the point where he will no longer be a good credit risk a few years hence is often not the bank's concern—*until a few years hence when the man's credit stops* because his land is worn out. But by then the damage has been done and all Puerto Rico has suffered a loss through the loss of some of its soil. A government agency, on the other hand, may be able to give credit on lower terms, for longer periods, and to use such credit as a means of forcing the farmer to adopt good agricultural practices which will conserve his soil and eventually yield him greater returns—even though his immediate returns may be smaller than they would be if he forced and ruined his soil with the help of private credit.

In recent years there has been a pronounced trend toward the drafting of an over-all agricultural plan, integrated with the total almighty Puerto Rican effort. In July, 1950, Muñoz Marín sent a request to the then U.S. Secretary of Agriculture, Charles F. Brannan, suggesting that the drafting of such a plan be undertaken jointly by agencies of the Puerto Rican government and the United States Department of Agriculture. Under the energetic leadership of Mr. Nathan Koenig, Assistant to Washington's Secretary of Agriculture, fourteen task teams studied as many phases of Puerto Rico's agricultural problem and drafted an impressive report, published in 1953 by the two governments. It is an excellent analysis of

Puerto Rico's agricultural problems and makes many sound recommendations as to ways in which those problems may be solved. It cannot, however, be regarded as a working plan.

A working plan, for agriculture or anything else, cannot stand alone. It must be an integral part of the great master plan for the island. Each of its recommendations may be eminently sound and would undoubtedly, if carried out, redound to the island's benefit. But the implementation of any one of the plan's many phases would also cost millions of dollars and require much human effort and energy, in a society in which only a limited number of dollars, and a limited number of trained men, are available. Agriculture is not the only field of Puerto Rican endeavor which needs extension and improvement. How much of the available budget should be spent on agriculture, and how much on roads, industrialization, education, public health, and all the other thousand things with which a pioneering government must always concern itself? Where and how does some admirable plan for agriculture conflict with an equally admirable plan for public works, education, or industrialization? How can they be integrated, one with the other?

Such diverse and complex problems, being faced by one small society, should give pause to the many geographers and land-use experts who today talk glibly about the need for improving the world's food supply by improving agricultural production in places like India and Africa. Most of them talk and think only in technical terms, aware only that modern methods of agriculture could greatly increase the supply of available foodstuffs, impatient with the "backward" people who fail to apply such methods. I doubt that there is a single backward farmer in Puerto Rico or elsewhere who wouldn't welcome a chance to increase his income and security through the adoption of modern methods. The chances are, however, that he also knows—as many of our land-use prophets do not— that agriculture cannot stand alone in any one society, divorced from industry, banking, and the over-all social scene. The Puerto Ricans know that they cannot modernize their agriculture without at the same time modernizing all other aspects of their life and economy. As those aspects progress, so will farming—no faster and no more slowly.

CHAPTER XV

Power and Industry

ACCORDING TO an old economic swindle still preached by some scholars, it was apparently decreed by God that only a few of the world's societies should engage in the industrialized processing of goods; the remainder must, without competing commercially with the great powers, provide foods and raw materials—in the past under conditions of outright slavery, and later under the freedom supported by wages of ten cents per day, or seventeen cents, or the twenty-seven cents which Liberia's workers are today earning for the purposes of paying their oppressive taxes and buying the products of our factories. The fact that they cannot buy many such products is now beginning to make some of our manufacturers unhappy; it is in part responsible for the slowly spreading interest in the task of raising standards of living and purchasing power in the so-called underdeveloped parts of the world; it helps to focus realistic attention on the filth, ignorance, hunger, disease, and resulting overpopulation which are every bit as great a threat to the great industrial countries as they are to the billion people who suffer them and are now growing weary of such suffering.

It is everywhere becoming apparent that industrialization is one of several interrelated solutions to that most pressing of all our current world problems. Not industrialization alone, of course. People have starved and do starve in industrialized Japan, East Prussia, and the relatively well-developed Union of South Africa. It must be industrialization plus a great many other things, including the kind of democracy which permits the worker to reap a fair share of the fruits of his labor. But when the aim is to permit our millions of former and present colonial subjects to improve their lives, industrialization of one kind or another must always come into the picture. The old economic swindle is rapidly disappearing from the intellectual and academic scene—if only because the world's stricken people have never quite believed it.

By the same token, it is everywhere increasingly apparent that the modernization of a present-day underdeveloped society demands the creation of an abundance of electric power, generated, distributed, and sold at the lowest possible cost. That power is needed for turning the wheels of the factories, for lighting the homes and the streets of the growing cities, for directing traffic on the crowded thoroughfares, for creating light in the rural homes so the children of the poor can read their schoolbooks, for lightening the individual burdens of the people and releasing them to take on other but lesser burdens in factories and on mechanized farms, for sustaining the radio stations and receivers through which the various governments labor to educate their people, for activating the motion-picture theaters which begin to play an increasing role in people's new social orientations—for all the multiple purposes of creation, recreation, and relaxation which, between them, do so much to combat the one alternative of exaggerated procreation.

When Senator Robert A. Taft visited Puerto Rico in 1943, he was annoyed with the various 150 per cent Americans who tried to tell him that the government's entry into the power field was unconstitutional. He didn't believe it, of course. It was a foolish thing to say to an eminent lawyer

whose father had not only been Chief Justice of the U.S.
Supreme Court but had previously, as President in 1912,
signed the first Federal Power Act ever passed by Congress.
Moreover, while Senator Taft did not like to see government
go into the power business, he agreed that in Puerto Rico
the government hardly had an alternative.

Before 1936 a number of Puerto Rican cities were served
with electric power—inadequately, poorly, and at high rates—
by a few private companies which lacked the means or the
financial incentives for expanding with those cities and had
not the vaguest intentions of expanding into the rural areas
where the majority of the people hadn't even the money to buy
kerosene for one miserable lamp each. But even then hydro-
generated government power had begun to prove itself and its
social benefits. Step by legal step, the private companies
had begun to be absorbed by the government, which was
working feverishly to generate ever more power and distribute
it to all parts of the island in an integrated system which is
today known as Puerto Rico's Little T.V.A. Today, virtually
the only privately owned electric power plants existing on the
island are those of the sugar mills, with their large but seasonal
loads which would overtax the common network during four
or five harvest months and make no demands on it whatever
during the rest of the year. And some of these have now begun
to sell their surplus power—whatever they don't happen to
need for turning the mills—to the government for resale to the
over-all society at the lowest possible rates.

Although the great Puerto Rican effort began with the
election of 1940, it was aided immeasurably by a number of
facts which date back to far before that revolutionary year.
One was Puerto Rico's inclusion within the American economic structure; another was the freedom of the Puerto Rican
government to retain and invest the excise taxes on the rapidly
growing rum industry; a third was undoubtedly the fact that

the government's generation and distribution of low-cost electric power had long before been legally established as a principle, through several bitter court cases, and physically implemented by power plants and transmission lines.

In 1925, and entirely as a by-product of irrigation, the government generated and sold a little more than 10,000,000 kilowatt hours. In 1951 the figure was almost 700,000,000 produced in an interlocked island-wide system of new hydro-electric and steam plants and sold for a gross revenue of some $14,000,000. The 325 new industries which had been established with government help between 1948 and 1954 (the figure grows weekly, and whatever I put down at the time of writing will be far out of date by the time of publication), giving employment to some 25,000 workers with a potential of 8,000 additional jobs, were in part attracted by that power network; all of Puerto Rico's cities and towns are served by it today; approximately 75,000 rural residents, living in 15,000 homes, small and large, formerly without any source of electric power, enjoyed the multiple benefits of rural electrification at the time of writing—many more will enjoy them at the time of reading; rates for domestic and industrial services are about one tenth as high as they were fifteen years ago. The Puerto Rico Water Resources Authority, which produces and distributes all that power, is a businesslike organization, financially autonomous, which floats its own bond issues and operates in a businesslike fashion out of profits earned.

There are still those in the United States who decry that kind of government business as creeping socialism, inimical to private enterprise. However, the owners and operators of factories on the island, whose lucrative private enterprises are in part made possible and sustained by government power, do *not* so decry it; nor do the private-enterprise manufacturers, wholesalers, and retailers of some $18,000,000 worth of electrical machinery and apparatus, of motors, bulbs, neon signs, electric irons, and washing machines, which were imported from the mainland in 1952.

In 1908 the insular legislature created the Puerto Rico Irrigation Service for the purpose of increasing agricultural production in the island's southeast. The organization's first project was completed in 1915, bringing water down from four reservoirs in the mountains and incidentally generating the electricity needed for running irrigation pumps. The surplus power was wired into the district's towns and rural areas, which had previously received nothing at all from private companies; it created so clamorous a demand and proved socially so effective in the improvement of living standards, that the generation and distribution of low-cost electric power, in the beginning a by-product of irrigation, eventually became a major activity of the government.

The PRRA built a few hydro plants with federal funds and turned them over to the Puerto Rican government against long-term repayment. One by one, sometimes painlessly and sometimes at considerable trouble, the various privately operated plants were bought by the government. The Tugwell administration changed the administrative setup by creating the Puerto Rico Water Resources Authority as an autonomous entity. New hydro plants were built where it was physically and financially possible. A floating steam plant was bought during the war, towed to San Juan harbor, and put to work generating power. A new steam plant was later built for the San Juan area. All generating plants were tied together by an island-wide network of transmission lines, soaring exuberantly from mountain to mountain, across wide and fertile valleys. Local distribution lines were extended into one rural or industrial district after another. Engineering staffs, airplanes, and a helicopter were acquired to facilitate the management of that system and the investigation of new potential sites for expansion as permitted by financial considerations—in an organization that must exist and grow through its own operations, sustained by fair profits.

As part of a government which has achieved remarkable co-ordination and integration of all its branches, the Water Resources Authority co-operates closely with a number of other agencies. As described, for instance, by Antonio Lucchetti, its head at that time, in a brief paper prepared in 1950, the Authority submits all of its new projects to the Insular Planning Board for approval—for weighing the undertaking's merits and gauging its place in the master developmental plans for the entire island. There is close liaison between the Industrial Development Company and the Authority with regard to the establishment of new industries as they may affect the demand for electric energy. Where highways are affected by the construction of new hydroelectric projects, where they must be relocated or new ones built, the Insular Department of the Interior steps into the picture to assure that the new construction is in line with the Interior Department's plans and is technically in accord with the department's standards. When new potentialities are created for irrigation to improve the island's agricultural production, the university's Agricultural Experiment Station makes preliminary studies of soil characteristics to determine the amounts of water needed for optimum productivity, drainage characteristics, degree of salinity for determining leaching requirements, and other factors. The Government Development Bank, created in 1945, is called in for assistance in the negotiations for financing programs. The fact that the Puerto Rico Aqueduct and Sewer Authority and the Water Resources Authority must both develop water resources to carry out their programs requires close co-ordination between the two agencies. Some of the lands to be irrigated through new projects now belong to the Land Authority, which can there, in co-ordination with the Water Resources Authority, plan its future operations from the start. Jointly with the Economic

Development Administration, which has need for geological information, the Authority has made an agreement for investigational services with the United States Geological Survey.

The Lajas Valley project, now under construction in the island's southwest, illustrates well the Authority's multiple benefits to the over-all society. There, besides generating power for rural, urban, and industrial electrification and providing irrigation water to double the agricultural production on some 26,000 acres of land, the Authority will also provide sources of safe, potable water for a number of towns and for the ever-spreading rural acqueducts which have today begun to ease the burden and improve the health of thousands of country-dwelling Puerto Ricans. In the field of agriculture alone, that one project promises added incomes, out of the land's improved productivity, of between one and two million dollars annually for a relatively small section of Puerto Rico. It will, moreover, permit local industrialization, as perhaps in the processing of the increased agricultural production. It will extend the blessings of low-cost domestic electricity to tens of thousands of people. It will do much to accelerate the present drop in Puerto Rico's disease and death rates which has already made the island, statistically speaking, one of the most healthful places in the Western Hemisphere.

The town of Vega Baja is on the north coastal plain, about twenty miles west of San Juan. In 1949 a small proportion of its 8,000-odd employable residents found work almost exclusively in sugar, in the cane fields and the near-by mills. The rest had no work at all. Most of those who did have jobs were idle well over half of every year, and between them they created a net income of some $70,000 annually for the town, or about nine dollars for every employable person. Picturesque Vega Baja resembled a number of Puerto Rican towns in that it was little more than a beautiful slum. *News-*

week reports that "countless hundreds of impoverished towns-men used to climb the chipped stone stairs to the mayor's office monthly in search of help. He used to hand out bus fares to men who wanted to leave Vega Baja to look for jobs. For a while he had to buy as many as one hundred caskets a month for the dead."

In 1948, however, the Puerto Rican government had changed its industrialization policies away from government ownership and management toward the active encouragement of industrialization by private capital aided by the government. Of the many new industries which then began to be established on the island, four were persuaded by Vega Baja's mayor, Angel Sandín, to settle in his town: a chinaware plant, two makers of electronic components, and a manufacturer of nuts, bolts, and aircraft parts. These plants did not entirely solve the employment problems; they provided jobs for 700 people, but some 3,000 of Vega Baja's potential earners were still unemployed in 1953. They did, however, do wonders for the town as a whole. Between them, the factory workers alone earned almost $800,000 in 1953, as compared with a total town income of $70,000 four years previously. Reporting on the chinaware factory, owned and operated by the Crane Corporation, Stuart Chase writes that "it buys local supplies amounting to $150,000 annually, food for the cafeteria, and so on. The new flood of purchasing power, moreover, reverses the emotional climate of the community, from resignation to ambition."

In reporting the results of Vega Baja's industrialization, *Newsweek* says: "A dry-goods-store owner reported last week: 'I've got more business than any time for twenty years.' Household-appliance sales have doubled in two years. One shop sold thirty-nine refrigerators at Christmas and forty for Mother's Day. A sprinkling of fairly expensive autos are now beginning to dot the narrow streets." In addition, efforts of the Puerto Rican government are doing much to improve life in the town. Reports *Newsweek* further: "A tidy new hospital with thirty-four beds was completed six months ago. A low-cost apartment house, for 148 families, opened last month. Thirty-one permits to build new homes have been issued in the last year."

Vega Baja's experiences are typical of the things which have begun to happen in dozens of Puerto Rican towns. Virtually every week at least one new factory is opened somewhere on the island; the total number of these during 1952–53 was eighty-two with thirty-seven more under construction in July, 1953. These figures apply to factories erected with some form of government help. Their total is 326, built between 1948, when the present policy was formulated, and May, 1954. The newly created social and economic climate, however, is also healthy for the growth of certain kinds of manufacture without any government help whatever. The total number of new factories which sprang up in Puerto Rico during the thirteen years which followed the revolutionary year of 1940—with or without help from the government—is 1,388. Most of those which were started without government help are small affairs, housed in old buildings and employing few workers. They nevertheless represent an appreciable start toward industrialization. The island's net income from manufacture was $26,000,000 in 1940, and $118,000,000 in 1952.

Because private capital was not forthcoming for industrialization the government industries created during the Tugwell regime were sold to Luis Ferré in 1950, when the pump had been primed and private capital had begun to come forward. Government had had its troubles while operating the plants. Government could easily provide technical management, but sales management, the commercial distribution of products, was more difficult. Moreover, it was unavoidable that management decisions must often be made with an eye to politics, Teodoro Moscoso, head of the Economic Development Administration, writes of this period: "Although the operations of the Development Company never became, as has often been the case in other countries, an object for political spoils and favoritism, over-all government orientation undoubtedly did influence the administrative policies of the company. Its production workers, for instance, were among the most highly paid in Puerto Rico. While desirable as a goal of economic development, this political determination of wage levels in plants under government ownership generally impaired the freedom of management in making such decisions, because of their political repercussions. This contributed to the difficulty of putting the plants on a profitable operating basis, thus limiting the earnings that could be reinvested.

"This experience vividly illustrates the problem in a 'mixed economy' . . . in which the legislators and government supporters tend to be unwilling on the one hand to see government enterprises pursue a vigorous management policy, yet on the other insist that such enterprises be profitable and solvent."

The glass factory, which had been able to produce only at a rate considerably lower than capacity because of the extreme shortage of soda ash in the American market, was tied up for months through a disastrous strike; this, in turn, had caused the rum industry to look elsewhere for its bottles during the last two years of government operations—when expectations of profits brought only increasing losses.

The paperboard mill had lost money under government operation, though giving employment and helping, through the containers manufactured, to sustain the rum industry.

Under Ferré's private management, the various ex-government plants stopped having labor difficulties, and their new owner began to make a good profit out of them almost immediately. Ferré also bought two steamers, which are used for carrying cement and bottles, for sale, to the mainland and to the various Caribbean countries and possessions, as well as for bringing machinery, steel, and other materials back to Puerto Rico. Besides "exporting" many new industrial products other than the traditional sugar, Puerto Rico now has the nucleus of a merchant marine which may someday grow to considerable proportions as the island's industrialization continues to grow. Profits on shipping have already begun to flow into Puerto Rican bank accounts, instead of exclusively into the treasuries of absentee steamship companies. The latter, however, don't seem to be unhappy about the matter. They are doing more business than ever before and the Puerto Rican-owned steamers are taking only a small part of the vast new shipping business which has in recent years been generated through the island's over-all effort.

The monies received from the sale of the plants are regarded as a kind of revolving fund, to be used, together with appropriated funds, for accelerating industrial development through private capital. A Commonwealth law forbids the government from being a minority stockholder in business ventures, as it can be, and often is, in such Latin American countries as Chile and Venezuela. The government may not participate financially in the operation of any industrial venture which it does not control, and the present general policy is against the creation of industries owned and operated by the government. Occasionally, however, a "vicious circle" situation makes it advisable to use government capital, and so to apply a touch of state socialism, for the purpose of furthering industrialization by private capital. It was pointed out in Chapter XIV that the Commonwealth government is building, at the time of the present writing, a great new market and food-processing plant in the San Juan area, at a cost of some $23,000,000. Agriculture cannot be stimulated without adequate marketing facilities; such facilities will not be provided by private capital until they are justified by a sufficiency of agricultural products. When the new market is a going concern, having stimulated enough agricultural production for its own support, the government may well sell it to a private operator and use the money so obtained for priming the pump somewhere.

The new Caribe Hilton hotel resulted from a similar situation. A tourist industry was deemed desirable as one of many ways of improving economic conditions; tourists would not go to Puerto Rico in appreciable numbers until there were good hotels; private capital would not build such hotels unless and until the tourists were there to warrant the investment. Hence the government spent $7,200,000 for a hotel which is now one of the show places of the Caribbean and made arrangements with the Hilton Hotel Corporation for operating it on a profit-sharing basis—two thirds to go the Commonwealth and one third to the Hilton Company. The hotel is today an outstanding financial success, and much new private capital is pouring into the tourist business in Puerto Rico as a result. Now there is talk of the government's selling the Caribe Hilton and using the money somewhere else.

Studies are being made, for instance, on the advisability of erecting a government-owned tool and die works. A number of industries which might otherwise be attracted will not establish themselves in Puerto Rico because there is no tool and die works; the lack of such industries as potential customers precludes its establishment by private capital; the government may therefore yet build a tool and die works, operate it for the purpose of helping to attract other industries, and sell it to private interests when it is a going concern.

As the island's industrialization progresses, its problems also become increasingly complex. Dozens and hundreds of problems, involving important policy decisions, pour in daily to the Economic Development Administration, to be weighed and sifted in a continuous research program devoted to the careful evaluation of all the factors involved.

Early in its efforts to attract continental and local capital for new industries, the government began to spend considerable money and effort on research and fact finding to help specific potential investors. On the continent, long industrialized and highly organized, with the labors of dozens of fact-finding agencies piling up results year after year, such governmental services are not needed; on an island which is only now emerging from its former status as an agrarian society geared almost exclusively to the production of sugar, and which cannot wait for industrialization to take place under the processes commonly regarded as normal, they play a vital part in economic growth.

As reported by Stuart Chase, in his National Planning Association booklet, "Operation Bootstrap in Puerto Rico," almost all new and potential investors in the Puerto Rican scene have enjoyed the finest possible relations with the Economic Development Administration and its Industrial Development Company and have been more than pleased with the investigational and advisory services rendered to them by that organization. Altogether, reports Chase, "If you are thinking of establishing a branch plant in Puerto Rico, here are the services which Fomento is prepared to furnish: (1) Round up, screen, test, and train your prospective workers; (2) plan your transportation problems—ocean, highway, air; (3) arrange to connect you with all public utilities—power, water, telephone, etc.; (4) help with housing, schools, hospitals for your workers, also for any managers and technicians brought down from the mainland; (5) relieve you in full of all taxes until 1959, and partially until 1962; (6) furnish economic research for your production and marketing problems, also chemical research if you need it; (7) and perhaps most important of all, assume that you are a *friend*, rather than a suspicious character with profiteering designs on the people."

Moreover, the government builds factories for new industries, renting them at nominal rates for a period of years and then selling them to the manufacturers at cost. That, of

course, takes much of the financial risk out of the establishment of a new industry. If the venture fails, the operator is
not saddled with a costly factory building. The government,
on the other hand, is enriched by the possession of a new plant
which it can always rent later to somebody else.

Finally, the Economic Development Administration carries on a ceaseless campaign of advertising and promotion on
the continent, in part to attract new industries, in part to sell
Puerto Rican rum, which contributes so much to the Commonwealth's finances, in part to attract tourists.

Much thought and study have been given to the perplexing
question of what kinds of industries should be created on an
island which is so dramatically lacking in raw materials. In
the days of the PRRA we made studies of Puerto Rico's external trade and drafted plans for manufacturing on the island
a number of things which were being imported from the
mainland, so thinking to relieve the urgent unemployment
problem, cut down the export of funds, pile up profits on the
island, and improve the economic situation considerably. In
view of Puerto Rico's colonial subjugation, most of those
plans were then academic. Under the circumstances, it did
not occur to us that the sugar industry was selling its product
throughout the United States and that it might become possible for Puerto Rico to become a center for manufacturing
certain goods for equally wide distribution.

The cement factory, built by the PRRA and turned over to
the Puerto Rican government—which very soon repaid its entire cost to Washington—was the first step in the modern program of industrialization as we envisaged it then. Needed
everywhere, for building homes, factories, dams, and highways, needed in ever-increasing quantities as the society
grows and builds, cement was an excellent product with
which to begin.

The various factories which the government built or projected during the Tugwell regime were based on the same

philosophy of greater material self-sufficiency. The government's shoe factory was an early proof that the philosophy was too narrow for Puerto Rico's needs. In theory it was eminently possible for one factory to turn out all the shoes bought in Puerto Rico; in practice it proved impossible for one factory to turn out all the various styles, shapes, and sizes bought there. Operated by the government for the purpose of meeting local demands, the factory proved uneconomical. It became eminently sound, however, when it was leased to a continental manufacturer who makes shoes for sale in the vast continental market.

With its shortage of minerals, metals, and fuels, Puerto Rico cannot, of course, expect to develop heavy industries, but it has ample potentialities for many more light and medium ones through the processing of its agricultural products, full exploitation of its few minerals, and expansion of industries based on imported raw materials, low-cost power, and the presence of abundant labor. Moscoso says: "No one has the wisdom to make a detailed blueprint of a large-scale industrial development, particularly when we operate within the framework of free private enterprise." He does, however, warn prospective investors against too great an interest in labor-oriented industries, meaning that they should not count on a growing and lasting supply of cheap labor. He goes on to say: "We know that we must try to industrialize the products of the land—pineapples, citrus fruits, tobacco, vegetables, and other minor crops. This we are on the way to accomplishing."

By and large, says Moscoso, "The best industry for Puerto Rico is any industry. Anyone willing to take a risk on us will be cordially welcome. A good entrepreneur should know enough about his own industrial activity to be able to determine with a reasonable degree of certainty his chances of success on the island. So far, the mortality rate of our new industries is considerably lower than that in mainland United States."

The processing of sugar is still the largest industry, but dairy products and the canning and preserving of fruits and vegetables are becoming increasingly important. There is now under construction (1953) in Ponce a plant for canning tuna fish. The deep waters around Puerto Rico, to be sure, do not permit commercial fishing anywhere near the island, but fishing boats from the Galápagos Islands and elsewhere will soon be hauling their catches to Ponce for industrial processing. The pulp and paper, chemical, metal and machinery, cement, glass, and shoe industries are well started, and nobody can at present foresee an end to the rapid industrial growth—under a government which has set itself the goal of 100,000 industrial jobs by 1960.

Official figures show that in 1940 the unemployed workers on the island totaled 112,000; by 1952, despite an appreciable increase in the total population, the number of unemployed had been reduced to 76,000. In discussing the problem of unemployment relief in his famous message of February, 1950, on priorities in budgeting, Governor Muñoz Marín said: ". . . The dilemma lies between investing and spending [as for relief]. The more that is spent, the less there is to invest. The more that is invested, the more there is to spend later on. Spending is the easier alternative, and, furthermore, the results of spending, though more temporary, are more immediately visible. Therefore we must exercise our will power in order to invest as much as possible and spend as little as possible, since that is the way to put an end to the present situation, to enable our people to free themselves from want as quickly as possible, and achieve a modest degree of prosperity and security."

The industrialization of an agrarian society demands drastic new orientations in the educational system to create a body of industrial workers, plus an increasingly effective public-health program to keep them on the job and reduce absenteeism. Those phases of the insular effort are discussed in Chapters XVII and XVIII. Suffice it here to say that the island's new industrial workers, who ten years ago were, as often as not, illiterate, half-starved cane cutters, sick with a variety of ailments that were directly or indirectly connected with malnutrition, have by now achieved a productivity, in terms of unit output per man, which compares favorably with that on the continent.

Studies and industrial performance show that, taken by and large, the Puerto Rican workers are quick to acquire mechanical and operational skills requiring dexterity and precision; they are less quick than are those on the mainland in developing an integrated, over-all mechanical sense. That is not because there is anything wrong with Puerto Ricans as such. It is because, as children in a stricken agrarian society, they were never given Erector Sets or other mechanical toys, because, as teen-agers, they could never acquire old automobiles and tinker them into running shape as hot rods.

The Department of Education has in recent years revised itself drastically for the purpose of keeping pace with modern needs. More emphasis than ever before is put on the vocational training which creates skilled workers for the new factories and plays so important a role in Puerto Rico's modern drastic culture changes. In 1940, some 450 students received vocational training; today, in the various vocational schools scattered over the island, about 10,000 students are learning a number of industrial trades, while another 8,000 are being trained by the government in its special program to attract and help specific new industries. Most of these will remain on the island to contribute to the program of industrialization; many will undoubtedly, after being trained, migrate to the mainland or to various Latin American countries. No matter! Emigration is today contributing considerably to the solution of Puerto Rico's pressing problems; there is a great difference between exporting thousands of poor, unskilled, bewildered Puerto Ricans, to be abused, cheated, maltreated, and crowded into the slums of Harlem, and exporting skilled workers who can stand on their own feet, will give Puerto Rico a good name abroad, and will thereby make Puerto Ricans welcome instead of resented.

CHAPTER XVI

The Tourist Industry

BACK IN 1936 some of us occasionally went to Fajardo, chartered a small and dirty boat, and spent the day at sea, dragging lines in the water, hauling in an occasional fish not astonishing in size, and making free with the case or two of chilled beer that we had brought with us. We called it "fishing," but we recognized the term as a euphemism. We were out to enjoy fresh air, beer, and good company—and especially to escape San Juan's tensions.

It was almost axiomatic that the fishing in Puerto Rican waters was worth nobody's time and effort. Here and there, to be sure, a few professional fishermen went to sea, and at various points along the coast one saw (and still does) men with their pants rolled up, wading in the water and skillfully tossing their graceful casting nets. But such activities did little except to offer a bare subsistence to a few. Their catches were small, of no commercial importance, and had to be disposed of very shortly after being taken out of the water. There were and are no industrialized facilities for storing, freezing or otherwise preserving, and distributing the fish. No waters in Puerto Rico's vicinity are sufficiently rich in desirable marine fauna to warrant the investment of capital in such facilities.

Partly for that reason, partly because, in the early days, it was dangerous for the people of Puerto Rico to venture on the surrounding waters "lest the Dutchman catch them" in his war on Spain, partly because their Spanish rulers had not allowed them to have ships of their own lest they compete with Spanish shipping, the Puerto Ricans have never developed any close identification with the sea. Indeed, only two decades ago, shunning the sea seemed to be a cultural trait. Sailing and ocean bathing were not Puerto Rican sports and were indulged in largely by mad Americans. At San Juan, Puerto Ricans who could afford it confined their swimming to various pools, built and operated by clubs and other organizations, or to the then popular Escambrón Beach Club—which was recently renovated, remodeled, and reopened as a swanky resort and recreation center. There one could rent a room or apartment and live by the sea; one could eat, drink, and dance in the public café; one could gamble at the illegal roulette wheel; one could swim in a small section of the ocean which had been fenced off against sharks and barracudas. The excitement was, of course, intense the time a storm damaged the fence and a shark got inside—and the management had the devil's own time getting him out again.

Everywhere, in those days, one ran into a deep and general fear of undertows and reefs, of harm supposedly resulting from undue bodily exposure to salt water and sun, of sting rays, sharks, and barracudas. Occasionally one still hears, repeated over the radio as folklore, a *plena* that was popular twenty years ago, about the patriotic barracuda which, according to the song, ate a lawyer of the Guanico Sugar Company—although in reality it had merely bitten off his leg. The island's several beautiful beaches were shunned by all but a few children of the very poor—who didn't know any better. At San Juan there was reason for such shunning. There was a slaughterhouse in those days, in the La Perla slum section, which threw its waste products into the sea and attracted hungry sharks. Elsewhere there was less reason beyond the general cultural orientation which made the sea an enemy of Puerto Ricans.

Today all that is changing rapidly. Sailing, motorboating, water skiing, and other sports are now increasingly popular. The old San Juan slaughterhouse has been removed, and more and more people are using the city's various sections of beach, with no ill effects. In line with its policy of providing good recreation facilities for the people, the government, in the early 1940's established beautiful Luquillo Beach—twenty miles from San Juan—as a popular swimming resort, policed, kept clean, and provided with bathhouses and picnic tables. It is now crowded every Sunday and half of the weekdays. As Puerto Rico loses its former cultural isolation, so it has also begun to lose its former fear of the sea.

As Puerto Rico becomes increasingly popular as a tourist center, too, its surrounding waters must also become increasingly popular. The government knows well that if it is to create a real tourist industry, it cannot content itself with merely seeing to it that visitors are housed in first-class hotels at first-class prices; they must also have something sporting to do after they get there. Hence, although it is still known that Puerto Rican waters are too deep for commercial fishing, the government undertook some years ago to investigate the concomitant dogma that those waters were not good for sport fishing either.

In 1951, the Development Company's Visitors Bureau sent to Miami for a fishing captain with boat and crew, for the purpose of discovering whether or not the things the Puerto Ricans had been saying about their waters for four centuries were actually true. The man who came was Ernest Hemingway's former skipper—not the old man of the sea who successfully rassled his brother only to be defeated by sharks—but the man, or one of them, who had skippered the novelist on his modest exploits to prove that sport fishing is every bit as close to godliness as are mountain climbing and killing bulls in fancy ways. According to all reports, he was enthusiastic about the results of his investigation; seldom had he seen such good waters for his trade. Today several Miami sport skippers go to Puerto Rico annually with their boats, incidentally teaching their specialized trade to Puerto Ricans, who will in turn expand the business as they acquire the needed capital.

Since that survey, sport fishing has become a major Puerto Rican activity. Two fishing tournaments are held every year under the sponsorship of the Visitors Bureau, with entrants from all parts of the United States as well as Puerto Rico. By 1954, according to an article in the San Juan paper, *El Mundo,* nine official world's records had been broken in Puerto Rican waters, and Puerto Rico ranks second among all localities in the establishment of such records. These records are for fish of various sizes, caught on lines of various weights, as for instance Estéban Bird's bonito, which weighed twenty-nine pounds and was pulled in on a thirty-pound line. The article does not name the fishing waters which top Puerto Rico's in the establishment of such records. It does quote Bird—today a leading Puerto Rican banker who seems to have become quite a fisherman since he and I made women's underwear together in the PRRA days—as saying that the apparently flourishing business of breaking records is good for Puerto Rico, not only in that it helps to build up the tourist industry, but also in that it gives the island publicity.

A few decades ago the idea of fostering a Puerto Rican tourist industry of commercial importance seemed mad indeed. Governor Winship's idea of planting flowers and staging public spectacles for the purpose of attracting tourists looked like that of a poor, tired Army man who could think of nothing else to improve economic conditions. There were no acceptable hotels, in any event, in which to house fastidious visitors whose tastes had been shaped in some of the world's best resort centers.

That lack of good hotels also impeded other phases of the great Puerto Rican effort. The island's leaders and people wanted to attract businessmen interested in investing money in Puerto Rico's development; they did not want to make a bad first impression by housing those businessmen in hotels which were second rate by world standards, relatively shabby and poorly staffed. Hence, in 1948, and because private capital was not forthcoming for adequate tourist facilities on an island which had no tourists to speak of, the government decided to invest $7,200,000 in an outstanding hotel.

The Caribe Hilton Hotel, designed by the Puerto Rican firm, Toro, Ferrer, and Torregrosa, is today not only a tourist attraction but also a fine example of the modern architecture which has begun to change the cultural landscape of several of San Juan's sections. Just as Brazil, when it decided to modernize itself, began to discard old, traditional, colonial forms of architecture, and to go in for beautiful new ventures in functionalism, so Puerto Rico today shows the sometimes startling (in an old Spanish colony), but always impressive, influence of thirteen architects and firms who have departed from old Spanish styles and are now striking out boldly along ultramodern lines.

A bold and colorful slab of a building on the outskirts of old San Juan, strikingly decorated inside with murals by various Puerto Rican artists, provided with all the usual facilities, including a casino, a kidney-shaped swimming pool, and an ocean beach, the Caribe Hilton adjoins the site of a small historic fortress which is said to be connected by tunnels with the larger fort of San Cristóbal, and which at one time played an historic role in Spain's early wars against the North Europeans. The government's troubles concerning that fortress is indicative of some of the troubles inherited from the colonial past.

It seems that, during the Harding regime, which was notoriously careless with public property, there was a commander in the U.S. Navy who thought that the Washington government owed him something. Accordingly, the Washington administration repaid its debt by giving him a 999-year lease on the Puerto Rican fortress—to be used as a private residence—*for a dollar a year*. He was living there, by the sea, surrounded by park land, in the capital's best spot, when the Puerto Rican government began to build its hotel. Correctly, the government decided that historic old forts belong to the people, should not be owned by private individuals, and should never have been given away by an irresponsible Washington administration. The one under consideration, especially, was wanted as part of the new hotel's environment. Getting the Navy commander out of his home again was, however, a difficult proposition. Apparently his lease was legally sound; lawsuits brought no results. Finally he settled for a cash payment of $464,000.

When the Caribe Hilton Hotel was opened, the Puerto Rican government also began its systematic promotional campaign. Direct advertising, press releases, promotion stunts, motion pictures, and other means are used constantly for the purpose of making the American world aware of Puerto Rico's tourist attractions as well as Puerto Rico's rum. Influential visitors are invited to the island by the government; travel agents are flown down at no cost to themselves. A flourishing tourist industry is now well started. Week after week goes by every summer when the Caribe Hilton Hotel and the Condado Beach Hotel in San Juan are filled 100 per cent with guests. The average load carried by the Caribe Hilton throughout the year is now 80 per cent of capacity; that of the Condado Beach Hotel is 90 per cent.

That dramatic flow has, of course, stimulated investment in other hotel facilities. Several attractive apartment hotels have in recent years been built in the San Juan area by private capital; most of them are filled almost all of the time.

The problem of luring tourists into the mountainous interior, however, is more difficult and received a major setback in 1954 when the new Hotel Barranquitas went bankrupt. Their imaginations fired by the outstanding success of the resort business at San Juan, a group of local businessmen had built a mountain hotel and resort center near the inland city of Barranquitas. The fact that they failed financially means only that there are risks also in the hotel business. However, their establishment is due to be reopened soon under the auspices of the government, which is thinking also of making it a central training place for hotel employes. It may well prove successful after the bankruptcy has squeezed a large part of the dollar value out of the capital evaluation. Certainly, Puerto Rico is richer by a beautiful set of buildings, looking down from a mountaintop on one of the island's most beautiful cities.

The hotel was designed by Henry Klumb, a disciple and former student of Frank Lloyd Wright, who has done much to change Puerto Rico's architectural landscape. The Barranquitas Hotel, the new library of the University of Puerto Rico, and the new church at Cataño, across the bay from San Juan, are among his greatest achievements. The story of the church is worth repeating as indicative of Puerto Rico's new directions.

There was a group of Dutch priests at Cataño who were interested in modern art and had for years bothered Klumb to build them a church. For years the latter had refused, on the grounds that he did not believe in organized worship and that any church designed by him had a good chance of not being consecrated by the bishop. The priests kept after him, however, the bishop made no objections, and Klumb finally agreed—on condition that he be given a completely free hand to express in concrete his own idea of the spirit of worship. The single-story, stark, but beautiful Cataño church is the result. The structure is irregularly rounded, with a flat façade from which all ornamentation is missing. One whole rounded side and part of the opposite side have no walls at all; there are only fixed concrete louvres with outside covering screens of flowering vines. Everything inside is simple, unadorned, starkly dignified. There are no saints, no pictures, no colored windows—no windows whatever. The light comes in between the louvres, filtered by the outside vines. The priests had a difficult time persuading Klumb to add, on the outside, a place from which to hang a bell. Beyond that bell, there is only one indication that the edifice is a church. Standing by itself, some fifty feet in front, is a great, plain wooden cross made of two square wooden beams fastened together.

When Klumb was asked to design the Barranquitas Hotel, the only instructions he was given dealt with such matters as size, desired facilities, and cost; in all other matters he was given a free hand. The result, in dignified modern style, blends with the rolling landscape and adapts itself to it. The hotel grounds comprise four hundred acres. In order to attract capital, Waldemar Lee, the promoter, offered a hundred one-acre lots to investors who bought $3,000 worth of stock. Private residences are now springing up on those lots, making the mountain hotel a future resort center.

The bankruptcy of the Barranquitas venture—perhaps because it was too small to carry the large load of its original capitalization, perhaps because Puerto Rico's interior has not yet been as well publicized as has San Juan—has not discouraged plans for other potential ventures to scatter and diversify the tourist trade. Studies are now being made for another mountain hotel, perhaps to be erected at Aguas Buenas at a cost of some $4,000,000. The possibilities for a resort center near the dramatic "Phosphorescent Bay" on the south coast are being investigated. Everywhere, the government is trying to encourage Puerto Ricans to open attractive guest homes for visitors who shy away from the great luxury resorts.

All this is not to imply that the visitor can find no place to go outside of San Juan. There are good hotels in such cities as Mayagüez and Ponce; resorts like Coamo Springs in the south and Treasure Island near Cidra are excellent for all who don't demand a maximum of sophisticated swank. By and large, however, such resorts are patronized more by Puerto Ricans and American residents of Puerto Rico than by tourists. As far as the tourist industry is concerned, they make small impressions on the Commonwealth's economy.

An unfortunate and puzzling cultural innovation which results from the acceleration of the tourist business concerns the treatment of Negroes in the luxury hotels. It is not easy to describe the attitude toward race in the free and democratic society which had once, as told in Chapter I, caused Mrs. Park to cry over being where she could forget all about being a Negro. There is a certain amount of subtle race prejudice in Puerto Rico, especially in the upper social circles where racial intermarriage is frowned upon and Negroes are usually excluded from social functions. But there is no segregation of any kind, and many Puerto Ricans are not even aware that they are relatively dark skinned until they come to the States and are treated as Negroes are here. Often skin color is used as a description of social position rather than of actual appearance. A Negro, high enough socially to travel first class, may arrive in Puerto Rico by steamer and be accosted by a white porter who wants to carry his suitcase. The latter is quite apt to address him as "*blanco*," or "white man," because he is a first-class passenger. The segregation which was introduced in Puerto Rican units of the army after the United States had taken over the island—and is now happily abolished—was foreign and baffling to the Puerto Ricans. At

the popular swimming resort of Luquillo Beach, maintained
by the government, there is not a trace of segregation, or even
color-consciousness. Nor is there in any part of the public-
school system.

That the growth of the tourist business poses problems in
race relations is shown by a story from Brazil, which is also
extremely lenient in racial matters and prides itself on its
color blindness when it comes to people. It seems that a
traveler from Alabama or Georgia registered in one of Rio de
Janeiro's most fashionable hotels. In the dining room, at his
first meal there, he spotted a colored man eating at a nearby
table. Indignantly he called the manager to object to such
uncivilized practices. He didn't want to eat in the same room
with Negroes. It turned out, however, that the colored gentleman was a cabinet member in the Brazilian government, as
Negroes have often held, and now hold, high positions in the
executive and legislative branches of Puerto Rico's government.

Negroes may today stay in the Caribe Hilton, the Condado
Beach Hotel, and all others. They may rent rooms, eat in the
dining room, drink in the bars, play in the casinos, tip the
bellboys, and attend special private functions to which they
have been invited. They may not, however, sun themselves on
the hotels' beaches or swim in the hotels' ocean. Lolling on
the sand on hotel property and swimming in the sea from
that property are reserved for the members of the hotels'
"Beach Clubs," which are exclusive only insofar as they are
color-conscious.

In 1953 one of our national magazines published a survey
of organized gambling in the Caribbean area. It was not surprising to read in that article that Puerto Rico's various casinos are not only the best managed of them all, but are the
only ones in the Caribbean area which are scrupulously
honest.

In 1936 I spent considerable time, and more money, at the roulette wheel in the Condado Beach Hotel. That wheel and others like it were popular institutions, patronized largely by Puerto Ricans. When I arrived on the island in December, 1948, to attend that tremendous opening of the new era— Muñoz' first inauguration as governor—several of my old friends informed me joyfully that the first government license for a casino had just been issued to the Condado Beach Hotel —on condition that the hotel add a new wing to double its capacity, that it improve its swimming facilities, and modernize itself in various other ways. I don't know whether or not the former wheel had been operated illegally; I do know that such gambling facilities are now licensed and scrupulously supervised by the government—which will stand for no cheating.

(The above statement irked my editor when he saw it in my first draft. "A roulette wheel which does not cheat," he wrote in comment, "is like a perpetual-motion machine. You can dream about it, but don't ask me to believe it. What you mean is that the cheating is moderate, or state-supervised." He may, of course, have something there. It may be that the one, or two, or three zeros which assure the management its cut on the gambling and make casinos profitable amount to a legal form of cheating. What the Puerto Rican government does is to make sure that the cheating goes no further.)

The government's Visitors Bureau manages a school in which croupiers and other casino operators are trained at the expense of the hotels which desire their services. Honesty is there drilled into them with the same relentlessness with which they are taught skills, poise, and manners.

Like almost everything else on the island, the matter of honesty in gambling was some years ago dramatized by one of Governor Muñoz' many bon mots. It seemed that one of Puerto Rico's wealthiest men, and one of the bitterest enemies of Muñoz and the Popular Democratic party, had won the government-operated lottery's annual grand prize of several hundred thousand dollars. Informed of the matter, Muñoz said: "That proves that our lottery is fair, even though God is not."

The tourist industry resembles all others in that, no matter how fine its physical plant may be, it is no better than are the skilled workers who operate that plant. One cannot take illiterate workers out of the cane fields, stuff them into uniforms, and expect them to function as waiters, bellhops, and the like. Exactly as the government is today training thousands of machinists and other skilled workers for the growing manufacturing plant, so it is also training Puerto Ricans in all the skills which, together, make a hotel a smoothly running organization. The course, which employs Swiss teachers to turn out skilled hotel employees, from bellboys to cashiers, takes ten months and includes a thorough drilling in the English language. During that time, students are paid twenty dollars per month, are given uniforms, and are fed at least one good meal per day. However, they don't all stay in Puerto Rico after they graduate. Many of them find jobs in the southwestern states, where there is also a demand for skilled bilingual hotel employees. The tourist industry of the Dominican Republic makes strong bids for their services, as does Brazil. Indeed, all of Latin America is becoming increasingly tourist-conscious; Puerto Rico is becoming known as an excellent source of trained workers. The government does not mind. Trained Puerto Ricans who earn a good reputation elsewhere improve Puerto Rico's reputation wherever they go.

In view of the strong resentments which had been aroused in earlier years by Washington's policy of ramming English down the throats of the bewildered Puerto Rican school children, it is significant to note the avidity with which prospective hotel employees and many others now study the lan-

guage. Some years ago I discussed the matter with Waldemar
Lee, then working for a dollar a year as the director of the
Tourist Bureau. "All that," he said, "is part of our over-all
revolution. It is astonishing how eager our people now are to
learn English. Everybody wants to learn it. Pretty soon we
plan to get to the point where no taxi driver can get a license
unless he knows English. We will probably have to open a
school or some night classes for them, but we will have no
trouble in finding enthusiastic students."

The Visitors Bureau has begun a long-term program under
which the old walled city of San Juan, now a small part of the
whole complex and sprawling capital, was first legally declared a historic monument and is now to be preserved and
restored as a beautiful old Spanish urban center. The same
men who some years ago were in charge of restoring old
Williamsburg were invited to Puerto Rico to make preliminary studies and plans. They saw the old walls, the forts, the
massive gates, the cathedral and other old churches, the cob-
blestoned streets, the many fine old government buildings,
the ancient coffee house, La Mallorquina, many fine and
solidly built houses—now mostly filled to overflowing by
crowded slum dwellers—and they were enthusiastic about
the wealth of impressive colonial material available for their
work.

The work of restoration goes hand in hand with city zoning
to prevent any modern buildings from being erected in old
San Juan; street cobblestones may no longer be torn up and
replaced with concrete; if a man insists on having a neon
sign for his business, he must move to the capital's Santurce
section, which has, in any event, grown to be the real business
center.

Some years ago, too, the Visitors Bureau created legislation
under which no more billboards may be erected along the
country roads and highways, and all those that now exist

must be removed within a few years' time—after their services have presumably repaid the monies invested in them.

Despite such steps Puerto Rico is still far behind the more advanced resort centers in the attractions which it offers the many visitors who demand organized entertainment. The men who are directly in charge of pioneering a tourist industry are acutely aware, for instance, of the fact that excursions from San Juan to other parts of the island are still scanty and poorly organized. San Juan itself offers swimming, fishing, gambling, baseball, basketball, some sight-seeing in the old city and the old forts, and not much of anything else.

There are no halls which can accommodate large conventions. There is only one night club (Jack's, but recommended) at which convention delegates can relax in the evening.

As far as the visitor from the United States is concerned, there is another great problem which seems to be insuperable. That is the problem of shopping. Puerto Rico has never had a tradition of producing any quantities of the handicrafted articles which tourists often demand because they are quaint and relatively inexpensive. Indeed, more often than not, an abundance of such articles indicates a low standard of living geared to home industries; a society which is rapidly industrializing for the improvement of living standards cannot afford to sponsor them in competition with its factory-made goods.

There are a few small shops which sell handicraft articles, but most of the things which the visitor can buy in San Juan are exactly the same things which he can buy, at lower prices and in a greater profusion of varieties, in New York.

Partly to offset that drawback, the Puerto Rican Visitors Bureau therefore works closely with the Virgin Islands government for the promotion of tourism. Literature describing the attractions of the Virgin Islands is freely available in all the Puerto Rican tourist centers; on the continent, the Virgin

Islands representatives, coming from a society which is even poorer than is Puerto Rico, are invited to share the office space of the Puerto Rican tourist representatives; visitors to Puerto Rico can at any time take a morning plane for a half-hour flight to Charlotte Amalie and return in the evening after a spree in one of the Caribbean's great shopping centers; if they would rather stay there, because they like the beaches or the hotels better, or because they are attracted to the more picturesque "natives," or because they want quick divorces, that is perfectly all right with the Puerto Rican government—which takes the reasonable stand that anything which attracts visitors to that general corner of the American Union is good for both societies.

If Puerto Rico, however, offers inadequate shopping facilities to visitors from the continental United States, it is by the same token becoming a shopping Mecca for visitors from such near-by countries as Venezuela. As Puerto Rican development and prosperity mount, as the goods in San Juan's stores multiply and diversify accordingly because the Puerto Ricans can every year buy more, better, and costlier goods, it is becoming increasingly important as such a Mecca. People in Caracas have discovered that it requires only a few hours for them to fly the five hundred miles which separate them from San Juan. They have begun to come in ever-increasing numbers to spend their money on American goods. They buy thousands of dollars' worth of suits of clothing, women's dresses, automobiles, refrigerators, deep freezers, washing machines, radios.

Despite its many disadvantages Puerto Rico's tourist industry flourishes and grows. More conventions, of organizations small enough to be accommodated in the existing halls, are held there every year. More cruise ships put in at San Juan than ever before, attracted by the old city and the unique reputation which Puerto Rico has won in recent years for its great over-all social effort. Statistics on the numbers of tourists received are lacking, but general statistics on arrivals in Puerto Rico reveal the growing interest shown in the island. In 1937 there was a total of about 24,000 arrivals— Puerto Ricans, mainland Americans, and aliens. In 1945 there were 32,000, and in 1949, 135,000. By 1953, the figure had grown to 230,000. All of San Juan's hotels together were 75 per cent filled on an average throughout the year, and nearly 100,000 people registered in those hotels.

Puerto Rico has become America's crossroad in the Caribbean.

CHAPTER XVII

Public Health

THERE IS A SCHOOL of thought which holds that tropical diseases impede successful development in the tropics—and will always so impede it because it is more difficult to control illness in the tropics than in the middle latitudes. The uniform warm and humid climate, argue the adherents of that school, is ideal for the propagation of disease germs as well as of insects and other vectors which spread such germs. There may or may not be some grains of truth in what they say. Their philosophy is nevertheless vicious in that it is fatalistic and therefore defeatist. It is opposed and refuted by many public-health experts who actually work in the tropics.

It is nonsense, say the latter, to lay the blame for tropical illnessess on the natural climate when the man-made social and economic climate is so obviously bad in the tropics that health conditions must be bad to correspond. In the middle latitudes, in the countries which are economically developed, standards of living are sufficiently high so that malnutrition of the majority is not a health problem. The majority, moreover, takes an adequate sanitary environment so for granted that they ignore it and feel free to credit their supposedly superior natural climate for their grantedly superior health. They are surrounded by municipal, state, and national health organizations, alerted, equipped, and financed to deal immediately with any threat to the public health. Much money is spent, and great care is taken, to see that their water and sewage facilities are not sources of infection. Their meat and other foods are inspected. Their restaurants are inspected. They have sufficient doctors, hospitals, clinics, and sufficient income to support them—usually with private funds, but with public funds where private income is inadequate.

The humid tropics, on the other hand, have long been the world's colonial regions par excellence, exploited as such. To be sure, capital outflow from the ruling countries to the colonies has been great, but profit returns have been greater. Whatever was left behind was not sufficient to raise wages above the twelve cents per person per day about which Estéban Bird complained, to assure diets and ways of life for the majority which are conducive to general health, to give the tropical society a budget sufficient for creating an adequate sanitary environment, medical services sufficient to meet existing needs, education geared in part to problems of hygiene, and over-all income large enough to support all that out of taxes.

Under such conditions, with such great differences in the man-made social climates, it is futile to blame the natural climate for observed differences between the health of many tropical peoples and that of residents in the so-called temperate regions. "Public health," say doctors of the U.S. Public Health Service, "is a purchasable commodity. The amount you get is the amount that you can, or are willing to, pay for." It is a good working principle which says, in effect, that public health is a function of an intangible called standards of living. Modern Puerto Rico is among the several societies (Australia's Queensland is another) which have shown that a tropical society which tackles its health problems by improving the man-made social climate which in its entirety is called the standard of living, instead of trying to change the natural climate, is likely to achieve notable results.

My own re-education on tropical health began in 1931 when I stopped in Puerto Rico en route to the Amazon, and Muñoz brought me word one day that Dr. Bailey Ashford wanted to see me. I had heard of Ashford as one of the American pioneers in tropical medicine. He had won world fame by being the first in the Western Hemisphere to isolate the parasite of hookworm, or ancylostomiasis; for the U.S. Army he had headed the first (unsuccessful) campaign to eradicate hookworm in Puerto Rico; people had begun to go to him from many parts of the American tropics because of his fame for curing the "incurable" tropical sprue—through the simple means (I discovered years later) of feeding his patients lean and fat meat.

He was a sick man himself in 1931, near the end of his life. I was delighted to go to his office, but considerably surprised by my reception. As soon as the handshaking was over, he said: "I have a big bone to pick with you people."

That was baffling. I could not fathom what bone he might want to pick with a man who was going forth merely to check on the behavior of the earth's magnetism and the idiosyncracies of the compass in various remote parts of the world. But before I could express my bewilderment, he went on.

"It's about hookworm. You fellows go all over the world, trying to clean it up, but you go at things wrong. You tell people to wear shoes, which they can't afford, and to build outhouses, which they can't afford either. You dose your hookworm patients with carbon tetrachloride, which, in their weakened condition, is worse than the disease itself. If you will examine their stools you will see that nature is constantly trying to pass off the parasite. Why don't you give nature a chance? Feed the people; improve their strength, and you won't have to worry about hookworm."

Astonished, I explained to him as politely as I could that I represented the Carnegie Institution of Washington, which had no direct interest in tropical medicine. Then it developed that two doctors of the Rockefeller Foundation, en route to start a hookworm campaign in some other part of the world's tropics, were in San Juan at the same time, and that he had mistaken me for one of them.

I had a long talk with him, in which he indicated his strong conviction that not only hookworm, but most of the other so-called tropical diseases as well, were actually diseases of low standards of living with their attendant evils of poverty, filth, crowding, malnutrition, and bad sanitary environment.

Twenty years later, at a reception in Washington, I met Dr. Juan Pons, then and now Puerto Rico's amiable and energetic Secretary of Health. I told him about my interest in the tropics and all their problems and congratulated him on the remarkable progress which Puerto Rico had made in matters of health. This time there was no doubt about the problem's real nature.

"Look," said Pons. "Let's not talk about tropical medicine, because there is no such thing. There is only a medicine of low standards of living and another of higher. Our experience in Puerto Rico and the entire world's disease pattern bear that out."

In 1952, as an outstandingly successful tropical medico and health official, Pons was invited to contribute to a definitive work on tropical medicine and its problems. He wrote back that he would gladly do what he could, but that he didn't know what tropical medicine was. Did those gentlemen really mean to ascribe to the tropical climate such ailments as malaria, gastrointestinal diseases, hookworm, and tuberculosis, which had plagued Puerto Rico for many decades? Pons ascribed them to the malnutrition and filth of abject poverty; he wanted to inform his colleagues that those and related diseases were found in all parts of the world, regardless of natural climate, where living standards resembled those of pre-1940 Puerto Rico, and that, moreover, his own experience showed that they begin to disappear as the poverty begins to be abolished and standards of living go up.

His heretical letter was never answered. He did not contribute to the book.

Twenty years ago, malaria was a scourge in Puerto Rico, as it also was in India, Africa, the Amazon basin, and many other tropical countries, and as it once had been in Washington, D.C., as far north as Ohio, and at Saratoga, New York. According to an unpublished report prepared in 1936 by the Planning Division of the PRRA, Puerto Rico's annual mortality from malaria was at that time nearly 200 deaths per 100,000 inhabitants, or six times as many as in the malaria belt in Alabama, Florida, Mississippi, and South Carolina. The statistics of 1940 showed that there were in that year 97 deaths from malaria per 100,000, or a total of nearly 2,000, and 24,000 cases of malaria, or nearly 1,300 per 100,000 inhabitants; actually there must have been many more—possibly two or three times as many—since thousands of ill Puerto Ricans in those days went nowhere near the doctors.

As a result of a vigorous health campaign, begun in 1941 by Dr. Antonio Fernós Isern and now carried forward by Dr. Pons, malaria has by now been eliminated from the Puerto Rican scene. In 1951, a greatly improved and far more efficient statistical service reported a total of 88 cases of malaria, or about four per 100,000; deaths from the disease had been reduced to .09 per 100,000—meaning that in that year two people died of malaria in Puerto Rico. By the time of the present writing, cases of malaria are so sporadic that the illness has become a medical rarity.

The 1936 report stated that Puerto Rico's mortality from tuberculosis was 308 to 337 per 100,000, or seven times that of Connecticut. In 1940, over 9,000 Puerto Ricans, nearly 500 per 100,000, suffered from tuberculosis, which proved fatal to well over half of that number. Ten years later, despite a marked population growth and a greatly improved health service which spotted and treated thousands of patients who would previously have gone unnoticed and unreported, the total number of tuberculosis cases had been reduced to 6,000, while deaths from the disease had gone down to 112 per 100,000. In 1952 the tuberculosis mortality was 90 per 100,-000 and still dropping rapidly.

The same statistical behavior is found in gastrointestinal diseases, which have long been, and are still, Puerto Rico's greatest killers. In 1936 the mortality from that cause was 360 per 100,000, or fifty times that of Connecticut and ten times that of Hawaii. In 1940 the figure was 405 per 100,000; in 1951 it was 127.

In partial explanation of its distressing figures on public health, the 1936 report went on to say: "The Puerto Rican laborers are subject to a process of slow starvation which for hosts of unemployed becomes habitual pressing hunger. Meat and milk, for example, are such luxuries that the daily per capita consumption is measured in ounces and spoonfuls."

Undoubtedly today's improved health is attributable in part to the fact that Puerto Rico's poor now eat better than they did then. Much of the improvement must, however, be ascribed to the direct efforts of the Department of Health.

The graphs in Dr. Pons's office move steadily downward; the malaria graph has hit bottom; those for tuberculosis and gastrointestinal diseases—commonly lumped under the shotgun diagnosis of diarrhea and enteritis—are steadily heading for the bottom. As they decline, so does the over-all death rate.

In 1906, Governor Beekman Winthrop wrote: "Although it may be possible, through the introduction of more advanced sanitary mediums, to reduce Puerto Rico's death rate, this rate is not excessive for a tropical island." In that year it was 23 per thousand. In 1940, some 35,000 Puerto Ricans died on their island, or 18.4 per thousand. When the mortality rate dropped to 12 per thousand in 1947, Dr. Pons thought that things had gone about as far as a public-health program could bring them. In his report for that year he wrote that the tuberculosis rate might be reduced slightly through direct action, that minor improvements in the over-all health picture could be expected here and there, but that the death rate was leveling off. "I expect," he wrote, "that at this point in our accomplishment any marked reduction in our mortality rates in the years to come must be in proportion to the improvement in economic level at which our population struggles, rather than to any increase in our direct health-promoting efforts; and that the smallest unfavorable change in our economy will have an immediate effect on those rates."

There was no unfavorable change; the economy kept improving, though not rapidly enough to suit the impatient Secretary of Health. Budgets for public health increased; efforts to reduce illness and death increased to correspond. In 1951, deaths on the island totaled 21,000, and the death rate was 9.4 per thousand. The following year the death rate had gone down to 9.0 per thousand, which was lower than that of the continental United States. It is still dropping at the time of the present writing.

At this point the thoughtful reader may well detect what seems to be a flaw in the argument that public health, in the tropics as elsewhere, is a function of standards of living. By that argument, since Puerto Rico's death rate is now lower than is that of the United States, Puerto Rico's standards of living should be higher than are those of the United States. That is, of course, absurd. Puerto Rico's per capita average annual income is still less than half of that of our poorest state, Mississippi; wages are considerably lower than in the United States; there is still, proportionally, more unemployment and more, and greater, poverty.

The absurdity, however, points up the greater absurdity of striving for simple correlations in the manner beloved and often demanded by scholars but seldom justified by the lives of people. If we now, because the correlation with standards of living seems to break down, return to that with the tropical climate, we are in danger of arriving at the even more absurd conclusion that the tropical climate is more healthful than is that in the middle latitudes.

"How have we lengthened our lives so much in such a short time?" asked Muñoz in a nation-wide radio broadcast on Columbus Day, 1953. "Largely by involving the people themselves in the determination of their own destiny."

Dr. Jacques May, who is in charge of the American Geographical Society's studies in Medical Geography, became aware of those matters some years ago and has formulated an ambitious, systematic program of research in Puerto Rico, aimed at arriving at possible conclusions regarding the complex interrelations between public health on the one hand, and, on the other, such matters as economic indexes, employment, manners of individual living, cultural mores, ways of living together, attitudes and habits of government, sanitary environment, psychological environment—and possibly natural climate as well. May he find the financing he needs! His study will help to clarify man's understanding of the relations between himself and his environment—of which man himself is the most important component.

According to all of Dr. Pons's public-health rules, the death rate had no business to continue to drop after 1947—considering the aggravating—to Pons—slowness with which the rest of the government was improving economic conditions. But it does continue to drop—so rapidly that Pons now envisions a situation in the near future, when deaths from tuberculosis and gastrointestinal diseases will have come down to the same levels that are found in the continental United States. When that has happened, says Pons, the over-all Puerto Rican death rate will be 7.6 per thousand—one of the lowest to be found anywhere in the world.

The life expectancy of the average Puerto Rican was 32 years in 1900, 42 in 1930, 46 in 1940, had risen to 61 in 1952, and as yet shows no sign of arresting its climb.

Such figures, I know, distress a number of demographers who seem today to be terrified by the word overpopulation. It is therefore well to point out that Puerto Rico's "explosive" birth rate was 39 per thousand in 1940, 41 in 1941, and 43 by 1947; by 1951 it had fallen to 37.3; in 1952 it was 35.2, and it is today still dropping rapidly. The death rate is nearing a minimum which is made irreducible by the fact that people do die of old age. The drop in the birth rate has just begun—for reasons dealt with in Chapter XX. The two are still out of phase, but the gap has begun to close.

As Puerto Rico begins to achieve real social and economic health, it is also moving toward a proper balance between population numbers and the developed resources sustaining the population; as the Puerto Ricans, year by year, produce more to eat, they have also begun to produce fewer Puerto Ricans to share the food. That is as it should be, in line with demographic trends often observed in many parts of the world, and also in line with the theory advanced by Dr. Josué de Castro in the latter's book *The Geography of Hunger*. According to that theory, for which the author, the Executive Director of the United Nations' Food and Agricultural Organization, reaped vituperative abuse from many scholars, human fertility tends to rise with malnutrition and to go down as nutritional standards rise.

The social mechanics through which Puerto Rico's current drop in birth rates is accomplished are among the most fascinating of the Commonwealth's current culture changes and are discussed in Chapter XX.

Adequate and energetic medical treatment is, of course, only one phase of any public-health effort. The provision of an adequate sanitary environment is another. The quality of drinking water available to the people is one of several indexes of such an environment.

To judge by his book, *The Stricken Land*, Governor Tugwell seems to have been greatly preoccupied with San Juan's untrustworthy water supply. He seems to have considered it symptomatic of all of Puerto Rico's ills; at times his book reads as though having to put up with it, having to boil and filter his drinking water, was among the worst of the hardships that he had to endure in a backward and improvident society.

He wrote about conditions during 1942–46, which were infinitely better than they had been when the United States first stepped into the Puerto Rican scene. In contrast to his complaints, however, it is significant that, since 1950, the San Juan water supply has been approved for interstate commerce. That means that steamers and airplanes putting in at the capital may now fill their tanks from the city water system with no thought of further purification, with no danger that their crews and passengers will thereafter catch diseases from polluted water. It also means that the life of some future Tugwell will be far easier and less worrisome in the capital. If you should move there tomorrow, you may throw away most or all of the common advice, oral and printed, about how to stay healthy in the tropics. Precisely as you may forget about the daily quinine pills for prophylaxis against malaria, so you may now drink from the common water supply, from anybody's tap, in any hotel or restaurant, without having to go through the common tropical ritual of boiling, filtering, and adding so many chlorazene pills that it smells worse than Chicago water. In fact, if you come from some place other than Chicago or Milwaukee, you may even be bothered by the fact that the San Juan water already smells and tastes of chlorine. You won't be bothered long, however; Chicagoans have long since become accustomed to it, and so will you. A little chlorine is better than a lot of typhoid and dysentery.

In his report of 1950–51, Dr. Pons stated that by then no

fewer than fifteen municipalities, including San Juan, had adequate treating plants serving safe water to an urban population of over 700,000. He also reported much progress in other urban communities, plus the fact that 164 new rural aqueducts had by then begun to bring safe water to nearly 400,000 rural residents whose women had previously lugged questionable water from polluted springs or streams, in old gasoline cans and sometimes over long distances. An active program of sanitation, always straining with its human energies against the rigid bounds imposed by limited budgets, is devoted to public water supplies and sewer systems, to stream-purification, industrial hygiene, food sanitation, soil sanitation, and municipal sanitation. Public and private water supplies are now sampled periodically for bacteriological examination; sewer systems are inspected regularly. The Department of Health—closely co-ordinated with all the rest of the government—works with the island's Aqueduct and Sewer Authority, and with the insular and municipal housing authorities, in making plans and deciding the all-important question of priorities in the execution of those plans. No new low-cost housing project, rural or urban, is allowed to be built unless and until the Department of Health and all others concerned (working always through the Planning Board) are satisfied that its water and sewer system are adequate for the health needs of both today and the years to come. Factories, new and old, are inspected regularly for possible deficiencies in temperature and humidity, ventilation, illumination, atmospheric contaminants, and sanitary facilities. The owners' compliance with the recommendations for improvement made by the Department of Health seems to be a voluntary matter; however, most of the owners and managers, forced and carried along by the increasing popular demand for better health, do comply without undue resistance.

Through such means, and through the periodic inspection of restaurants, ice plants, bottling works, and the like—to say nothing of private homes—and a campaign to teach the rudiments of sanitation to the individual poor, the over-all sanitary environment has been drastically improved since 1941.

Puerto Rico's present low death rate seems all the more remarkable when one remembers that over 80 per cent of the island's people are still, despite rising standards of living, medically indigent—and that of that 80 per cent an appreciable number are still medically all but inaccessible, in part because they live in remote sections of the hills, and in part because they superstitiously follow the hocus-pocus of *curanderos* or *curanderas*—male or female folk healers who flourish in all the world's isolated and poverty-stricken communities.

That means that, despite the fact that there were some five hundred doctors on the island in 1940 as compared to well over a thousand today, over 80 per cent of the medicine practiced in Puerto Rico must be public medicine, and so a drain on a budget already low and overstrained when compared with those of the various states.

In addition to managing six tuberculosis hospitals and five general hospitals, the department maintains seventy-six public-health units in the various districts. Each of these is a clinic (though some have small hospitals attached to them) for the treatment of such diseases as tuberculosis, syphilis, and heart trouble. Each unit, however, is also an important educational center in which doctors and nurses constantly talk to patients about various health problems, as well as a field outpost of various such sub-organizations as the Bureaus of Tuberculosis, Venereal Disease, Maternal and Infant Hygiene, Crippled Children, Malaria and Insect Control, Public-Health Nursing, and Sanitation. It is largely through these centers, and through its Division of Social Welfare, that the department manages to reach a large number of the rural poor who also, because of their poverty, constitute the greatest single reservoir of disease.

The over-all aim is, through the public-health units, the department's Division of Public Welfare, the Division of Hospitals, and through close co-operation with the educational system for health instruction, school lunches, and public milk stations, to reach into all walks of Puerto Rican life, and all of the interlocking phases of any one walk of life. Always the work comes back to education in its manifold forms—and to pioneering in education. One unique but gratifyingly successful practice is to talk about general health problems to patients in hospitals—where they and their visitors are more receptive to such talks than at any other time.

Mrs. Glenola Rose was one of my students in the area-studies course that I had the honor to conduct in Puerto Rico in 1952. A mature woman—she will not mind my saying that she is older than I—an interested woman with a vast variety of experiences in matters of public health in many parts of the world, she had this to say about the Rio Piedras public-health unit—in the term paper that she wrote for the course:

"Among the seventy-six public-health units one is unique, that at Rio Piedras. It is the training center for all personnel for all public-health units in Puerto Rico."

After describing the plant, staff, and varied activities of this unit, which include the offering of services to the community in prenatal, well baby, preschool, and school clinics, control programs for tuberculosis and venereal disease, malaria and communicable diseases, programs for cancer and heart disease, education in nutrition and all other matters of health, she calls attention to what is undoubtedly one of the greatest factors in the Puerto Rican success. "One is impressed with the enthusiasm and response from every person involved, both patients and staff, from the janitor up. This atmosphere appears to result from the insistence that each and every person is valuable in his own right—true democracy. One of the ways of giving satisfaction is the custom of giving a diploma at graduation to anyone finishing a course of training. The

Puerto Ricans are eager to be educated, take pride in securing an education. Janitors as well as other employees get diplomas. But, so do mothers, who are taught how to care for themselves and their families. There are constant graduation ceremonies. The people are being taught to want what they should have and to be proud of wanting it!"

In describing his program to the second regional meeting of the American College of Physicians, in November, 1950, Pons said: "It is imperative that we put into the attitude of people, into their everyday conscious thinking, that illness and infirmity are to a very large measure preventable, that they are cancelable liabilities, and that it is unnecessary to suffer them. . . . We must teach people to seek the services that prevent them, rather than those that remedy them. We must see that the communities co-operate in a constructive manner with the agencies dedicated to the promotion of health. When we accomplish this, then we shall have the greatest of any progress in medicine to report."

While Pons's report on the problems and achievements of Puerto Rico's Department of Health was noteworthy, I doubt if the American College of Physicians liked hearing it—at a time when virtually all the doctors in the United States were shivering in their boots over the bogey of socialized medicine.

Despite the notable achievements of his department, despite the dramatic recent drop in mortality from virtually all causes, as well as in the incidence of diseases of various kinds, and in line with the fact that the casual visitor to Puerto Rico today can still be appalled by the conditions of poverty and illness that he encounters, Dr. Juan Pons is in no way a booster of the chamber-of-commerce kind. He still complains openly, publicly, and healthily about his troubles and problems. Every time I see him he is on the verge of resigning his job and returning to private practice. The following year, when I see him again, he is still on the job and still about to resign, in part because he can earn more money in private practice, in part because the island's over-all effort is too slow to suit him, not sufficiently effective to help and permit him to do the job he wants to do and believes he should do. At the time of the present writing, that has been going on for four years, but Pons is still Puerto Rico's Secretary of Health—and still impatient.

"It is interesting indeed," he said to the American College of Physicians, "that a small epidemic outbreak in Puerto Rico brings forth all our might to prevent a few deaths in as many days and that public opinion becomes manifestly impatient if that might is not immediately forthcoming; yet, there is no great worry over the fact that some 60,000 women give birth each year (164 daily) in dingy, substandard homes in the rural areas without any of the benefits of present-day medicine. Certainly a small epidemic outbreak offers no greater urgency than the fact that hundreds of children do not have a wholesome home and appropriate food; the death of a few during an epidemic outbreak is not a more serious matter than the fact that hundreds of families are each month left to suffer hunger and misery upon the death or infirmity of the breadwinners."

Continuing in that vein, and dealing with the obstacles that result from limited budgets, he said: "We now have on the waiting list of the Crippled Children's Bureau, 1,009 children waiting for orthopedic treatment of one kind or another, 556 children waiting for plastic surgery, and 1,358 waiting for treatment of remediable ocular conditions; most of them have been waiting for much too long, and we do not know just when they can be taken care of. We know of 824 cerebral palsied children who are receiving little if any expert care.

"Screening surveys have shown that our schools, with an approximate enrollment of 400,000 children, contain some 38,000 with visual difficulties readily correctable, and some 25,000 children who are hard of hearing; little is being done about them. One study has indicated that there are no fewer than 400 children under eighteen years of age who are blind, most of them from causes that could have been prevented."

Dr. Pons's positive and open distress about such matters, his complaints about the limitations which prevent him from tackling the problems indicated, are themselves signs of a new Puerto Rico with new social orientations. A few decades ago the crippled children of the poor, and those with defective eyesight, and those hard of hearing, and the palsied, were generally not treated at all—except for the few who received help from inadequate private charities. I doubt that they were even counted and that they received much more attention than shrugs of pity on being seen by accident.

Pons's complaints of 1950 are the expressions of an impatient man, personifying in his field a society impatient to get things done. But even while he and the society complain, Puerto Rico keeps soaring ahead in its public-health affairs, with statistical results which are probably not even approached anywhere else—in terms of positive achievements made in a few brief years.

And all that is only a beginning. What will Puerto Rico's statistics on morbidity and mortality, on death rates and life expectancy, look like some decades from now when the programs for agriculture, for industrialization, for education—now in their incipient stages—swell into full activity, bringing with them the public-health program which will have available ever larger budgets, ever more personnel, ever more ideas and enthusiasms, as the over-all effort keeps gaining momentum?

Perhaps the most important single explanation of Puerto Rico's remarkable success in matters of public health is found in the fact that the island's Department of Health not only subscribes to, but also abides by, Craig's dictum that "the days of monastery medicine and the ivory tower are gone." Medicine, to Howard Reid Craig, in his book *Introduction to Social*

Medicine, is "an integral, interrelated, and interdependent part of a functioning social and economic system which to be viable must exist in a continuing state of flux."

Pons's vision of a future Puerto Rico with the world's lowest death rate and one of the world's best climates of sanitation and health is not necessarily a vision of the distant future. As yet, the figures, curves, and charts, dealing with mortality and incidence of various diseases, with infant mortality and maternal deaths in childbirth, have shown no indication of discontinuing their dramatic drops. The vision of a Puerto Rico with the world's lowest death rate, is realizable in the near or immediate future of another decade or two—barring a local catastrophe or a world calamity.

CHAPTER XVIII

Education

A<small>N EDUCATIONAL SYSTEM</small>, taken in its entirety, is a mirror of the total society in which it functions. The over-all aims of that society, its intentions toward itself and its citizens, are all reflected in some ways—either positively or negatively—in its education. Those who shape educational policies, those who disagree with policies, those who confuse curricula and methodologies with policies, those who argue over subject matter versus techniques, dogma versus freedom of thought, educational leadership versus administrative policing, all of them together, and many more, reflect the sum total of their society's culture. It was shown in Chapter III that when that culture is cramped and circumscribed by colonialism, its educational system is also cramped and circumscribed; its educators may be excellent men, skilled in their trade, but they are not permitted to express themselves as such; the results are apt to be "confusion compounded by resentment and mounting toward chaos." When the society shakes off the lethargy and anguish of its colonialism, when it begins to reshape itself, it also re-examines its educational system, revitalizes it, expands it, reshapes it in line with the society's total human aims.

When the United States took over the island in 1899 it

found an educational system extremely limited and church controlled. Commissioners from Washington were appointed to reorganize it according to continental patterns and with a complete disregard of local mores, customs, and needs. They changed and expanded the system, but their prime aim seemed to be that of making what they considered good Americans out of the Puerto Ricans. As early as 1900, Dr. M. G. Brumbaugh, the first Commissioner of Education under the American flag, proudly reported to the U.S. government that the average Puerto Rican child knew more about Washington, Lincoln, Betsy Ross, and the American flag than did the average child in the United States. The question of whether he knew as much as he should about the responsibilities involved in taking his place as a Puerto Rican in the Puerto Rican society seems to have been of secondary importance.

Puerto Rican teachers were, of course, dissatisfied with that state of affairs. Among themselves they groped for new orientations, but that did them little good in a system in which educational policy rested in the hands of an American appointed by Washington—who could, moreover, be at any time replaced by another American with radically different policies and orientations. Opposite the Commissioners of Education most teachers kept prudently quiet.

In 1930, however, Hoover appointed Dr. José Padín as Commissioner of Education. A progressive, liberal educator, Padín began to re-examine the island's entire educational philosophy and to encourage all his teachers to do the same. Nineteen hundred and thirty marked the turning point for a trend which has not yet run its full course, a turning away from a philosophy of education based on tradition in theory, and routine in practice, to a philosophy based on a diagnosis of the Puerto Rican educational system from the viewpoint of Puerto Rico's needs. Spanish became again the medium of instruction; English a required subject of study.

But the vital and stimulating Padín period was ended by the shots which killed Col. Riggs. After that, it will be remembered, Washington turned on Puerto Rico as if in revenge. Dr. Gruening, according to the Ickes diary, wanted again to ram English down the throats of the Puerto Rican children. Padín resigned, and Gallardo was appointed for the implementation of Washington's return to outmoded, reactionary policies. As told in Chapter IX, Inés Mendoza, then a high-school teacher and now the wife of Muñoz Marín, was dropped from the school system for daring to testify at the Hays hearings that she considered the old practice of doing all the teaching in English as bad pedagogy. Those events, and the general air of reaction and psychological fatigue which marked the period 1936–40, again put a brake on effective local inquiry into the effectiveness of the school system. Teachers continued to discuss such matters, but they went underground as far as Washington was concerned.

The hiatus after Gallardo's resignation in 1945, when for a time there was no responsible commissioner because no qualified educator would accept the job under the political terms laid down by Congress, was again marked by much re-examination and several elaborate surveys designed to lead toward self-determined educational policies, to be adopted when and if Puerto Rico should win the power to determine its own policies. The act of Congress under which the people were permitted to elect their own governor in 1948, and the latter could appoint a Commissioner of Education responsible to him and the people rather than to Washington, released a flood of energies and ideas. Under the leadership of Commissioner (now Secretary) Mariano Villaronga, the entire society, from the loftiest professor down to the lowliest *jíbaro*, began to be education-minded as never before. The system of public instruction began to be revitalized and expanded to fit modern needs.

In an address delivered in 1947 in Atlantic City at a convention of the Middle States Association of Colleges and Secondary Schools Dr. Jaime Benítez, chancellor of the University of Puerto Rico, said: "In my opinion, the key educational problem in Puerto Rico is not that we need more schools—which we do; or more teachers—which we do; or that our students should be willing and able to stay longer with us—which they should. I believe it is far more important to give to the whole educational system a sense and purpose in terms of the realities and potentialities of our life."

In the same vein in a Puerto Rican-prepared article in the Cuban magazine *Carteles*, April 26, 1953, we read that the aims of the island's public instruction are: "to improve the pupils' physical, mental, and spiritual health; to raise the living standard of the Puerto Rican people; to educate the people in the optimum utilization of available resources, in the improvement of domestic and individual economy, in the frugal life, and in the spirit which shapes and tempers attitudes toward material necessities; to teach that the maximum fruition of man is through creation rather than acquisition; to improve the tone of human relations through instruction as well as practical examples of collaboration in matters of respect and consideration for others; to develop skills for communication and the solution of problems through the wise administration of various curricular materials such as reading and writing, the natural sciences, mathematics, the social sciences, and vocational arts; and finally to develop firm sets of values and respect for the same."

Puerto Rico has come a long way since the days when the principal aim of its education was to teach pupils English and to see to it that they knew more than did children in the United States about Washington, Lincoln, Betsy Ross, and the American flag.

In 1899 the number of Puerto Rican children of school age totaled 290,000, of whom 22,000, or 8 per cent, actually attended schools; in 1940, 50 per cent of a total of 586,946 children between the ages of six and eighteen were able to attend schools; in 1952, almost 500,000 children, or 67 per cent of the total population of school age, received an education—the following year the total figure was up to 520,000. When the United States took over Puerto Rico only 15 per cent of all Puerto Ricans ten years of age or older were literate; by 1940 the figure had climbed to 68.5 per cent; today it is nearly 80 per cent. Not only because of the growing demand for education and because the older illiterates will die before long, but also because there is now a strong legislative push in that direction—in accordance with plans developed by the Department of Education—will the disease of illiteracy soon be as dead as malaria is today.

The fact that Puerto Rico's budget for public education is today nearly a third of the total budget—with all other branches of the government clamoring for ever more money—indicates a lively and vital interest. The expenditure per pupil of $71 annually, as compared with the $24 that were spent in 1940, is another indication of the growth of that preoccupation—even when the devaluation of the dollar is considered. However, the fact that New York and New Jersey spend about $200 per pupil every year shows that Puerto Rico still has a long way to go in bringing up its educational effort as the over-all Operation Bootstrap brings increasing results and increasing budgets.

Fifteen years ago Puerto Rican public education was commonly regarded as being better than that found in most colonial possessions and in almost any underdeveloped area as poor as was Puerto Rico. Today it is correctly recognized as being much better than it was then. Nevertheless, the Commonwealth's public education is still below the best, and even the average, found on the continent. Teachers are paid salaries ranging from $105 to $150 per month; they and many of the schools are overworked through double and interlocking enrollment because neither teaching power nor facilities exist to reduce teaching loads to the point demanded by good pedagogy; there are not nearly enough teachers available even though their number has grown from about 6,000 in 1940 to over 10,000 today. Those are indications of relatively low standards. On the other hand, the facts that those teachers have banded together in an association and that that association makes constant studies and carries on constant lively discussions on the problem of improving education, are signs of an admirable vitality in Puerto Rico's school system.

In general, the debaters or educators fall into two classes: those who would immediately extend education with the utmost speed to all Puerto Ricans, by any and all means, and those who have their eyes on quality, on educational standards, and insist that the monies available be used for raising those standards, even if it means slowing down the extension of education and the immediate eradication of illiteracy.

The Superior Council of Education, which directs the overall educational effort, carries on constant research and issues publications devoted to problems, improvement, and extension. Consultants from the continent are invited to make surveys and recommendations; at times Puerto Rican teachers have been so enraged by their reports that they have written criticisms which have in themselves been valuable contributions to the analysis of the island's educational problems. Men and women who claim correctly that almost any high-school graduate can teach the rudiments of the three R's to children and adults, and that such youngsters could be hired cheaply for an invaluable extension of education at the lowest levels, are opposed by those who believe that such practices would amount to a lowering of standards, that the real need is for the constant and more effective training of more and better teachers and the construction of more and better schools. The Planning Board, which will not permit a school or other public building to be erected unless it meets the board's specifications of being hurricane resistant, sanitary, and otherwise in line with the island's new material plant, is opposed by those who bewail the investment of so much money in mere buildings, who insist that a school consists of a teacher and pupils even though they sit on a log, and that wooden schools will in many cases serve the current needs of a poor society with still too many children out of school, and still too many illiterate adults, even though the wooden schools may blow down at the first hurricane.

The organization of the Department of Education reflects its determination to reach effectively into every phase and aspect of the Commonwealth's life and problem. The established school system is composed of an elementary school of six years, a three-year junior high school, rural and urban (the two differ in their approaches and curricula because of the varying demands made on them), and a high school. There are, moreover, vocational schools which are making important contributions to the industrialization program, schools for adult education, evening high schools, a Division of Community Education whose remarkable program is discussed in Chapter XIX, and a system of free music schools. In addition, the Department of Education carries on orientation programs, a program of vocational rehabilitation, of school lunchrooms and free lunches for children, of veterans' education, and an information service for students and teachers.

In 1950, the Carnegie Library administration turned over to the department its libraries in San Juan and Santurce. In addition to managing these, the school system operates three bookmobiles at the time of the present writing, taking books to education-hungry people in the country, and will probably, by the time of publication, have realized its plan of operating a bookmobile unit in every one of the eight educational districts.

The department manages a radio station for the purpose of reaching all of the island's people in one way or another. It operates a photographic laboratory which pictorially records every aspect of Puerto Rico's life and growth. One of its most vital new innovations is the Department of Education Press.

Teachers and departments on the continent have a wealth of instructional material to draw on. Dozens of publishing houses produce textbooks by the hundreds of titles, dealing variously with American educational problems and the American way of life. Except for some local variations, language differences do not exist; regional differences are not so great that hundreds of pamphlets, periodicals, films, and other visual aids do not serve Delaware's educational system virtually as well as California's.

Such materials served the needs of earlier Commissioners of Education, determined to Americanize Puerto Rican children through the use of American books and materials; they do not serve the needs of modern Puerto Rico. The urge toward a real adjustment to the American way of life and the concomitant knowledge of English is today stronger than ever, but it cannot be met by rejecting old Puerto Rican ways of life and culture values. The realization of that fact creates a need for new instructional materials, written in Spanish, which take into account Puerto Rico's cultural origins and present transformations, its changing mores, its history, its specific problems—local as well as in relation to the United States and all the rest of the world.

Such materials cannot be bought from existing publishers. Puerto Rico's Department of Education has therefore gone into the publishing business for the purpose of creating teaching materials geared to existing and changing needs.

Dr. Antonio Colorado, who heads the press, was in New York during World War II, where he did valuable work for the Office of War Information. Many a time, in preparing material for broadcasting to our Allies in Latin America, he saved the OWI from the error of merely, enthusiastically but also chauvinistically, shouting hurrah for America's power and undoubted democracy. As well as anybody on the island, he knows that the Puerto Ricans know about our power and democracy; what they want to learn is how to handle their own problems as Americans *and* Puerto Ricans.

Among the activities of the press, which has its own printing and production plant, is the publication of a weekly paper, *Escuela*, for free distribution to the pupils in the elementary and high schools. It deals with literature, art, science, general information, the English language, biographies, school notes, and recreation. Alternate editions, alternately slanted, go to the elementary and high schools, 300,000 of the one and 100,-000 of the other.

The monthly periodical *Educación* is prepared for distribution to teachers. Besides discussing educational problems and progress, in Puerto Rico as well as on the continent and abroad, it keeps track of meetings, projects and studies, and offers guidance to teachers in doing their work and meeting their specific problems.

In addition, during the first five years after its establishment in 1948, the press published more than 125 textbooks, plans of study, monographs on Puerto Rico's agricultural, economic, and sociological problems, didactic materials for teachers. Besides writing its own texts and publishing appropriate discourses by various Puerto Rican lecturers, it cooperates with the large publishing firms on the continent toward adapting their books to Puerto Rican use. All the publications go to all libraries and important institutions of learning in the United States and Latin America. Both here and in the various Latin American republics they have begun to have a marked influence toward understanding of the Puerto Rican problem. In the twenty American nations south of the Rio Grande they also help to improve understanding of, and relations with, the United States.

Never before, for instance, has there been available in Spanish an objective and scholarly school text on the history of the United States which states the facts and does not offend by waving the flag. In August, 1953, Ginn and Company published one, written by Muzzey and Kidger and translated by Colorado, beautifully illustrated, printed, and bound. It was prepared for use in Puerto Rican schools; the publisher will find a growing demand for it in many parts of Latin America; the Department of State will be correspondingly grateful.

It is truly said that Puerto Rico is the meeting place of Latin American and North American cultures and can do much toward reconciling the two. One of the island's educational innovations which has been copied in many parts of Latin America, though the need for it is today diminishing in Puerto Rico, is the Second Unit Rural School, established under Padín during the 1930's.

Previous to the establishment of those schools, most of the educational effort had been confined to the towns and cities; the rural areas had a few poor equivalents of the Little Red Schoolhouse in which the three R's and other subjects were taught by rote. That was bad, of course, in a society which was still predominantly rural, and one whose human strength consisted largely of the impoverished peasantry, the *jíbaros*. The new program of the Second Unit Rural Schools began with detailed studies of all the various rural areas in which they were established, of their type or types of agriculture, their health conditions, their relative isolation from the rest of Puerto Rico, their social conditions in general. Those studies then became, each in its way according to the communities served, the bases for the schools' operations and educational programs—which were closely interrelated with the communities they served.

Each school had (and has) a farm on which the boys, in addition to their regular academic subjects, are taught agriculture. Facilities exist for teaching the girls cooking, canning, and other branches of domestic science; the social studies taught were in the early days aimed primarily at the understanding of the particular communities in which the schools were located; much emphasis was placed on vocational training; instruction in health and hygiene was made an essential part of the curriculum. Boys and girls, as today, were encouraged to join such organizations as the Future Farmers of America, so becoming, through devotion to their own particular problems, also identified with the vast agricultural world beyond Puerto Rico.

The work of the schools soon became intimately tied in with that of the Insular Office of Public Welfare. Social workers attached to them strove to help the children and their parents and to bring about a close relationship between the school and the community's various individuals. Mothers' clubs and parent-teacher associations strengthened that relationship. The school so became, also, a community center; its influence on adult life came to be felt widely, as for instance through night classes for adults, the organization of co-operatives, and the joint tackling of many other community problems.

Those things were revolutionary in Puerto Rico a quarter of a century ago. The facts that the Second Unit Rural Schools have been drastically modified by now, that they are today largely rural junior high schools with some vocational aspects added, mean only that Puerto Rico has changed. The psychological and cultural division between city and country is today not nearly so drastic as it was two decades ago; people by the thousands have flocked to the towns to take industrial jobs; new roads have united city and country more than ever before; the growth of literacy, the radio, and other means of communication have brought about accelerated exchanges of information.

The stress which Padín placed on health and hygiene in the

Second Unit Rural Schools has now been greatly intensified in all of the island's schools. The phenomenal success of the Department of Education in reducing the death rate is due in no small measure to the increased emphasis on health and hygiene in all the schools, and to the island-wide program for training teachers for health instruction and group dynamics devoted to such matters as nutrition, mental health, cancer, and tuberculosis. Health is further improved by the fact that about $8,000,000 per year, including a sizable amount from the federal government, is spent on school lunches and milk stations. The program does not yet reach all the children who need it, but the department is planning soon to extend it everywhere. Meanwhile, as shown in Chapter XIX, individual communities, through community action, are themselves extending it.

Vocational training, even of the most rudimentary type, was a welcome innovation when the Second Unit Rural Schools were established. Today all of Puerto Rico is vocation-minded to such an extent that individual public schools can no longer cope with the problem of vocational training in an industrializing society.

After World War II the Puerto Rican government bought a wealth of war surplus machinery and equipment and used it for founding what was at the time the world's largest single vocational school, designed to fit the many needs of an agrarian society that was industrializing and badly needed skilled workers. Located in the San Juan area, this school was in the beginning managed by the university, and some three thousand students soon began to learn fifty different trades, ranging from welding to cooking, from carpentry to electronics, from blacksmithing to auto mechanics. In 1950, however, the school was taken over by the Department of Education and decentralized for the purpose of better serving all of Puerto Rico's people. The San Juan unit, known as the Miguel Such School, is still the largest, but other units are located in other Puerto Rican cities. As stated in Chapter XV, the total attendance in those schools is today nearly 20,000; among these are some seventy-five students from near-by Caribbean islands who receive their training on scholarships, at Puerto Rico's expense.

The Second Unit Rural Schools may be moribund as such, but the spirit in which they were established is not. In his report of 1950–51, Dr. Villaronga describes several rural projects as being designed, "(a) to adapt the curriculum to the realities of rural environment; (b) to awaken in the community the desire to study and attack its own problems; and (c) to develop in our rural areas a genuine leadership capable of developing projects that are of real benefit to the community."

He goes on to say that "these projects are being carried out with the co-operation of the respective municipal governments, the Agricultural Extension Service, the Social Programs Administration of the Department of Agriculture and Commerce, and our Division of Community Education.

"Committees composed of representatives of community groups and the schools have been organized at each of the selected centers. The representatives of the government agencies and the local school authorities act as technical consultants.

"The committees take charge of directing the study of the community; of discussing, evaluating, and co-ordinating their own activities; of stimulating community action; and of helping to solve the problems which arise.

"The work which is being done reflects a more complete understanding of the community and its needs and interests; better utilization of its available resources; and effective articulation of the school activities and the community projects undertaken. A growing number of persons have become interested in the projects, many of whom are potential leaders."

The study of English is stressed throughout the school system. The difference there, between today and a mere decade ago, is that it has been taken completely out of the hands of the politicians and placed in the hands of those who are expert in the matter of language instruction.

One of the marked features of Puerto Rico's changing culture is the present swelling demand for instruction in English—by taxi drivers and waiters who serve a swelling stream of continental customers, by Puerto Ricans who work in factories managed by continentals, by Puerto Ricans who plan to migrate to the continent either permanently or temporarily as members of harvest gangs, by men and women in all walks of life as well as by their children. Under current systems and orientation, it will not be many years before all Puerto Ricans are bilingual.

The structure, administration, and orientations of the university, too, have, during the past decade, under Chancellor Jaime Benítez, been drastically revised to serve better than before the needs of an emerging society. More stress than ever before is put on the sciences, and much research is done in the university laboratories on problems directly affecting Puerto Rico's life and potentialities. Engineering and agricultural research and extension have acquired new importance and popularity. The university's Social Science Research Center engages in a program of constant inquiry for the purpose of clarifying the island's real problems. Finally—in part for the purpose of preventing the faculty from becoming ingrown, in part to bring in a steady stream of new ideas, attitudes, and methods, in part for the broader purpose of promoting closer relationships with the continental educational world—a considerable number of visiting professors from the mainland United States and Latin America are invited to Puerto Rico every year to teach in the university.

The total enrollment in the university was 5,000 in 1940; it is nearly 11,000 today, and growing.

Not everybody in Puerto Rico, however, is unqualifiedly

happy over present vital trends in education. Cultural changes don't take place that easily. The most powerful voice of dissent in Puerto Rico is Bishop McManus of Ponce, who has repeatedly claimed that all of Muñoz' Operation Bootstrap is materialistic and therefore virtually immoral.

The Bishop's attitude toward current trends in education is expressed in the following acrimonious terms: "The present system is said to be democratic. It is just the contrary. It is antidemocratic and in addition antireligious. It is the special system of a minority group who talk a great deal about democracy, as well as liberty, equality, and brotherhood, and thus conceal, even from themselves, their hatred of God and Religion, and who try to impose on the majority a system that denies the rights of the majority—a wrong permissible to them when God is excluded from human life."

Another violent attack on the principle of separation of Church and State, which has the bishop's authorization, reads as follows: "One consequence of thus eliminating God from both public and private life is that religious faith, or its lack, becomes the personal affair of each individual; that the Church is only a private society tolerated by law; and if different religious sects develop, then all are of equal worth, not only before the State but in themselves. And this doctrine is utilized to destroy the work of Jesus Christ, who founded but one Church, *the only true Church.*"

Nevertheless, the government and its school system insist on the rigid separation of Church and State, not because the government and its officials are in any way antireligious, but on the ground that "in a democracy man must be guaranteed complete freedom of conscience in both the political and religious spheres of his life."

In an address on "Religion and the Public Schools," Secretary Villaronga, in 1951, expressed himself as follows: "No one would dare deny that religious experience and belief are an integral part of life and culture. Nor would anyone deny the merit of organized religions as interpreters and moral guides for mankind. But these have nothing to do with the vital principle that the school of the people and for the people should not lend itself to sectarian indoctrination except at the imminent risk of endangering its own position as a free agent of democracy in the community.

"There are those who persistently deny this simple proposition. It is these people who are responsible for the current violent criticism of our public school. Yet, though this group has become very vociferous recently over the much discussed question as to whether or not to eliminate Article 19 * from our constitution, we must realize that they are merely expressing an attitude whose origin may clearly be traced to the past. They have characterized our public-school system as atheistic, antireligious, immoral, and antidemocratic. They have even claimed that the public school is the principal cause of many of the social evils besetting not only our island but the whole twentieth century. Essentially this criticism comprises the single argument that since the public school does not offer sectarian religious instruction, it is devoid of all moral principles, all religious belief, and all idea of a relationship with a Supreme Being, the source and end of all things."

In the same speech, the Secretary of Education went on to say: "... In order to preserve democracy, not merely as a form of government but as the one true bulwark of personal freedom, the State is ... forced to maintain its functions and those of the Church absolutely and completely separate.

"For this reason the democratic State refuses to regulate or interfere with the various forms of religious communions and creeds. At the same time, it is constantly on guard against any

* NOTE: The article referred to was Article 19 in an early draft of the constitution, which was being prepared but had not yet been adopted at the time Villaronga made his address. In the constitution as adopted later, it is Section 3 of the Bill of Rights, which in turn is Article II. It reads: "No law shall be made regarding an establishment of religion or prohibiting the free exercise thereof. There shall be complete separation of Church and State."

possible sectarian influence or interference with the duties of the government. The State cannot permit the teaching of any form of institutionalized religion in the public-school system, pay for such instruction, or offer the use of any facilities for that purpose. As a democratic State, it must maintain perfect impartiality toward all organized religions, neither granting favors to anyone, nor denying to any person, because of his religious beliefs, any of the rights of citizenship.

"Nevertheless, this does not mean that the State cannot or should not recognize the universality of religious experience and belief, or encourage the development and affirmation of the universal belief which, as expressed or embodied in the great religions, especially Christianity, paved the way for democracy."

One of the outstanding features of Puerto Rico's new orientations is the increasing contribution which the island is making to world affairs. That contribution, regardless of whether it is made by educators or by technicians in other fields who were educated on the island, is a direct and visible result of the current determination to orient all education, not only toward Puerto Rico's specific problems per se, but also toward its problems as a member of the human world—able and privileged to contribute to the affairs of that world.

Both the public-school system and the university for instance, annually give scholarships to a large number of foreign students, especially from Latin America, eager to acquire the attitudes and various skills needed for the development of their own countries. Those scholarships form a part of Puerto Rico's considerable contribution to the Point IV trend in which the Commonwealth has been and is so notable a pioneer.

Chancellor Benítez, of the university, is a member of the United States Committee on Education for UNESCO and has several times attended UNESCO meetings as the United

States' delegate. Dr. Ismael Rodriguez Bou, permanent secretary of Puerto Rico's Superior Council on Education, was
a delegate for UNESCO and the Organization of American
States at the 1949 seminar in Rio de Janeiro on rural and adult
education. As the most effective of all the delegates there, he
was selected to go as technical adviser for UNESCO to a similar seminar in Mysore, India, the following year. Later he
was sent by UNESCO on an educational mission to a large
number of Latin American republics.

In many of the latter, in Bolivia, Paraguay, El Salvador,
Costa Rica, Mexico, Venezuela, and others, Rodriguez Bou
found Puerto Rican professionals, experts on diet, education,
agriculture—and especially on social growth and development. Some had been hired by the governments concerned;
some worked for the United Nations; some for various U.S.
government agencies; some for the Organization of American
States.

During the past decade, Puerto Ricans, representing both
their own small society and the United States as a whole, have
played a vital and constructive role in the affairs of the international Caribbean Commission.

When Cuzco was wrecked by earthquake some years ago,
the Peruvian government called in Dr. Rafael Picó, chairman
of the Puerto Rico Planning Board for consultation on effective rebuilding, consonant with good city planning. After the
1953 election of Don José Figueres as President of Costa Rica,
Picó was called to that country for the purpose of setting up
a planning board, Puerto Rican style. In January, 1953, the
United Nations sent him to New Delhi as one of the discussion
leaders in an international conference on housing in underdeveloped countries.

In its general cultural orientations, Puerto Rico is today far
more—and more constructively—internationally minded than
are most American states—certainly more so than is my own
state of Delaware.

And that, it must be remembered, is brand new. When Muñoz, in 1949, offered Puerto Rico's help and services to President Truman for the implementation of Point IV, most of the island was skeptical. What *could* Puerto Rico offer—a crowded small society with few resources, struggling desperately with its scarce materials to solve abundant and pressing economic, social, and political problems?

In an address on United Nations Day, October 24, 1951, Dr. Rodriguez Bou listed some of the many contributions that Puerto Rico was making to the work and ideals of a united and developing world, and said: "We have entered the field of international relations with very little previous experience, with almost no organization for the purpose, but we are providing examples of a good attitude and service."

Never again can Puerto Rico return to its condition of a few short years ago, psychologically isolated from the world, neglected, suffering not only material want but also from the devastating sense of inferiority which plagues many colonial subjects and helps to maintain and prolong the institution of colonialism.

CHAPTER XIX

Civic Employment

WHEN DR. RAFAEL PICÓ, in 1954, attended the international conference on housing in New Delhi, he and his exhibits aroused great interest among the delegates from India and other underdeveloped countries of southeastern Asia. The Germans, the British, and other advanced nations had much to say and show about low-cost housing for the people. Their architectural design may have been better than was that displayed by the Puerto Ricans. Their methods of construction may have been technically more efficient than those used on the island. But the new Puerto Rican rural homes, built under the government's resettlement program, cost only three hundred dollars and were therefore within the financial range of people living in underdeveloped lands. The social techniques used in Puerto Rico for constructing those houses were studied eagerly by all the conference delegates. Indians and several other delegates asked Dr. Picó to arrange to send Puerto Rican technicians to various countries in Africa and Asia for the purpose of spreading those techniques.

The one aspect of the Puerto Rican effort which most interests the Point IV observers who go to the island is the program of civic employment which was listed by Governor Muñoz

Marín as the sixth of the government's sources of income. Pioneered by the Social Programs Administration on lands administered by the Commonwealth's Department of Agriculture, that activity has already, in five years, resulted in the construction of more than 25,000 sturdy and sanitary rural homes. It has created new roads, built by the people themselves, community houses, co-operatives, schools, and the like. On all the lands under government control, it has changed Puerto Rico's cultural landscape—at minimum cost to the government and with maximum returns in the release of human energies for the improvement of human existence.

There was no reason, however, why such action should be confined to lands administered by the government. The attitudes, the norms, the social techniques required for community action should be taught to all the people in an organized educational effort; once acquired, they would be valuable assets for the entire society and each of its individual members. That led to the creation, in 1949, of the Division of Community Education within the Commonwealth's Department of Education.

Outside Puerto Rico, that division is now becoming known for the excellence of the documentary films which it makes and uses for the purpose of arousing civic consciousness. The latest film to be completed at the time of the present writing is *El Puente* (*The Bridge*). The New York office of the Commonwealth's Department of Labor lends it and others like it to schools and other institutions throughout the United States, where it is greatly in demand and does much to enhance Puerto Rico's good name. Simply, but with a high degree of technical and artistic excellence, it portrays the story of how and why a group of poor country people built a footbridge over the Botijas River.

A small stream, easily forded in good weather, the Botijas flows near the city of Barranquitas. About a hundred children who live in the township of Barrio Botijas #2 have to cross it twice daily on their way to and from school, as do their parents bound to or from the city or their sporadic jobs. In rainy weather, however, the crossing used to be dangerous, if not impossible, because the river becomes torrential. Flash floods roaring down from the mountains have in the past threatened the lives of several people who were caught on the stepping stones of the fords; a few years ago a schoolboy was swept downstream by such a flood and narrowly escaped either drowning or being battered on the rocks. If it rained while the children were in school on the other side, they couldn't get back—sometimes for days at a stretch. The result was that, if it even looked like rain, mothers would not permit their children to go to school, while many of the men in the sixty families affected also had to stay at home and lose working days and wages.

It is estimated that, before the bridge was built, a hundred children lost about half of their school time. For decades, the people affected had clamored to various government officials for a bridge. Once the neighbors had built a makeshift wooden bridge, but it was washed down the river in the first flood.

Then, in 1949, the Division of Community Education selected Domingo Torres Mattei, one of the most respected men in the entire district, brought him to San Juan for a training period, and sent him back with the title of Group Organizer.

He began to talk with the people about community problems and to distribute thousands of booklets on life in Puerto Rico, on health, on new ways of doing things, on many subjects that were very interesting but didn't add up to a bridge. He visited everybody for miles around, driving a jeep on the often all-but-impassable roads, and after a while he began to paper his district with colorful posters announcing free movies on certain nights. On those occasions he set up a portable screen on a hilltop, turned on a portable generator he had in the back of his jeep, and showed a film of Puerto

Rican life to the assembled people, many of whom had never seen motion pictures before. The films were fascinating, but they still didn't add up to the bridge that was on everybody's mind.

In December, 1950, a group of twenty-four neighbors called on him to discuss the problem and to wonder about a government which spent so much money on movies but not a cent for providing safe passage across a river that constantly cut into their earning power and the education of their children. He listened sympathetically and hinted that the community's people might build the bridge themselves. That was not exactly a new idea, but it was staggering in its implications and almost an impossibility to isolated countryfolk who had no money and few if any of the required technical skills. But Domingo kept encouraging them, and from the time of the first discussion the bridge became the central theme of his conversations in the community. His district included a lot more territory, but Torres Mattei returned to the barrio again and again and held meetings twice a month, between January and July, 1951, to discuss the bridge from all angles. These meetings began to result in action.

Members of the community raised $125 among themselves in pennies, nickels, and dimes. One man had had some construction experience; under Domingo's encouragement he designed a concrete bridge, specifying for reinforcement two old truck chassis that he had seen in a junk yard in Barranquitas and that they might hope to obtain as a gift. The design was submitted to the local district engineer of the island's Department of Interior; he checked the plans, improved on them here and there, and gave advice for construction. A school was being repaired near by, with some old lumber left over; the people asked for this lumber and obtained it as a donation. People waited on the mayor of Barranquitas and persuaded him to contribute eighty bags of cement and six hundred pounds of iron rods from the city's stock. Other donations, of cement, nails, tools, and of the two truck chassis, began to come in. By July, 1951, the people of Barrio Botijas #2 had gathered all the materials they needed for their bridge.

Under Domingo's leadership they elected one of their neighbors as project foreman. He began his work on July 12, sending out daily calls on how many helpers he would need for the job—after regular working hours in the fields, on Saturdays and Sundays—whenever people had a few hours or a day to spare. He had no labor problems. When he called for ten helpers, fifty were likely to come, men, women, and children, eager and interested.

The bridge was completed after twenty-two days, during which some sixty people had contributed their work, and even the dedication, attended by the entire community, was something new in Puerto Rican affairs. The local *politicos* were present only as welcome guests, not to make speeches. The little boy who had been swept down the river the year before made the principal speech, and a mother cut the ribbon. Representatives of the Division of Community Education were there only to make motion pictures.

After the bridge's completion, the division's staff in San Juan got busy on a new documentary film, depicting the entire story, from the troubled school situation that had existed before the bridge had been built, the misadventure of the boy who had nearly drowned in a flash flood, the anguish of the parents when the weather looked threatening, through the first talks of the group organizer, the talks in the community, the gradual growth of community determination, the efforts to obtain materials—to the actual construction and dedication. The script was written carefully and the picture was made on the scene with no professional actors, with the community's people playing the same parts that they had played while planning and building. Incidental music was composed for the picture; posters were painted and reproduced by the silk-screen method.

Today there are one or two copies of the film in the States, while a number of other copies are being shown in Puerto Rico to country people in various parts of the island for the purpose of stimulating various other kinds of community action.

Had the Puerto Rican government built the bridge in the first place, it would have cost about $4,000. Critics of the Division of Community Education make much of the fact that the films and other materials which had been used to stir the people of Barrio Botijas #2 into action, the wages of the group organizer, his jeep, generator and projector, his posters, books and leaflets, the effort in San Juan to produce all that, cost a great deal more. What those critics overlook or ignore, however, is the enormous value of an aroused community spirit which, having built the bridge, can now go on to other means of improving community life. The government's budget for community education is an investment calculated to pay large eventual dividends in the channeled efforts of Puerto Rico's people to help themselves.

Important in itself, the new bridge across the Botijas River is infinitely more important as a part of the ferment that has begun to stir in all parts of Puerto Rico. The Division of Community Education was created by legislative action on May 14, 1949; it started from scratch, with no staff, no materials, with nothing but a vital idea blessed by the governor and the legislature, and with inadequate funds for implementing the idea. By the time of the present writing it has stimulated and gotten under way no fewer than 105 projects of community action in as many parts of the island. Forty-nine of them have been completed.

In Barrio Mariana, in the sugar zone, where most workers earn their poor livings by cutting cane, individual farming is almost unknown. The people, however, wanted to augment their food supply. The group organizer encouraged them, through talks that went on for months and covered every phase of the problem, to create a community garden. They obtained land from the local school, in return for the promise of vegetables for the school lunches. They sent soil samples to the Agricultural Extension Agency, had them analyzed, and requested advice on proper practices from that agency and the Soil Conservation Service. They obtained good seeds from the university's experiment station, on their promise to set aside a portion of the garden for growing seeds for future years. They took up a collection of pennies and dimes for the purchase of fertilizers and the materials that went into the fence which was needed to keep cattle out of the garden. The entire community turned out to prepare the soil and cultivate the garden under the direction of an elected foreman. Among the results were: (1) crops so large that they astonished members of the community; (2) an education in proper agricultural practices, which, coming through direct experience, voluntarily sought and intimately tied up with the community's problems, was far more effective than any mere lecture course could have been; (3) close liaison between the community and the various agricultural agencies which promises large returns in the years to come; (4) marked improvement in individual gardens of the neighbors and some decrease in cash expenditure for food; and (5) increases of the school lunches given to children.

Barrio Santa Olaya in Bayamón had only two one-room schools serving the first four grades. For fifth grade and up, children had to walk a long distance to another school and cross rivers which were sometimes in flood. This meant that few children in the barrio ever went beyond the fourth grade. The hard-pressed government had no money available for the construction of another school, but under the group organizer's stimulation the decision was reached to build a school for the fifth and sixth grades. Committees were appointed to consult with various agencies on the proper plans for such a project. One group went to San Juan to visit the Planning Board, not only obtaining much valuable technical help and advice, but also returning to spread the message among their rural neighbors of what the Planning Board, always an august body in the eyes of simple farmers, meant to the people of Puerto Rico. The Department of Education promised to provide a teacher as soon as the school was finished. Collections were taken up. Since the barrio was poor and was able to raise only eighty dollars in two months' time, it was decided to build a wooden school instead of the concrete building that had been planned in the beginning. Wood, nails, tools, paint, were gathered wherever they could be found, and the barrio's entire population turned out to do the work, the women preparing hot meals while the men labored.

The planning of this venture had begun in March, 1951. In September of the same year, the school was inaugurated. As usual, the community itself conducted the inauguration, but one of its members was a Puerto Rican soldier from Santa Olaya, recently returned from the Korean War. He made the main speech, expressing his pride over being able to participate in that one example of the things he had fought for on the other side of the world.

Now the community of Santa Olaya has begun to study other problems. Its people have talked of their need for a water tank for the school and have considered the building of a community center.

In Barrio Maricao Afuera, some five hundred people had no drinking water locally available; their women had to trudge long distances to obtain and carry water in old gasoline tins converted into pails. They began to discuss the problem systematically in January, 1951—as usual spending much more time on the important task of talking the project through than on the actual work. Finally they borrowed and rented equipment, and in September, after several discouraging failures, they had an excellent eight-inch well, three hundred feet deep. Then the government was persuaded to run a power line into the district, and a motor and pump were obtained to bring the water to the surface. Now the community not only has adequate water but electricity as well for home use. It would have cost the government about $4,000 to drill the well by orthodox methods; it cost the community $660, plus a lot of rewarding labor.

In another part of the island, the government had completed a dam, and so created a new reservoir which was stocked with fish. Government experts, however, explained to near-by residents that they must not fish in the reservoir for at least a year, no matter what their hunger. If they wanted the reservoir to serve as a permanent supply of food, they would first have to give the fish a chance to reproduce. The problem was discussed with the group organizer, with the result that the entire community became a body of voluntary game wardens. Not only did the people agree to refrain from doing any fishing themselves (incidentally watching each other to prevent backsliding), but they discouraged others from elsewhere from fishing in the reservoir. For a whole year they took turns in watching all parts of the reservoir, and when somebody, anybody, started to do any fishing, they persuaded him to desist—using the gentle, dignified, polite, but always firm and even stubborn methods for which the Puerto Rican *jíbaro* is famous. Those who know the poverty of rural Puerto Rico, the incessant struggle for food, can realize what a miracle of co-operation that project was. Now that part of the country not only has a permanent source of proteins, but has also learned a valuable lesson in conservation—in the most effective manner possible.

The Statement of Motives of the bill creating the Division of Community Education, written by Muñoz Marín himself, says in part that this agency is to give "to the communities and to the Puerto Rican community in general the wish, the tendency, and the way of making use of their own aptitudes for the solution of many of their own problems. . . ." The statement goes on to say: "The community should not be civically unemployed. The community can be constantly and usefully employed in its own services, in terms of pride and satisfaction for the members thereof."

Fred G. Wale, formerly with the Julius Rosenwald Fund, was appointed head of the division, and with him were two other Americans, Edwin Rosskam, an expert photographer, and Jack Delano, a motion-picture director who can turn his hand to anything that goes into the making of a film, including photography, script-writing, and the composition of incidental music. From the start, however, the policy was to train and encourage Puerto Ricans to take over all phases of the work, and today only Wale is left of the original trio of non-Puerto Ricans; he himself works as half of a team; the other half consists of his Puerto Rican wife, Carmen Isales, a former social worker.

The directives called for the use of "motion pictures, radio, books, pamphlets and posters, phonograph records, lectures and group discussions," and one of the first steps was the rental of an old market hall which was converted into a studio, office building, and general workshop. While one group in the division began the important work of selecting and training an adequate staff for work in the field, another group in the studios and shops turned out materials for those representatives to use. A similar organization in the mainland United States would be able to obtain a wealth of such materials at little cost in the form of rented films and educational pamphlets and posters, turned out by the thousands in Washington and various other cities. But in Puerto Rico the need was for materials in Spanish, dealing in the simplest possible terms with various aspects of the Puerto Rican problem. It was therefore necessary to start from scratch to create such materials. This was done with the help of a group of young Puerto Rican writers, artists, composers, photographers, printers, and other craftsmen, who were thereby granted new outlets for their own creative impulses.

The old market is today a beehive of activity. The booklets that are there produced include an annual almanac stressing the Puerto Rican scene and dealing with such special subjects as good land use, health, etc. The almanac form assures that thousands of country people refer to it again and again throughout the year. There are special booklets on health; there is one on life in various parts of Puerto Rico for the benefit of those many rural people who have never in their lives been far beyond their own valleys; there is another on how people live in various other parts of the world, how they work and how they shape their environments toward the improvement of life.

The series of films began with one called *From the Clouds,* describing life throughout Puerto Rico with the help of bird's-eye views from a plane. Now there are shorts on land use, on health, on Puerto Rican music as it differs from one part of the island to another. While such shorts are being produced, the planning and production of the longer documentary films go constantly forward.

One of the latter, *Los Peloteros* (*The Ballplayers*), depicts the trials and successful efforts of a group of boys to raise money for uniforms for their baseball team. Only two of its actors are professionals; the boys themselves and half of the town of Comerío turned out to play in the film. There are no professionals whatever in *A Voice in the Mountain.* It is the true story of an illiterate laborer who wanted an education, of his troubled efforts to organize a night class for himself and his neighbors, and of the countryside's elation when one of its oldest and most beloved inhabitants finally learned to write his name.

In 1952 this film won the signal honor of being selected for showing at the International Film Festivals in Venice and Edinburgh.

Several such films are always in the discussion or production stages. They use simple themes, played by the country people themselves with the island's natural beauty as background. Their lessons are grasped immediately by the men and women who nightly stand in the open air on hilltops to see the first motion pictures of their lives.

There are a few chauvinistic Puerto Ricans who still lament the realistic rural simplicity of the films and clamor for scenes of grand public buildings, telephones and new factories, historical achievements and political leaders in action. There are educators who would like to do away with the films entirely and substitute less expensive posters and lectures on how and why children should brush their teeth, why contour plowing is important, and why it is often wise to boil drinking water. Meanwhile, however, the films are beginning to be recognized as an art form new in Puerto Rico and as major cultural contributions of the Commonwealth's modern era, while their effectiveness in stimulating people to group action increases daily.

Distressed by the fact that Jack Delano left his organization, Fred Wale went to the continent in 1952 in search of a new director. He got in touch with a group of Americans outstanding in the field of documentary films—men who had created such masterpieces as *The River*, and *The City*. He showed them *A Voice in the Mountain*, which had been planned, written, directed, photographed, and edited entirely by young Puerto Ricans. The continental experts told Wale that he didn't need anybody else. Instead of hiring a man from the mainland to work with Puerto Ricans, he should send his young men to the States to improve documentary films here.

For effective use of the materials created in San Juan, Puerto Rico is divided into forty rural areas, each with its group organizer equipped with a jeep, projector, generator, and other needed equipment. Mrs. Wale, Doña Carmen Isales, is in charge of the important work of selecting and training field representatives. Hundreds of applicants have been interviewed; most of them were turned down. The hard lessons that the successful candidates have had to learn is that it is not at all their job to persuade people to build bridges, schools, roads, to create gardens or organize night classes. It is to encourage people to develop the initiatives, the ability to plan, and the needed disciplines, voluntarily accepted, which will in the end result in community-created bridges and the like. At first it is always difficult for prospective group organizers, being trained in San Juan, to realize that they are not leaders or teachers, that they are merely catalytic agents whose job it is to encourage people to develop and act upon their own ideas. A group organizer may be firmly convinced that the thing his people need most is a new and pure water supply. But he says nothing about it, and if they develop a desire for a kitchen in which school lunches may be cooked for their children, or an improved road, or a community center, he encourages them to translate that idea, and not his own, into action. The basic concept there is that community spirit and enterprise have a much better chance of growing around an idea that springs from the community itself than around something that a government employee preaches as being for the people's good.

I asked Doña Carmen about her standards for selecting organizers. She said: "They must be respected at home, catch on to the general idea, dedicate themselves to it, and prove their ability to work along our lines. We don't discriminate against Ph.D.'s, or M.A.'s. Two of our men have graduated from the university. One of our best, however, only finished eighth grade. He has the confidence of his people, his work is outstandingly effective, and he has by now, through sheer interest in his work, learned to write analytical reports that any highly trained social worker could be proud of."

In 1952 I attended a hilltop meeting with Mr. and Mrs. Wale. It was in a remote section, and we barely managed to reach it by car—over a rudimentary dirt road. In some sections the organizers have to load their generators and other equipment on horses in order to reach the specified spots. Several hundred men, women, and children stood about, watched the film *The Ballplayers*, laughed here and there, and exclaimed with wonder that the actors were just simple people like themselves. It ran for an hour and a half, and afterward the people wouldn't go home. They stood about talking, and after a while some of them started singing—into the microphone that the organizer had set up—the old *decimas* beloved in the Puerto Rican hills. Then they got into singing contests of the classical type, in which each participant makes up a verse extemporaneously about some current local subject. They take turns to carry on the story until one of them fumbles and loses.

I have seen and heard such contests among African tribesmen and in remote parts of the Amazon basin; they were a dying art in Puerto Rico, but are now reviving spontaneously through the respect for the common man's creative impulses which the Division of Community Education is fostering. Otto Mallery of Philadelphia, organizer and for years president of the American Recreation Association, attended one of the hilltop meetings and said that he had never dreamed, from his own experience, that such spontaneous reaction was possible. Another American, trained and experienced in group dynamics, hadn't thought it possible either; he accused the division bluntly of having rehearsed the whole thing for weeks in advance in order to put on a show for his benefit.

Through such singing, or other group response to a stimulating film, the group organizer tries to arouse the first spark of the latent community creative spirit, which he then nurses carefully and tries to guide toward future constructive enterprises. The films, the books, the conscious attitudes of the organizers, are all aimed primarily at one simple thing—to help people to develop faith in themselves and their own aspirations and latent abilities. As that faith is translated into successful action to build bridges and roads, schools and gardens, wells and night classes for illiterate adults, it inevitably creates more faith as well as a growing store of community pride.

In the latest report of the division we read such things as the following:

"In a barrio of Hatillo . . . we have watched the people move from a pressure group, demanding that the mayor . . . solve their problems, to a position where they applauded when a neighbor stated that this was a matter that we ourselves must solve. . . .

"We were present at a meeting when the members of a community refused graciously but firmly the gift of a large sum of money from a well-to-do person outside their barrio because, they said, they wished to have the opportunity to raise the money in nickels and dimes from their own pockets. . . .

"We have watched an influential neighbor try to block a road-building project when he found that the community did not intend to have it pass his store. And then we watched the community win him over to its way of thinking."

After Puerto Rico had turned the corner with the election of 1940, one heard poor people everywhere on the island say of Muñoz Marín: "He is our leader who has given us faith in ourselves." The Division of Community Education was created for the purposes of helping that faith to grow and of channeling it into constructive action. A number of Puerto Ricans, who are today justifiably concerned over the problem of Muñoz Marín's successor, have begun to agree with Doña Inés, the governor's wife, who said to me in 1951: "That is the program which will produce the island's future leaders."

CHAPTER XX

Culture Changes and the Population Problem

BY ANY DEFINITION Puerto Rico is a crowded island, with a density of population resembling that of Japan or the United Kingdom. In 1952 its population was approximately 2,285,000, its density 668 per square mile. Kingsley Davis reports that Puerto Rico has 1,473 persons per square mile of arable land, whereas the mainlaind United States has only 220. "Furthermore," he goes on, "Puerto Rico depends on its agricultural land for the support of its people more heavily than does the mainland. As of 1940 it had 58.3 per cent of its occupied males in agriculture, as compared with 22.3 in continental United States. The crowded character of its agriculture can be seen from the fact that Puerto Rico has approximately 170 agriculturally employed per square mile of arable land as compared with 9.6 on the mainland."* However, in another study Davis points out that the distribution of Puerto Rico's population is changing rapidly. People are streaming from the country into the cities and are thereby contributing to the improvement of the demographic picture.

* Annals of the American Academy of Political and Social Science, January, 1953.

As stated in Chapter XVII, the birth rate has dropped somewhat in recent years, but the death rate has dropped phenomenally. Davis points out that the "rate of natural increase—the excess of births over deaths in relation to population—has . . . recently been one of the highest in the world. The average rate for the decade 1942-51 is so high that, if continued without migration, it would double the population in approximately 26 years. This would give the island nearly 9,000,000 inhabitants by the end of the century, nearly 18,-000,000 in 75 years, and soon there would literally be standing room only."

Just as it has been fashionable in recent years to use figures of that kind, applied to other parts of the world, for the purpose of oversimplifying the great modern world problem, so it was long fashionable to use them for oversimplification in Puerto Rico. Various advocates of planned parenthood have insisted that the entire effort to improve standards of living is futile because it was not preceded and accompanied by an effective, island-wide, organized campaign for birth control— was in fact accompanied until recently by a startling increase in fertility. Albizu Campos has long claimed that the entire concept of overpopulation is a fraud encouraged by the imperialistic United States as an excuse for setting out to exterminate the Puerto Ricans entirely. Officials and continental employees of the sugar industry used to claim smugly that nothing was wrong with the island except that it contained too many Puerto Ricans who, since they stubbornly persisted in having children, deserved no better than the fate that sugar was meting out to them. When the Chardón Commission drafted its classic plan which led to the creation of the PRRA, it was more realistic in that it advocated economic reform as a means of handling the problem. It began its report: "The economic problem of Puerto Rico, in so far as the bulk of its people is concerned, may be reduced to the simple terms of progressive landlessness, chronic unemployment, and implacable growth of the population," and added an appendix to show "the appalling increase in population, with an increase in birth rate from 20.4 to 39.0 in twenty-five years and a decrease in death rate of 36.7 to 22.4." Chardón and his associates would have been horrified in 1934 had they realized that by 1947, and despite economic improvements far more drastic than any they envisioned when they wrote their plan, the birth rate would climb to forty-three per thousand and the death rate would drop to nine a few years later.

If Puerto Rico shows anything, however, it shows that human affairs are too complex to lend themselves to oversimplification for purposes of special pleading of one kind or another. Societies act as living organisms, in which everything interacts with everything else, in a manner in which cause and effect can never be clearly distinguished. Except through the application of techniques whenever and wherever the demand arises from within any one society, the population problem cannot be handled per se apart from all other problems. It is an integral and integrated part of the larger over-all problem of improving standards of living. Indeed, a good case can be made for the claim that the condition known as overpopulation is at the root of all human progress.

Societies tend to handle their population problems in three ways, which are interrelated and go hand in hand. In a triple assault, they cannot truly be separated, one from the other. One is economic development to raise standards of living—in all its complex manifestations as discussed in this book. Another is migration, which is discussed in Chapter XXI. The third is the application of birth-control methods as (but not before) the demand for such application grows because the ideal of the small family tends to rise with standards of living.

In his excellent study, *Puerto Rico's Economic Future*, Harvey Perloff says: "Raising living standards to relatively high levels would seem to be the most desirable and the most [permanently] effective method of limiting population growth. . . .

Higher living levels bring about a growing feeling of responsibility among parents for the education and prospects of their children, wider knowledge and better methods of birth control, and the wish to raise personal consumption levels by keeping the family small." He cites a study by Dr. Lydia Roberts, which shows that Puerto Rican mothers who have finished childbearing, in families with incomes of less than $500, have an average of 5.24 children each, that the number of children decreases steadily with increases in income, and that those with incomes of $2,000 and over have 3.57 children each.

By that criterion, of course, everything that is done by the government to improve standards of living is indirectly also done to reduce the growing number of Puerto Ricans who share those standards.

The Roberts study, moreover, demonstrates for Puerto Rico a relationship which has long been established in demographic studies—that between education and family limitation. Puerto Rican mothers who have had no schooling at all have an average of 6.1 children each; those who have attended school only a year or two have 5.0; those who went through eighth grade have 3.4; those with high-school diplomas have 2.4.

Again, everything that is done by the government to extend and improve education, to wipe out illiteracy, is apparently also done to reduce the birth rate.

The average number of children per mother, throughout Puerto Rico, is 4.90. In rural areas it is 5.49, in urban areas 4.09, shading down from 4.51 for those with incomes of $500 or less to 3.09 for those with $2,000 or more.

Against the background of those figures, Davis says: "Such differences are precisely the kind found at the beginning of a period of declining fertility, for it is the urban, white-collar, and literate classes that first begin to limit their reproduction." He cites the astonishing modern growth of Puerto

Rico's cities as another index of reduced fertility. "The low fertility classes are being steadily augmented. Although still thought of as rural, Puerto Rico is actually quite urban and is fast becoming more so. By 1940 the proportion of people who dwell in urban places had risen to 30 per cent, and by 1950 it had reached 40 per cent. In fact, the gain in urban percentage during the 1940–50 decade was as great as it had been during the thirty years previously."

But within cities, too, as indicated by the Roberts findings on the relations between fertility and such matters as income and education, there is a definite distribution of fertility groups. Poor, illiterate people living in filthy slums have more children than do those whose housing has been improved and who have begun to climb up the economic ladder.

Before the early 1930's, when the PRERA and the PRRA began to build low-cost housing projects, the growth of the cities had been prompted largely by desperation and had therefore been haphazard and often terrible in its effects. People had swarmed into the cities from the stricken rural areas in the frantic search for some means of sustenance. Crowding by the hundreds into existing houses which had originally been built for a few families each, they had transformed the beautiful old walled city of San Juan into one great slum. They had pre-empted filthy, malodorous swamps and other waste areas. Using scraps of lumber, tin, rags and anything else that would hold together, at times using the debris resulting from hurricanes, they had built filthy, unsanitary shacks, unfit for human habitation but still overfilled by men and women and the ever-growing number of their children. In San Juan, the slum areas of La Perla (The Pearl) and El Fanguito (The Mudhole) became notorious as being among the worst to be found anywhere on earth.

That situation was a great challenge to the new government which took over in 1941. The Planning Board, which was first organized as the Planning, Zoning, and Urbanization

Board, still devotes a major part of its efforts to effective city planning—made difficult by the fact that modern Puerto Rico has inherited from the past a conglomeration of more or less messy urban centers, well laid out in the beginning by the first Spanish settlers (who had a genius for city planning), but later grown haphazard, crowded, poorly managed, beggar infested, and often dirty.

The Economic Development Administration today creates city jobs through industrialization and thereby raises a special problem, undreamed of a few years ago. The desirability of decentralizing the new industrial plant, of scattering it to all parts of the island, is well recognized; however, continental managers of factories erected with continental capital often don't like to take their complaining wives to live in small inland towns with sleepy semi-Spanish cultures, with picturesque slums, but without clubs, bars, swimming pools, golf courses, or movies adequate for continental managers and their wives. That problem must be taken into consideration by the city planners, whose job it is to improve the cultural atmosphere of *all* Puerto Rican cities.

In an almighty effort, the government plans and builds low-cost housing projects, decent, sanitary, sturdy, the inhabitants of which are charged rent according to their ability to pay. One such project, within the city limits of San Juan, comprises 7,000 concrete houses and is considered the largest single low-cost housing project to be built anywhere in the Western world; it amounts to the building, in one great mass-production operation, of a city of between 20,000 and 30,000 people, with stores, schools, movies, roads, bus lines, paved streets, sewer facilities, running water, electric light and power, adequate sanitary and health environment, and all the other things that go into a modern urban settlement. Slum clearance projects, decently designed and priced apartment dwellings, spring up in all the various cities, one by one as plans are completed and money is available with the help of federal aid.

Various branches of the government devote themselves to creating decent parks, to fostering baseball, basketball, and other forms of recreation, to helping people, through the efforts of social workers, to adjust themselves to new surroundings and new ways of life. The Department of Education must constantly revise its curriculums to keep pace with changing needs.

Even the problem of persuading people to move out of the slums into better neighborhoods is not always easily solved. Slums are themselves a way of life. There is a certain social and economic freedom in living in a miserable shack which one has erected by one's own effort over a fetid swamp. It may cost less than does life in even the lowest of low-cost housing projects. On the whole it often involves less bother from the government's social workers who tell you not to throw your garbage and slops out the front door, or the government's health inspectors or truant officers. In the slum, a man usually owns his own house and is therefore not threatened by a rise in rent just because another of his sons joined the army and is sending home an extra allotment. The slum home may be within walking distance of his place of work, while the new home provided by the government may well entail the bothersome and relatively expensive transportation to the job by bus.

But the slums are being eliminated as rapidly as funds and man power permit. In the cities, as everywhere else, the Puerto Rican government is creating a new cultural environment conducive to the lowering of the birth rate in response to popular demand. As a man has to pay more rent for every child born, as his children demand shoes and decent clothes when they go to school, as the children learn in school about the details of a decently improved life, as the women learn the same things, so inexorably, the new Puerto Rican ideal of the small family must spread to even the poorest of urban and rural Puerto Ricans. In those conditions lies the explanation for the current drop in birth rate from 43 per thousand in 1947 to 35.2 in 1952, with no slowing down in sight.

There is no doubt that the small-family ideal is spreading; there is, in fact, a certain amount of astonishment over the fact that it spreads as rapidly as it does. For the over-all Puerto Rican effort is still in its infancy, and its statistics to date indicate how much is still to be accomplished. To be sure, the average per capita income has doubled since 1941, in terms of purchasing power, but figures published in 1949 by Lydia Roberts and Rosa Luisa Stefani indicate how much still remains to be done. According to those figures, 44 per cent of Puerto Rico's families still have annual incomes of less than $500 each, nearly two-thirds have less than $750, and three-fourths have less than $1,000. Seventeen per cent of the families have incomes ranging between $1,000 and $1,999, while only 8 per cent have $2,000 or more.

What all that means, again, in relation to current demographic trends, is that fine correlations between cause and effect are not feasible in human affairs. The island's current and growing demand for small families is an expression of the same general, aroused human conscience which has created and energized the Battle for Production and Operation Bootstrap, for improving the means and qualities of human existence.

Childbirth and everything related to it are such intimate matters that the question of whether or not to have children is in every case up to the conscience of the individuals who play direct and important roles in the matter. That conscience, of course, may differ radically from the conscience of the busy modern prophets of demographic doom who make careers out of proclaiming that the modern world's only trouble is that it is too full of foreigners, who, perversely enough, refuse to practice birth control for the purpose of safeguarding our American standards of living which they have never been permitted to sample. The conscience of the individual who has the children may be rudimentary or virtually atrophied, as in the case of the *jíbaro* described by Bailey Ashford and quoted in Chapter II; it may be poorly informed—with the government making every effort to make it well informed; it may be well informed already; it may be torn by the old and ubiquitous struggle between Church and State; the principle is the same—in a democracy that conscience, and it only, can in the long run determine fertility trends.

And that conscience of the individual, multiplied by the hundreds of thousands to be expressed as a social force, is the highest expression of a people's ever-changing culture. By culture I don't mean religion; I don't mean music, painting, or folklore; I don't mean education; I don't mean economic or political circumstances; I don't mean geographic environment, racial heritage, class distinction, or any other one thing. I mean all those things together, and many more, interacting, each with all the others at all times in a vital and complex manner. A people's collective conscience which tends to regulate birth rates through the exercise of the individual conscience of every single one of its members is shaped by the complex interaction of "Ways of living and working; the forward-looking habits in a community; the religious vision; the land and its crops, and the factories, and the tools, and the techniques, and the raising of children, and the cultivation of the understanding, and science, and art, and recreation, and health habits, and sustenance, and clothes, and sheltering roof, and justice, and generosity, and serenity" in whatever strength or measure all of those things, and many others, including political freedom, may play a vital role in the community at any one time in its life.

Puerto Rico's birth rate is going down today because the people of Puerto Rico demand such a drop. Kingsley Davis reports that "many Puerto Ricans are anxious to limit the size of their families." The government has legalized the dissemination of birth-control information and the sterilization of women in cases where childbirth is mortally dangerous, but a large part of the public clamors for more help along those lines than the government is giving. As reported in Chapter IV, even in 1936 the public demand for help toward the limitation of families was considerable. But in those days Puerto Rico was at the political mercy of Washington; today the Commonwealth has a free hand.

In 1951 the city of San Juan was enlarged to take in what had formerly been the neighboring city of Rio Piedras. Doña Felisa Rincón de Gautier, San Juan's city manager, invited my wife, a social worker and an old friend, to accompany her on her first conferences and hearings in the newly acquired administrative territory. My wife returned, impressed with the number of women who had asked Felisa only for help toward being sterilized. Every mayor of every city and town on the island is constantly under pressure from his constituents to expand the facilities for birth control and sterilization.

On June 29, 1951, the newspaper, *El Imparcial*, came out with screaming headlines, covering half the front page, announcing that five hundred women had been sterilized in the municipal hospital in Lajas. The story was presented as an energetic attack on the government for such diabolical practices. On reading it, however, one found that the doctor involved was in trouble with the government, not for having sterilized women, but because he had charged them $35.00 each, which he had not been supposed to do, and because he had pocketed the money, which, as a municipal employee, he hadn't been supposed to do either.

I discussed the story with a high government official, and found him not at all unhappy about it.

"Imagine what this means," he said. "In two years' time at least five hundred women went to him alone, with thirty-five dollars, to be sterilized. Think of what thirty-five dollars means to those women—in terms of labor, in terms of depriving themselves and their children of food, in terms of going without the very necessities of life. Think of the saving and scrounging and deprivation that was behind every single one of the fees that that fellow collected. What it means is that the demand for sterilization is becoming so overwhelming that the government must take greater and more active cognizance of it. This story dramatizes that demand, again calls it to the attention of my people and my government, and will so, by that much, help all the women of Puerto Rico who today want to do right by their children and themselves through limiting their families."

In a society in which 85 per cent of the people are Roman Catholics, the Catholic Church is apparently powerless opposite that swelling popular demand. Indeed, the Bishop of Ponce has himself complained that the church is losing ground in Puerto Rico. Stycos and Hill report that "for the lower classes, at least, Catholicism has become a series of rituals to be combined with social festivities, and a cult of saints to bring good fortune." The same two reported in January, 1953, in the Annals of the American Academy of Political and Social Science, that "in the past two years, scores of articles attacking birth control, sterilization, and the overpopulation thesis have appeared in the insular newspapers, and several religious organizations have devoted all or a large share of their efforts to anti-birth-control activity." They go on to report that the *Independentista* party, or at least its leader, has used anti-birth-control propaganda as a political weapon for attacking the *Populares* with nonsensical accusations of class genocide—the attempt to solve the problem of poverty by eliminating the poor. But it doesn't seem to work as planned. Every attack also contains information which is avidly grasped by many of the poor, who subsequently go to the clinics to request birth-control help.

As reported in Chapter VIII, it was difficult for the federal government to manage the rural resettlement projects which the PRRA had started. A group of Quakers was therefore asked to manage the Castañer project on contract with Washington. At the end of their first year of such management, the Quakers stated in their official report that, in their hospital, they had in one year sterilized some three hundred women, who as a group, before asking for sterilization, had added more than two thousand children to Puerto Rico's population. The stir in Congress was considerable; immediately after receipt of the report, Washington sent a peremptory order that there must be no more sterilizations on federal property. The reaction in Puerto Rico was significant.

On hearing what the Quakers had done, the Bishop of Ponce sent to every priest on the island, with orders that it be read from the pulpit on a certain Sunday, a pastoral letter dealing with the evils of sterilization and contraception as well as with the Godless Protestants who were killing Puerto Rican children. The priests obeyed, but the letter misfired. Thousands of women, good Catholics, said: "This is wonderful. Where can we learn more? Where can we find that kind of help?" After that historic Sunday, doctors were swamped with requests for sterilization.

Officially, the government has formulated no policies and made no statements on the birth-control problem per se. There may well be political reasons for that silence. There may also be the reason that Muñoz Marín always thinks in terms of the individual and always respects the conscience of the individual. He strives to make it a "conscience which is well informed," but he respects it even when it is poorly informed. In dealing with a matter as intimate as is that of childbirth, there is always the question of how far one may decently go toward shaping and forcing that conscience toward the specific, socially desirable end of having fewer children; by the same token there is also the question of how far a democratic government may go toward thwarting the expression of an aroused conscience which demands information and help for birth control.

But if the government and the Popular Democratic party are officially silent on those matters, some of their highest officials, speaking as private individuals and within their rights of free speech, are not. Several of them have in recent years made ringing public speeches calling for an energetic government program to aid the people in the limitation of their families. Social justice, they claim, demands such a program. The rich have no difficulty in limiting their families; they can get all the medical help they want; it is time that the same facilities be extended to at least those many of the poor who demand it. It is also time, they say, to start an energetic education program to make the poor want it. One official went so far as to state in a public speech that the situation was sufficiently serious to call for the sterilization of men.

For such pronouncements they have been immediately excommunicated. It seems to have accomplished little, except, perhaps, to strengthen the cause for birth control through the resulting publicity. The officials affected are still at their posts, still doing their work of improving the island's social and economic life. Neither they nor the Popular Democratic party of which they are members seem to have lost popularity as a result of the excommunications.

Stycos and Hill remark that "the tabloid catering to the lowest class of readers has produced the largest headlines condemning the government's program. Copies of this newspaper are often passed from family to family and have undoubtedly been a major source of information for lower-class families." They are in no doubt that "the majority of Puerto Ricans desire to limit their families" and conclude that "superstitious fears, modesty complexes, marital mistrust, lack of equality in marriage, and so forth," are the principal obstacles to the general substitution of the—by now rapidly growing—small-family ideal for that of the large family, which prevailed until a few decades ago. They advocate expansion of present facilities for family limitation, a co-ordinated program of sex education and premarital counseling, and a greater and more active interest in birth control on the part of doctors and nurses.

"Without such measures," they conclude, "Puerto Ricans will achieve their family ideals slowly but surely. With such measures, a rapid drop in the birth rate may be predicted."

A number of demographers who today deal pessimistically with world trends in population within the world setting of resources sustaining populations keep insisting that it is dangerous if not fatal to raise standards of living in the so-called underdeveloped lands, without insisting that population growth be first reduced through universal adoption of an energetic birth-control program—at least among the poor. Dr. Josué de Castro, Executive Director of the Food and Agricultural Organization of the United Nations, has advanced the theory that hunger itself leads to overpopulation in that it increases human fertility. He cannot prove his theory, nor can his many enemies disprove it, but it has the great advantage of working out as a social reality. We cannot, anywhere, abolish or alleviate human hunger without, as in Puerto Rico, so reshaping the society in question that conditions are created which lead to a drop in birth rates. Nevertheless, De Castro's theory, published in his book *The Geography of Hunger*, enrages a large number of demographers and conservationists. Fairfield Osborn, in his *The Limits of the Earth*, says: "A theory that the birth rate is highest among the ill fed, and more particularly among those who lack protein in their diet, is not supportable as a uniform biological principle for mankind. There exists an overwhelming mass of evidence which confirms the self-evident fact that well-nourished people have the highest fertility potential. . . ."

He may be right, of course, but it is not the *fertility potential* which counts in human affairs, not the fecundity, but the actual fertility, the actual number of children born. Osborn says later: "The infinitely tragic fact is that starvation is at present the only controlling factor to constantly increasing human numbers in a vast portion of the world." Puerto Rico seems to refute him and to support De Castro. It is not always easy to comprehend exactly what alarmists of the Osborn type are driving at. They seem to feel that people whose living standards are high enough to give them enough to eat have more children than do those with low standards of living—accompanied, as always, by malnutrition. In their calculations they place emphasis on space and resources, rather than on what man does with space and resources. They reject the concept that it is never a land which is overpopulated, in terms of inhabitants per square mile; it is always an economy in terms of inhabitants per square meal. They tend to regard man's creative energies as being applied almost exclusively to the biological process of creating more men; through such warped reasoning, they seem to arrive at the odd conclusion that the divine spark in man, his creativeness, is more destructive, and more dangerous to human societies, than are the energies released by nuclear fission.

Puerto Rico's experience is merely one of many which show that man is and always must be a creative animal. Bottle up his creative energies, as through the complex restrictive institutions of colonialism, prevent him from using them for making a better life for himself and succeeding generations, and they will find an outlet in the one form left to man—namely the production of children. Release those energies, put them to work on the task of improving life, and the number of children produced will begin to go down.

The so-called demographic problem cannot be separated from all the other social problems which beset man. Social life on earth cannot be reduced to simple correlations in sixth-grade arithmetic. As one creates a better life, so one also creates conditions which tend eventually to limit the number of people who enjoy that better life.

CHAPTER XXI

Migration

AT THE BEGINNING of the nineteenth century, when the French began to have serious troubles with their Haitian slaves, a number of Frenchmen left Haiti to re-establish themselves in Spain's peaceful colony of Puerto Rico. After the Louisiana Purchase in 1803, many Creoles, Frenchmen, and Spaniards left the affected teritory and moved to Puerto Rico to escape being ruled by the Protestant, Republican United States. For decades after the outbreak of the Latin American revolutionary wars, beginning with Miranda's ill-fated expedition from New York to Venezuela in 1806 and ending with the establishment of the various Latin American republics in the 1820's, thousands of Spanish royalists left the revolting Spanish colonies and sought refuge in royalist Puerto Rico. Many Corsicans came after Napoleon's fall.

The flow of people was in those days into Puerto Rico. The island's population grew dramatically, swelled constantly by newcomers. For varying reasons, but centuries after the 1530's, when the governor thought it necessary to threaten the death penalty for anybody who was so inflamed by the news of Pizarro's exploits in Peru that he wanted to leave and get in on the conquest and the loot, relatively few Puerto Ricans left their island. Most of them were always desperately poor, but they stayed in Puerto Rico. For several hundred years they were hemmed in by the North Europeans, who harassed the Spanish on the Caribbean Sea. After that, they were busily assimilating their thousands of immigrants, opening the interior mountains for settlement, creating a distinctly Puerto Rican culture of their own.

Being poor, Puerto Rico was also overpopulated, since poverty is the only possible measure of overpopulation. However, the island's inhabitants were also easygoing and democratic; neither the push from within nor the pull from without was as yet sufficiently strong to cause any appreciable emigration. Not until the 1890's was there a recorded outward movement of any appreciable size. The Puerto Rican sugar agriculture had been ruined by the imposition of a U.S. tariff on sugar. Thousands of Puerto Ricans were left, not only poor and unemployed, but landless as well. But Hawaii, about to be joined to the United States, had already received large amounts of American capital for its industrializing agriculture and needed field hands. Puerto Ricans were recruited to go to Hawaii, where their colony today numbers about 10,000.

During the early years of American rule, a number of Puerto Ricans were sporadically recruited for agricultural labor in the United States. Most of them were unhappy—especially the dark-skinned. It was difficult for people coming from their patriarchal society, where a man's color was hardly noticed and he could be a person no matter how poor, to adjust to their treatment by American employers—to be pushed around and treated as Spanish-speaking, second-class, colored cheap labor. However, some did come to find new homes in the United States, of which all Puerto Ricans became citizens in 1917. The 1930 census reported Puerto Ricans in all of the forty-eight states. Some also moved to the American Virgin Islands, while a minor trickle went to the various Latin American republics. But their numbers were insignificant compared to those of the migrants to the mainland United

States. Practically all of the latter who went to stay came from cities and moved to cities.

By 1940, their numbers had become appreciable. New York by then had 63,000 Puerto Ricans. However, it was not until after World War II that the streams of out-migrants* became so large that it began to have an appreciable effect on Puerto Rico's population problem. By 1952, the maximum annual out-flow amounted to 53,000, or about 85 per cent of that year's total increment in population as calculated by the difference between births and deaths. Clarence Senior reports that the direct loss for the decade 1942-51 was 249,918. In addition, the stream of farm workers who went to the States, earned money, sent money home, and returned to Puerto Rico for the winter, swelled from about 3,000 in 1947 to possibly 15,000 in 1952.

At the time of the present writing, the out-stream is decreasing and there is an appreciable increase of those who are returning to Puerto Rico from the mainland. Conditions continue to improve on the island, while the job opportunities are becoming fewer in the states. Nevertheless, the total out-migration is of considerable importance to those who plan and carry out Puerto Rico's over-all development. In its report, "Economic Development, 1940-1960," the Planning Board reports: "From April 1940 to April 1950, the labor force on the island was increased by 160,000. Sufficient work opportunities were created to absorb that increase and an additional 11,000 of the balance of unemployed at the beginning of the decade. Without emigration during the decade . . . unemployment would have amounted to 201,000 as compared to the actual unemployment figure of 101,000 in June, 1950."

It is significant that the number of Puerto Ricans who left their island swelled to really large proportions at precisely

---

* A clumsy term, but one commonly used for Puerto Ricans moving to the United States. "Emigrants" does not fit the situation, since the Puerto Ricans are American citizens.

the time when things were improving at home as never before, when a fever for development gripped the entire population, when job opportunities were increased by the thousands
annually and even the unemployed were better off—because
of more effective relief—than they had ever been before.

That is to be expected, since the Commonwealth's improvement of its social-economic conditions rides on the wave of
individual interest in self-improvement. Hundreds of thousands who two decades ago would have suffered their poor
lots in lethargy because the institutions and psychology of
colonialism provided few opportunities for improvement,
while malnutrition left little energy for it, have now been
aroused to look and strive for means of bettering their lives.
The same newly released energies which prompt thousands
of Puerto Ricans to build new homes for themselves in the
agricultural resettlement programs, and new bridges and
schools under the Division of Community Education, prompts
other thousands to move to the mainlaind. Jobs and wages
have multiplied dramatically in Puerto Rico since 1941; they
have multiplied even more dramatically in the States.

At the same time direct ties between the island and the
States have been strengthened since 1941, if only through the
extension of education, the spread of the English language,
the reduction of illiteracy, the new influx of American capital,
and the swelling stream of letters and financial remittances
from those Puerto Ricans who have moved to the States to
those who stayed behind. The extent to which Puerto Rico is
losing its former psychological isolationism is also the extent
to which thousands of modern Puerto Ricans have begun to
see the United States as a land of opportunity rather than as
the imperialistic octopus. That is an important part of the current culture change.

As every New Yorker knows, the life of the Puerto Rican
on the continent is still no bed of roses. It was no bed of roses,
either, for the 40,000,000 immigrants who preceded him—

from various European countries—also with the vision of a land of opportunity. That means, according to studies made by the Puerto Rican government, that the best, the most courageous, the most enterprising Puerto Ricans are often those who leave their island in search of new opportunities. The Commonwealth's gain through their departure, as reflected in demographic statistics, is therefore not wholly without drawbacks. The statistical gain means a human loss in the cream of the manpower. Moreover, as Senior points out, most of the migrants come from the cities where the Puerto Rican people have achieved the most pronounced part of their current drop in fertility. Those who come to the states have in most cases already embraced the small-family ideal, leaving the more fertile behind.

There is a persistent rumor to the effect that the Puerto Rican government encourages migration to the States as one means of reducing population pressure at home. Actually, the government neither encourages nor discourages such migration. It does, however, take an active interest in those who plan to move, do move, or have moved. It maintains offices, largely for their benefit, in New York, Washington, Chicago, Los Angeles, and San Juan. It makes never-ending studies toward easing the lots of Puerto Ricans on the mainland. It collaborates closely with the authorities of New York City and other centers toward handling the social problems created by the Puerto Rican migrants. For such purposes it spends thousands of dollars annually, badly needed on the island itself.

The law of 1947, regulating labor contractors, is a case in point. Previous to that year there had been many abuses. Unscrupulous agents, working hand in glove with new, small air lines which at times charged as little as thirty-five dollars for passage to New York, opened offices in San Juan. They painted glowing pictures of life in the United States, talked about jobs on the mainland, arranged for the shipment of whole plane-loads, and charged fees for their services. On several occasions, the second-hand planes were wrecked over the Atlantic and dozens of Puerto Ricans were killed. At times the agents shipped their clients to places on the continent where no work existed for them; then the problem arose in those places of how to care for the penniless newcomers.

The 1947 law, however, abolished fee-charging agencies in Puerto Rico. It stipulated that all contracts for workers recruited on the island must be approved by the insular Secretary of Labor. "One basic policy decision," according to Clarence Senior's article in the Annals of the American Academy of Political and Social Sciences, "was that no Puerto Rican worker could be recruited for the continent unless a labor shortage was certified by the responsible local, state, and federal labor officials."

Today, moreover, no planes except those of the regular, scheduled air lines may be used for transporting Puerto Rican labor to the States, unless they have been certified by the Puerto Rican as well as the federal officials.

After some eight men had been jailed on the island for violating the new regulations, the law began to work well for the protection of Puerto Rican migrants.

Moreover, when a Puerto Rican wants to migrate to the mainland today, the government, through the university and other branches, offers all possible help to prospective migrants who request it, in teaching them a certain amount of English and acquainting them with the conditions they will find on the continent.

Those seasonal laborers who make good in the States—and in my state of Delaware Puerto Ricans as such have won a good reputation as workers—make their own arrangements with their employers, come back again and again, and don't need the services of recruiting agents. All of them together, too, add directly to the island's economic well-being. Says Senior: "The seasonal farm workers under contract in 1951 earned about $6,300,000. This amount was earned during a period when the vast majority would have had no income whatever. Not only did they support themselves; they sent home to their families between 2 and 2½ million dollars.

"Money orders from both rural and urban migrants have helped to reverse the balance of payments in the section of remittances. The 1949-50 money order payments were $12,-635,832; the following year they had risen to $16,983,235."

Of the urban migrants, of those who move north with their families for the purpose of establishing new homes for themselves on the continent, by far the majority go to New York first of all. Only slowly, after they have managed in New York to get a foothold in the economy, do they drain out from there to New Jersey; Gary, Indiana; Connecticut; Chicago; St. Louis —as jobs become available for them elsewhere, as the Puerto Rican government's efforts to disperse them bear fruit, as Puerto Ricans who have gone ahead write letters back to New York urging others to follow them.

To the average resident of a Puerto Rican city, New York virtually is the United States. There is a New York department store in San Juan; most of the steamers and planes from the island go to New York; most of the letters and checks from transplanted Puerto Ricans come from New York; the 375,000 Puerto Ricans who are there now—though stratified in class and torn between themselves in regional, social, political, and at times religious dissensions—are nevertheless a relatively comforting group to land into, as Puerto Ricans who know at least some of the ropes in the city and also know the problems of newcomers from their own island.

Besides, the current wave of Puerto Ricans into New York is nothing new. Except for the fact that they are already U.S. citizens when they arrive, they differ little from several other ethnic groups which have come to the United States during the decades preceding 1920. As the country's principal gate of entry and *entrepôt* for newcomers, New York City has seen wave after wave of immigrants, of millions of men and women coming successively from such lands as Ireland, Poland, Lithuania, Russia, etc. Many of them made their homes in the city's slums, at least for a time, until they could establish themselves somehow in the American economy. In the beginning they usually, and understandably, clung together; only gradually did they begin to disperse to such centers as Pittsburgh, Chicago, Detroit, and St. Louis. Poor, bewildered, ignorant of our language and customs, they began at the bottom of the economic ladder. They were vulnerable to all kinds of frauds and swindles, perpetrated by unscrupulous landlords, employers, confidence men, gangsters, and political ward heelers who fished for votes in various ethnic puddles. Only as they became linguistically and culturally acclimatized, as they joined labor unions, as they discovered social tools and weapons for their own protection, as they became more or less Americanized and so shed the need for clinging together, as their second generations grew up in the American scene, did their lots begin to improve and they to make their large contributions to America's strength.

Many of today's Puerto Rican arrivals in New York are every bit as bewildered, every bit as ignorant of our language and customs, every bit as much prey to mass swindles, as were their predecessors from Europe. Their plight, problems, and progress were well dealt with in 1950, in a survey conducted by C. Wright Mills, Clarence Senior, and Rose Kohn Goldsen, sponsored by Columbia University and published by Harpers under the title *The Puerto Rican Journey*.

Upon arrival in the States, as pointed out in that report and later again by Mr. Joseph Monserrat of the New York office of the Commonwealth's Department of Labor, "The Puerto Rican must make many adjustments. The weather is more extreme, being very hot in summer and very cold in winter. The pace is extremely rapid. . . . The Negro and darker-skinned Puerto Rican who has not known discrimination before suddenly finds that his ability to make a living is often based on the color of his skin and not upon his ability to do the job. The Puerto Rican comes from a patriarchal society where the father is the main breadwinner and rules the roost. Upon arrival in the States, the family structure is often changed. The father finds it difficult to earn enough or even to find a job. His wife, however, is often wanted for her skilled needlework and very often becomes the main breadwinner. She no longer need be completely dependent upon her husband and becomes more independent. The children's position within the family undergoes a change. Very often the parents know little or no English. The children, however, have learned some English either in the schools of Puerto Rico or on the continent. When their parents have need to conduct business in English the children are often brought along as interpreters. No longer are they 'seen but not heard'; now they are the very center of social interaction.

"A study of Puerto Rican delinquent boys provides us with further insight into the difficulties parents and children go through during the adjustment process. The study indicated that Puerto Rican youngsters were not involved in many major crimes. A disproportionate number of them, however, had been institutionalized for incorrigibility. This is not difficult to understand since these youngsters were suffering from 'second generationitis.' These children find themselves caught between cultures; their parents and homes on one side; the school and the street on the other. A young girl whose parents have been brought up in the tradition that a girl must not go out alone with boys and that she should be kept close at home is bewildered and rebels when her schoolmates invite her to a settlement dance and her parents refuse her permission. She tells her mother that she is going to visit a friend and sneaks off to the dance. When she returns and is questioned as to her whereabouts she lies again. This innocent lying often leads to more serious deceptions and soon the youngster is on the road to delinquency. The parent, on the other hand, is hurt and bewildered by the child's action, complaining that youngsters are allowed 'too much liberty here.' The great tragedy here is the sincere and honest belief of both parents and children that they are right and the other wrong. More tragic is the fact that each is right, depending on the frame of reference used."

Most of them, too, are victims of the prevailing housing shortage. Tenement buildings, already overcrowded the day they were designed, are divided and subdivided by their landlords. Often, two or three Puerto Rican families must perforce live in apartments designed for one. For that they at times reap shallow contempt for living "like animals." Sometimes, too, the building had been condemned even before the landlord rented space in it to Puerto Ricans; no sooner is it filled than it is torn down on the city's insistence, and the newcomers have to move elsewhere to overcrowd other living quarters.

The government of New York City is doing everything in its power to cope with the Puerto Rican problem, but many New Yorkers, seeing one neighborhood after another invaded by Puerto Ricans, are irritated and fearful. To some, the Puerto Ricans are convenient whipping boys. Thefts, robberies, and murders are not new in New York, but three times during the month before the present writing I heard New York Puerto Ricans, as "they," blamed for specific crimes. In some quarters it has become fashionable to blame "them" for the recent rise in juvenile delinquency, to claim that "they" are unhealthy, shiftless, dirty, and lazy and that "they" come to New York largely for the purpose of going on the city's relief rolls.

The studies made by Senior and his associates refute all that. It is also true that the New York Puerto Ricans today contribute considerably to the city's life and activities. As pointed out by Monserrat, fewer than 5 per cent of the New York Puerto Ricans are on relief, while "building maintenance, garment, clothing and textile factories, hotels and restaurants, toy, novelty and plastic plants, and many other aspects of the city's economy would be critically injured if all the Puerto Ricans elected to go elsewhere. Furthermore, whatever ethnic group came to replace them would be faced by the same problems of housing, health, etc., which are faced by the Puerto Ricans. They would also create the same kinds of difficulties caused by those members of the Puerto Rican community who are the latest arrivals and are therefore on the bottom rung of the occupational ladder.

"Moreover, the Puerto Rican migration is, in effect, only a small part of the internal movement of American citizens. Between April 1, 1950, and the same date of 1951, almost five and a quarter million American citizens moved their residences across state lines; Puerto Ricans made up only 38,000 of that number. The Southerners are in a position similar to that of the Puerto Ricans, and many times as many persons annually migrate northward from the South as from Puerto Rico."

As stated before, one great advantage that the Puerto Rican migrants have over those from the South and over the waves of Europeans who preceded them is that their home government continues to take an active interest in them. Imagine Governor Byrnes asking the mayor of New York for a conference on how to ease the lot of the South Carolinians who have moved to Harlem! It is also true that New York City shows a more concerted and constructive interest in its Puerto Ricans than it has in any previous wave of immigrants. There have long been a Mayor's Committee on Puerto Rican Affairs as well as a number of private and semiofficial groups devoted to helping the Puerto Ricans.

Every year, for a number of years, the University of Puerto Rico has given scholarships and other aid to groups of teachers and social workers who deal with Puerto Ricans in New York. These go to the island for summer workshops, gain in the knowledge required for their work, and incidentally develop a high respect for what Puerto Ricans are accomplishing for themselves on the home ground. If for no other reason than that of the island's enhanced reputation, the money is considered well spent.

In March, 1953, at the Commonwealth's expense, there was held an important conference in San Juan, called to discuss the problem of Puerto Ricans in New York City. The quality of New York's thirteen delegates, who met with Puerto Ricans of the same high level, indicated on the one hand the situation's gravity and on the other New York's eagerness to deal with it. The delegates included the president of the Borough of Manhattan, the chief city magistrate, the planning commissioner, the commissioners of health, welfare, hospitals, and of housing and buildings, the presiding justice of the Domestic Relations Court, and high-level representatives of the city's educational system, housing authority, and the like.

At that conference, New York City pledged itself to do certain things, the city and the Commonwealth agreed to do other things jointly, and the Commonwealth undertook to intensify its programs to help actual and prospective migrants.

Those programs include counseling service to migrants regarding job opportunities, housing, climate, clothing needs, etc., to be given by and through the eight local offices of the Puerto Rican Employment Service, affiliated with the United States Employment Service. They offer special health advice to all prospective migrants, medical examinations such as chest X-rays, as well as the good offices of the Commonwealth in trying to persuade tuberculars to stay on the island for treatment instead of taking their illness to the continent.

Through orientation programs, using lectures, films, film strips, and all other available means, the Commonwealth pledged itself, whenever possible, to acquaint prospective migrants with the realities they will have to face in the States, with the differences in living habits, job opportunities in various places and especially outside of New York City, hazards to health and welfare arising from the critical housing shortage. It proposed to show motion pictures "about life in the continental United States, with emphasis on areas outside of New York City, so that Puerto Ricans will have a concept of the United States as a whole rather than of only one spot in it."

The City of New York agreed to develop courses of in-service training for employees in all city departments who deal with Puerto Ricans, in order to help dispel the many derogatory myths about the New York Puerto Ricans, "substitute facts for them and to point up the economic and social contributions to the end that they may be prepared to give Puerto Ricans services equal to those given to other residents." It also agreed to develop and extend the policy of adding qualified Spanish-speaking personnel to its various staffs and organizations.

Together with the federal and state departments of labor, the city pledged itself to remain active in helping to enforce the minimum-wage and other laws; it regretted that "the federal government has abolished the positions of two Spanish-speaking minimum-wage investigators whose activities in a little over two years had resulted in the recovery for Puerto Rican workers of over $200,000 in wages of which they had been deprived"; because labor organizations are in a particularly valuable position to help dispel prejudicial myths and to speed up the adjustment processes, the city delegation joined with the Puerto Ricans in expressing satisfaction over "the recent holding of two conferences of A. F. of L. and C.I.O. unions of New York City and the organization of a continuing committee on the unionization of Puerto Rican and other Spanish-speaking workers."

The two units agreed, as for instance through the exchange of professional personnel, to continue fostering and developing possibilities for closer co-operation between various Puerto Rican endeavors, as in health, education, hospitals, and social work, and corresponding New York activities. The University of Puerto Rico agreed to increase the number of its maintenance scholarships granted to American teachers for their annual summer workshop on the island, conducted jointly with New York University.

In view of the proven success of Puerto Rico's local self-help programs, it was mutually agreed to try to extend such programs to the Puerto Ricans in New York, to encourage the latter to take the lead in community programs and various self-help projects, including other ethnic groups where desirable, for the purposes of improving the "blighted and deteriorating areas in which Puerto Rican and other new working-class arrivals in New York City are forced to live," and of changing as rapidly as possible the cultural habits built up in earlier environments which may be inadequate in the new one.

Full co-operation was pledged in such matters as urging New York Puerto Ricans to attend night classes and participate in the activities of settlement houses, labor unions, church groups, parent-teacher associations, and other neighborhood and city-wide civic groups so that they may make their contributions "to the day-to-day functioning of our common American democracy."

Among the Commonwealth's constant efforts to disperse the Puerto Rican migrants and find them jobs outside New York, the success of the early action at Gary, Indiana, was both notable and significant. In 1948 there was a drastic shortage of manpower in the steel mills of the Gary area. Five hundred workers were therefore flown in from Puerto Rico, carefully screened by the mills, and as carefully indoctrinated by their own government, which urged them to learn English as rapidly as possible, join labor unions, participate in union and civic affairs, and finally to disperse and not to hang together clannishly as a Puerto Rican community-within-a-community.

Six months later, the Gary, Indiana, *Post Tribune* made a survey of the situation and published six articles about it, in

which it expressed considerable surprise that the experiment
had succeeded beyond all expectations. The Puerto Ricans,
said the paper, learned their work rapidly and well. Absenteeism was not a problem among them. The crime wave
that some had expected to develop after their arrival never
materialized; indeed, Puerto Rican names were almost not
to be found on the police blotters. They fitted well into the
community, and non-Puerto Rican members of the community
took them in readily. They liked baseball and apparently, according to the paper, loved their wives. They saved their
money and were good American citizens.

The success of the first five hundred Gary Puerto Ricans
opened doors, of course, for many more. The number of
Puerto Ricans now in the Gary area runs into the thousands.

The Gary experience is today becoming relatively common.
A number of industries in various parts of the United States
have in recent years filled their labor shortages with Puerto
Ricans—sometimes with much trepidation in view of the lat-
ters' reputation in New York—but usually with excellent
results. The same good qualities which Muñoz Marín has
harnessed on the island to reshape Puerto Rico's entire life,
seem, from the letters I have seen in the Department of Labor,
to be discovered increasingly today by American employers
who hire Puerto Ricans.

Moreover, whatever tensions and problems are today
created by hundreds of thousands of Puerto Ricans in the
States are due to disappear by themselves in the natural
course of events. As standards of living and opportunities for
employment go up on the island, as the birth rate continues
to drop, there will be less need every year for out-migration
to seek a better life. As standards of living rise, too, as the
health of the Puerto Ricans improves, as they learn various
industrial and other skills, as they become bilingual at home,
as they learn more about the United States, those who do

come will be increasingly welcome and decreasingly noticed (the two often go together).

The problems now created by migrant Puerto Ricans in the United States represent only a phase of the early stages of Puerto Rico's great transition.

CHAPTER XXII

Where Now?

IN 1953 the United States officially reported to the United Nations that Puerto Rico was no longer a dependent territory and that Washington would no longer report on it as such. Momentarily, the United Nations headquarters became a Puerto Rican debating ground. Representatives of the Independence party went to New York to protest against the move on the ground that Puerto Rico was still, in effect, a colony. They were opposed by representatives of the Puerto Rican government, who claimed that the Commonwealth had entered freely and of its own accord into the compact with Washington defining its present political status, that it had achieved self-government within the framework of the American Union, and that it was, in fact, no longer a dependent territory. A small flurry was stirred by the debate. Fear of Nationalist terrorism caused the bodyguard of Henry Cabot Lodge, America's delegate to the United Nations, to be increased. President Eisenhower made a statement to the effect that Puerto Rico could have national sovereignty whenever it so desired. Muñoz Marín made an answering statement, thanking the President for his generosity but disavowing in the name of his people a desire for what he calls "separate independence."

In January, 1954, Roger Baldwin of the American Civil Liberties Union was invited to Puerto Rico by the governor to make an investigation. While he found considerable unanimity over a number of matters such as the fact that Puerto Ricans are still subject to laws in the drafting of which they have no voice, he also found differences of opinion on how such matters should be handled. The *Populares*, he reported, are determined to work, through evolutionary processes, toward increases in the island's autonomy; the *Independentista* party and (Baldwin thinks) also the Statehood, cling to their avowed goals and oppose all compromise measures leading to greater autonomy.

With some exceptions, notably that of the Popular Democratic party, it has long been the custom of Puerto Rico's political parties to include status planks in their platforms. So, for instance, the Republican party has always stood for eventual statehood; in 1948, in fact, it changed its name to the Statehood party, *Partido Estadista Puertorriqueño*, popularly known as the PEP. The now defunct Liberal party, to which Muñoz Marín belonged until his expulsion in 1937, campaigned in part for eventual independence. The present Independence party, *Partido Independentista Puertorriqueño*, popularly known as the PIP, campaigns primarily for independence.

In line with the custom of identifying various parties with various kinds of eventual status, it has also long been the custom of political leaders to claim that votes for their parties constituted votes for their kinds of status. For instance, the elections of 1932 and 1936 were won by the Coalition of Republican and Socialist parties, of which the one stood officially for statehood and the other, while favoring statehood, refrained from making status a campaign issue. The two parties, together, polled 54 per cent of the total vote cast in 1932, a fact which leaders of the Republican party interpreted as meaning that well over half of the island's population favored statehood for Puerto Rico. On the other hand, the *Liberales* polled more votes than did any other single party in that election, gaining 44 per cent of the total vote cast. Its leaders claimed that that fact, plus the fact that the Socialist party had not made status a campaign issue, meant that the majority of Puerto Ricans were for independence. They were in turn answered by the Republican leaders, who pointed out that the violent Nationalist party, which had campaigned openly and exclusively for independence, had polled only 2 per cent of the total vote, which they chose to interpret as meaning that only 2 per cent of Puerto Rico's people favored eventual independence.

As pointed out in Chapter V, the 1932 election was the first and only one in which Albizu Campos' Nationalist party participated. Failing to win the 10 per cent of total which was then required for the party to remain a party (today it is 5 per cent), it thereafter shrank to its present condition of an odd small group of fanatical terrorists. Albizu, however, explained his 1932 defeat as having been caused by colonialism's economic pressures. A colonial election, he argued, could never be a free and truly indicative one because the economic system was so stacked that a man might well lose his job if he voted the wrong way. He insisted that the majority of Puerto Rico's people are essentially "patriotic" in that they desire national sovereignty above all else, and that their vote would show them to be that way were it not for restrictive economic conditions.

The results of the 1948 election would seem, on the surface, to bear him out to some extent. Whatever the advocates of independence might say about Puerto Rico's still being a colony, everybody concedes that that election was much more fair than had been the one of 1932. The custom of buying votes had been abolished. Muñoz had made much headway with his constant efforts to educate his people politically, toward the point where their votes would really represent their feelings on important issues. Nineteen hundred and forty-eight was the first time that the Independence party went to the polls, campaigning officially for a kind of independence which was to be won in a peaceful fashion through mutual agreement with Washington. In that year it won 66,141 votes, or 10 per cent of the total. The fact that it won 125,734 votes four years later, or 19 per cent of the total, is interpreted by its leaders as meaning either that the desire for independence is growing rapidly at the same time that Puerto Rico's economic and social affairs are showing their present phenomenal improvement, or that that desire has always been large but is only now, because of improved conditions and a growing political awareness, being reflected in the vote.

The 1952 election represented the death knell of the Socialist party, which had actually been a labor party, identified with the A. F. of L. rather than with state socialism as such. In 1936 it had polled the respectable sum of 144,294 votes, or 26 per cent of the total. After that year, Muñoz' Popular Democratic party, with its promises to labor and the common man, and its even greater achievements, had steadily taken votes away from the Socialists and others. In 1952 the Socialist party polled only 21,655 votes, or 3 per cent of the total; its loss meant the gains of both the *Populares* and the *Independentistas*. In that year the Statehood party won 85,172 votes, or 12 per cent. The Popular Democratic party won 65 per cent of the total, with 429,064 votes. Since the latter party stands firmly for Puerto Rico's present commonwealth status, though consistently refraining from making status a campaign issue, the 1952 election might be, and often is, interpreted as meaning that the Puerto Rican people are overwhelmingly in favor of the status they have now and have decisively rejected both statehood and independence as the alternate but ultimate solutions of their political problem.

But general elections are poor indices of popular feelings on such matters. I have heard several people say that they are good *Populares,* or members of the Popular Democratic party, but not *Muñocistas,* or followers of Muñoz in the latter's ideas on status. It is quite possible for a man to vote for Muñoz and his party because he is for the program of social and economic reform which is today transforming Puerto Rico, while still hoping that someday in the near future Puerto Rico will become either a sovereign nation or one of forty-nine, or fifty, or fifty-one (depending on what happens meanwhile to Alaska and Hawaii) states which together comprise the United States of America. Similarly, as pointed out in an earlier chapter, many men and women have voted for the Independence party, and some for the Statehood party, not because they wanted either independence or statehood for their island, but because they were angry at the government and wanted to register a protest vote. Laborers on the government-owned proportional profit farms have been known to vote for the Independence party because the government was mechanizing its farms for greater efficiency and was therefore throwing laborers out of work. One prominent member of the Independence party, Sr. Rafael Arjona Siaca, began his political life with the Republican party, advocating statehood, switched to the *Populares* with their striving toward commonwealth status, and then bolted Muñoz' party in favor of the *Independentistas.*

A referendum or plebiscite, in which political status is the only issue, is of course a far more reliable index of popular feeling than is a general election. But even there, while the details of statehood are clearly defined in the American scheme of things, independence is so nebulous a concept that the referendum, to be worth anything, would have to deal with some specific form of independence rather than with the idea in the abstract. It will be remembered from Chapter IX that in 1936 the Tydings bill proposed such a plebiscite. Had it passed in Congress, and had it been a decent bill, with workable terms giving Puerto Rico an opportunity for transform-

ing its colonial economy into a strong economy of independence, the people of Puerto Rico might well, in that year, have
voted for independence. The general feeling for independence, going hand in hand with a general feeling of hopelessness about colonialism, was much stronger in those days of
abysmal suffering than it is today. Muñoz Marín—even then
the island's outstanding leader in the hold he had on people
and their loyalties—was himself for eventual independence
and would probably have campaigned accordingly. But the
Tydings bill, providing only a ten-year interval for economic
transformation, and in other ways, too, making an effective
transformation impossible, merely offered the people of
Puerto Rico a choice between the bad colonial status that they
already had and a far worse kind of independence. In that dilemma, in which a vote for independence looked like a vote
for collective suicide, while a vote against independence
could well have been interpreted as a vote for continued slow
starvation as a colony, the people of Puerto Rico were indignant over what they considered Washington's bad faith and
glad that Congress failed to pass the bill.

Obviously, thousands of Puerto Rican voters today cast
their votes for a party which favors eventual independence.
Respected throughout the world as a noble ideal, independence in the abstract possibly has even more Puerto Rican adherents who have never voted for the party espousing it. But
1936 taught the Puerto Ricans, with a shock, that there are
many possible kinds of independence; if they were to vote on
the issue in a plebiscite, they would not only have to have the
particular kind spelled out to them, but would also have to
know about Washington's willingness to give it to them.

Gilberto Concepción de Gracia, the head of the Independence party, thinks that he can persuade Washington to grant
a workable kind of independence, preceded by an interim period of perhaps fifty years for developing an economy of
sovereignty. Should he ever win an election, he would un-

doubtedly work on Washington to offer something of the kind. If Washington did offer it, which seems doubtful, he would probably have to arrange for a plebiscite to accept or reject the offer. In such an event it would not be at all surprising, Puerto Rican politics being what it is, to see the voters, after electing Concepción on an independence platform, emphatically rejecting the kind of independence that he managed to offer them.

What it boils down to is the futility of regarding the status question per se, out of context of the changing over-all scene, and drawing conclusions about desires for this or that kind of status from election returns or from what one hears from the man on the street. In his first inaugural speech, Muñoz pointed out that the question of political status must be regarded as an integral part of the life of the people and that it cannot be seperated from consideration of that life as a complex whole. Puerto Rican scholars today write about "the evolution of the status thesis," meaning that it changes with changing social and economic conditions, with one kind of status more meaningful at one time in the life of the people, and another at another, and with the evolution of that life also, inevitably, developing the form of status which best fits existing conditions.

The present commonwealth status was developed as a result of an evolutionary process. Unique in world political affairs, with no precedent on earth or in history, it grew directly out of Puerto Rican experiences rather than out of the cerebrations of political scientists dealing with ideas in the abstract. It is unique in part because it developed, not through legislation passed in Washington and handed down to the Puerto Ricans, but through a proposal made by Puerto Rico to Washington for a compact by which the people of Puerto Rico and the government of the United States would mutually and in friendship establish the terms of their future relationship. Public Law 600, passed by Congress and approved on July 3, 1950, recognized the principle of "government by consent," stated specifically that it was in the nature of a compact and was a unique piece of federal legislation in that, by its own terms, it was not to become law until the people of Puerto Rico had voted on accepting or rejecting it; by a "no" vote, a small colonial society could have invalidated a law passed by the Congress of the then ruling country. The law, and so also the compact, was accepted by the Puerto Rican voters in a referendum in 1951, with a vote of 387,016 to 119,169, which was, on the one hand, a strong vote for continuation of political relations with the United States and, on the other, a vote against separate independence. In the campaign preceding the referendum, the Independence party had done most of the talking against the compact, which weakened the chances for independence by voluntarily affirming continued political relations with Washington. Those who were for Puerto Rico's statehood had fewer objections to the compact because it in no way precluded, and in some ways even improved, the chances for, eventual statehood.

Under Public Law 600, the modus operandi of the federal government in Puerto Rico and the relationships between the government and people of Puerto Rico and the United States continue as before. The United States continues to operate the army, navy, air force, post office, customs service, and various such federal agencies as the Soil Conservation Service in Puerto Rico. Excise taxes collected on goods manufactured in Puerto Rico and duties collected in Puerto Rican ports continue to be returned to the Puerto Rican treasury instead of being paid into the federal treasury. Incomes earned in Puerto Rico continue to be exempt from federal income tax, on the principle of "no taxation without representation." Puerto Rico continues to be represented in Congress by only one resident commissioner who has a voice but no vote. Puerto Rico remains within the economic structure of the United States.

In all matters pertaining to local government, however, Puerto Rico was given a free hand under the compact of Public Law 600, subject only to control, on the grounds of constitutionality, by the U.S. Supreme Court. In passing the compact law, Congress also voluntarily surrendered its imperialistic authority. The law provided that the people of Puerto Rico should draft their own constitution, which should, on its acceptance by the Puerto Rican voters as well as by Congress, become the basic law of the emerging political unit, which is officially called a Commonwealth in English, and an *Estado Libre Asociado*, or Free Associated State, in Spanish. The Puerto Ricans elected members of a constituent assembly to draft the constitution. When the assembly had finished its work, a Puerto Rican referendum accepted the constitution by a vote of 375,594 to 82,877.

Congressional approval of the new constitution was not granted without a certain amount of haggling. At one time certain members of Congress tried to stipulate, through an amendment to the new constitution, that Puerto Rico should never be allowed to amend it without specific consent from Congress. That raised a storm of protest. Puerto Ricans said: "What goes on here? First they enter into a compact, giving us the right to rule ourselves under our own constitution, and then they turn around and try to amend that constitution without asking us, in such a way that we cannot handle our affairs in the future without continuing to be beggars at the doors of Congress." There were some who thought that the proposed Congressional amendment to Puerto Rico's constitution was perhaps in itself not very serious, but that a profound moral issue was at stake. The feeling of indignation ran so high that the majority of Puerto Ricans might well, at that moment, have voted to drop the whole matter unless the Congressional amendment was withdrawn, to stay in their former status until some future Congress could be persuaded to co-operate without trying to nullify the entire spirit of a compact of free association.

Muñoz Marín cabled to Washington: ". . . People here are dismayed with amendment that nullifies the significance of the whole constitutional process. To the limitations rightfully imposed on state constitutions and the Puerto Rican constitution, the amendment adds an obvious colonial touch. The people of Puerto Rico in voting to accept Law 600 in the nature of a compact, in which the principle of government by consent was 'fully recognized,' certainly had no idea they were consenting to any trace of colonialism. No self-respecting people would. Free men may live under such circumstances but they will certainly not go to the polls and vote that they love and cherish them. I fear that if the matter cannot be remedied in conference, great moral harm will be done to our people and some moral harm to the good name of the United States in the world. You can rely on us to protect the good name of the United States."

Fortunately, the Congressional amendment, governing amendments to Puerto Rico's constitution, was stricken out. Congress, however, did remove from the Bill of Rights certain provisions which some congressmen called unworkable and others labeled "socialistic," "communistic," and contrary to American ideals of government. These were provisions under which the government acknowledged certain responsibilities toward the people and defined eventual goals toward which government and people should strive jointly. They were taken almost verbatim from the Universal Declaration of Human Rights of the United Nations, although they were in no way new in Puerto Rico. For years before the writing of the constitution, the Puerto Rican government had acted in conformance with their terms, had *lived* them without debate, as though they had already been put on paper as the basic law of the land.

Under the provisions struck out by Congress, the Commonwealth recognized the right of every individual to an education, to obtain work, to an adequate standard of living, to social protection in the event of unemployment, sickness, old age, or disability, to special care and assistance for motherhood and childhood. The Commonwealth government pledged itself to do everything in its power "to promote the greatest possible expansion of the system of production, to assure the fairest possible distribution of economic output, and to obtain the maximum understanding between individual initiative and collective co-operation." The Congressional action of eliminating those sections baffled the Puerto Ricans, since the Universal Declaration of Human Rights had been approved by the General Assembly of the United Nations—and so also by the United States—on December 10, 1948. Puerto Rico's leaders, however, were not too disturbed. Since they are now free to amend their own constitution without interference, they can at any time put the various sections once eliminated by Congress back in again.

As pointed out by Pedro Muñoz Amato, Congress ceded much of its authority when it passed Law 600 and accepted the constitution drafted subsequently. In general, the people of Puerto Rico now have self-government under their own constitution, but two closely related matters still remain to be cleared up. The island still has no voting representation in Congress, although Congressional laws apply to it, and there is no provision for amending the so-called Federal Relations Statute, defining relations between the Commonwealth and the federal government. If, in the future, provisions are to be made for voting representation in Congress, and for other changes in the Federal Relations Statute, shall such provisions be made unilaterally, by Congress alone, or jointly, "in the nature of a compact," by Puerto Rico and Washington? If, in the future, it is decided that Puerto Rico shall contribute to the expenses of the federal government, that excise taxes

on goods made in Puerto Rico shall no longer be returned to
the Commonwealth, that Puerto Ricans shall pay federal income tax, shall the decision be made by Congress alone or
shall the government and people of Puerto Rico be consulted
on the question of whether or not they can afford such contributions without crippling their present energetic program
to raise standards of living and extend the benefits of education and public health to all the island's people? There is no
provision for the answer to these vitally important questions
in Public Law 600 or anywhere else, and the extent to which
they persist and plague those who want to place the Commonwealth's political status on a sound basis is also the extent
to which Puerto Rico still lacks control over its own destiny
as a part of the American Union. It was undoubtedly that situation which has caused Muñoz Marín on several occasions
to raise the question of potential contributions to the federal
treasury. If, when the time comes, the Commonwealth voluntarily offers to make such contributions and presents a bill
in Congress providing for such contributions, then Puerto
Rico will automatically have something to say about the manner in which things are handled—in the nature of a compact.
Until something like that is done, or until the entire matter
has been clarified—perhaps through the U.S. Supreme Court—
Puerto Rico still has insufficient control over its own destiny,
must still be aware of a Damoclean sword over its head. It
is conceivable that Congress can still pass legislation which
vitally affects Puerto Rico without the consent of the Commonwealth. A Congress which is ignorant of Puerto Rican
affairs, like those which in earlier years cramped the island's
educational system, or a Congress which may for the moment
be vindictively inclined toward the island—perhaps because
of a recurrence of terroristic activities on the part of the Nationalists—seems now to have the power to amend the Federal Relations Statute unilaterally in such a way that the great

Puerto Rican efforts at transformation would be crippled or seriously retarded.

Meanwhile, and with such matters still remaining to be cleared up, the evolution of the status thesis has progressed remarkably since the Popular Democratic party won the election of 1940. As long as the party continues to exercise strong leadership in the matter, its consistent gains in strength would seem to imply a concomitant increase in the desire of the Puerto Ricans to remain under the American flag, as American citizens—continuing to progress in an evolutionary fashion from their former sufferings as colonial subjects. In 1952, the *Populares* polled 429,064 votes, or 65 per cent of the total. The opposing parties did not manage to elect a single member of the legislature or a single municipal official in any of the towns and cities. They are represented in the legislature only because the Commonwealth's constitution, recognizing the dangers of a one-party government, provides for such representation on a proportional basis.

The strength of the Popular Democratic party is recognized as being not an unmixed blessing. In effect, in its local affairs and since the two opposition parties stand primarily for changed relations with the United States, Puerto Rico does have a one-party government—not by choice, but because Muñoz Marín, his party, and his policies, are so overwhelmingly popular that nobody has been able to challenge them. Muñoz' political enemies may challenge this or that minor point in his program. They may claim, for instance, that an agency such as the Division of Community Education spends too much money for the results achieved. But they cannot, without committing political suicide, challenge the Popular Democratic party's program as a whole, its social and economic aims, its energetic activities for increasing employment, improving health, spreading and improving education, its imaginative leadership which appeals to the people's deepest and best emotions.

Muñoz' enemies use that fact to bolster their claim that he is a dictator, but refrain from pointing out that he has been freely elected by the people again and again, and that Puerto Rican elections are today more free, more honest, and cleaner than they have ever been before—and more so than are elections in many parts of the continental United States.

Usually, however, charges of dictatorship are made in the mainland press by visiting American journalists and later reproduced in the Puerto Rican papers. And occasionally the journalists seem to have prostituted themselves. There is the story, for instance, of the American operator, who must here, for obvious reasons, remain nameless, but who had gone to Puerto Rico during Piñero's governorship to do some very lucrative work, both for the government and on his own. He thought he was entitled to tax exemption under the new law, but was told that the matter was entirely up to the judgment of the Executive Council. The 1948 election took place before the matter was settled. The operator went to candidate Muñoz during the campaign, told him that he felt it his duty to contribute to campaign expenses, and offered him $25,000 in cash. Muñoz refused the money, but, on the other's insistence, agreed to have his party treasurer accept it, against a receipt and on condition that it be returned after the election in case the Popular Democratic party did not need it. The American protested that he did not want a receipt. Muñoz laughed and said: "You just try to give my party treasurer one dime without taking a receipt. If you succeed, I will immediately have a new treasurer."

The money was paid. The party did not need it for the campaign. The money was returned in check form. The Executive Council later decided, on the merits of the case, that the American was not entitled to tax exemption. The latter tried to see the newly elected governor but failed to get into the *Fortaleza*. Then some of his local representatives came to me, and others, to beg us to intercede with Muñoz because their boss was working himself into a rage and was about to do "something terrible" to Puerto Rico unless the whole matter could be straightened out. We didn't intercede—at least I didn't. Muñoz continued not to see the man. About that time there arrived in Puerto Rico several free-lance journalists of the more flamboyant kind, living in swank in the Caribe Hilton Hotel. The articles of one of them, published in obscure American newspapers, were to the effect that Muñoz was a dictator running a one-party government and a coward to boot, a prisoner of the police who was afraid of the Nationalists, had lost touch with the people, and no longer attended public meetings for fear of being shot. Whereupon I gave an interview stating that I had, during the preceding few weeks, attended three public meetings with Muñoz, that he had attended several others without me, that I had invited the writer of the article to one such meeting, that he had refused to go, and that it had been the writer, and not the governor, who refused to attend public meetings.

Of such stuff are the charges of dictatorship made. Whether or not the two journalists concerned were in the pay of the large-scale operator who had threatened to do "something terrible" to Puerto Rico, is, of course, a moot question. What is important is that most Puerto Ricans thought they were.

When the constitution was being drafted, a number of people, afraid of Muñoz' continuing popularity, wanted to insert a provision limiting any one man's governorship to two terms. At that time Muñoz said to me: "I am perfectly willing to have them do that as far as I am concerned. But, damn it, I am not willing to grant it as a principle. If one man is capable of doing things for the people and with the people, and if he continues term after term to win the people's votes, he should be allowed to serve for as many terms as the people want. It is undemocratic to limit a governor's services to two terms when he does so good a job that the people want him for three, or four, or six terms. The real job is to see to it that the election machinery functions well, that nobody is allowed to tamper with the vote, that the vote actually does represent the true choice of the voters, freely expressed. As long as that is done, there can be no fear of dictatorship."

The constitution did not limit even Muñoz to two terms, and today there is widespread speculation on who his successor might be. Muñoz himself, as far as I know, has not indicated any personal choice for such a successor. The possibility exists, and is often heard discussed on the island, that he will run again and again in response to popular demand, be elected again and again, and will die in office—like Roosevelt. A number of Puerto Ricans believe that Puerto Rico will achieve a real two- or three-party system then—and not until then. It seems possible that Muñoz' eventual removal from the scene may split the Popular Democratic party into various factions as several of its present leaders begin to compete for the governorship.

Meanwhile, just as the government saw to it that opposition parties are represented in the legislature even though they do not manage to have their representatives elected, it also saw to it that parties can survive longer than they could formerly. The change in law, under which a party now needs to poll only 5 per cent of the total vote in any one election in order to remain a political party and be able to go to the next elections as such, as compared with the 10 per cent required formerly, was made specifically because the Popular Democratic party was running away with everything and needed opposition to be healthy in a healthy, democratic society.

Despite the recent gains of the Independence party, a number of observers, myself included, feel that the desire for independence is waning rapidly, and also that any kind of independence achieved under conditions as they are today would be a calamity for the island.

An incident related to the Korean War, in which the 65th

Regiment of Puerto Rican Infantry distinguished itself, with 3,000 casualties, shows a decided swing in modern Puerto Rico's orientations. Shortly before the election of 1952, the head of the Statehood party made a public statement to the effect that presidential candidate Eisenhower had called the war an Asian war and had hinted a willingness to leave it to the Asians and withdraw American troops. He called for joint action on the part of the leaders of Puerto Rico's political parties, endorsing that statement and petitioning Washington to withdraw Puerto Rican troops from the conflict. The head of the Independence party immediately issued his own statement, endorsing the PEP stand, claiming that the Korean War was not Puerto Rico's (as a colony) and asserting his eagerness to act jointly with the other party heads in a united Puerto Rican front to have the 65th regiment withdrawn. Muñoz refused, answering to the effect that he thought Eisenhower wrong, that it was not an Asian war, that it was a war against aggression and for the democratic way of life, and that the people of Puerto Rico, who had begun to share so notably in that way of life, should be willing to fight to uphold it.

Not only did the statement not cost him a single vote as far as anybody can tell—the victory of the *Populares*, a few days later, was overwhelming—but it brought him a flood of mail, nearly all of it saying, in effect, "Thank God for such a leader." Within an hour after Muñoz' statement appeared in the papers, an old taxi driver rushed up to the *Fortaleza* with a letter which he wanted to give Don Luis personally. The letter said that two of the old man's sons had already been killed in Korea and that his third and last son was even then in the army, training to go to Korea. It thanked the governor for his statement and expressed the writer's indignation over the actions of the Statehood and Independence leaders as being an insult to the memory of his two dead sons and the integrity of the remaining one. Most of the letters that poured into the *Fortaleza* were in the same vein, from people who had lost boys in Korea and thanked the governor for defending their memory and integrity.

Except in that it disturbed the advocates of independence by robbing their arguments of a certain amount of validity, the Congressional fairness through which the commonwealth status was brought about did little to strengthen the desire for independence. On the contrary. On the whole, the hundreds of thousands of Puerto Ricans now in the States, bad as their lot often is in centers like New York, the manner in which their lives are constantly improving, the manner in which they are socially and economically accepted in places like Gary, Indiana, the letters and remittances which they send home, undoubtedly strengthen ties to the United States and diminish the validity of the independence thesis. The very thought of being able to come and go freely within the United States, as American citizens, coupled with the thought of what might well happen to Puerto Rico economically and to jobs in Puerto Rico in the event of independence, is widely regarded as a powerful argument against potential independence.

Muñoz abandoned his early stand in favor of independence largely because he could see no way in which any Congress, no matter how benevolently inclined, could possibly give duty-free entry into the United States to Puerto Rican products. The imposition of a tariff on sugar would ruin the sugar industry, which was then, as it still is, the island's economic mainstay. The entire program of economic development which has during the past decade and a half made such notable advances is based firmly on continued relations with the United States, as part of the American Union, within the framework of the American economic structure. If independence should come, and with it the need for paying duty on goods sent to the States, what will happen to the hundreds of new industries, established largely with American capital, for the production of goods for nation-wide distribution?

The advocates of independence have no good answers to such questions, except to hope, on the one hand, that some future Congress will grant political sovereignty to Puerto Rico while still leaving it within the American economic structure, and to point out, on the other, that an independent Puerto Rico will be able to make its own foreign-trade agreements and will be able to buy goods more cheaply outside the U.S. tariff structure. The opponents answer them by saying that it is very well to be able to make one's own foreign-trade agreements, but it is economically futile to have the power to make such agreements when a little pin point of an island has to compete in them with the vast United States. They claim that in that event Puerto Rico will revert to being a producer and exporter of a few things such as sugar, but that its growing industrial plant, now an integral part of the efficient United States plant, will collapse and shrink down to just a few factories devoted largely to making goods for consumption by the Puerto Ricans themselves.

The prevailing economic thinking on statehood was dramatized a few years ago by one of Muñoz' famous quips. He said: "Let us see what statehood would cost us. So much in excise taxes, so much in customs receipts, so much in income taxes. Altogether about $80,000,000. That is just about our total budget this year. We would have to find ways of doubling our budget if we want to survive. And what would we get out of it? Two senators and six representatives in Congress. Since when are eight politicians worth $80,000,000 a year?"

Sr. Luis Ferré, the industrialist and vice president of the Statehood party, has answered such arguments with an elaborate presentation of his own, claiming that the Commonwealth's present financial advantages, in the form of federal subsidies, the return of excise taxes and customs receipts, etc.—but ignoring federal income tax—amount to only $37,-500,000, while the added financial advantages resulting from statehood would total more than $275,000,000. He mentions social security as a federal activity not now applied in Puerto Rico, vastly increased federal subsidies if the island were a state, increases to be expected in the sugar quota, relinquishment of the present ruling which restricts the refinement of sugar in Puerto Rico, and a vast acceleration of the industrial program, which should add an extra $120,000,000 to Puerto Rico's budget.

These are rosy figures, based largely on guesswork. Many a state, such as Mississippi, does not have a flourishing program of industrialization merely because it is a state. Ferré points out that Oklahoma and Washington, states with populations comparable to that of Puerto Rico, received much more federal aid during 1949 than did Puerto Rico; his opponents answer that the federal aid given to Oklahoma in that year was 11.1 per cent of the state's total financial contribution to the federal government, that Washington recovered, in federal aid, only 7.8 per cent of its federal contributions, and that Puerto Rico, making no contributions to the management of the federal government, therefore received much more than did either of the two states.

As I write I have before me two lists prepared by the federal government, the one showing housing projects approved for development with federal money, as of December 31, 1953, the other listing similar projects approved for final planning. The total for both lists, for Puerto Rico, comes to eighteen projects. It is a tribute both to federal generosity and to the energy with which Puerto Rico is tackling its serious housing problem. The leading state in the first list, according to which Puerto Rico has sixteen projects now under way, is New York, with eight projects; the leading state in the second list is Pennsylvania, with fourteen projects. When it comes to housing, therefore, Puerto Rico is well at the top in the number of projects receiving federal aid.

One suspects that the Statehood party, the renamed former Republican party, supported largely by the island's leading bankers and industrialists, is in favor of statehood largely as a hedge against the possibility of some future swing toward independence. The Civil War established the principle of once a state always a state, the principle under which no state or group of states can secede to form an independent nation. President Eisenhower's statement offering the Puerto Ricans independence, if they wanted it, at the time of the arguments before the United Nations, brought out the fact that the present commonwealth status may be regarded as being temporary, leading in the future to statehood, independence, or an indefinite continuation of commonwealth status, possibly modified from time to time as the evolutionary processes create new conditions.

Nobody can at this stage say what the future will bring. Rexford Tugwell is convinced that Puerto Rico should begin to move toward statehood; the advocates of independence are certainly not silent and have no reason to be silent at the present time. Muñoz Marín has come out openly in favor of keeping the situation fluid, of making changes as need arises and opportunity presents itself, of chancing whatever "bad" laws opposite Puerto Rico some future Congress may pass. He states that the understanding between the former colony and the Congress is now so good, and the pact of mutual consent has worked out so well, that Puerto Rico's situation is now better than ever before in history, and rapidly improving. What he favors is an indefinite continuation of the commonwealth status, aimed at making it permanent through the application of the mutual-consent principle applied to working things out with Congress.

Whatever may be said, and until some other party with other ideas wins control of the government, that seems to be the way it will be. As long as Muñoz retains the political power, the island's political status will undoubtedly remain essentially what it is while undergoing various evolutionary changes through the application of the powers and principles which are basic to what it is today.

Meanwhile Puerto Rico remains a working advertisement of American democracy. To date not the slightest sign of a change is apparent in the condition which made Chester Bowles, as Ambassador to India, repeatedly invite Muñoz to visit him in India because he could do more than could any other American to further good relations between India and the United States. There is no sign of change in the feeling which prompted Muñoz to cable Congress in 1951: "You can rely on us to protect the good name of the United States."

Many important problems still remain to be solved in the relations between Puerto Rico and the United States, but the method of solving them has been established, in a free and democratic manner—at the very time the United States was under vicious attack from the communist side of the world as a grasping imperialist. With the world in a turmoil over the twin problems of abolishing colonialism and raising standards of living for a billion people who are today on the verge of actual starvation, Puerto Rico, with Washington's full co-operation, has set an important example of the manner and manners in which those problems can be solved.

With the world torn between two fundamentally different basic philosophies, thousands of visitors to the island, from all parts of the free world, see what Puerto Rico has done and is doing, and go home again, saying, "This is America's answer to communism." And that expresses Puerto Rico's greatest importance to the United States and the modern world.

Index

ABOUT THE AUTHOR

EARL PARKER HANSON *was born in Berlin, Germany, of American parents in 1899. He was graduated from the University of Wisconsin and has done graduate work in geography at the University of Chicago and Columbia University. At various times during his life he has been an engineer, explorer, lecturer, and writer. He is the author of many distinguished books in the general field of geography and has contributed frequently to geographical and scholarly magazines. He is presently chairman of the Department of Geography and Geology at the University of Delaware. The author's interest in Puerto Rico began in 1935 when he served there as planning consultant in the early stages of the work which is now being carried on by the Puerto Rico Planning Board.*

4/6/55